7-6-89

D0079392

U.S. National
Security Policy
and Strategy

U.S. NATIONAL SECURITY POLICY AND STRATEGY

Documents and Policy Proposals

Sam C. Sarkesian
with
Robert A. Vitas

Greenwood Press
New York • Westport, Connecticut • London

Library of Congress Cataloging-in-Publication Data

U.S. national security policy and strategy : documents and policy
   proposals / [edited by] Sam C. Sarkesian with Robert A. Vitas.
      p. cm.
   Bibliography: p.
   Includes index.
   ISBN 0-313-25482-6 (lib. bdg. : alk. paper)
   1. United States—National security. I. Sarkesian, Sam Charles.
II. Vitas, Robert A. III. Title : US national security policy and
strategy.
UA23.U235 1988
355'.033573—dc19   88-10244

British Library Cataloguing in Publication Data is available.

Library of Congress Catalog Card Number: 88-10244
ISBN: 0-313-25482-6

First published in 1988

Greenwood Press, Inc.
88 Post Road West, Westport, Connecticut 06881

Printed in the United States of America

The paper used in this book complies with the
Permanent Paper Standard issued by the National
Information Standards Organization (Z39.48-1984).

10 9 8 7 6 5 4 3 2 1

Contents

Series Foreword

Policymakers and strategists alike share a common view that in
the nuclear age issues of U.S. national security policy are
increasingly complex and open to a variety of policy and strategic interpretations and options. More study is needed to
define terminology, to clarify issues, and to provide a historical background for understanding concepts, varying perspectives, and the process of policy development in terms of
national security.

Greenwood Press is publishing a series of Public Policy
Formation reference volumes in different issue-oriented areas.
The three volumes dealing with a particular issue-oriented
area will include a work giving analytical profiles of public
information and interest groups that have played a major role
in the field, with an emphasis on the period since 1960; a
collection of documents and policy proposals during that
period; and an annotated bibliography. These volumes are designed for college students, teachers, researchers, and professionals in organizations, government, and the media.

While the three volumes dealing with national security
policy and strategy do not claim to be all-encompassing in
surveying and analyzing groups, documents, and publications in
the field, they provide a real sense of history and a solid
background for studying the subject. They contribute to a
unique new reference series that opens up significant new
lines of research in the field, and they offer guidelines for
future study.

Sam C. Sarkesian
Series Editor for the collection
dealing with U.S. national
security policy and strategy issues

Preface

The purpose of this volume is to try to establish (or reestablish) a sense of history and perspective in the study and teaching of national security. In so doing, it will also try to bring a sense of balance to current debates on national security policy. This is done by providing the reader with a series of selected official U.S. documents covering the past thirty years. A careful reading will provide valuable insights not only into the policy process, but also on the meaning of American values, national interests, and national strategy--at least insights on how officials of the U.S. government saw these and the way they tried to implement them. In this respect, the documents speak for themselves.

However, this is not intended to substitute for the many excellent studies of national security and those that examine specific security issues. A serious study of U.S. national security will surely require critical reading of such studies. Yet there is a valuable place for the study of materials emanating directly from the U.S. government, particularly those that articulate intentions, perceptions, and policy goals. There is no substitute for examining these primary sources. At the very least, they can establish the necessary background for understanding U.S. national security policy and for critical analyses of serious studies of the subject.

To be sure, the selection of documents in itself reflects a certain view of U.S. national security. To minimize the problems that may evolve in this regard, an attempt is made to follow a systematic and balanced approach in categorizing U.S. national security periods and in selecting documents appropriate to them.

There are a number of points that should be made in this respect. First, the period covered in this volume is generally from the 1950s to the middle 1980s, although we begin with the National Security Act of 1947. In outline, the volume ends with the end of the first term of President Reagan, although some references will be made, for example, to the Iran-Contra affair. Additionally, some material is included that is specifically on national security policy and strategy that goes beyond the middle 1980s. These are included because of their relevance in clarifying U.S. national security posture. Second, a number of excellent foreign and national security policy volumes were used as background and guides. These are listed in the Select Bibliography. Third, no attempt was made to be comprehensive; presumably this could not be done in one volume. That is, the purpose of this volume is not to provide all of the important documents relevant to U.S. national security policy. Selections attempt to portray the critical reference points in any given period or event, with an eye towards identifying the attitudes and mind-sets of the times. Fourth, and finally, within the context of the first three, the purpose of this volume is to provide a picture of the landscape of U.S. national security policy over the past three decades that can serve as a road map for its study and teaching.

There are a number of scholarly pitfalls in editing a volume such as this. Some will not agree with the categorizations. Others will dispute the focus of some of the categories. Still others will surely criticize the selection of documents. Finally, there will be those who will argue about the cohesiveness and conceptual basis of the volume. Nonetheless, there is value in such a volume, even one with a modest purpose. Students and serious readers should have access to selected documents, not only to restore a sense of history, but to provide a research framework for the study of U.S national security policy. Further, as suggested earlier, a selected collection of documents touching on events over the past three decades may assist in establishing a more balanced and accurate view for critically analyzing public debates and policy positions on national security. Finally, this volume may even assist policymakers in assessing current policy more accurately and in developing future policy.

There are several editorial matters that require explanation. Most of the material contained here is excerpted from the original documents. Several shorter documents are reproduced in their entirety, but this is the exception rather than the rule. Additionally, only those documents that are available through public sources are included. This is to identify documents that can be readily obtained. Further, the public character of these documents allows extensive quotation without prior permission.

The source is placed at the bottom of the page on which the document begins. If more than one document begins on the same page, the page will provide all the sources. However, complete citations are generally not provided, but are included in the Reference List at the end of the book. For example, many documents are from the Public Papers of the Presidents or from the Department of State Bulletin. These are identified as such, but the complete citation appears only in the Reference List. A select bibliography of published books that are considered important in the study of U.S. national security is also included.

An important part of the book is the study by Robert A. Vitas, "Sources in the Study of National Security." That study provides the details and guidelines used in researching national security and in compiling the material for this volume. This should be useful to those who contemplate working in the field.

Finally, the utility of this volume is found in its attempt to identify documents that provide signposts and reference points to important periods in U.S. national security, as well as in providing critical substantive dimensions to them. Additionally, by categorizing U.S. national security according to issues, events, and important periods, rather than only chronologically, a clearer pattern emerges: continuity, a sense of history and a balanced perspective.

Chicago, Illinois   S.C.S.
September, 1988   R.A.V.

U.S. National
Security Policy
and Strategy

1

The Study of U.S. National Security

Sam C. Sarkesian

The complexity of the international order and the politics it generates has made the study of national security not only difficult, but increasingly ambiguous. The problems faced by the United States, and open systems in general, in the latter part of the 1980s have created new dimensions and challenges to the traditional concepts of national security. International terrorism, unconventional conflicts, and the changing nature of U.S.-USSR relationships, to name but a few considerations, demand new insights and concepts in coming to grips with US national security. But the problems go beyond the international security setting and have to do with the idea of national security itself. There is little agreement, for example, among scholars and practitioners regarding the meaning of national security and its conceptual dimensions.

Compounding the problem is the fact that there is little consensus in the United States on national security policy, the meaning of American values in the external environment, and the nature of national interests. This a reflection not only of complexities in the international security setting, but also of the persistence of the Vietnam and Watergate experiences in the United States. Further, changing demographics and dynamics in the U.S. political system have tended to increase social and political heterogeneity, fragment political organizations within and among each other, and magnify the diversity of political views. Single issue politics has become fashionable. In the aggregate, these factors have made it extremely difficult for any administration of recent memory to establish and maintain a consensus on national security policy for any length of time.

In an earlier work, this author summed up these problems as follows:

> The problems are compounded by the fact that the previously held consensus on U.S. defense policy has disappeared and has been replaced by confrontations between political actors regarding defense and nondefense spending, serious disagreements on moral issues of U.S. strategy, and difficulties in developing an acceptable military posture that is commensurate with objectives and strategy.[1]

What has been lost in the process is a sense of history. That is, many tend to forget the continuities of American national security policy and its historical commitment to certain national interests. The arguments, pro and con, regarding US policy in Central America and the Caribbean are illustrative of a focus on the "immediate," with concomitant lack of historical perspective, as well as neglect of long-range perceptions. In other words, there is neither a retrospective nor a prospective focus.   Many have forgotten (or perhaps neglect to consider), for example, that the Kennedy Administration in the early 1960s established policies regarding the U.S. and the Caribbean that are parallel to those being pursued today. The point is that many national security issues facing the U.S. today owe their inception to what may have occurred one or more decades ago. Yet little reference is made to these in current debates.

One reason for this neglect may well be that questions of national security were rather narrowly defined until World War II. Protection of the U.S. homeland and the integrity of its borders were almost the sole objective of national security policy. The two oceans not only provided a relatively effective barrier to foreign adversaries, but were cornerstones of our policy. Indeed, prior to World War II, the United States viewed itself as "Island America," shaping its national security strategy accordingly. The essence of this strategy rested on sea power and, later, on air power. National security was thus influenced--as were American mind sets.

NATIONAL SECURITY: DEFINITIONS AND CONCEPTS

In following these guidelines, we are faced with the problem of defining, and conceptualizing about, national security. There is little scholarly agreement when dealing with the two. Some stress the need to link domestic security with external security. Others argue that national security must include domestic economic capability of allies as well as adversaries in the national security equation. A more focused approach is on military capability in response to external threats. There is also a tendency for some to use defense policy and national security policy synonymously. And finally, foreign and national security policy are often intermixed. Add to this the lack of agreement on the meaning of national interests, vital interests, and American values as they are projected into the external world, and one can readily see the problems of trying to come to grips with national security policy.

These observations point out the problem in trying to study U.S. national security. As one scholar states, "No formal definition of national security as a field has been generally accepted; none may be possible."[2] Another states that national security "is a rather unsatisfactory label for a field whose boundaries and chief structural features remain to be identified."[3] The same author further states that national security is an "abbreviation of 'National Military Security' and [he takes] this term to denote a field of study concerned primarily with the generation of national military power and its employment in interstate relationships."[4]

In any case, some systematic design must be adopted for identifying the critical points in the national security landscape. These considerations lead us to the following definition:

National security policy is that part of government policy primarily concerned with formulating and implementing national strategy to create a favorable military environment for U.S. national interests. An integral part ofthis is to prevent the effective use of military force by the nation's adversaries or potential adversaries in obstructing or denying the ability of the United States to pursue its national interests.[5]

The selection and placement of documents are guided by this definition. Chronological order was also a consideration, although not overriding. The national security issue or event, as well as the category, were primary in this regard. For example, Chapter Two includes documents ranging from the National Security Act of 1947 to the Goldwater-Nichols Department of Defense Reorganization Act of 1986. By grouping these various documents in one category, a reasonably accurate picture is portrayed of the evolution of the national security establishment. To assist in this portrayal, each chapter includes a brief introduction to the period and events in question and their national security implications.

THE PRESIDENT, CONGRESS, AND NATIONAL SECURITY

The focal point of this volume is the Oval Office. The incumbent in that office is at the center of the national security policy process. Each president since the end of World War II has functioned with similar legal and political power in national security policy. This is not to deny the changes in Executive-Legislative relations brought on by Vietnam (War Powers Act), Watergate (Hughes-Ryan Amendment of 1974 constraining intelligence activities), and some events in the latter part of the 1980s. Indeed, even a brief glance at the events following the Vietnam War and a cursory reading of the relevant documents reveal attempts by Congress to exert increasing influence and control over national security--matters that have traditionally been reserved to the Executive. In 1987, for example, the Joint Congressional Hearings on the Iran-Contra affair were fundamentally an attempt by the Democrat-controlled Congress to inject itself into an area of policy that has been outside its purview.

According to some, however, the increased confrontation between Congress and the Executive is symptomatic of the changing nature of the presidential office. One authority concludes, for example,

> that the presidency not only has begun a period of decline but that the office is becoming increasingly unworkable as a result of a number of emerging forces in the domestic and international political environments. If the imperial presidency was the proper metaphor for that period (1930s to the 1960s), the fitting catchword for today might well be the impossible presidency.[6]

But the fact remains that legal and political power

embodied in constitutional provisions and practices are supposed to give the President dominance in national security affairs. It is doubtful that the 535-member Congress can exercise leadership and initiative in such matters, regardless of the position of individual members. Further, many argue that it is only the President who is elected to <u>national</u> office, in contrast to specific constituencies represented in Congress. Finally, others argue that the Supreme Court put the issue to rest with its decision that only the President can represent the United States in foreign affairs.[7] Nonetheless, in the late 1980s, it is clear that the issue is far from resolution.

This brief view of the problems inherent in Congress-Executive relationships with respect to national security is important in terms of this volume's focus. There is much in the volume that concentrates on statements by those occupying the Oval Office. Additionally, there is a great deal of material reflecting the views and policies of cabinet officers and officials in the executive office. Throughout the volume, however, there are major legislative initiatives that have an important impact on the presidential role in national security. It is the interplay between presidential initiatives and policy-making, and the reactions and responses by Congress, that provides the dynamics in national security policy-making.

Notes

1. Sam C. Sarkesian, "The President and National Security: An Overview," in Sam C. Sarkesian, ed., <u>Presidential Leadership and National Security: Style, Institutions and Politics</u> (Boulder, Col.: Westview Press, 1981), p. 3.

2. Donald M. Snow, <u>National Security: Enduring Problems of U.S. defense Policy</u> (New York: St. Martin's Press, 1987), p. 3.

3. Klaus Knorr, "National Security Studies: Scope and Structure of the Field," in Frank Trager and Philip S. Kronenberg, eds., <u>National Security and American Society: Theory, Process, and Policy</u> (Lawrence: University of Kansas Press, 1973), p. 5.

4. Knorr, pp. 5-6.

2

The National Security Establishment

INTRODUCTION

The basis for America's post-World War II national security establishment evolved from the National Security Act of 1947. Prior to World War II, decentralization and department autonomy characterized the U.S. national security system and the military structure. For all practical purposes, the national security establishment did not take shape until immediately after World War II. Yet efforts were made as early as the 1920s to establish a unified military department.

The U.S. experience in World War II emphasized the need for a centralized command and control system for the defense effort. A Joint Chiefs of Staff was created after America's entry into World War II and emerged as one of the most important bodies in the planning and supervision of the U.S. military effort.

Building on this experience, the National Security Act of 1947 created a unified military establishment. In addition, the U.S. Air Force was established as a separate military organization. The position of Secretary of Defense was also created, to serve as the president's principal assistant in all national security matters. Equally important, the National Security Council and Central Intelligence Agency were established.

However, a number of problems soon surfaced, primarily as a result of the inherent conflict between established decentralized structures, department autonomy, and the drive for centralization. The Secretary of Defense, for example, presided over a unified military establishment, but there was no single executive department for defense. Each military department retained its executive-department status, with all this suggested with respect to the power of the secretaries of the various military services. The Secretary of Defense emerged primarily as a "coordinator" rather than the head of an executive department. Bureaucratic power struggles were inevitable in such an arrangement.

The 1949 Amendment to the National Security Act was an attempt to solve some of these problems. It established a single executive Department of Defense, downgrading the military services to military departments. The position of Chairman was created to serve as the corporate head of the Joint Chiefs of Staff.

However, organizational shortcomings again surfaced, prompting President Eisenhower to request additional changes. The 1958 change led to the granting of substantial power to the Secretary of Defense to supervise and control the military establishment. He was given authority to deal directly with unified and specified commands, for example. Although the national security establishment retained its original shape, the Secretary of Defense became its most powerful member.

It was not until 1986 that another major defense reorganization took place with the passage of Public Law 99-433, known as the Goldwater-Nichols Department of Defense Reorganization Act of 1986. It is interesting to note that this new reorganization was initiated by Congress. The prime purpose of the Act is to expand the authority of the Chairman of the Joint Chiefs by making him the principal military adviser to the President, the National Security Council, and the Secretary of Defense. It also increases the Chairman's role in budgetary matters and in setting strategic directions, among other things. It is also interesting to note that the Act created the position of Assistant Secretary of Defense for Special Operations and Low Intensity Conflict- a position that was still not filled by the middle of 1988. As of this writing, it was too early to determine what impact the 1986 reorganization would have on the national security establishment over the long run.

It is also important to recognize that the concept of covert operations was established in the late 1940s. In an attempt to respond to and counter the Soviet Union's broad undercover activities, covert operations, and propaganda, the United States established its own covert operations policy. NSC 10/2, June 1948, set out the policy and ground rules. This has been in place, with only minor changes, for four decades. Covert operations are included here because of their long-range impact on the national security establishment and their importance in shaping U.S. political-military policy and strategy.

DOCUMENTS

National Security Act of 1947

DECLARATION OF POLICY

SEC. 2. In enacting this legislation, it is the intent of Congress to provide a comprehensive program for the future security of the United States; to provide for the establishment of integrated policies and procedures for the departments, agencies, and functions of the Government relating to the national security; to provide three military departments for the operation and administration of the Army, the Navy (including naval aviation and the United States Marine Corps), and the Air Force, with their assigned combat and service components; to provide for their authoritative coordination and unified direction under civilian control but not to merge them; to provide for the effective strategic direction of the armed forces and for their operation under unified control and for their integration into an efficient team of land, naval, and air forces.

* * * * *

COORDINATION FOR NATIONAL SECURITY

National Security Council

SEC. 101. (a) There is hereby established a council to be known as the National Security Council (hereinafter in this section referred to as the "Council").

The President of the United States shall preside over meetings of the Council: Provided, That in his absence he may designate a member of the Council to preside in his place. The

Source: United States Statutes at Large, 1947, vol. 61, part 1, pp. 496-505.

function of the Council shall be to advise the President with respect to the integration of domestic, foreign, and military policies relating to the national security so as to enable the military services and the other departments and agencies of the Government to cooperate more effectively in matters involving the national security.

The Council shall be composed of the President; the Secretary of State; the Secretary of Defense, appointed under section 202; the Secretary of the Army, referred to in Section 205; the Secretary of the Navy; the Secretary of the Air Force, appointed under section 207; the Chairman of the National Security Resources Board, appointed under section 103; and such of the following named officers as the President may designate from time to time: The Secretaries of the executive departments, the Chairman of the Munitions Board appointed under section 213, and the Chairman of the Research and Development Board appointed under section 214; but no such additional member shall be designated until the advice and consent of the Senate has been given to his appointment to the office the holding of which authorizes his designation as a member of the Council.

(b) In addition to performing such other functions as the President may direct, for the purpose of more effectively coordinating the policies and functions of the departments and agencies of the Government relating to the national security, it shall, subject to the direction of the President, be the duty of the Council—

(1) to assess and appraise the objectives, commitments, and risks of the United States in relation to our actual and potential military power, in the interest of national security, for the purpose of making recommendations to the President in connection therewith; and

(2) to consider policies on matters of common interest to the departments and agencies of the Government concerned with the national security, and to make recommendations to the President in

connection therewith.

(c) The Council shall have a staff to be headed by a civilian executive secretary who shall be appointed by the President, and who shall receive compensation at the rate of $10,000 a year. The executive secretary, subject to the direction of the Council, is hereby authorized, subject to the civil-service laws and the Classification Act of 1923, as amended, to appoint and fix the compensation of such personnel as may be necessary to perform such duties as may be prescribed by the Council in connection with the performance of his functions.

(d) The Council shall, from time to time, make such recommendations, and such other reports, to the President as it deems appropriate or as the President may require.

Central Intelligence Agency

SEC. 102. (a) There is hereby established under the National Security Council a Central Intelligence Agency with a Director of Central Intelligence, who shall be the head thereof. The Director shall be appointed by the President, by and with the advice and consent of the Senate, from among the commissioned officers of the armed services or from among individuals in civilian life....

THE NATIONAL MILITARY ESTABLISHMENT

ESTABLISHMENT of the NATIONAL MILITARY ESTABLISHMENT

SEC. 201. (a) There is hereby established the National Military Establishment, and the Secretary of Defense shall be the head thereof.

(b) The National Military Establishment shall consist of the Department of the Army, the Department of the Navy, and the Department of the Air Force, together with all other agencies created under title II of this Act.

Secretary of Defense

SEC. 202. (a) There shall be a Secretary of Defense, who shall be appointed from civilian life by the President, by and with the advice and consent of the Senate: <u>Provided</u>, That a person who has within ten years been on active duty as a commissioned officer in a Regular component of the armed services shall not be eligible for appointment as Secretary of Defense. The Secretary of Defense shall be the principal assistant to the President in all matters relating to the national security. Under the direction of the President and subject to the provisions of this Act he shall perform the following duties:

(1) Establish general policies and programs for the National Military Establishment and for all of the departments and agencies therein;

(2) Exercise general direction, authority, and control over such departments and agencies;

(3) Take appropriate steps to eliminate unnecessary duplication or overlapping in the fields of procurement, supply, transportation, storage, health, and research;

(4) Supervise and coordinate the preparation of the budget estimates of the departments and agencies comprising the National Military Establishment; formulate and determine the budget estimates for submittal to the Bureau of the Budget; and supervise the budget programs of such departments and agencies under the applicable appropriation Act.

<u>Provided</u>, That nothing herein contained shall prevent the Secretary of the Army, the Secretary of the Navy, or the Secretary of the Air Force from presenting to the President or to the Director of the Budget after first so informing the Secretary of Defense, any report or recommendation relating to his department which he may deem necessary; <u>And provided further</u>,

That the Department of the Army, the Department of the Navy, and the Department of the Air Force shall be administered as individual executive departments by their respective Secretaries and all powers and duties relating to such departments not specifically conferred upon the Secretary of Defense by this Act shall be retained by each of their respective Secretaries.

(b) The Secretary of Defense shall submit annual written reports to the President and the Congress covering expenditures, work, and accomplishments of the National Military Establishment, together with such recommendations as he shall deem appropriate.

Military Assistants to the Secretary

SEC. 203. Officers of the armed services may be detailed to duty as assistants and personal aides to the Secretary of Defense, but he shall not establish a military staff....

War Council

SEC. 210. There shall be within the National Military Establishment a War Council composed of the Secretary of Defense, as Chairman, who shall have power of decision; the Secretary of the Army; the Secretary of the Navy; the Secretary of the Air Force; the Chief of Staff, United States Army; the Chief of Naval Operations; and the Chief of Staff, United States Air Force. The War Council shall advise the Secretary of Defense on matters of broad policy relating to the armed forces, and shall consider and report on such other matters as the Secretary of Defense may direct.

Joint Chiefs of Staff

SEC. 211. (a) There is hereby established within the National Military Establishment the Joint Chiefs of Staff, which shall consist of the Chief of Staff, United States Army; the Chief of Naval Operations; the Chief of Staff, United States Air Force; and the Chief of Staff to the Commander in Chief, if there be one.

(b) Subject to the authority and direction of the President and the Secretary of Defense, it shall be the duty of the Joint Chiefs of Staff--

(1) to prepare strategic plans and to provide for the strategic direction of the military forces;

(2) to prepare joint logistic plans and to assign to the military services logistic responsibilities in accordance with such plans;

(3) to establish unified commands in strategic areas when such unified commands are in the interest of national security;

(4) to formulate policies for joint training of the military forces;

(5) to formulate policies for coordinating the education of members of the military forces;

(6) to review major materiel and personnel requirements of the military forces, in accordance with strategic and logistic plans; and

(7) to provide United States representation on the Military Staff Committee of the United Nations in accordance with the provisions of the Charter of the United Nations.

(c) The Joint Chiefs of Staff shall act as the principal military advisers to the President and the Secretary of Defense and shall perform such other duties as the President and the Secretary of Defense may direct or as prescribed by law.

Joint Staff

SEC. 212. There shall be, under the Joint Chiefs of Staff, a Joint Staff to consist of not to exceed one hundred officers and to be composed of approximately equal numbers of officers from each of the three armed services. The Joint Staff, operating under a Director thereof appointed by the Joint Chiefs of Staff, shall perform such duties as may be directed by

the Joint Chiefs of Staff. The Director shall be
an officer junior in grade to all members of the
Joint Chiefs of Staff.

NATIONAL SECURITY ACT AMENDMENTS of 1949

SEC. 2. In enacting this legislation, it
is the intent of Congress to provide a
comprehensive program for the future security of
the United States; to provide for the
establishment of integrated policies and
procedures for the departments, agencies, and
functions of the Government relating to the
national security; to provide three military
departments, separately administered, for the
operation and administration of the Army, the
Navy (including naval aviation and the United
States Marine Corps), and the Air Force, with
their assigned combat and service components; to
provide for their authoritative coordination and
unified direction under civilian control of the
Secretary of Defense but not to merge them; to
provide for the effective strategic direction of
the armed forces and for their operation under
unified control and for their integration into
an efficient team of land, naval, and air forces
but not to establish a single Chief of Staff
over the armed forces nor an armed forces
general staff (but this is not to be interpreted
as applying to the Joint Chiefs of Staff or
Joint Staff).

Change in the Composition of the National
Security Council

SEC. 3. The fourth paragraph of section
101 (a) of the National Security Act of 1947 is
amended to read as follows:

"The Council shall be composed of--

"(1) the President;
"(2) the Vice President;
"(3) the Secretary of State;
"(4) the Secretary of Defense;

Source: United States Statutes at Large, vol.
63, part 1, 1950, pp. 579-583.

"(5) the Chairman of the National Security Resoures Board; and

"(6) the Secretaries and Under Secretaries of the other executive departments and of the military departments, the Chairman of the Munitions Board, and the Chairman of the Research and Development Board, when appointed by the President by and with the advice and consent of the Senate, to serve at his pleasure."

Conversion of the National Military Establishment into an Executive Department

"SEC. 201. (a) There is hereby established, as an Executive Department of the Government, the Department of Defense, and the Secretary of Defense shall be the head thereof.

"(b) There shall be within the Department of Defense (1) the Department of the Army, the Department of the Navy, and the Department of the Air Force, and each such department shall on and after the date of enactment of the National Security Act Amendments of 1949 be military departments in lieu of their prior status as Executive Departments, and (2) all other agencies created under title II of this Act....

"(d) The Secretary of Defense shall be the principal assistant to the President in all matters relating to the Department of Defense. Under the direction of the President, and subject to the provisions of this Act, he shall have direction, authority, and control over the Department of Defense....

"(4) The Departments of the Army, Navy, and Air Force shall be separately administered by their respective Secretaries under the direction, authority, and control of the Secretary of Defense...

"(6) No provision of this Act shall be so construed as to prevent a Secretary of a military department or a member of the Joint Chiefs of Staff from presenting to the Congress, on his own initiative, after first so informing the Secretary of Defense, The National Security Council, any recommendation relating to the Department of Defense that he may deem proper.

"(d) The Secretary of Defense shall not less often than semi-annually submit written reports to the President and the Congress covering expenditures, work and accomplishments of the Department of Defense, accompanied by (1) such recommendations as he shall deem appropriate, (2) separate reports from the military departments covering their expenditures, work and accomplishments, and (3) itemized statements showing the savings of public funds and the eliminations of unnecessary duplications and overlapping that have been accomplished pursuant to the provisions of this Act....

"SEC. 211. (a) There is hereby established within the Department of Defense the Joint Chiefs of Staff, which shall consist of the Chairman, who shall be the presiding officer thereof but who shall have no vote; the Chief of Staff, United States Army; the Chief of Naval Operations; and the Chief of Staff, United States Air Force. The Joint Chiefs of Staff shall be the principal military advisers to the President, the National Security Council and the Secretary of Defense.

"(b) Subject to the authority and direction of the President and the Secretary of Defense the Joint Chiefs of Staff shall perform the following duties in addition to such other duties as the President or the Secretary of Defense may direct:

"(1) preparation of strategic plans and provisions for the strategic direction of the military forces;

"(2) preparation of joint logistic plans and assignment to the military services of logistic responsibilities in accordance with such plans;

"(3) establishment of unified commands in strategic areas;

"(4) review of major materiel and personnel requirements of the military

forces in accordance with strategic and logistic plans;
"(5) formulation of policies for joint training of the military forces;
"(6) formulation of policies for coordinating the military education of members of the military forces; and
"(7) providing United States representation on the Military Staff Committee of the United Nations in accordance with the provisions of the Charter of the United Nations.

"(c) The Chairman of the Joint Chiefs of Staff (hereinafter referred to as the 'Chairman') shall be appointed by the President by and with the advice and consent of the Senate, from among the Regular officers of the armed services to serve at the pleasure of the President for a term of two years and shall be eligible for one reappointment, by and with the advice and consent of the Senate, except in time of war hereafter declared by the Congress when there shall be no limitation on the number of such reappointments...

"(d) While holding such office he shall take precedence over all other officers of the armed services: Provided, That the Chairman shall not exercise military command over the Joint Chiefs of Staff or over any of the military services.

"(e) In addition to participating as a member of the Joint Chiefs of Staff in the performance of the duties assigned in subsection (b) of this section, the Chairman shall, subject to the authority and direction of the President and Secretary of Defense, perform the following duties:

"(1) serve as the presiding officer of the Joint Chiefs of Staff;
"(2) provide agenda for meetings of the Joint Chiefs of Staff and assist the Joint Chiefs of Staff to prosecute their business as promptly as practicable, and;
"(3) inform the Secretary of Defense and, when appropriate as determined by the President or the Secretary of Defense, the

President, of those issues upon which agreement among the Joint Chiefs of Staff has not been reached...."

(c) Section 212 of the National Security Act of 1947 is amended to read as follows:
"SEC. 212.   There shall be, under the Joint Chiefs of Staff, a Joint Staff to consist of not to exceed two hundred and ten officers and to be composed of approximately equal numbers of officers appointed by the Joint Chiefs of Staff from each of the three armed services. The Joint Staff, operating under a Director thereof appointed by the Joint Chiefs of Staff, shall perform such duties as may be directed by the Joint Chiefs of Staff. The Director shall be an officer junior in grade to all members of the Joint Chiefs of Staff."

PUBLIC LAW 15
April 4, 1953

An Act to Amend the National Security Act of 1947 to authorize the appointment of a Deputy Director of Central Intelligence, and for other purposes.

Be it enacted by the Senate and House of Representatives of the United States of America in Congress assembled, That subsections (a) and (b) of section 102 of the National Security Act of 1947, as amended, is amended to read as follows:
"SEC. 102.   (a) There is hereby established under the National Security Council a Central Intelligence Agency with a Director of Central Intelligence who shall be the head thereof, and with a Deputy Director of Central Intelligence who shall act for, and exercise the powers of, the Director during his absence or disability. The Director and the Deputy Director shall be appointed by the President, by and with advice and consent of the Senate, from among the commissioned officers of the armed services, whether in an active or retired status, or from

Source: United States Statutes at Large, 1953, vol. 67, pp. 19-20.

among individuals in civilian life: Provided,
however, That at no time shall the two positions
of the Director and Deputy Director be occupied
simultaneously by commissioned officers of the
armed services, whether in an active or retired
status.

"(b) (1) If a commissioned officer of the
armed services is appointed as Director, or
Deputy Director, then--

"(A) in the performance of his duties
as Director, or Deputy Director, he shall be
subject to no supervision, control, restriction,
or prohibition (military or otherwise) other
than would be operative with respect to him if
he were a civilian in no way connected with the
Department of the Army, the Department of the
Navy, the Department of the Air Force, or the
armed services or any component thereof; and

"(B) he shall not possess or exercise
any supervision, control, powers, or functions
(other than such as he possesses, or is
authorized or directed to exercise, as Director,
or Deputy Director) with respect the armed
services or any component thereof, the
Department of the Army, The Department of the
Navy, or the Department of the Air Force, or any
branch, bureau, unit, or division thereof, or
with respect to any of the personnel (military
or civilian) of any of the foregoing.

REORGANIZATION PLAN NO. 6 OF 1953
DEPARTMENT OF DEFENSE

Section 1. Transfers of functions.(a) All
functions of the Munitions Board, the Research
and Development Board, the Defense Supply
Management Agency and the Director of
Installations are hereby transferred to the
Secretary of Defense.
(b) The selection of the Director of the
Joint Staff by the Joint Chiefs of Staff, and
his tenure, shall be subject to the approval of
the Secretary of Defense.

Source: United States Statutes at Large, 1953,
vol. 67, pp. 19-20 and 638.

(c) The selection of the members of the Joint Staff by the Joint Chiefs of Staff, and their tenure, shall be subject to the approval of the Chairman of the Joint Chiefs of Staff.

(d) The functions of the Joint Chiefs of Staff with respect to managing the Joint Staff and the Director thereof are hereby transferred to the Chairman of the Joint Chiefs of Staff....

Sec. 3. <u>Assistant Secretaries of Defense</u>. Six additional Assistant Secretaries of Defense may be appointed from civilian life by the President, by and with the advice and consent of the Senate. Each such Assistant Secretary shall perform such functions as the Secretary of Defense may from time to time prescribe and each shall receive compensation at the rate prescribed by law for assistant secretaries of executive departments.

PUBLIC LAW 85-599
DEPARTMENT OF DEFENSE REORGANIZATION ACT OF 1958

An Act to promote the national defense by providing for reorganization of the Department of Defense, and for other purposes.

<u>Be it enacted by the Senate and House of Representatives of the United States of America in Congress assembled</u>, That this Act may be cited as the "Department of Defense Reorganization Act of 1958."

Sec. 2. In enacting this legislation, it is the intent of Congress to provide a comprehensive program for the future security the United States; to provide for the establishment of integrated policies and procedures for the departments, agencies, and functions of the Government relating to the national security; to provide a Department of Defense, including the three military Departments of the Army, the Navy (including naval aviation and the United States Marine Corps), and the Air Force under the direction, authority, and control of the Secretary of Defense; to provide that each military depart-

_____

Source: <u>United States Statutes at Large</u>, 1958, vol. 71, part 1, pp. 514-518.

ment shall be separately organized under its own Secretary and shall function under the direction, authority, and control of the Secretary of Defense; to provide for their unified direction under civilian control of the Secretary of Defense but not to merge these departments or services; to provide for the establishment of unified or specified combatant commands, and a clear and direct line of command to such commands; to eliminate unnecessary duplication in the Department of Defense, and particularly in the field of research and engineering by vesting its overall direction and control in the Secretary of Defense; to provide more effective, efficient, and economical administration in the Department of Defense; to provide for the unified strategic direction of the combatant forces, for their operation under unified command, and for their integration into an efficient team of land, naval, and air forces but not to establish a single Chief of Staff over the armed forces nor an overall armed forces general staff.

Strengthening the Direction, Authority,
And Control of the Secretary of Defense

SEC. 3. (a) Section 202 (c) of the National Security Act of 1947, as amended (5 U.S.C. 171a (c)), is amended to read as follows:
"(c) (1) Within the policy enunciated in section 2, the Secretary of Defense shall take appropriate steps (including the transfer, reassignment, abolition, and consolidation of functions) to provide in the Department of Defense for more effective, efficient, and economical administration and operation and to eliminate duplication....
"(7) Each military department (the Department of the Navy to include naval aviation and the United States Marine Corps) shall be separately organized under its own Secretary and shall function under the direction, authority, and control of the Secretary of Defense. The Secretary of a military department shall be responsible to the Secretary of Defense for the operation of such department as well as

its efficiency. Except as otherwise specifically provided by law, no Assistant Secretary of Defense shall have authority to issue orders to a military department unless (1) the Secretary of Defense has specifically delegated in writing to such an Assistant Secretary the authority to issue such orders with respect to a specific subject area, and (2) such orders are issued through the Secretary of such military department or his designee. In the implementation of this paragraph it shall be the duty of each such Secretary, his civilian assistants, and the military personnel in such department to cooperate fully with personnel of the Office of the Secretary of Defense in a continuous effort to achieve efficient administration of the Department of Defense and effectively to carry out the direction, authority, and control of the Secretary of Defense.

"(8) No provision of this Act shall be so construed as to prevent a Secretary of a military department or a member of the Joint Chiefs of Staff from presenting to the Congress, on his own initiative, after first so informing the Secretary of Defense, any recommendations relating to the Department of Defense that he may deem proper...."

"(a) There is under the Joint Chiefs of Staff a Joint Staff consisting of not more than 400 officers selected by the Joint Chiefs of Staff with the approval of the Chairman. The Joint Staff shall be selected in approximately equal numbers from-

"(1) the Army;
"(2) the Navy and the Marine Corps; and
"(3) the Air Force....

"(b) The Chairman of the Joint Chiefs of Staff in consultation with the Joint Chiefs of Staff, and with the approval of the Secretary of Defense, shall select the Director of the Joint Staff.... The Director must be an officer junior in grade to each member of the Joint Chiefs of

Staff.

"(c) The Joint Staff shall perform such duties as the Joint Chiefs of Staff or the Chairman prescribes. The Chairman of the Joint Chiefs of Staff manages the Joint Staff and its Director, on behalf of the Joint Chiefs of Staff.

"(d) The Joint Staff shall not operate or be organized as an overall Armed Forces General Staff and shall have no executive authority. The Joint Staff may be organized and may operate along conventional staff lines to support the Joint Chiefs of Staff in discharging their assigned responsibilities."

(b) Section 202 of the National Security Act of 1947, as amended, is amended by adding at the end thereof the following new subsection:

"(j) With the advice and assistance of the Joint Chiefs of Staff the President, through the Secretary of Defense, shall establish unified or specified combatant commands for the performance of military missions, and shall determine the force structure of such combatant commands to be composed of forces of the Department of the Army, the Department of the Navy, the Department of the Air Force, which shall then be assigned to such combatant commands by the departments concerned for the performance of such military missions. Such combatant commands are responsible to the President and the Secretary of Defense for such military missions as may be assigned to them by the Secretary of Defense, with the approval of the President. Forces assigned to such unified combatant commands or specified combatant commands shall be under the full operational command of the commander of the unified combatant command or the commander of the specified combatant command. All forces not so assigned remain for all purposes in their respective departments. Under the direction, authority, and control of the Secretary of Defense each military department shall be responsible for the administration of the forces assigned from its department to such combatant commands. The responsibility for the support of forces assigned to combatant commands shall be vested in one or more of the military departments as may be directed by the Secretary of Defense. Forces assigned to such unified or specified combatant commands shall be transferred therefrom only by authority of and under procedures established by the Secretary of Defense, with the approval of the President."

PUBLIC LAW 99-433

GOLDWATER-NICHOLS

DEPARTMENT of DEFENSE REORGANIZATION ACT of 1986

An Act to reorganize the Department of Defense and strengthen civilian authority in the Department of Defense, to improve the military advice provided to the President, the National Security Council, and the Secretary of Defense, to place clear responsibility on the commanders of the unified and specified combatant commands for the accomplishment of missions assigned to those commands and ensure that the authority of those commanders is fully commensurate with that responsibility, to increase attention to the formulation of strategy and to contingency planning, to provide for more efficient use of defense resources, to improve joint officer management policies, otherwise to enhance the effectiveness of military operations and improve the management and administration of the Department of Defense, and for other purposes....

151. Joint Chiefs of Staff: composition; functions

Source: Public Law 99-433, 99th Congress, October 1, 1986.

(a)   COMPOSITION.--There   are   in   the Department of Defense the Joint Chiefs of Staff, headed by the Chairman of the Joint Chiefs of Staff. The Joint Chiefs of Staff consist of the following:
>   (1) The Chairman.
>   (2) The Chief of Staff of the Army.
>   (3) The Chief of Naval Operations.
>   (4) The Chief of Staff of the Air Force.
>   (5) The Commandant of the Marine Corps.

(b) FUNCTION AS MILITARY ADVISERS.--(1) The Chairman of the Joint Chiefs of Staff is the principal military adviser to the President, the National Security Council, and the Secretary of Defense.

>   (2) The other members of the Joint Chiefs of Staff are military advisers to the President, the National Security Council, and the Secretary of Defense....

(d) ADVICE AND OPINIONS OF MEMBERS OTHER THAN CHAIRMAN.--
>   (1) A member of the Joint Chiefs of Staff (other than the Chairman) may submit to the   Chairman   advice   or   an   opinion   in disagreement with, or advice or an opinion in addition   to,   the   advice   presented   by   the Chairman to the President, the National Security Council, or the Secretary of Defense. If a member submits such advice or opinion, the Chairman shall present the advice or opinion of such member at the same time he presents his own advice to the President, the National Security Council, or the Secretary of Defense, as the case may be.
>   (2)   The   Chairman   shall   establish procedures to ensure that the presentation of his own advice to the President, the National Security Council, or the Secretary of Defense is not unduly delayed by reason of the submission of the individual advice or opinion of another member of the Joint Chiefs of Staff.

(e) ADVICE ON REQUEST.--The members of the Joint   Chiefs   of   Staff,   individually   or collectively,   in   their   capacity   as   military advisers, shall provide advice to the President, the National Security Council, or the Secretary of Defense on a particular matter when the President, the National Security Council, or the Secretary requests such advice....

154. Vice Chairman

(a) APPOINTMENT.--(1) There is a Vice Chairman of the Joint Chiefs of Staff, appointed by the President, by and with the advice and consent of the Senate, from the officers of the regular components of the armed forces.
(2) The Chairman and Vice Chairman may not be members of the same armed force. However, the President may waive the restriction in the preceding sentence for a limited period of time in order to provide for the orderly transition of officers appointed to serve in the positions of Chairman and Vice Chairman.
(3) The Vice Chairman serves at the pleasure of the President for a term of two years and may be reappointed in the same manner for two additional terms. However, in time of war there is no limit on the number of reappointments....
(d) FUNCTION AS ACTING CHAIRMAN.--When there is a vacancy in the office of Chairman or in the absence or disability of the Chairman, the Vice Chairman acts as Chairman and performs the duties of the Chairman until a successor is appointed or the absence or disability ceases....
(3) Selection of officers of an armed force to serve on the Joint Staff shall be made by the Chairman from a list of officers submitted by the Secretary of the military department having jurisdiction over that armed force. Each officer whose name is submitted shall be among those officers considered to be the most outstanding officers of that armed force. The Chairman may specify the number of officers to be included on any such list....

(d) OPERATION OF JOINT STAFF.--The Secretary of Defense shall ensure that the Joint Staff is independently organized and operated so that the Joint Staff supports the Chairman of the Joint Chiefs of Staff in meeting the congressional purpose set forth in the last clause of section 2 of the National Security Act of 1947 (50 U.S.C. 401) to provide--

(1) for the unified strategic direction of the combatant forces;

(2) for their operation under unified command; and

(3) for their integration into an efficient team of land, naval and air forces.

(e) PROHIBITION OF FUNCTION AS ARMED FORCES GENERAL STAFF.-The Joint Staff shall not operate or be organized as an overall Armed Forces General Staff and shall have no executive authority. The Joint Staff may be organized and may operate along conventional staff lines....

(e) The Chairman (or in his absence the Vice Chairman) of the Joint Chiefs of Staff may, in his role as principal military adviser to the National Security Council and subject to the direction of the President, attend and participate in meetings of the National Security Council....

(4) Except as otherwise directed by the Secretary of Defense, all forces operating within the geographic area assigned to a unified combatant command shall be assigned to, and under the command of, the commander of that command. The preceding sentence applies to forces assigned to a specified combatant command only as prescribed by the Secretary of Defense.

(b) Chain of Command.--Unless otherwise directed by the President, the chain of command to a unified command or specified combatant command runs--

(1) from the President to the Secretary of Defense; and

(2) from the Secretary of Defense to the commander of the combatant command.

#163. Role of Chairman of Joint Chiefs of Staff

Subject to the limitations in section 152(c) of this title, the President may--

(1) direct that communications between the President or the Secretary of Defense and the commanders of the unified

and specified combatant commands be transmitted through the Chairman of the Joint Chiefs of Staff; and

(2) assign duties to the Chairman to assist the President and the Secretary of Defense in performing their command function.

(b) OVERSIGHT BY CHAIRMAN OF JOINT CHIEFS OF STAFF.--The Secretary of Defense may assign to the Chairman of the Joint Chiefs of Staff responsibility for overseeing the activities of the combatant commands. Such assignment by the Secretary to the Chairman does not confer any command authority on the Chairman and does not alter the responsibility of the commanders of the combatant commands prescribed in section 164(b)(2) of this title.

(2) Subject to the authority, direction and control of the Secretary of Defense, the Chairman of the Joint Chiefs of Staff serves as the spokesman for the commanders of the combatant commands, especially on the operational requirements of their commands....

(d) AUTHORITY OVER SUBORDINATE COMMANDERS.--Unless otherwise directed by the President or the Secretary of Defense--(1) commanders of commands and forces assigned to a combatant command are under the authority, direction, and control of, and are responsible to, the commander of the combatant command on all matters for which the commander of the combatant command has been assigned authority under subsection (c);...

(a) In General.--The Secretary of Defense, with the advice and assistance of the Chairman of the Joint Chiefs of Staff, shall provide for the administration and support of forces assigned to each combatant command.

(b) Responsibility of Secretaries of Military Departments. Subject to the authority, direction, and control of the Secretary of Defense and subject to the authority of commanders of the combatant commands under section 164(c) of this title, the Secretary of a military department is responsible for the

administration and support of forces assigned by
him to a combatant command....

#661. Management of Policies for joint
speciality officers

(a) Establishment.--The Secretary of
Defense shall establish policies, procedures,
and practices for the effective management of
officers of the Army, Navy, Air Force, and
Marine Corps on the active-duty list who are
particularly trained in, and oriented toward
joint matters. Such officers shall be identified
or designated (in addition to their principal
military occupational speciality) in such manner
as the Secretary of Defense directs. For
purposes of this chapter, officers to be managed
by such policies, procedures, and practices are
referred to as having, or having been nominated
for, the 'joint speciality.'
(b) Numbers and Selection.--(1) The number
of officers with the joint speciality shall be
determined by the Secretary. Such number shall
be large enough to meet the requirements of
subsection (d).
(2) Officers shall be selected for the
joint speciality by the Secretary of Defense
with the advice of the Chairman of the Joint
Chiefs of Staff. The Secretaries of the military
departments shall nominate officers for
selection for the joint speciality....
Section 619 is amended by adding at the
end the following new subsection:
"(e)(1) An officer may not be selected for
promotion to the grade of brigadier general or
rear admiral (lower half) unless the officer has
served in a joint duty assignment.
(2) Subject to paragraph (3), the
Secretary of Defense may waive paragraph (1)--

(A) when necessary for the good of the
service;
(B) in the case of an officer whose
proposed selection for promotion is based
primarily upon scientific and technical
qualifications for which joint requirements do
not exist;..."

ANNUAL NATIONAL SECURITY STRATEGY REPORT

SEC. 104. (a)(1) The President shall transmit to Congress each year a comprehensive report on the national security strategy of the United States (hereinafter in this section referred to as a 'national security strategy report').

(2) The national security strategy report for any year shall be transmitted on the date on which the President submits to Congress the budget for the next fiscal year....

(b) Each national security strategy report shall set forth the national security strategy of the United States and shall include a comprehensive description and discussion of the following:

(1) The worldwide interests, goals, and objectives of the United States that are vital to the national security of the United States.

(2) The foreign policy, worldwide commitments, and national defense capabilities of the United States necessary to deter aggression and to implement the national security strategy of the United States.

(3) The proposed short-term and long-term uses of the political, economic, military, and other elements of the national power of the United States to protect or promote the interests and achieve the goals and objectives referred to in paragraph (1).

(4) The adequacy of the capabilities of the United States to carry out the national security strategy of the United States, including an evaluation of the balance among the capabilities of all elements of the national power of the United States to support the implementation of the national security strategy.

(5) Such other information as may be necessary to help inform Congress on matters relating to the national security strategy of the United States.

NSC 10/2
A REPORT TO THE NATIONAL SECURITY COUNCIL

June 18, 1948

National Security Council Directive on Office of
Special Projects

    1. The National Security Council, taking cognizance of the various covert activities of the USSR, its satellite countries and Communist Groups to discredit and defeat the aims and activities of the United States and other Western powers, has determined that, in the interests of world peace and U.S. national security, the overt foreign activities of the U.S. government must be supplemented by covert operations.

    2. The Central Intelligence Agency is charged by the National Security Council with conducting espionage and counter-espionage operations abroad. It therefore seems desirable, for operational reasons, not to create a new agency for covert operations, but in time of peace to place the responsibility for them within the structure of the Central Intelligence Agency and correlate them with espionage and counter-espionage operations under the over-all control of the Director of Central Intelligence....

    d. The Director of Central Intelligence shall be responsible for:
    (1) Ensuring, through designated representatives of the Secretary of State and of the Secretary of Defense, that covert operations are planned and conducted in a manner consistent with US foreign and military policies and with overt activities. In disagreements arising between the Director of Central Intelligence and the representatives of the Secretary of State or the Secretary of Defense over such plans, the matter shall be referred to the National Security Council for decision....

Source: "NSC 10/2: A Report to the National Security Council" by the Executive Secretary of the Office on Special Operations, June 18, 1948.

5. As used in this Directive, "covert operations" are understood to be all activities (except as noted herein) which are conducted or sponsored by this Government against hostile foreign states or groups or in support of friendly foreign states or groups but which are so planned and executed that any U.S. Government responsibility for them is not evident to unauthorized persons and that if uncovered the US Government can plausibly disclaim any responsibility for them.... such operations shall include any covert activities related to: propaganda; economic warfare; preventive direct action, including sabotage, anti-sabotage, demolition and evacuation measures; subversion against hostile states, including assistance to underground resistance movements, guerrillas and refugee liberation groups, and support of indigenous anti-communist elements in threatened countries of the free world. Such operations shall not include armed conflict by recognized military forces, espionage, counter-espionage, and cover and deception for military operations....

3

Global Commitments and the New Look

INTRODUCTION

The optimistic view of the World War II allies that they would carry their cooperative spirit into the post–World War II period came to a clear end in 1948 with the Communist coup in Czechoslovakia. To be sure, there were earlier signs of impending U.S.–USSR confrontations, such as the Greek Civil War and the earlier Soviet intervention in Iran. The Truman Doctrine and George Kennan's "Mr. X" article on containment were forerunners of the policy articulated by the National Security Council in 1950 (NSC 68) with respect to the Soviet threat and US response. The Marshall Plan and NATO firmed up the Western allies' posture against a monolithic Soviet and Eastern European bloc. Thus, with the Czechoslovakia coup and the consolidation of Eastern Europe by the Soviet Union, the U.S. and its allies were faced with a bipolar world, led by the U .S. on one side and the Soviet Union on the other. Each superpower represented a distinctly different ideology and political system. What made the problem particularly threatening was the Communist takeover of mainland China in 1949. However, Stalin's death in 1952 changed the character of U.S.–USSR relationships and eventually had an impact on the international security environment.

National Security Council Paper No. 68 defined the Soviet threat and pointed out the direction and purpose of Stalin's policy directly threatening the United States. Any Soviet expansion, the paper stated, would be a clear defeat for open systems. NSC 68 called for increases in defense spending with appropriate cuts in

nondefense spending in order to build the necessary
military strength to counter the Soviet threat. Coming
almost on the heels of World War II, this position was in
direct contrast to the mood of Congress and the American
people.

The Korean War was a turning point for the United
States. The Korean War was a limited war, with limited
objectives and limited commitments. Although it signalled
a new era in modern warfare, it was not seen as such by
most Americans, including the military. The war did
signal a change in U.S. public attitudes, however,
regarding the Soviet and Communist threat. Declaring that
North Korea had broken the peace by invading South Korea,
the United Nations demanded the withdrawal of all North
Korean forces from the South and called for assistance
from other member states. After three years of conflict,
with the U.S. providing the major combat units for the
UN, stability was restored essentially along the same
lines as prior to the war.

Following the Korean War, the U.S. established a
new strategy called the "new look." Formulated under the
Eisenhower Administration, massive nuclear retaliation
replaced conventional response to aggression. Further, in
addition to containment, the Eisenhower Administration
adopted a policy of liberation of captive nations.
Articulated by Secretary Dulles, this was based on the
premise that the U.S. would not accept coexistence with
Communism. Rather, the U.S. was committed to "rolling
back" the Communist tide by supporting the liberation of
Communist--dominated states. The threat to use massive
retaliation against opponents lead to domestic
accusations, charging Secretary Dulles with
"brinksmanship." The U.S. inability (or reluctance) to
support the Hungarian Revolution eroded the credibility
of the liberation policy.

Developments in the Third World also characterized
the post-Korean War period. The Eisenhower Administration
broadened the policy of containment to encompass a number
of Third World states. These set the stage for U.S.
security interests into the next several decades. It was
in this context that United States viewed the French
withdrawal from Indochina, the Algerian Revolution,
followed by the Castro-led Cuban Revolution.
Revolutionary war and limited war were becoming primary
characteristics of the post-World War II period.

Paralleling these developments were the conflicts
emerging in the Middle East and the struggle over the
Suez Canal. Although the British, French, and Israeli

forces were militarily successful in the Suez operation in 1956, it was a political failure. This spelled the end of "colonial type" interventions. Turmoil in Iran added to the confusing Middle East picture. The Shah returned to power and set the stage for major events three decades later.

The United States became militarily involved, albeit temporarily, in the Middle East with the deployment of over 15,000 troops in Lebanon to maintain law and order on behalf of the Lebanese government. Britain also deployed about 3,000 troops. The decision by President Eisenhower to commit U.S. forces followed a request by Lebanese President Chamoun to help defend Lebanese independence. Earlier, a coup in Iraq had deposed the monarchy and led to the death of a number of pro-Western leaders. Fear of an attempt against Lebanon by the newly formed forces in Iraq prompted the Lebanese request to both the United States and Britain for help.

Events on the other side of the world also began to get the attention of the United States. Threats of conflict in the Taiwan Straits between Communist China and Nationalist China (in Formosa) led to U.S. naval intervention. Other events in the Asian area, specifically in Southeast Asia, led to the creation of the Southeast Asian Treaty Organization (SEATO). The "domino theory," focusing particularly on Southeast Asia became the watchword of the Eisenhower Administration. These events in the aggregate, encompassing a variety of Third World states and the Middle East led to the establishment of the "Eisenhower Doctrine," proclaiming U.S. support of any nation determined to preserve its freedom, particularly in the face of Communist aggression. This included the use of military force, if necessary. This was the basis for the U.S. response to the Suez Crisis and the deployment of troops into Lebanon in 1958.

Two other important events characterized the Eisenhower period. The U-2 incident, in which U.S. pilot Gary Powers was shot down and captured by the Soviet Union, proved to be an international embarrassment for the Eisenhower Administration. Powers was brought to trial in the Soviet Union and received wide international coverage. Premier Khrushchev cancelled his participation in the 1960 Paris Summit over the incident. The second was the U.S. break with Cuba after Castro had established a Marxist-Leninist system.

President Eisenhower's farewell address, parts of which are often quoted today, ended one era and opened another. Throughout the last part of the 1950s, the American people, in the main, displayed a sense of well-being and enjoyed prosperity, even with the emerging external security issues.

DOCUMENTS

NATIONAL SECURITY COUNCIL 68 (NSC 68), 1950

On the one hand, the people of the world yearn for relief from the anxiety arising from the risk of atomic war. On the other hand, any substantial further extension of the area under the domination of the Kremlin would raise the possibility that no coalition adequate to confront the Kremlin with greater strength could be assembled. It is in this context that this Republic and its citizens in the ascendency of their strength stand in their deepest peril.

The issues that face us are momentous, involving the fulfillment or destruction not only of this Republic but of civilization itself. They are issues which will not await our deliberations. With conscience and resolution this Government and the people it represents must now take new and fateful decisions...

In a world of polarized power, the policies designed to develop a healthy international community are more than ever necessary to our own strength.

As for the policy of "containment," it is one which seeks by all means short of war to (1) block further expansion of Soviet power, (2) expose the falsities of Soviet pretensions, (3) induce a retraction of the Kremlin's control and influence and (4) in general, so foster the seeds of destruction within the Soviet system that the Kremlin is brought at least to the point of modifying its behavior to conform to generally accepted international standards.

It was and continues to be cardinal in this policy that we possess superior overall power in ourselves or in dependable combination with other like-minded nations. One of the most

Source: Department of State, <u>Foreign Relations of the United States, 1950</u>, vol. I, pp. 237-265.

important ingredients of power is military strength. In the concept of "containment," the maintenance of a strong military posture is deemed to be essential for two reasons: (1) as an ultimate guarantee of our national security and (2) as an indispensable backdrop to the conduct of the policy of "containment." Without superior aggregate military strength, in being and readily mobilizable, a policy of "containment"--which is in effect a policy of calculated and gradual coercion--is no more than a policy of bluff....

In "containment" it is desirable to exert pressure in a fashion which will avoid so far as posible directly challenging Soviet prestige, to keep open the possibility for the U.S.S.R. to retreat before pressure with a minimum loss of face and to secure political advantage from the failure of the Kremlin to yield or take advantage of the openings we leave it.

We have failed to implement adequately these two fundamental aspects of "containment". In the face of obviously mounting Soviet military strength ours has declined relatively....

The United States now possesses the greatest military potential of any single nation in the world. The military weaknesses of the United States vis-a-vis the Soviet Union, however, include its numerical inferiority in forces in being and in total manpower. Coupled with the inferiority of forces in being, the United States also lacks tenable positions from which to employ its forces in event of war and munitions power in being and readily available....

It is quite clear from Soviet theory and practice that the Kremlin seeks to bring the free world under its dominion by the methods of the cold war. The preferred technique is to subvert by infiltration and intimidation. Every institution of our society is an instrument which it has sought to stultify and turn against our purposes. Those that touch most closely our material and moral strength are obviously the prime targets: labor unions, civic enterprises, schools, churches, and all media for influencing opinion. The effort is not so much to make them serve obvious Soviet ends as to prevent them from serving our ends, and thus to make them sources of confusion in our economy, our culture and our body politic. The doubts and diversities that in terms of our values are part of the merit of a free system, the weaknesses and the problems that are peculiar to it, the rights and privileges that free men enjoy, and the disorganization and destruction left in the wake of the last attack on our freedoms, all are but opportunities for the Kremlin to do its evil work. Every advantage is taken of the fact that our means of prevention and retaliation are limited by those principles and scruples which are precisely the ones that give our freedom and democracy its meaning for us. None of our scruples deter those whose only code is "morality is that which serves the revolution...."

The risk of having no better choice than to capitulate or precipitate a global war at any of a number of pressure points is bad enough in itself, but it is multiplied by the weakness it imparts to our position in the cold war. Instead of appearing strong and resolute we are continually at the verge of appearing and being alternately irresolute and desperate; yet it is the cold war which we must win, because both the Kremlin design and our fundamental purpose give it the first priority...

But there are risks in making ourselves strong. A large measure of sacrifice and discipline will be demanded of the American people. They will be asked to give up some of the benefits which they have come to associate with their freedoms. Nothing could be more important than that they fully understand the reasons for this. The risks of a superficial understanding or of an inadequate appreciation of the issues are obvious and might lead to the adoption of measures which in themselves would jeopardize the integrity of our system. At any point in the process of demonstrating our will to make good our fundamental purpose, the Kremlin may decide to precipitate a general war, or in testing us, may go too far. These are risks we will invite by making ourselves strong, but they are lesser risks than those we seek to avoid. Our fundamental purpose is more likely to be defeated from lack of the will to maintain it, than from any mistakes we may make or assault we may undergo because of asserting that will. No people in history have preserved their freedom who thought that by not being strong enough to protect themselves they might prove inoffensive to their enemies....

Finally, the absence of good faith on the part of the U.S.S.R. must be assumed until there is concrete evidence that there has been a decisive change in Soviet policies. It is to be doubted whether such a change can take place without a change in the nature of the Soviet system itself....

In the light of present and prospective Soviet atomic capabilities, the action which can be taken under present programs and plans...becomes dangerously inadequate, in both timing and scope, to accomplish the rapid progress toward the attainment of the United States political, economic, and military objectives which is now imperative.

A continuation of present trends would result in a serious decline in the strength of the free world relative to the Soviet Union and its satellites. This unfavorable trend arises from the inadequacy of current programs and plans rather than from any error in our objectives and aims. These trends lead in the direction of isolation, not by deliberate decision but by lack of the necessary basis for a vigorous initiative in the conflict with the Soviet Union.

Our position as the center of power in the free world places a heavy responsibility upon the United States for leadership. We must organize and enlist the energies and resources of the free world in a positive program for peace which will frustrate the Kremlin design for world domination by creating a situation in the free world to which the Kremlin will be compelled to adjust. Without such a cooperative effort, led by the United States, we will have to make gradual withdrawals under pressure until we discover one day that we have sacrificed positions of vital interest.

It is imperative that this trend be

reversed by a much more rapid and concerted build-up of the actual strength of both the United States and the other nations of the free world. The analysis shows that this will be costly and will involve significant domestic financial and economic adjustments.

The execution of such a build-up, however, requires that the United States have an affirmative program beyond the solely defensive one of countering the threat posed by the Soviet Union. This program must light the path to peace and order among nations in a system based on freedom and justice, as contemplated in the Charter of the United Nations. Further, it must envisage the political and economic measures with which and the military shield behind which the free world can work to frustrate the Kremlin design by the strategy of the cold war; for every consideration of devotion to our fundamental values and to our national security demands that we achieve our objectives by the strategy of the cold war, building up our military strength in order that it may not have to be used. The only sure victory lies in the frustration of the Kremlin design by the steady development of the moral and material strength of the free world and its projection into the Soviet world in such a way as to bring about an internal change in the Soviet system. Such a positive program--harmonious with our fundamental national purpose and our objectives--is necessary if we are to regain and retain the initiative and to win and hold the necessary popular support and cooperation in the United States and the rest of the free world.

This program should include a plan for negotiation with the Soviet Union, developed and agreed with our allies and which is consonant with our objectives. The United States and its allies, particularly the United Kingdom and France, should always be ready to negotiate with the Soviet Union on terms consistent with our objectives. The present world situation, however, is one which militates against successful negotiations with the Kremlin for the terms of agreements on important pending issues would reflect present realities and would therefore be unacceptable, if not disastrous, to the United States and the rest of the free world. After a decision and a start on building up the strength of the free world has been made, it might then be desirable for the United States to take an initiative in seeking negotiations in the hope that it might facilitate the process of accommodation by the Kremlin to the new situation. Failing that, the unwillingness of the Kremlin to accept equitable terms or its bad faith in observing them would assist in consolidating popular opinion in the free world in support of the measures necessary to sustain the build-up.

In summary, we must, by means of a rapid and sustained build-up of the political, economic, and military strength of the free world,...[bolster] the determination and ability of the free world to frustrate the Kremlin design of a world dominated by its will. Such evidence is the only means short of war which eventually may force the Kremlin to abandon its present course of action and to negotiate acceptable agreements on issues of major importance.

The whole success of the proposed program hangs ultimately on recognition by this Government, the American people, and all free peoples, that the cold war is in fact a real war in which the survival of the free world is at stake. Essential prerequisites to success are consultations with Congressional leaders designed to make the program the object of non-partisan legislative support, and presentation to the public of a full explanation of the facts and implications of the present international situation. The prosecution of the program will require of us all the ingenuity, sacrifice, and unity demanded by the vital importance of the issue and the tenacity to persevere until our national objectives have been attained.

THE KOREAN WAR

The Outbreak of Hostilities in Korea; Response to Events in Korea, June 24-30, 1950

Source: Department of State, Foreign Relations of the United States, 1950, vol. VIII, p. 211.

Telegram from the Ambassador in Korea (Muccio)
to the Secretary of State, June 25, 1950

According to Korean army reports which
partly confirmed by KMAG field advisor reports,
North Korean forces invaded ROK territory at
several points this morning. Action was
initiated about 4 a.m. Ongjin blasted by North
Korean artillery fire. About 6 a.m. North Korean
infantry commenced crossing parallel in Ongjin
area, Kaesong area, Chunchon area and amphibious
landing was reportedly made south of Kangnung on
east coast. Kaesong was reportedly capturerd at
9 a.m., with some 10 North Korean tanks
participating in operation. North Korean
forces, spearheaded by tanks, reportedly closing
in on Chunchon. Details of fighting in Kangnung
area unclear, although it seems North Korean
forces have cut highway. Am conferring with KMAG
advisors and Korean officials this morning re
situation.

It would appear from nature of attack and
manner in which it was launched that it
constitutes all out offensive against ROK.

Resolution Adopted by the United Nations
Security Council
(U.N. Document S/1511)

June 27, 1950

Having determined that the armed attack
upon the Republic of Korea by forces from North
Korea constitutes a breach of the peace; and

Having called for an immediate cessation
of hostilities; and

Having called upon the authorities of
North Korea to withdraw forthwith their armed
forces to the 38th parallel; and

Having noted from the report of the United
Nations Commission for Korea that the
authorities in North Korea have neither ceased
hostilities nor withdraw their armed forces to
the 38th parallel, and that urgent military
measures are required to restore international

Source: Department of State, <u>Foreign Relations
of the United States, 1950</u>, vol. VIII, p. 211.

peace and security; and

Having noted the appeal from the Republic of Korea to the United Nations for immediate and effective steps to secure peace and security,

Recommends that the Members of the United Nations furnish such assistance to the Republic of Korea as may be necessary to repel the armed attack and to restore international peace and security in the area.

President Harry Truman's Radio and Television Address to the American People on the Situation in Korea
July 19, 1950

On Saturday, June 25th, Communist forces attacked the Republic of Korea.

This attack has made it clear, beyond all doubt, that the international Communist movement is willing to use armed invasion to conquer independent nations. An act of aggression such as this creates a very real danger to the security of all free nations.

The attack upon Korea was an outright breach of the peace and a violation of the Charter of the United Nations. By their actions in Korea, Communist leaders have demonstrated their contempt for the basic moral principles on which the United Nations is founded. This is a direct challenge to the efforts of the free nations to build the kind of world in which men can live in freedom and peace.

It is important for all of us to understand the essential facts as to how the situation in Korea came about.

Before and during World War II, Korea was subject to Japanese rule. When the fighting stopped, it was agreed that troops of the Soviet Union would accept the surrender of the Japanese soldiers in the northern part of Korea, and that American forces would accept the surrender of the Japanese in the southern part. For this purpose,

---

Source: <u>Public Papers of the Presidents of the United States</u>, Harry S. Truman, 1950, pp. 537-538. Hereafter referred to as <u>Public Papers of the Presidents.</u>

the 38th parallel was used as the dividing line.

Later the United Nations sought to establish Korea as a free and independent nation. A commission was sent out to supervise a free election in the whole of Korea. However, this election was held only in the southern part of the country, because the Soviet Union refused to permit an election for this purpose to be held in the northern part. Indeed, the Soviet authorities even refused to permit the United Nations Commission to visit northern Korea.

Nevertheless, the United Nations decided to go ahead where it could. In August 1948, the Republic of Korea was established as a free and independent nation in that part of Korea south of the 38th parallel.

In December 1948, the Soviet Union stated that it had withdrawn its troops from northern Korea and that a local government had been established there. However, the Communist authorities never have permitted the United Nations observers to visit northern Korea to see what was going on behind that part of the Iron Curtain.

It was from that area, where the Communist authorities have been unwilling to let the outside world see what was going on, that the attack was launched against the Republic of Korea on June 25th. That attack came without provocation and without warning. It was an act of raw aggression without a shadow of justification....

Fifty-two of the 59 countries which are members of the United Nations have given their support to the action taken by the Security Council to restore peace in Korea.

These actions by the United Nations and its members are of great importance. The free nations have now made it clear that lawless aggression will be met with force. The free nations have learned the fateful lesson of the 1930s. That lesson is that aggression must be met firmly. Appeasement leads only to further aggression and ultimately to war....

The fact that Communist forces have invaded Korea is a warning that there may be similar acts of aggression in other parts of the world. The free nations must be on their guard, more than ever before, against this kind of sneak attack.

It is obvious that we must increase our military strength and preparedness immediately. There are three things we need to do.

First, we need to send more men, equipment, and supplies to General MacArthur.

Second, in view of the world situation, we need to build up our own Army, Navy and Air Force over and above what is needed in Korea.

Third, we need to speed up our work with other countries in strengthening our common defenses.

To help meet these needs, I have already authorized increases in the size of our Armed Forces. These increases will come in part from volunteers, in part from Selective Service, and in part from the National Guard and the Reserves.

President Eisenhower's Radio and Television Address to the American People Announcing the Signing of the Korean Armistice

July 26, 1953

My fellow citizens:

Tonight we greet, with prayers of Thanksgiving, the official news that an armistice was signed almost an hour ago in Korea. It will quickly bring an end to the fighting between the United Nations forces and the Communist armies. For this Nation the cost of repelling aggression has been high. In thousands of homes it has been incalculable. It has been paid in terms of tragedy.

With special feelings of sorrow--and of solemn gratitude we think of those who were called to lay down their lives in that far-off land to prove once again that only courage and sacrifice can keep freedom alive upon the earth. To the widows and orphans of this war, and to those veterans who bear disabling wounds, America renews tonight her pledge of lasting

Source: <u>Public Papers of the Presidents</u>, Dwight D. Eisenhower, 1953, pp. 520-521.

devotion and care.

Our thoughts turn also to those other Americans wearied by many months of imprisonment behind the enemy lines. The swift return of all of them will bring joy to thousands of families. It will be evidence of good faith on the part of those with whom we have signed this armistice.

Soldiers, sailors, airmen of 16 different countries have stood as partners beside us throughout these long and bitter months. America's thanks go to each. In this struggle we have seen the United Nations meet the challenge of aggression--not with pathetic words of protest, but with deeds of decisive purpose. It is proper that we salute particularly the valorous armies of the Republic of Korea, for they have done even more than prove their right to freedom. Inspired by President Syngman Rhee, they have given an example of courage and patriotism which again demonstrates that men of the West and men of the East can fight and work and live together side by side in pursuit of a just and noble cause.

And so at long last the carnage of war is to cease and the negotiations of the conference table are to begin. On this Sabbath evening each of us devoutly prays that all nations may come to see the wisdom of composing differences in this fashion before, rather than after, there is resort to brutal and futile battle. Now as we strive to bring about that wisdom, there is, in this moment of sober satisfaction, one thought that must discipline our emotions and steady our resolution. It is this: we have won an armistice on a single battleground--not peace in the world. We may not now relax our guard nor cease our quest.

NATIONAL SECURITY POLICY: NSC 162/2

October 30, 1953

Basic Problems of National Security Policy

Source: Department of State, Foreign Relations of the United States, 1952-1954, vol. II, part 1, pp. 577-597.

To meet the Soviet threat to U.S. Security.

In doing so, to avoid seriously weakening the U.S. economy or undermining our fundamental values and institutions.

Nature of the Soviet Threat

With increasing atomic power, the Soviets have a mounting capability of inflicting very serious and possibly crippling damage on the United States. The USSR will also continue to have large military forces capable of aggressive action against countries of the free world. Present estimates are, however, that the USSR will not deliberately initiate general war during the next several years, although general war might result from miscalculation. In the absence of general war, a prolonged period of tension may ensue, during which each side increases its armaments, reaches atomic plenty and seeks to improve its relative power position.

A sound, strong, and growing U.S. economy is necessary to support over the long pull a satisfactory posture of defense in the free world and a U.S. capability rapidly and effectively to change to full mobilization. The United States should not weaken its capacity for high productivity for defense, its free institutions, and the incentives on which its long-term economic growth depends.

Defense Against Soviet Power and Action

In the face of these threats, the United States must develop and maintain, at the lowest feasible cost, requisite military and on military strength to deter and, if necessary, to counter Soviet military aggression against the United States or other areas vital to its security.

The risk of Soviet aggression will be minimized by maintaining a strong security posture, with emphasis on adequate offensive retaliatory strength and defensive strength. This must be based on massive atomic capability, including necessary bases; an integrated and effective continental defense system; ready forces of the United States and its allies suitably deployed and adequate to deter or initially to counter aggression, and to discharge required initial tasks in the event of general war; and an adequate mobilization base; all supported by the determined spirit of the U.S. people.

This strong security posture must also be supported by an effective U.S. intelligence system, an adequate manpower program, superior scientific research and development, a program of limited defense mobilization, reasonable internal security, and an informed American people.

Such a strong security posture is essential to counter the Soviet divisive tactics and hold together the coalition. If our allies were uncertain about our ability or will to counter Soviet aggression, they would be strongly tempted to adopt a neutral position, especially in the face of the atomic threat....

In Western Europe, a position of strength must be based on British, French, and German cooperation in the defense of the continent. To achieve a stronger Europe, the United States should support, as long as there is hope of early success, the building of an integrated European Community (including West Germany and if possible a united Germany), linked to the United States through NATO. The United States should press for a strong, united, stable Germany, oriented to the free world and militarily capable of overcoming internal subversion and disorder and also of taking a major part in the collective defense of the free world against aggression. The United States must continue to assist in creating and maintaining mutually agreed European forces, but should reduce such assistance as rapidly as United States interests permit.

In the Far East, strength must be built on existing bilateral and multilateral security arrangements until more comprehensive regional arrangements become feasible. The United States should stress assistance in developing Japan as a major element of strength. The United States should maintain the security of the off-shore island chain and continue to develop the defensive capacity of Korea and Southeast Asia in accordance with existing commitments.

In the Middle East, a strong regional grouping is not now feasible. In order to assure during peace time for the United States and its allies the resources (especially oil) and the strategic positions of the area and their denial to the Soviet bloc, the United States should build on Turkey, Pakistan, and, if possible, Iran, and assist in achieving stability in the Middle East by political actions and limited military and economic assistance, and technical assistance, to other countries in the area.

In other areas of the free world the United States should furnish limited military aid, and limited technical and economic assistance, to other free nations, according to calculated advantages of such aid to the U.S. world position.

As presently deployed in support of our commitments, the armed forces of the United States are over-extended, thereby depriving us of mobility and initiative for future military action in defense of the free world....

In the event of hostilities, the United States will consider nuclear weapons to be as available for use as other munitions. Where the consent of an ally is required for the use of these weapons from U.S. bases on the territory of such ally, the United States should promptly obtain the advance consent of such ally for such use. The United States should also seek, as and when feasible, the understanding and approval of this policy by free nations....

Reduction of the Soviet Threat

The United States must seek to improve the power position of itself and the rest of the free world in relation to the Soviet bloc.

The United States must also keep open the possibility of negotiating with the USSR and Communist China acceptable and enforceable agreements, whether limited to individual issues now outstanding or involving a general settlement of major issues, including control of armaments....

The policy of the United States is to prevent Soviet aggression and continuing domination of other nations, and to establish an effective control of armaments under proper safeguards; but is not to dictate the internal political and economic organization of the USSR.

As a means of reducing Soviet capabilities for extending control and influence in the free world, the United States should:

Take overt and covert measures to discredit Soviet prestige and ideology as effective instruments of Soviet power, and to reduce the strength of communist parties and other pro-Soviet elements.

Take all feasible diplomatic, political, economic and covert measures to counter any threat of a party or individuals directly or indirectly responsive to Soviet control to achieve dominant power in a free world country.

Undertake selective, positive actions to eliminate Soviet-Communist control over any areas of the free world...

In the face of the developing Soviet threat, the broad aim of U.S. security policies must be to create, prior to the achievement of mutual atomic plenty, conditions under which the United States and the free world coalition are prepared to meet the Soviet-Communist threat with resolution and to negotiate for its alleviation under proper safeguards. The United States and its allies must always seek to create and sustain the hope and confidence of the free world in the ability of its basic ideas and institutions not merely to oppose the communist threat, but to provide a way of life superior to Communism.

The foregoing conclusions are valid only so long as the United States maintains a retaliatory capability that cannot be neutralized by a suprise Soviet attack.

THE NEW LOOK
The Evolution of Foreign Policy
Address by Secretary Dulles, January 12, 1954

Source: Department of State Bulletin, January 25, 1954, pp. 107-110.

The Soviet Communists are planning for what they call "an entire historical era," and we should do the same. They seek, through many types of maneuvers, gradually to divide and weaken the free nations by overextending them in efforts which, as Lenin put it, are "beyond their strength, so that they come to Source: practical bankruptcy." Then, said Lenin, "our victory is assured." Then, said Stalin, will be "the moment for the decisive blow."

In the face of this strategy, measures cannot be judged adequate merely because they ward off an immediate danger. It is essential to do this, but it is also essential to do so without exhausting ourselves.

When the Eisenhower administration applied this test, we felt that some transformations were needed.

It is not sound military strategy permanently to commit U.S. land forces to Asia to a degree that leaves us no strategic reserves.

It is not sound economics, or good foreign policy, to support permanently other countries; for in the long run, that creates as much ill will as good will.

Also, it is not sound to become permanently committed to military expenditures so vast that they lead to "practical bankruptcy."

Change was imperative to assure the stamina needed for permanent security. But it was equally imperative that change should be accompanied by understanding of our true purposes. Sudden and spectacular change had to be avoided. Otherwise, there might have been panic among our friends and miscalculated aggression by our enemies. We can, I believe, make a good report in these respects.

We need allies and collective security. Our purpose is to make these relations more effective, less costly. This can be done by placing more reliance on deterrent power and less dependence on local defensive power.

This is accepted practice so far as local communities are concerned. We keep locks on our doors, but we do not have an armed guard in every home. We rely principally on a community security system so well equipped to punish any who break and steal that, in fact, would-be-aggressors are generally deterred. That is the modern way of getting maximum protection at a bearable cost.

What the Eisenhower administration seeks is a similar international security system. We want, for ourselves and the other free nations, a maximum deterrent at a bearable cost.

Local defense will always be important. But there is no local defense which alone will contain the mighty landpower of the Communist world. Local defenses must be reinforced by the further deterrent of massive retaliatory power. A potential aggressor must know that he cannot always prescribe battle conditions that suit him. Otherwise, for example, a potential aggressor, who is glutted with manpower, might be tempted to attack in confidence that resistance would be confined to manpower. He might be tempted to attack in places where his superiority was decisive.

The way to deter aggression is for the free community to be willing and able to respond vigorously at places and with means of its own choosing.

So long as our basic policy concepts were unclear, our military leaders could not be selective in building our military power. If an enemy could pick his time and place and method of warfare-and if our policy was to remain the traditional one of meeting aggression by direct and local opposition-then we need to be ready to fight in the Arctic and in the Tropics; in Asia, the Near East, and in Europe; by sea, by land, and by air; with old weapons and with new weapons....

Now the Department of Defense and the Joint Chiefs of Staff can shape our military establishment to fit what is our policy, instead of having to try to be ready to meet the enemy's many choices. That permits of a selection of military means instead of a multitude of means. As a result, it is now possible to get, and share, more basic security at less cost....

We do not, of course, claim to have found some magic formula that insures against all forms of Communist successes. It is normal that at some times and at some places there may be setbacks to the cause of freedom. What we do expect to insure is that any setbacks will have only temporary and local significance, because they will leave unimpaired those free-world assets which in the long run will prevail....

If we rely on freedom, then it follows that we must abstain from diplomatic moves which would seem to endorse captivity. That would, in effect, be a conspiracy against freedom. I can assure you that we will never seek illusory security for ourselves by such a "deal."

The President's News Conference
March 17, 1954

Question: Mr. Dulles has outlined the policy of retaliation, and in some quarters that has been interpreted as meaning that if you have a local war or local situation that the retaliation might be against Moscow or Peking or some major point. Could you discuss the question of the local warlike situation?

The President:...there is one thing I can tell you about war, and almost one only, and it is this: no war ever shows the characteristics that were expected; it is always different. What we are trying to say now is to express a generalization that would apply in an infinite variety of cases, under an infinite variety of provocations, and I just don't believe it is possible. I think that what has got to be decided is how deeply the safety and security of America is involved.

We do know that there are weapons now in being that give more than ever to the attacker a tremendous advantage, the man who attacks by surprise. The element of surprise, always important in war, has been multiplied by the possibility of creating such widespread destruction quickly. Therefore, any President should be worse than impeached, he should be hanged, I should say, if he didn't do what all America would demand that he do to protect them in an emergency.

Source: <u>Public Papers of the Presidents</u>, Dwight D. Eisenhower, 1954, pp. 325-331.

But when it comes to saying that where on the fringe or the periphery of our interests and of wherever we may be, that any kind of an act on the part of the enemy would justify that kind of thing, that I wouldn't hold with for a moment; I don't think anybody else would.

Question: I would like to go back to the matter of Secretary Dulles and the doctrine of "massive retaliation." As you [said], you can't foresee the things you might do under varying circumstances. Perhaps we are confused, because we have been led to believe that Secretary Dulles had enunciated some new doctrine. Is it a new doctrine, sir?

President: Oh, not, not at all.

Question: Then there is nothing new about that?

President: After all, let's remember this: the American
sailors tried to fight back at Pearl Harbor, didn't they?

Question: Yes.

President: Well, that was an act of war; it was an act of violence, at least. We would have been amazed had they not done so.

If you can imagine such things happening on a larger scale, who is the man who has to act quickly? The President of the United States, as the Commander in Chief of the Armed Forces; he has got to do something. But when it comes down to saying that merely because in some corner of the world our vital interests are hurt, we are going to decide in advance such great and extraordinary action that Congress really has no way of backing up, that wouldn't be right.

Question: Last week, Mr. President, you said you didn't particularly care for slogans, but we have had this, we have been hearing now about the "new look," the "new look" in defense, "new look" in foreign policy; is it true, sir, would we be wise to assume that nothing new has happened in the matter of the military....

President: "New Look": now what do we mean? We mean this: we are not fighting with muzzle-loaders in any of the services. Every single day things change in this world, and any staff or any group of leaders doing his job is re-examining the world situation, the advances of science, the whole situation, geographic and otherwise, of our country and of others, to see what it is that we now need most to insure our security and our peaceful existence.

You cannot possibly say that kind of a unit and organization that I took to war or took over across the Channel in 1944 would have any usefulness today whatsoever. For example, you will recall we landed on June 6; we got out of that narrow little beachhead on about July 25. All right; behind that we built up two artificial harbors and we were landing over the beaches. What would two atomic bombs have done to the whole thing?

So you just simply can't take, in warfare or in any contemplation of war or preparation for war, take old patterns and say that is by which we live.

All that the "new look" is is an attempt by intelligent people to keep abreast of the times; and if you want to call your today's clothes the "new look" as compared to what Lincoln wore, all right, we are in the "new look." But I just don't like this expression because it doesn't mean much to me.

I mean that we are striving our best to meet the grave responsibilities that are placed upon those people whose job is to protect this country. Let me point this out: I hear people say "bigger army." Now, our most valued, our most costly asset is our young men. Let's don't use them any more than we have to.

For 40 years I was in the Army, and I did one thing: study how can you get an infantry platoon out of battle. The most terrible job in warfare is to be a second lieutenant leading a platoon when you are on the battlefield.

If we can do anything to lessen that number--remember this: we are planning right now the greatest peacetime army we have ever held, one million men in time of peace.

What are we talking about? It is, I think, there is too much hysteria. You know, the world is suffering from a multiplicity of fears. We fear the men in the Kremlin, we fear what they will do to our friends around them; we are fearing what unwise investigators will do to us here at home as they try to combat subversion or bribery or deceit within. We fear depression, we fear the loss of jobs. All of these, with their impact on the human mind, make us act almost hysterically, and you find hysterical reactions.

We have got to look at each of those in its proper perspective, to understand what the whole sum total means. And remember this: the reason they are feared and bad is because there is a little element of truth in each, a little element of danger in each. That means that finally there is a little residue that you can meet only by faith, a faith in the destiny of America; and that is what I believe is the answer.

This "new look"--the "new look" is just our effort to solve in one field, that of direct military attack, to produce the best results we can for the protection of America. To call it revolutionary or to act like it is something that just suddenly dropped down on us like a cloud out of the heaven, is just not true, just not true.

THE DOMINO PRINCIPLE

The President's News Conference
April 7, 1954

Question: Mr. President, would you mind commenting on the strategic importance of Indochina to the free world?

President: You have, of course, both the specific and the general when you talk about such things.

First of all, you have the specific value of a locality in its production of materials that the world needs.

Then you have the possibility that many human beings pass under a dictatorship that is inimical to the free world.

Finally, you have broader considerations that might follow what you would call the "falling domino" principle. You have a row of dominoes set up, you knock over the first one, and what will happen to the last one is

Source: Public Papers of the Presidents, Dwight D. Eisenhower, 1954, pp. 325-331.

certainty that it will go over quickly. So you could have a beginning of a disintegration that would have the most profound influences.

Now, with respect to the first one, two of the items from this particular area that the world uses are tin and tungsten. They are very important. There are others, of course, the rubber plantations and so on.

Then with respect to more people passing under this domination, Asia, after all, has already lost some 450 million of its people to the Communist dictatorship, and we simply can't afford greater losses.

But when we come to the possible sequence of events, the loss of Indochina, of Burma, of Thailand, of the Peninsula, and Indonesia following, now you begin to talk about areas that not only multiply the disadvantages that you would suffer through--losses of materials, sources of materials, but now you are talking about millions and millions and millions of people.

Finally, the geographical position achieved thereby does many things. It turns the so-called island defensive chain of Japan, Formosa, of the Philippines and to the southward; it moves in to threaten Australia and New Zealand.

It takes away, in its economic aspects, that region that Japan must have as a trading area or Japan, in turn, will have only one place in the world to go--that is, toward the Communist areas--in order to live.

So, the possible consequences of the loss are incalculable--to the free world.

THE PACIFIC CHARTER AND THE SOUTHEAST ASIA TREATY ORGANIZATION

The Pacific Charter, Manila, September 8, 1954

The Delegates of Australia, France, New Zealand, Pakistan, the Republic of the Philippines, the Kingdom of Thailand, the United

Source: United States Treaties and Other International Agreements, vol. 6, part 1, 1955, p. 91.

Kingdom of Great Britain and Northern Ireland,
and the United States of America,

Desiring to establish a firm basis for
common action to maintain peace and security in
Southeast Asia and the Southwest Pacific,

Convinced that common action to this end,
in order to be worthy and effective, must be
inspired by the highest principles of justice
and liberty,

Do Hereby Proclaim:

First, in accordance with the provisions
of the United Nations Charter, they uphold the
principle of equal rights and self-determination
of peoples and they will earnestly strive by
every peaceful means to promote self-government
and to secure the independence of all countries
whose people desire it and are able to undertake
its responsibilities;

Second, they are each prepared to continue
taking effective practical measures to ensure
conditions favorable to the orderly achievement
of the foregoing purposes in accordance with
their constitutional processes;

Third, they will continue to cooperate in
the economic, social and cultural fields in
order to promote higher living standards,
economic progress and social well-being in this
region;

Fourth, as declared in the Southeast Asia
Collective Defense Treaty, they are determined
to prevent or counter by appropriate means any
attempt in the treaty area to subvert their
freedom or to destroy their sovereignty or
territorial integrity.

SOUTHEAST ASIA COLLECTIVE DEFENSE
September 8, 1954

The Parties to this Treaty,

Recognizing the sovereign equality of all the
Parties,

Reiterating their faith in the purposes
and principles set forth in the Charter of the

Source: United States Treaties and Other
International Agreements, 1955, vol. 6, part 1,
pp. 82-86.

United Nations and their desire to live in peace with all peoples and all governments,

Reaffirming that, in accordance with the Charter of the United Nations, they uphold the principle of equal rights and self-determination of peoples, and declaring that they will earnestly strive by every peaceful means to promote self-government and to secure the independence of all countries whose people desire it and are able to undertake its responsibilities,

Desiring to strengthen the fabric of peace and freedom and to uphold the principles of democracy, individual liberty and the rule of law, and to promote the economic well-being and development of all peoples in the treaty area,

Intending to declare publicly and formally their sense of unity, so that any potential aggressor will appreciate that the Parties stand together in the area, and

Desiring further to coordinate their efforts for collective defense for the preservation of peace and security,

Therefore agree as follows:

ARTICLE I

The Parties undertake, as set forth in the Charter of the United Nations, to settle any international disputes in which they may be involved by peaceful means in such a manner that international peace and security and justice are not endangered, and to refrain in their international relations from the threat or use of force in any manner inconsistent with the purposes of the United Nations.

ARTICLE II

In order more effectively to achieve the objectives of this Treaty, the Parties, separately and jointly, by means of continuous and effective self-help and mutual aid will maintain and develop their individual and collective capacity to resist armed attack and to prevent and counter subversive activities directed from without against their territorial integrity and political stability.

ARTICLE III

The Parties undertake to strengthen their free institutions and to cooperate with one another in the further development of economic measures, including technical assistance, designed both to promote economic progress and social well-being and to further the individual and collective efforts of governments toward these ends.

ARTICLE IV

1. Each Party recognizes that aggression by means of armed attack in the treaty area against any of the Parties or against any State or territory which the Parties by unanimous agreement may herafter designate, would endanger its own peace and safety, and agrees that it will in that event act to meet the common danger in accordance with its constitutional processes. Measures taken under this paragraph shall be immediately reported to the Security Council of the United Nations.

2. If, in the opinion of any of the Parties, the inviolability or the integrity of the territory or the sovereignty or political independence of any Party in the treaty area or of any other State or territory to which provisions of paragraph 1 of this Article from time to time apply is threatened in any way other than by armed attack or is affected or threatened by any fact or situation which might endanger the peace of the area, the Parties shall consult immediately in order to agree on the measures which should be taken for the common defense.

3. It is understood that no action on the territory of any State designated by unanimous agreement under paragraph 1 of this Article or any territory so designated shall be taken except at the invitation or with the consent of the government concerned.

THE MANILA PACT AND THE PACIFIC CHARTER (SEATO)

Address by Secretary Dulles, September 15, 1954

Our quest for peace took us last week to Manila. There, eight nations met to create unity for security and peace in Southeast Asia and the Southwestern Pacific....

Australia, France, New Zealand, Pakistan, the Philippines, Thailand, the United Kingdom, and the United States met together. We negotiated as full and equal partners and in the end signed a treaty for defense both against open armed attack and against internal subversion.

The treaty provides that, in the case of aggression by armed attack, each of the countries will act to meet the common danger.

A council is established for consultation with regard to military planning and other planning.

The treaty recognizes also the danger of subversion and indirect aggression. It deals with this difficult problem more explicitly than any other security treaty that has been made. In this respect, the treaty represents an important forward step, because subversion and indirect aggression have been principal tools of international communism.

The treaty provides that if any party believes that the integrity of the treaty area is menaced by other than armed attack, the parties shall consult immediately to agree on measures which should be taken for the common defense. These measures will, of course, never involve intervention in the purely internal affairs of another state.

The United States was in a special position at Manila, because it was the only one of the signatories which did not have territorial interests in the treaty area. For the others, the pact was not only an anti-Communist pact but also a regional pact. Therefore, it dealt with any and all acts of aggression which might disturb the peace of the

Source: Department of State Bulletin, September 27, 1954, pp. 431-433.

area. We stipulated on behalf of the United
States, however, that the only armed attack in
that area which we would regard as necessarily
dangerous to our peace and security would be a
Communist armed attack.

Any significant expansion of the Communist
world would, indeed, be a danger to the United
States, because international communism thinks
in terms of ultimately using its power position
against the United States. Therefore, we could
honestly say, using the words that President
Monroe used in proclaiming his Doctrine, that
Communist armed aggression in Southeast Asia
would, in fact, endanger our peace and security
and call for counteraction on our part.

The treaty recognizes the importance of
economic welfare. But it does not commit the
United States to any "handout" program. We agree
to cooperate in the development of economic
measures which will promote economic and social
well-being. Congress this year had the vision to
see that there might be special needs in
Southeast Asia. So, by the Mutual Security Act,
Congress has already provided a fund to be
available in this area. Part of it will no doubt
be spent to assist the free governments in
Southeast Asia....

I believe that the Manila Pact will, in
fact, make a substantial contribution to
preserve free governments in Southeast Asia and
to prevent communism from rushing on into the
Pacific area, where it would seriously threaten
the defense of the United States....

In my opening address to the Conference, I
emphasized that one of the most effective
weapons of communism was to pretend that the
Western Powers were seeking to impose
colonialism on the Asian peoples. I said we must
make it abundantly clear that we intend to
invigorate independence. "Only then can the West
and the East work together in true fellowship."

This Manila Conference faced up to that
issue. It was the first conference where
representative nations of Asia and of the West
sat down together to work out a program of
mutual security. The result was the Pacific
Charter, which, in ringing terms, dedicates all
the signatories to uphold the principles of

self-determination, self-government, and independence for all countries whose peoples desire it and are able to undertake its responsibilities.

Whenever there arises in Asia a power that wants to conquer others, it adopts the motto: "Asia for the Asians." The Japanese, when they were dominated by the war lords, used that slogan. Today the Soviet and Chinese Communists have adopted it. They want to prevent the free countries of Asia from getting the help they need to preserve their independence.

The Pacific Charter, on which the East and the West did meet, may well prove to be the most momentous product of the Conference.

The Communists' attitude was shown, during the Conference, by vicious propaganda attacks and even more significantly by new military activities in a nearby area. Apparently they hoped to intimidate the members of our Conference and perhaps to prevent some from signing the security pact.

Efforts to intimidate by violence are typical of the Communist technique. When the Korean armistice negotiations were reaching their climax, the Chinese Communists opened their bloodiest assault against the United Nations position in Korea. Once it had been agreed to discuss peace in Indochina, the Communist forces of Ho Chi Minh, backed by Communist China, opened their murderous assault on Dien-Bien Phu. And as the Manila Conference opened, the Chinese Communists opened their artillery fire on Quemoy, an island which has been part of Free China ever since the end of World War II and which was only about 400 miles distant from the Philippines.

This effort to intimidate the Manila Conference was a total failure. All of the particpants signed the Manila Pact and the Pacific Charter with confidence that in so doing they were adding to their own security....

The Manila Pact is directed against no government, against no nation, and against no people. It is directed only against aggression. The fact that the Communists find that objectionable is tragically revealing of their ambitions.

THE EISENHOWER DOCTRINE: Statement by Secretary
Dulles before the House Committee on
Foreign Affairs

January 7, 1957

Since World War II, the United States has
had to meet a series of critical situations with
strong measures backed with national unity.

The dangers have been met in different
ways, as circumstances dictated. In some cases
there was economic aid alone. In some cases we
dealt only with the military aspect of the
problem. Also in some cases there was action by
the Congress by legislation. In some cases there
was action by treaty processes. And in some
cases the Executive acted with tacit
acquiescence of Congress.

But though these needs have been different
and the constitutional methods have been
different, there have been basic underlying
similarities.

In each case we proceeded from the premise
that, as it was put by President Truman in his
Greek-Turkey message, "totalitarian regimes
imposed upon free peoples, by direct or indirect
aggression, undermine the foundations of
international peace and hence the security of
the United States."

Also, all our treaty and legislative
action has been designed to promote peace by
making clear our position in advance and thus to
deter aggression and to prevent dangerous
miscalculations by would-be aggressors.

Also, in each case our resolve has been
impressive because of the national unity which
expressed it.

Also, in each case where we have so acted,
we have in fact preserved freedom.

Today we concern ourselves with the Middle
East. Few of us doubt that it would be a major
disaster for the nations and peoples of the
Middle East, and indeed for all the world, if
that area were to fall into the grip of
international communism.

Source: <u>Department of State Bulletin</u>, January
28, 1957, pp. 127-129.

The disaster would spread far beyond the confines of the Middle East itself. The economies of many free-world countries depended directly upon natural products of the Middle East and on transportation through the Middle East. And, indirectly, the entire free-world economy is concerned. Western Europe is particularly dependent upon the Middle East. The vast sacrifices the United States has made for the economic recovery of Europe and military defense of Europe would be virtually nullified if the Middle East fell under the control of international communism.

Finally, a Communist breakthrough in the Middle East would encourage the Soviet rulers to resort everywhere to more aggressive policies. It would severely weaken the pressures within the Soviet world for more liberal policies. It would be a severe blow to the struggling peoples of Hungary and Poland who are so valiantly striving for more independence. It would undo, throughout the world, much of the benefit of the earlier actions I have recalled.

For all these reasons, the United States must do whatever it properly can to assist the nations of the Middle East to maintain their independence.

After the most thorough consideration, President Eisenhower has concluded, and has recommended to the Congress, that action be taken which will first of all make unmistakably clear that it is the policy of the United States, declared by the Congress and the President, to cooperate with the nations of the Middle East to maintain their independence.

It would in the second place authorize the President to assist any nation or group of nations in the general area in the development of economic strength dedicated to the maintenance of national independence.

It would in the third place authorize the President to undertake military assistance programs with any such nation or group of nations, if they desired such assistance.

It would in the fourth place authorize the President to employ the armed force of the United States to secure and protect the territorial integrity and political independence of any such nation or group of nations requesting such aid against overt armed aggression from any nation controlled by international communism.

The proposed legislation is in the judgement of our President necessary to meet the danger.

The danger can take any one or more of several forms. There is the possibility of open armed attack. There is the possibility of subversion, a danger which is increased if there be a sense of insecurity. There is the danger that economic conditions be such as to make communism seem an attractive choice. Any program, to be adequate, must be prepared to meet all three of these dangers and any combination of them. Also, those needs cannot be met under present conditions unless we make clear now, in relation to the Middle East, what we have already made clear in relation to so many areas; namely, that armed Communist attack would have to be met, if need be, by the armed force of the United States.

You may feel--I do feel--that there is in fact no doubt as to what the Congress would do if international communism set out on a piecemeal conquest of the world by war. But until the Congress has actually spoken, there is doubt in the Middle East and there may be doubt in the Soviet Union. If those doubts persist, then the danger persists and grows. If we elect to wait and see and then decide, the waiting period will greatly heighten vulnerability to both direct attack by overwhelming force and to indirect aggression.

The purpose of the proposed resolution is not war. It is peace. The purpose, as in the other cases where the President and the Congress have acted together to oppose international communism, is to stop World War III before it starts.

JOINT RESOLUTION TO PROMOTE PEACE AND STABILITY
    IN THE MIDDLE EAST, March 1957

Source: <u>Department of State Bulletin</u>, March 25, 1957, p. 481.

<u>Resolved by the Senate and House of Representatives of the United States of America in Congress assembled</u>,

That the President be and hereby is authorized to cooperate with and assist any nation or group of nations in the general area of the Middle East desiring such assistance in the development of economic strength dedicated to the maintenance of national independence....

SEC. 2. The President is authorized to undertake, in the general area of the Middle East, military assistance programs with any nation or group of nations of that area desiring such assistance. Furthermore, the United States regards as vital to the national interest and world peace the preservation of the independence and integrity of the nations of the Middle East. To this end, if the President determines the necessity thereof, the United States is prepared to use armed forces to assist any such nation or group of such nations requesting assistance against armed aggression from any country controlled by international communism:

<u>Provided</u>, That such employment shall be consonant with the treaty obligations of the United States and with the Constitution of the United States....

SEC. 4. The President should continue to furnish facilities and military assistance, within the provisions of applicable law and established policies, to the United Nations Emergency Force in the Middle East, with a view to maintaining the truce in that region....

SEC. 6. This joint resolution shall expire when the President shall determine that the peace and security of the nations in the general area of the Middle East are reasonably assured by international conditions created by action of the United Nations or otherwise except that it may be terminated earlier by a concurrent resolution of the two Houses of Congress.

PRESIDENT EISENHOWER: FAREWELL RADIO
and TELEVISION ADDRESS to the AMERICAN PEOPLE
January 17, 1961

My Fellow Americans:

* * * * *

A vital element in keeping the peace is
our military establishment. Our arms must be
mighty, ready for instant action, so that no
potential aggressor may be tempted to risk his
own destruction.

Our military today bears little relation
to that known by any of my predecessors in
peacetime, or indeed by the fighting men of
World War II or Korea.

Until the latest of our world conflicts,
the United States had no armaments industry.
American makers of plowshares could, with time
and as required, make swords as well. But now we
can no longer risk emergency improvisation of
national defense; we have been compelled to
create a permanent armaments industry of vast
proportions. Added to this, three and a half
million men and women are directly engaged in
the defense establishment. We annually spend on
military security more than the net income of
all United States corporations.

This conjunction of an immense military
establishment and a large arms industry is new
in the American experience. The total influence-
-economic, political, even spiritual--is felt in
every city, every State house, every office of
the Federal government. We recognize the
imperative need for this development. Yet we
must not fail to comprehend its grave
implications. Our toil, resources and livelihood
are all involved; so is the very structure of
our society.

In the councils of government, we must
guard against the acquisition of unwarranted
influence, whether sought or unsought, by the
military-industrial complex. The potential for
the disastrous rise of misplaced power exists

Source: <u>Public Papers of the Presidents</u>, Dwight
D. Eisenhower, 1960-1961, pp. 1037-1039.

and will persist.

We must never let the weight of this combination endanger our liberties or democratic processes. We should take nothing for granted. Only an alert and knowledgeable citizenry can compel the proper meshing of the huge industrial and military machinery of defense with our peaceful methods and goals, so that security and liberty may prosper together.

Akin to, and largely responsible, for the sweeping changes in our industrial-military posture has been the technological revolution during recent decades.

In this revolution, research has become central; it also becomes more formalized, complex, and costly. A steadily increasing share is conducted for, by, or at the direction of, the Federal government.

... the free university, historically the fountainhead of free ideas and scientific discovery, has experienced a revolution in the conduct of research. Partly because of the huge costs involved, a government contract becomes virtually a substitute for intellectual curiosity. For every old blackboard there are now hundreds of new electronic computers.

The prospect of domination of the nation's scholars by Federal employment, project allocations, and the power of money is ever present--and is gravely to be regarded.

Yet, in holding scientific research and discovery in respect, as we should, we must also be alert to the equal and opposite danger that public policy could itself become the captive of a scientific-technological elite.

It is the task of statemanship to mold, to balance, and to integrate these and other forces, new and old, within the principles of our democratic system--ever aiming toward the supreme goals of our free society.

U.S.-CUBAN POLICY
Statement by the President Restating United States Policy Toward Cuba, January 26, 1960

Source: Public Papers of the Presidents, Dwight D. Eisenhower, 1960-1961, pp. 135-136.

The United States Government adheres strictly to the policy of non-intervention in the domestic affairs of other countries, including Cuba. This policy is incorporated in our treaty commitments as a member of the Organization of American States.

Second, the United States Government has consistently endeavored to prevent illegal acts in territory under its jurisdiction directed against other governments. United States law enforcement agencies have been increasingly successful in the prevention of such acts. The United States record in this respect compares very favorably with that of Cuba from whose territory a number of invasions directed against other countries have departed during the past year, in several cases attended with serious loss of life and property damage in the territory of those other countries. The United States authorities will continue to enforce United States laws, including those which reflect commitments under Inter-American treaties, and hope that other governments will act similarly. Our Government has repeatedly indicated that it will welcome any information from the Cuban Government or from other governments regarding incidents occurring within their jurisdiction or notice, which would be of assistance to our law enforcement agencies in this respect.

Third, the United States Government views with increasing concern the tendency of spokesmen of the Cuban Government, including Prime Minister Castro, to create the illusion of aggressive acts and conspiratorial acts aimed at the Cuban Government and attributed to United States officials or agencies. The promotion of unfounded illusions of this kind can hardly facilitate the development, in the real interest of the two peoples, of relations of understanding and confidence between their governments. The United States Government regrets that its earnest efforts over the past year to establish a basis for such understanding and confidence have not been reciprocated.

Fourth, the United States Government, of course, recognizes the right of the Cuban Government and people in exercise of their national sovereignty to undertake those social, economic and political reforms which, with due regard for their obligations under international law, they may think desirable. This position has frequently been stated and it reflects a real understanding of and sympathy with the ideals and aspirations of the Cuban people. Similarly, the United States Government and people will continue to assert and to defend, in the exercise of their own sovereignty, their legitimate interests.

Fifth, the United States Government believes that its citizens have made constructive contributions to the economies of other countries by means of their investments and their work in those countries and that such contributions, taking into account changing conditions, can continue on a mutually satisfactory basis. The United States Government will continue to bring to the attention of the Cuban Government any instances in which the rights of its citizens under Cuban law and under international law have been disregarded and in which redress under Cuban law is apparently unavailable or denied. In this connection it is the hope of the United States Government that differences of opinion between the two governments in matters recognized under international law as subject to diplomatic negotiations will be resolved through such negotiations. In the event that disagreements between the two governments concerning this matter should persist, it would be the intention of the United States Government to seek solutions through other appropriate international procedures.

Statement by the President on
Terminating Diplomatic Relations with Cuba
January 3, 1961

Between one and two o'clock this morning, the Government of Cuba delivered to the United States Charge d'Affaires ad interim of the United States Embassy in Habana a note stating

---

Source: <u>Public Papers of the Presidents</u>, Dwight D. Eisenhower, 1960-1961, p. 891.

that the Government of Cuba has decided to limit the personnel of our Embassy and Consulate in Habana to eleven persons. Forty-eight hours was granted for the departure of our entire staff with the exception of eleven. This unusual action on the part of the Castro Government can have no other purpose than to render impossible the conduct of normal diplomatic relations with that Government.

Accordingly, I have instructed the Secretary of State to deliver a note to the Charge d'Affaires ad interim of Cuba in Washington which refers to the demand of his Government and states that the Government of the United States is hereby formally terminating diplomatic and consular relations with the Government of Cuba. Copies of both notes are being made available to the press.

This calculated action on the part of the Castro Government is only the latest of a long series of harassments, baseless accusations, and vilification. There is a limit to what the United States in self-respect can endure. That limit has now been reached. Our friendship for the Cuban people is not affected. It is my hope and my conviction that in the not too distant future it will be possible for the historic friendship between us once again to find its reflection in normal relations of every sort. Meanwhile, our sympathy goes out to the people of Cuba now suffering under the yoke of a dictator.

Statement by James C. Hagerty
US Rights at Guantanamo Base

January 4, 1961

The termination of our diplomatic and consular relations with Cuba has no effect on the status of our naval station at Guantanamo. The treaty rights under which we maintain the naval station may not be abrogated without the consent of the United States.

Source: Department of State Bulletin, January 23, 1961, p. 104.

CRISIS: U-2 INCIDENT
Department of State Note

May 5, 1960

The Department has been informed by NASA that, as announced May 3, an unarmed plane, a U-2 weather research plane based at Adana, Turkey, piloted by a civilian has been missing since May 1. During the flight of this plane, the pilot reported difficulty with his oxygen equipment. Mr. Khrushchev has announced that a U.S. plane has been shot down over the U.S.S.R. on that date. It is entirely possible that having a failure in the oxygen equipment, which could result in the pilot losing consciousness, the plane continued on automatic pilot for a considerable distance and accidentally violated Soviet airspace. The United States is taking the matter up with the Soviet Government, with particular reference to the fate of the pilot.

Statement by Secretary Herter

May 9, 1960

On May 7 the Department of State spokesman made a statement with respect to the alleged shooting down of an unarmed American civilian aircraft of the U-2 type over the Soviet Union. The following supplements and clarifies this statement as respects the position of the United States Government.

Ever since Marshal Stalin shifted the policy of the Soviet Union from wartime cooperation to postwar conflict in 1946 and particularly since the Berlin blockade, the forceful takeover of Czechoslovakia, and the Communist aggressions in Korea and Viet-Nam the world has lived in a state of apprehension with respect to Soviet intentions. The Soviet leaders have almost complete access to open societies of the free world and supplement this with vast espionage networks. However, they keep

Sources: Department of State Bulletin, May 23, 1960, pp. 816-818. This citation is for both documents of May, 1960.

their own society tightly closed and rigorously controlled. With the development of modern weapons carrying tremendously destructive nuclear warheads, the threat of surprise attack and aggression presents a constant danger. This menace is enhanced by the threats of mass destruction frequently voiced by the Soviet leadership.

For many years the United States in company with its allies has sought to lessen or even to eliminate this threat from the life of man so that he can go about his peaceful business without fear. Many proposals to this end have been put up to the Soviet Union. The President's open skies proposal of 1955 was followed in 1957 by the offer of an exchange of ground observers between agreed military installations in the U.S., the U.S.S.R., and other nations that might wish to participate. For several years we have been seeking the mutual abolition of the restrictions on travel imposed by the Soviet Union and those which the United States felt obliged to institute on a reciprocal basis. More recently at the Geneva disarmament conference the United States has proposed far-reaching new measures of controlled disarmament. It is possible that the Soviet leaders have a different version and that, however unjustifiedly, they fear attack from the West. But this is hard to reconcile with their continual rejection of our repeated proposals for effective measures against surprise attack and for effective inspection of disarmament measures.

I will say frankly that it is unacceptable that the Soviet political system should be given an opportunity to make secret preparations to face the free world with the choice of abject surrender or nuclear destruction. The Government of the United States would be derelict in its responsibility not only to the American people but to free peoples everywhere if it did not, in the absence of Soviet cooperation, take such measures as are possible unilaterally to lessen and to overcome this danger of surprise attack. In fact the United States has not and does not shirk this responsibility.

In accordance with the National Security

Act of 1947, the President has put into effect
since the beginning of his administration
directives to gather by every possible means the
information required to protect the United
States and the free world against surprise
attack and to enable them to make effective
preparations for their defense. Under these
directives programs have been developed and put
into operation which have included extensive
aircraft, normally of a peripheral character but
on occasion by penetration. Specific missions of
these unarmed aircraft have not been subject to
Presidential authorization. The fact that such
surveillance was taking place has apparently not
been a secret to the Soviet leadership, and the
question indeed arises as to why at this
particular juncture they should seek to exploit
the present incident as a propaganda battle in
the cold war.

    This government had sincerely hoped and
continues to hope that in the coming meeting of
the Heads of Government in Paris Chairman
Khrushchev would be prepared to cooperate in
agreeing to effective measures which would
remove this fear of sudden mass destruction from
the minds of people everywhere. Far from being
damaging to the forthcoming meeting in Paris,
this incident should serve to underline the
importance to the world of an earnest attempt
there to achieve agreed and effective safeguards
against surprise attack and aggression.

The President's Radio and Television Report
to the American People on the Events in Paris

May 25, 1960

    ...as President, charged by the
Constitution with the conduct of America's
foreign relations, and as Commander-in-Chief,
charged with the direction of the operations and
activities of our Armed Forces and their
supporting services, I take full responsibility
for approving all the various programs

Source: Public Papers of the Presidents, Dwight
D. Eisenhower, 1960-1961, pp. 439, 441.

undertaken by our government to secure and evaluate military intelligence.

It was in the prosecution of one of these intelligence programs that the widely publicized U-2 incident occurred....

As to the timing, the question was really whether to halt the program and thus forego the gathering of important information that was essential and that was likely to be unavailable at a later date. The decision was that the program should not be halted.

The plain truth is this: when a nation needs intelligence activity, there is no time when vigilance can be relaxed. Incidentally, from Pearl Harbor we learned that even negotiation itself can be used to conceal preparations for a surprise attack.

Next, as to our government's initial statement about the flight, this was issued to protect the pilot, his mission, and our intelligence processes, at a time when the true facts were still undetermined....

As to the four-power meeting on Monday morning, he [Khrushchev] demanded of the United States four things: first, condemnation of U-2 flights as a method of espionage; second, assurance that they would not be continued; third, a public apology on behalf of the United States; and, fourth, punishment of all those who had any responsibility respecting this particular mission.

I replied by advising the Soviet leader that I had, during the previous week, stopped these flights and that they would not be resumed. I offered also to discuss the matter with him in personal meetings, while the regular business of the Summit might proceed. Obviously, I would not respond to his extreme demands. He knew, of course, by holding to those demands the Soviet Union was scuttling the Summit Conference.

4

New Defense Policies: Flexible Response and Counterinsurgency

INTRODUCTION

The inauguration of John Kennedy as President appeared to usher in a new era, not only in domestic politics but in the international security arena. Basing part of his election platform on the so-called missile gap (which proved to be false), the new President was quickly faced with problems, not with nuclear weapons, but with Cuba. The Bay of Pigs debacle seemed to open the door to a new and turbulent era in U.S. national security policy. Not only did important security problems develop in Third World areas extending from Southeast Asia to the Caribbean and into Black Africa, but U.S.-USSR relations took a decided turn for the worse. Nonetheless, the Kennedy Administration began with optimism and idealism touching many Americans and bringing a sense of purpose and direction to its policies and developing a sense of confidence in its allies.

The new administration moved away from the "new look" strategy of the previous administration and adopted a "flexible response." This new strategy was based on the view that the U.S. should be prepared to respond in a variety of ways across the conflict spectrum. Limiting response only to massive retaliation was, in the view of the new administration, a unidimensional strategy incapable of responding to nonnuclear conflicts.

The policy remained fixed in deterrence, but with an added conventional and unconventional dimension. At the same time, arms control efforts were pursued leading to a Limited Test Ban Treaty with the Soviet Union.

Further, a new posture developed with respect to

Latin America. The Alliance for Progress extended a helpful hand to governments in the South, based on the idea of economic assistance for developing democracy and in responding to poverty. In brief, the Kennedy policy seemed to broaden U.S. horizons considerably beyond Europe and the Soviet Union.

One of the most publicized efforts to help the Third World was the creation of the Peace Corps. The idea that a group of Americans skilled in the needs of the Third World would live and work with indigenous peoples caught the imagination of young Americans. The Peace Corps proved to be a reasonably successful effort, particularly in its early years. It remains an ongoing operation.

Even with all of these new dimensions, the early 1960s saw the emergence of serious challenges and crises, some of which remain today. Cuba was the center of two U.S. security episodes; one a failure, the other a reasonable success. The Bay of Pigs operation, inherited from the Eisenhower Administration, turned into a major national security failure. Vacillation regarding the degree of U.S. support that should be extended to the Cuban expeditionary force intent on overthrowing Castro, and misinterpretation of the internal situation in Cuba, led to a complete failure.

In the following year (1962), the Soviet Union began a secret effort to install offensive missiles in Cuba. Alerted by U.S. intelligence, the Kennedy Administration took steps to block the Soviet effort. The Cuban Missile Crisis is now a well-examined incident in U.S.-USSR relations. Eventually the United States and the Soviet Union avoided war, reaching accommodations regarding relations between the U.S. and Cuba. Although avoiding World War III, the Cuban Missile Crisis spurred the Soviet Union into a massive arms buildup eventually reaching "parity" with the U.S. In any case, the U.S. was evidently prepared to use military force if the quarantine of Cuba had failed. Many observers feel that this was one of President Kennedy's finest hours, although some recent scholarship seems to suggest that much was wrong with the way the Administration handled the Cuban Missile Crisis.

Soviet Premier Khrushchev tested the young president early on, beginning with the Kennedy-Khrushchev meeting in Vienna in 1961. The Berlin Crisis in the same year was precipitated by Khrushchev, who demanded that a peace treaty be concluded with Germany placing Berlin under the control of a sovereign German Democratic Republic (East

Germany). If the allies refused, the Soviet Union threatened to sign a separate peace with East Germany. From the end of World War II until 1961, two million East Germans had fled to the West, many of them through West Berlin. Khrushchev's view assumed that a sovereign East Germany would be able to stop the exodus. Although Khrushchev did not follow through with his threat of a separate peace treaty, the Berlin Wall was erected in the summer of 1961. Kennedy's famous "Ich bin ein Berliner" speech in Berlin in 1963 focused world attention on the "Wall" and proved to be a morale boost to West Berliners.

What ultimately became the most serious problem stemmed from the French return to Indochina after World War II. The problem evolved first in Laos and then in South Vietnam. The Communist regime in North Vietnam, after defeating the French, tried to expand its control of what was formerly French Indochina, by supporting and directing insurgents in Laos, but more ardently in South Vietnam. By 1963, the insurgency in South Vietnam had reached serious proportions. The U.S. advisory effort expanded from a few hundred to 16,000 by the middle of 1963. The Kennedy Administration, supportive of Eisenhower's domino principle, became increasingly concerned about the future of South Vietnam and the rest of Southeast Asia. Events moved rapidly in 1963 with the assassination of Premier Diem of South Vietnam by the South Vietnamese military. Many felt that the coup and assassination were indirectly supported by the Kennedy Administration. In November of the same year, Kennedy was assassinated. New leaders came onto the stage and the U.S. became increasingly bogged down in Southeast Asia.

In any case, the Kennedy era brought with it a new, more optimistic and dynamic posture towards the Third World. While most observers accepted the view that the Kennedy period was akin to King Arthur's Camelot, others argued that the security policies, particularly in Southeast Asia, opened the door to a variety of problems associated with wars of liberation. Kennedy's stress on counterinsurgency and the revitalization of U.S. Special Forces, signalled the shift of the U.S. effort towards Southeast Asia. This counterinsurgency era was reflected in the serious conflicts that took place in Southeast Asia following Kennedy's death. The optimism and hope that Kennedy brought with him to the presidency were dashed on the streets of Dallas and with his death a tragic era seemed to unfold for the United States.

DOCUMENTS

President Kennedy's Inaugural Address

January 20, 1961

The world is very different now. For man holds in his mortal hands the power to abolish all forms of human poverty and all forms of human life. And yet the same revolutionary beliefs for which our forebears fought are still at issue around the globe--the belief that the rights of man come not from the generosity of the state but from the hand of God.

We dare not forget today that we are the heirs of that first revolution. Let the word go forth from this time and place, to friend and foe alike, that the torch has been passed to a new generation of Americans--born in this century, tempered by war, disciplined by a hard and bitter peace, proud of our ancient heritage--and unwilling to witness or permit the slow undoing of those human rights to which this nation has always been committed, and to which we are committed today at home and around the world.

Let every nation know, whether it wishes us well or ill, that we shall pay any price, bear any burden, meet any hardship, support any friend, oppose any foe to assure the survival and the success of liberty.

This much we pledge--and more.

To those old allies whose cultural and spiritual origins we share, we pledge the loyalty of faithful friends. United, there is little we cannot do in a host of cooperative ventures. Divided, there is little we can do-- for we dare not meet a powerful challenge at odds and split asunder.

To those new states whom we welcome to the ranks of the free, we pledge our word that one form of colonial control shall not have passed away merely to be replaced by a far more iron tyranny. We shall not always expect to find them supporting our view. But we shall always hope to

Source: <u>Public Papers of the Presidents</u>, John F. Kennedy, 1961, pp. 1-2.

find them strongly supporting their own freedom--and to remember that, in the past, those who foolishly sought power by riding the back of the tiger ended up inside.

To those peoples in the huts and villages of half the globe struggling to break the bonds of mass misery, we pledge our best efforts to help them help themselves, for whatever period is required--not because the Communists may be doing it, not because we seek their votes, but because it is right. If a free society cannot help the many who are poor, it cannot save the few who are rich.

To our sister republics to the south of our border, we offer a special pledge--to convert our good words into good deeds--in a new alliance for progress--to assist free men and free governments in casting off their chains of poverty. But this peaceful revolution of hope cannot become the prey of hostile powers. Let all neighbors know that we shall join them to oppose aggression or subversion anywhere in the Americas. And let every other power know that this Hemisphere intends to remain master of its own house.

To that world assembly of sovereign states, the United Nations, our last best hope in an age where the instruments of war have far outpaced the instruments of peace, we renew our pledge of support--to prevent it from becoming merely a forum for invective--to strengthen its shield of the new and the weak--and to enlarge the area in which its writ may run.

Finally, to those nations who would make themselves our adversary, we offer not a pledge but a request: that both sides begin anew the quest for peace, before the dark powers of destruction unleashed by science engulf all humanity in planned or accidental self-destruction.

We dare not tempt them with weakness. For only when our arms are sufficient beyond doubt can we be certain beyond doubt that they will never be employed.

But neither can two great and powerful groups of nations take comfort from our present course--both sides overburdened by the cost of modern weapons, both rightly alarmed by the steady spread of the deadly atom, yet both racing to alter that uncertain balance of terror that stays the hand of mankind's final war.

So let us begin anew--remembering on both sides that civility is not a sign of weakness, and sincerity is always subject to proof. Let us never negotiate out of fear. But let us never fear to negotiate....

All this will not be finished in the first one hundred days. Nor will it be finished in the first one thousand days, nor in the life of this Administration, nor even perhaps in our lifetime on this planet. But let us begin.

In your hands, my fellow citizens, more than mine, will rest the final success or failure of our course. Since this country was founded, each generation of Americans has been summoned to give testimony to its national loyalty. The graves of young Americans who answered the call to service surround the globe.

Now the trumpet summons us again--not as a call to bear arms, though arms we need--not as a call to battle, though embattled we are--but a call to bear the burden of a long twilight struggle, year in and year out, "rejoicing in hope, patient in tribulation"--a struggle against the common enemy of man: tyranny, poverty, disease and war itself.

Can we forge against these enemies a grand and global alliance, North and South, East and West, that can assure a more fruitful life for all mankind? Will you join in that historic effort?

In the long history of the world, only a few generations have been granted the role of defending freedom in its hour of maximum danger. I do not shrink from this responsibility--I welcome it. I do not believe that any of us would exchange places with any other people or any other generation. The energy, the faith, the devotion which we bring to this endeavor will light our country and all who serve it--and the glow from that fire can truly light the world.

And so, my fellow Americans: ask not what your country can do for you--ask what you can do for your country.

My fellow citizens of the world: ask not what America will do for you, but what together we can do for the freedom of man.

Finally, whether you are citizens of America or citizens of the world, ask of us here the same high standards of strength and sacrifice which we ask of you. With a good conscience our only sure reward, with history the final judge of our deeds, let us go forth to lead the land we love, asking His blessing and His help, but knowing that here on earth God's work must truly be our own.

DEFENSE POLICY

President John F. Kennedy

Special Message to the Congress on the Defense Budget, March 28, 1961

The primary purpose of our arms is peace, not war--to make certain that they will never be used--to deter all wars, general or limited, nuclear or conventional, large or small--to convince all potential aggressors that any attack would be futile--to provide backing for diplomatic settlement of disputes--to insure the adequacy of our bargaining power for an end to the arms race. The basic problems facing the world today are not susceptible to a military solution. Neither our strategy nor our psychology as a nation--and certainly not our economy--must become dependent upon the permanent maintenance of a large military establishment. Our military posture must be sufficiently flexible and under control to be consistent with our efforts to explore all possibilities and to take every step to lessen tensions, to obtain peaceful solutions and to secure arms limitations. Diplomacy and defense are no longer distinct alternatives, one to be used where the other fails--both must complement each other....

Our arms will never be used to strike the first blow in any attack. This is not a confession of weakness but a statement of strength. It is our national tradition. We must

Source: <u>Public Papers of the Presidents</u>, John F. Kennedy, 1961, pp. 230-240.

offset whatever advantage this may appear to hand an aggressor by so increasing the capability of our forces to respond swiftly and effectively to any aggressive move as to convince any would-be aggressor that such a movement would be too futile and costly to undertake....

We shall never threaten, provoke or initiate aggression--but if aggression should come, our response will be swift and effective.

Our arms must be adequate to meet our commitments and ensure our security, without being bound by arbitrary budget ceilings. This nation can afford to be strong--it cannot afford to be weak. We shall do what is needed to make and to keep us strong....

The strength and deployment of our forces in combination with those of our allies should be sufficiently powerful and mobile to prevent the steady erosion of the Free World through limited wars; and it is this role that should constitute the primary mission of our overseas forces. Non-nuclear wars, and sub-limited or guerrilla warfare, have since 1945 constituted the most active and constant threat to Free World security. Those units of our forces which are staioned overseas, or designed to fight overseas, can be most usefully oriented toward deterring or confining those conflicts which do not justify and must not lead to a general nuclear attack. In the event of a major aggression that could not be repulsed by conventional forces, we must be prepared to take whatever action with whatever weapons are appropriate. But our objective now is to increase our ability to confine our response to non-nuclear weapons, and to lessen the incentive for any limited aggression by making clear what our response will accomplish. In most areas of the world, the main burden of local defense against overt attack, subversion and guerrilla warfare must rest on local populations and forces. But given the great likelihood and seriousness of this threat, we must be prepared to make a substantial contribution in the form of strong, highly mobile forces trained in this type of warfare, some of which must be deployed in forward areas, with a substantial airlift and

sealift capacity and prestocked overseas
bases....
     Our military position today is strong. But
positive action must be taken now if we are to
have the kind of forces we will need for our
security in the future. Our preparation against
danger is our hope of safety....

Special Message to Congress on Urgent National
                      Needs
                  May 25, 1961

     The adversaries of freedom did not create
revolution; nor did they create the conditions
which compel it. But they are seeking to ride
the crest of its wave--to capture it for
themselves.
     Yet their aggression is more often
concealed than open. They have fired no
missiles; and their troops are seldom seen. They
send arms, agitators, aid, technicians and
propaganda to every troubled area. But where
fighting is required, it is usually done by
others--by guerrillas striking at night, by
assassins striking alone--assassins who have
taken the lives of four thousand civil officers
in the last twelve months in Vietnam alone--by
subversives and saboteurs and insurrectionists,
who in some cases control whole areas inside of
independent nations.
     [The following paragraph was omitted in
the reading of the message, but appears in the
text transmitted to the Congress.]
     They possess a powerful intercontinental
striking force, large forces for conventional
war, a well-trained underground in nearly every
country, the power to conscript talent and
manpower for any purpose, the capacity for quick
decisions, a closed society without dissent or
free information, and long experience in the
techniques of violence and subversion. They make
the most of their scientific successes, their
economic progress and their pose as a foe of
colonialism and friend of popular revolution.
They prey on unstable or unpopular governments,

Source: Public Papers of the Presidents, John
F. Kennedy, 1961, pp. 397-401.

unsealed, or unknown boundaries, unfilled
hopes, convulsive change, massive poverty,
illiteracy, unrest and frustration.

With these formidable weapons, the
adversaries of freedom plan to consolidate their
territory--to exploit, to control, and finally
to destroy the hopes of the world's newest
nations; and they have ambition to do it before
the end of this decade. It is a contest of will
and purpose as well as force and violence--a
battle for minds and souls as well as lives and
territory. And in that contest, we cannot stand
aside....

There is no single simple policy which
meets this challenge. Experience has taught us
that no one nation has the power or the wisdom
to solve all the problems of the world or manage
its revolutionary tides--that extending our
commitments does not always increase our
security--that any initiative carries with it
risk of a temporary defeat--that nuclear weapons
cannot prevent subversion--that no free people
can be kept free without will and energy of
their own--and that no two nations or situations
are exactly alike....

A major part of our partnership for self-
defense is the Military Assistance Program. The
main burden of local defense against local
attacks, subversion, insurrection or guerrilla
warfare must of necessity rest with local
forces. Where these forces have the necessary
will and capacity to cope with such threats, our
intervention is rarely necessary or helpful.
Where the will is present and only capacity is
lacking, our Military Assistance Program can be
of help.

But this program, like economic
assistance, needs a new emphasis. It cannot be
extended without regard to the social, political
and military reforms essential to internal
respect and stability. The equipment and
training provided must be tailored to legitimate
local needs and to our own foreign and military
policies, not to our supply of military stocks
or a local leader's desire for military display.
And military assistance can, in addition to its
military purposes, make a contribution to
economic progress, as do our own Army

Engineers....
       I have directed a further reinforcement of
our own capacity to deter or resist non-nuclear
aggression. In the conventional field, with one
exception, I find no present need for large
levies of men. What is needed is rather a change
of position to give us still further increases
in flexibility.
       Therefore, I am directing the Secretary of
Defense to undertake a reorganization and
modernization of the Army's divisional
structure, to increase its non-nuclear
firepower, to improve its tactical mobility in
any environment, to insure its flexibility to
meet any direct or indirect threat, to
facilitate its coordination with our major
allies, and to provide more modern mechanized
divisions in Europe and bring their equipment up
to date, and new airborne brigades in both the
Pacific and Europe....
       In addition, our special forces and
unconventional warfare units will be increased
and reoriented. Throughout the services new
emphasis will be placed on the special skills
and languages which are required to work with
local populations.

Annual Budget Message to Congress
Fiscal Year 1963

January 18, 1962

       This budget carries forward the policies
instituted within the past 12 months to
strengthen our military forces and to increase
the flexibility with which they can be
controlled and applied. The key elements in our
defense program include: a strategic offensive
force which would survive and respond
overwhelmingly after a massive nuclear attack; a
command and control system which would survive
and direct the response; an improved anti-bomber
defense system; a civil defense program which
would help to protect an important proportion of
our population from the perils of nuclear

Source: Public Papers of the Presidents, John F.
Kennedy, 1961, pp. 22-29.

fallout; combat-ready limited war forces and the air and sealift needed to move them quickly to wherever they might have to be deployed; and special forces to help our allies cope with the threat of Communist-sponsored insurrection and subversion....

The budget provides for further significant increases in the capabilities of our strategic forces, including additional Minuteman missiles and Polaris submarines. These forces are large and versatile enough to survive any attack which could be launched against us today and strike back decisively....

Although a global war poses the gravest threat to our survival, it is not the most probable form of conflict as long as we maintain the forces needed to make a nuclear war disastrous to any foe. Military aggression on a lesser scale is far more likely. If we are to retain for ourselves a choice other than a nuclear holocaust or retreat, we must increase considerably our conventional forces. This is a task we share with our free world allies.

The budget recommendations for 1963 are designed to strengthen our conventional forces substantially. I am proposing:

An increase in the number of regular Army divisions from 14 to 16....

A substantial increase in the number of regular tactical fighter units of the Air Force....

...significant increases in procurement for all of our conventional forces. These forces must be equipped and provisioned so they are ready to fight a limited war for a protracted period of time anywhere in the world.

Remarks at West Point to the Graduating Class of
the U.S. Military Academy
June 6, 1962

The fact of the matter is that the period just ahead in the next decade will offer more opportunities for service to the graduates of this Academy than ever before in the history of

Source: <u>Public Papers of the Presidents</u>, John F. Kennedy, 1961, pp. 453-455.

the United States, because all around the world, in countries which are heavily engaged in the maintenance of their freedom, graduates of this Academy are heavily involved. Whether it is in Viet-Nam or in Laos or in Thailand, whether it is a military advisory group in Iran, whether it is a military attache in some Latin American country during a difficult and challenging period, whether it is the commander of our troops in South Korea--the burdens that will be placed upon you when you fill those positions as you must inevitably, will require more from you than ever before in our history. The graduates of West Point, the Naval Academy, and the Air Force Academy in the next 10 years will have the greatest opportunity for the defense of freedom that the Academies' graduates have ever had....

Therefore, I hope that you realize--and I hope every American realizes--how much we depend upon you. Your strict military responsibilities, therefore, will require a versatility and an adaptability never before required either in war or in peace. They may involve the command and control of modern nuclear weapons and modern delivery systems, so complex that only a few scientists can understand their operation, so devastating that their inadvertent use would be of worldwide concern, but so new that their employment and their effects have never been tested in combat conditions.

On the other hand, your responsibilities may involve the command of more traditional forces, but in less traditional roles. Men risking their lives, not as combatants, but as instructors or advisors, or as symbols of our Nation's commitments. The fact that the United States is not directly at war in these areas in no way diminishes the skill and courage that will be required, the service to our country which is rendered, or the pain of the casualties which are suffered. To cite one example of the range of responsibilities that will fall upon you: you may hold a position of command with our special forces, forces which are too unconventional to be called conventional, forces which are growing in number and importance and significance, for we now know that it is wholly misleading to call this "the nuclear age," or to say that our security rests only on the doctrine of massive retaliation....

This is another type of war, new in its intensity, ancient in its origin--war by guerrillas, subversives, insurgents, assassins, war by ambush instead of by combat; by infiltration, instead of aggression, seeking victory by eroding and exhausting the enemy instead of engaging him. It is a form of warfare uniquely adapted to what has been strangely called "wars of liberation," to undermine the efforts of new and poor countries to maintain the freedom that they have finally achieved. It preys on economic unrest and ethnic conflicts. It requires in those situations where we must counter it, and these are the kinds of challenges that will be before us in the next decade if freedom is to be saved, a whole new kind of strategy, a wholly different kind of force, and therefore a new and wholly different kind of military training.

But I have spoken thus far only of the military challenges which your education must prepare you for. The nonmilitary problems which you will face will also be most demanding, diplomatic, political, and economic....

Whatever your position, the scope of your decisions will not be confined to the traditional tenets of military competence and training....

In many countries, your posture and performance will provide the local population with the only evidence of what our country is really like. In other countries, your military mission, its advice and action, will play a key role in determining whether those people will remain free. You will need to understand the importance of military power and also the limits of military power, to decide what arms should be used to fight and when they should be used to prevent a fight, to determine what represents our vital interests and what interests are only marginal....

Our forces, therefore, must fulfill a broader role as a complement to our diplomacy, as an arm of our diplomacy, as a deterrent to our adversaries, and as a symbol to our allies of our determination to support them....

To talk of such talent and effort raises in the minds, I am sure, of everyone, and the minds of all of our countrymen, why--why should men such as you, able to master the complex arts of science, mathemathics, language, economy, and all the rest, devote their lives to a military career, with all of its risks and hardships? Why should their families be expected to make the personal and financial sacrifices that a military career inevitably brings with it? When there is a visible enemy to fight in open combat, the answer is not so difficult. Many serve, all applaud, and the tide of patriotism runs high. But when there is a long slow struggle, with no immediate visible foe, your choice will seem hard indeed....

But you have one satisfaction, however difficult these days may be: when you are asked by a President of the United States or by any other American what you are doing for your country, no man's answer will be clearer than your own. And that moral motivation which brought you here in the first place is part of your training here as well. West Point was not built to produce technical experts alone. It was built to produce men committed to the defense of their country, leaders of men who understand the great stakes which are involved, leaders who can be entrusted with the heavy responsibilities which modern weapons and the fight for freedom entail, leaders who can inspire in their men the same sense of obligation to duty which you bring to it.

DEFENSE ARRANGEMENTS of the NORTH ATLANTIC COMMUNITY

Secretary of Defense McNamara
Address at the University of Michigan
June 16, 1962

One of the most impressive lessons that Europe has provided us recently is the lesson of her revival from the ashes of destruction at the end of the Second World War. The national

Source: Department of State Bulletin, July 9, 1962, pp. 64-69.

economies of Europe were almost at a standstill
15 years ago. Their capital plant was largely
destroyed, either directly by bombing or
indirectly by years of neglect and patchwork
repair. The people were exhausted by 6 years of
war, and a large part of the most productive age
group had been wiped out. Yet in the last 10
years they have managed to increase the
production of steel and electricity by over 130
percent each, and this has been typical of the
recovery pattern.

The pump-priming help of the American
Marshall Plan came at a crucial time in the
process of European recovery. By the genius of
the plan, as envisaged by men like George
Marshall and Harry Truman, was to help the
Europeans help themselves.

At the same time that the nations of
Europe were rebuilding at home, they were going
through the difficult and often painful process
of reestablishing their relationships with the
peoples of Africa and Asia, no longer as master
and servant but as members of the human race,
all equally entitled to develop their individual
capabilities. This process of change is by no
means complete, and there are still difficult
times ahead. But the joint achievement of Europe
and its former colonies in revising their
relations with each other is at least as
impressive as the economic recovery of Europe
itself....

All of these achievements have been
accomplished under pressure from titanic forces
which make rational organization of human
society increasingly difficult both for the
Europeans and for ourselves. Let me mention some
of these forces.

We are confronted with a population
explosion resulting from our own success in
coping with disease and abnormalities and by now
threatening to double the earth's population by
the end of this century. Unless we can control
this explosion in the poor and resource-limited
countries, the effects of economic growth may be
canceled out by population growth, and
unsatisfied rising expectations, particularly in
the younger nations, may upset the delicate
balance of political stability.

We are borne along by the accelerating pace of science and technology. In this country alone, new inventions are patented at a rate of 50,000 a year. Our population of scientists and engineers has increased by more than 40 percent in the last 8 years. In fact, 80 percent of all scientists and engineers who have lived throughout history are alive today.

We are faced with an extraordinary increase in the number of national states. Since World War II, 35 new nations have been formed. Each new nation expresses the natural desire for self-determination and self-government. But their numbers complicate the problem of international diplomacy at the same time that military and economic developments increase our interdependence. Every nation is more and more directly affected by the internal situation of its neighbors, and the globe has shrunk to the point where we are all each other's neighbors.

Lastly, we live in the shadow of the Sino-Soviet drive for world domination--surely not the only shadow on the world today, but one of the longest and deepest. By itself it represents the most serious military force this nation has ever faced; by its exploitation of the entire world's troubles, it is a threat of a kind that is as new to the world as the rising technologies and populations and national sovereignties themselves.

In the face of all these challenges, the ultimate objective of the free world is to establish a system of peaceful world order, based on the dignity of the individual and dedicated to the free development of each man's capacities. The members of the North Atlantic community--the Europeans and ourselves--bear a special responsibility to help achieve this objective. This responsibility derives from the strength of our national institutions and the wealth of our material resources....

But we cannot hope to move toward our objective unless we move from strength. Part of that strength must be military strength. But I want to emphasize that we see our military strength, not as the means of achieving the kind of world we seek, but as a shield to prevent any other nation from using its military strength,

either directly or through threats and
intimidation, to frustrate the aspirations we
share with all free peoples of the world. The
aggressive use of military strength is foreign
to the best traditions of the United States.
And, as the President points out ..."the basic
problems facing the world today are not
susceptible of a final military solution."

What the military component of our
national power must do, and what we must see
that it is capable of doing, is to assure to the
peoples of the free world the freedom to choose
their own course of development.

Yet the nature and extent of the military
power base needed to meet the entire spectrum of
challenges confronting the free world is beyond
the capacity of any single nation to provide.
Since our own security cannot be separated from
the seecurity of the rest of the free world, we
necessarily rely on a series of alliances, the
most important of which is the North Atlantic
Treaty Organization....

A central military issue facing NATO today
is the role of nuclear strategy. Four facts seem
to us to dominate consideration of that role.
All of them point in the direction of increased
integration to achieve our common defense.
First, the alliance has overall nuclear
strength adequate to any challenge confronting
it. Second, this strength not only minimizes the
likelihood of major nuclear war but makes
possible a strategy designed to preserve the
fabric of our societies if wars should occur.
Third, damage to the civil societies of the
alliance resulting from nuclear warfare could be
very grave. Fourth, improved non-nuclear forces,
well within alliance resources, could enhance
deterrence of any aggressive moves short of
direct, all-out attack on Western Europe.

Let us look at the situation today. First,
given the current balance of nuclear power,
which we confidently expect to maintain in the
years ahead, a surprise nuclear attack is simply
not a rational act for any enemy. Nor would it
be rational for an enemy to take the initiative
in the use of nuclear weapons as an outgrowth of
a limited engagement in Europe or elsewhere. I
think we are entitled to conclude that either of

these actions has been made highly unlikely.

Second, and equally important, the mere fact that no nation could rationally take steps leading to a nuclear war does not guarantee that a nuclear war cannot take place. Not only do nations sometimes act in ways that are hard to explain on a rational basis, but even when acting in a "rational" way they sometimes, indeed disturbingly often, act on the basis of misunderstandings of the true facts of a situation. They misjudge the way others will react and the way others will interpret what they are doing.

We must hope--indeed I think we have good reason to hope--that all sides will understand this danger and will refrain from steps that even raise the possibility of such a mutually disastrous misunderstanding. We have taken unilateral steps to reduce the likelihood of such an occurence. We look forward to the prospect that through arms control the actual use of these terrible weapons may be completely avoided. It is a problem not just for us in the West but for all nations that are involved in this struggle we call the cold war.

For our part we feel we and our NATO allies must frame our strategy with this terrible contingency, however remote, in mind. Simply ignoring the problem is not going to make it go away.

The United States has come to the conclusion that, to the extent feasible, basic military strategy in a possible general nuclear war should be approached in much the same way that more conventional military operations have been regarded in the past. That is to say, principal military objectives, in the event of a nuclear war stemming from a major attack on the alliance, should be the destruction of the enemy's military forces, not of his civilian population.

The very strength and nature of the alliance forces make it possible for us to retain, even in the face of a massive surprise attack, sufficient reserve striking power to destroy an enemy society if driven to it. In other words, we are giving a possible opponent the strongest imaginable incentive to refrain from striking our cities.

The strength that makes these contributions to deterrence and to the hope of deterring attack upon civil societies even in wartime does not come cheap. We are confident that our current nuclear programs are adequate and will continue to be adequate for as far into the future as we can reasonably foresee. During the coming fiscal year the United States plans to spend close to $15 billion on its nuclear weapons to assure their adequacy. For what this money buys, there is no substitute.

In particular, relatively weak national nuclear forces with enemy cities as their targets are not likely to be sufficient to perform even the function of deterrence. If they are small, and perhaps vulnerable on the ground or in the air, or inaccurate, a major antagonist can take a variety of measures to counter them. Indeed, if a major antagonist came to believe there was a substantial likelihood of its being used independently, this force would be inviting a preemptive first strike against it. In the event of war, the use of such a force against cities of a major nuclear power would be tantamount to suicide, whereas its employment against significant military targets would have a negligible effect on the outcome of the conflict. Meanwhile the creation of a single additional national nuclear force encourages the proliferation of nuclear power with all of its attendant dangers.

In short, then, limited nuclear capabilities, operating independently, are dangerous, expensive, prone to obsolescence, and lacking in credibility as a deterrent. Clearly, the United States nuclear contribution to the alliance is neither obsolete nor dispensable....

For the kinds of conflicts, both political and military, most likely to arise in the NATO area, our capabilities for response must not be limited to nuclear weapons alone. The Soviets have superiority in non nuclear forces in Europe today. But that superiority is by no means overwhelming. Collectively, the alliance has the potential for a successful defense against such forces....

I want to remind you also that the

security provided by military strength is a
necessary, but not sufficient, condition for the
achievement of our foreign policy goals,
including our goals in the field of arms control
and disarmament. Military security provides a
base on which we can build free-world strength
through the economic advances and political
reforms which are the object of the President's
programs, like the Alliance for Progress and the
trade expansion legislation. Only in a peaceful
world can we give full scope to the individual
potential, which is for us the ultimate value.

CRISES
THE BAY OF PIGS
The President's News Conference, April 12, 1961

I want to say that there will not be under
any conditions, an intervention in Cuba by the
United States Armed Forces. This Government will
do everything it possibly can, and I think it
can meet its responsibilities, to make sure that
there are no Americans involved in any actions
inside Cuba....
The basic issue in Cuba is not one between
the United States and Cuba. It is between the
Cubans themselves. I intend to see that we
adhere to that principle and as I understand it
this administration's attitude is so understood
and shared by the anti-Castro exiles from Cuba
in this country.

President Kennedy's Message to Chairman
Khrushchev
Concerning the Meaning of Events in Cuba
April 18, 1961

Mr. Chairman:

You are under a serious misapprehension in
regards to events in Cuba. For months there has
been evident and growing resistance to the
Castro dictatorship. More than 100,000 refugees
have recently fled from Cuba into neighboring
countries. Their urgent hope is naturally to

Sources: <u>Public Papers of the Presidents</u>, John
F. Kennedy, 1961, pp. 258-259 and 286-287.

assist their fellow Cubans in their struggle for freedom. Many of these refugees fought alongside Dr. Castro against the Batista dictatorship; among them are prominent leaders of his own original movement and government.

These are unmistakable signs that Cubans find intolerable the denial of democratic liberties and the subversion of the 26th of July Movement by an alien-dominated regime. It cannot be surprising that, as resistance within Cuba grows, refugees have been using whatever means are available to return and support their countrymen in the continuing struggle for freedom. Where people are denied the right of choice, recourse to such struggle is the only means of achieving their liberties.

I have previously stated, and I repeat now, that the United States intends no military intervention in Cuba. In the event of any military intervention by outside force we will immediately honor our obligations under the inter-American system to protect this hemisphere against external aggression. While refraining from military intervention in Cuba, the people of the United States do not conceal their admiration for Cuban patriots who wish to see a democratic system in independent Cuba. The United States government can take no action to stifle the spirit of liberty.

I have taken careful note of your statement that the events in Cuba might affect peace in all parts of the world. I trust that this does not mean that the Soviet government, using the situation in Cuba as a pretext, is planning to inflame other areas of the world. I would like to think that your government has too great a sense of responsibility to embark upon any enterprise so dangerous to general peace.

I agree with you as to the desirability of steps to improve the international atmosphere. I continue to hope that you will cooperate in opportunities now available to this end. A prompt cease-fire and peaceful settlement of the dangerous situation in Laos, cooperation with the United Nations in the Congo and a speedy conclusion of an acceptable treaty for the banning of nuclear tests would be constructive steps in this direction. The regime in Cuba could make a similar contribution by permitting the Cuban people freely to determine their own future by democratic processes and freely to cooperate with their Latin America neighbors.

I believe, Mr. Chairman, that you should recognize that free peoples in all parts of the world do not accept the claim of historical inevitability for the Communist revolution. What your government believes is its own business; what it does in the world is the world's business. The great revolution in the history of man, past, present and future, is the revolution of those determined to be free.

U.N. General Assembly Debates Cuban Complaint
Statements by U.S. Representative Adlai E.
Stevenson, April 17, 1961

Dr. Roa, speaking for Cuba, has just charged the United States with aggression against Cuba and invasion coming from Florida. These charges are totally false, and I deny them categorically. The United States has committed no aggression against Cuba, and no offensive has been launchged from Florida or from any other part of the United States.

We sympathize with the desire of the people of Cuba--including those in exile who do not stop being Cubans merely because they could no longer stand to live in today's Cuba--we sympathize with their desire to seek Cuban independence and freedom. We hope that the Cuban revolution will succeed in doing what Castro's revolution never really tried to do: that is, to bring democratic processes to Cuba.

But as President Kennedy has already said,

...there will not under any conditions be...an intervention in Cuba by United States armed forces. This government will do everything it possibly can--and I think it can meet its responsibilities--to make sure that there are no Americans involved in any actions inside Cuba.

Source: Department of State Bulletin, May 8, 1961, pp. 667 and 676--cited for statements of April 17th and 18th.

I wish to make clear also that we would be opposed to the use of our territory for mounting an offensive against any foreign government.

April 18, 1961

But let me comment on the many accusations about activities in the United States. I repeat what I said yesterday: No invasion has taken place from Florida or any other part of the United States, and we are opposed to the use of our territory for launching a military attack against any foreign country. Dr. Roa has alleged, and others have faithfully repeated, countless instances of United States intervention in Cuba through air actions, arms, supplies, ships, and so forth. A careful examination of his speech will show, however, not one bit of evidence of United States involvement. But the facts, or the want of them, are evidently no deterrent to lurid rhetoric and accusation by some among us.

The whole world knows and no one denies that, since Dr. Castro betrayed his revolution, there has been a rising tide of discontent and resistance by Cubans both inside and outside of Cuba; sabotage, violence, and guerrilla fighting within Cuba have been daily news for many months. But it is not true, as the representative of Rumania claimed yesterday, that this has been caused by aircraft proceeding from United States territory and "piloted by Americans," to quote from his words.

It is not true any more than it is true, as Dr. Roa and others have repeated, that an invasion has been launched from Florida.

President John F. Kennedy
Address before the American Society
of Newspaper Editors, April 20, 1961

The President of a great democracy such as ours, and the editors of great newspapers such as yours, owe a common obligation to the people: an obligation to present the facts, to present

Source: <u>Public Papers of the Presidents</u>, John F. Kennedy, 1961, pp. 304-306.

them with candor, and to present them in perspective. It is with that obligation in mind that I have decided in the last 24 hours to discuss briefly at this time the recent events in Cuba.

On that unhappy island, as in so many other arenas of the contest for freedom, the news has grown worse instead of better. I have emphasized before that this was a struggle of Cuban patriots against a Cuban dictator. While we could not be expected   to hide our sympathies, we made it repeatedly clear that the armed forces of this country would not intervene in any way.

Any unilateral American intervention, in the absence of an external attack upon ourselves or an ally, would have been contrary to our traditions and to our international obligations. But let the record show that our restraint is not inexhaustible. Should it ever appear that the inter-American doctrine of non-interference merely conceals or excuses a policy of nonaction--if the nations of this hemisphere should fail to meet their commitments against outside Communist penetration--then I want clearly understood that this Government will not hesitate in meeting its primary obligations which are to the security of our Nation!

Should the time ever come, we do not intend to be lectured on "intervention" by those whose character was stamped for all time on the bloody streets of Budapest! Nor would we expect or accept the same outcome which this small band of gallant Cuban refugees must have known that they were chancing, determined as they were against heavy odds to pursue their courageous attempts to regain their Island's freedom.

But Cuba is not an island unto itself; and our concern is not ended by mere expressions of nonintervention or regret. This is not the first time in either ancient or recent history that a small band of freedom fighters has engaged the armor of totalitarianism.

It is not the first time that Communist tanks have rolled over gallant men and women fighting to redeem the independence of their homeland. Nor is it by any means the final episode in the eternal struggle of liberty against tyranny, anywhere on the face of the globe, including Cuba itself.

Mr. Castro has said that these were mercenaries. According to press reports, the final message to be relayed from the refugee forces on the beach came from the rebel commander when asked if he wished to be evacuated. His answer was: "I will never leave this country." That is not the reply of a mercenary. He has gone now to join in the mountains countless other guerrilla fighters, who are equally determined that the dedication of those who gave their lives shall not be forgotten, and that Cuba must not be abandoned to the Communists. And we do not intend to abandon it either!

The Cuban people have not yet spoken their final piece. And I have no doubt that they and their Revolutionary Council, led by Dr. Cardona--and members of the families of the Revolutionary Council, I am informed by the Doctor yesterday, are involved themselves in the Islands--will continue to speak up for a free and independent Cuba.

Meanwhile we will not accept Mr. Castro's attempts to blame this nation for the hatred with which his one-time supporters now regard his repression. But there are from this sobering episode useful lessons for us all to learn. Some may be still obscure, and await further information. Some are clear today.

First, it is clear that the forces of communism are not to be underestimated, in Cuba or anywhere else in the world. The advantages of a police state--its use of mass terror and arrests to prevent the spread of free dissent--cannot be overlooked by those who expect the fall of every fanatic tyrant. If the self-discipline of the free cannot match the iron discipline of the mailed fist--in economic, political, scientific, and all the other kinds of struggles as well as the military--then the peril to freedom will continue to rise.

Secondly, it is clear that this Nation, in concert with all the free nations of this hemisphere, must take an ever closer and more realistic look at the menace of external Communist intervention and domination in Cuba.

The American people are not complacent about Iron Curtain tanks and planes less than 90 miles from their shore. But a nation of Cuba's size is less a threat to our survival than it is a base for subverting the survival of other free nations throughout the hemisphere. It is not primarily our interest or our security but theirs which is now, today, in the greater peril. It is for their sake as well as our own that we must show our will.

The evidence is clear--and the hour is late. We and our Latin friends will have to face the fact that we cannot postpone any longer the real issue of survival of freedom in this hemisphere itself. On that issue, unlike perhaps some others, there can be no middle ground. Together we must build a hemisphere where freedom can flourish; and where any free nation under outside attack of any kind can be assured that all of our resources stand ready to respond to any request for assistance.

Third, and finally, it is clearer than ever that we face a relentless struggle in every corner of the globe that goes beyond the clash of armies or even nuclear armaments. The armies are there, and in large number. The nuclear armaments are there. But they serve primarily as the shield behind which subversion, infiltration, and a host of other tactics steadily advance, picking off vulnerable areas one by one in situations which do not permit our own armed intervention.

Power is the hallmark of this offensive-- power and discipline and deceit. The legitimate discontent of yearning people is exploited. The legitimate trappings of self-determination are employed. But once in power, all talk of discontent is repressed, all self-determination disappears, and the promise of a revolution of hope is betrayed, as in Cuba, into a reign of terror. Those who on instruction staged automatic "riots" in the streets of free nations over the efforts of a small group of young Cubans to regain their freedom should recall the long roll call of refugees who cannot now go back--to Hungary, to North Korea, to North Viet- Nam, to East Germany, or to Poland, or to any of the other lands from which a steady stream of refugees pours forth, in eloquent testimony to the cruel oppression now holding sway in their homeland.

We dare not fail to see the insidious nature of this new and deeper struggle. We dare not fail to grasp the new concepts, the new tools, the new sense of urgency we will need to combat it--whether in Cuba or South Viet-Nam. And we dare not fail to realize that this struggle is taking place every day, without fanfare, in thousands of villages and markets-- day and night--and in classrooms all over the globe.

The message of Cuba, of Laos, of the rising din of Communist voices in Asia and Latin America--these messages are all the same. The complacent, the self-indulgent, the soft societies are about to be swept away with the debris of history. Only the strong, only the industrious, only the determined, only the courageous, only the visionary who determine the real nature of our struggle can possibly survive.

No greater task faces this country or this administration. No other challenge is more deserving of our every effort and energy. Too long we have fixed our eyes on traditional military needs, on armies prepared to cross borders, on missiles poised for flight. Now it should be clear that this is no longer--that our security may be lost piece by piece, country by country, without the firing of a single missile or the crossing of a single border.

We intend to profit from this lesson. We intend to reexamine and reorient our forces of all kinds--our tactics and our institutions here in this community. We intend to intensify our efforts for a struggle in many ways more difficult than war, where disappointment will often accompany us.

For I am convinced that we in this country and in the free world possess the necessary resource, and the skill, and the added strength that comes from a belief in the freedom of man. And I am equally convinced that history will record the fact that this bitter struggle reached its climax in the late 1950's and the early 1960's. Let me then make clear as the

President of the United States that I am determined upon our system's survival and success, regardless of the cost and regardless of the peril!

CUBAN MISSILE CRISIS

Public Law 87-833

Joint Resolution, October 3, 1962

Expressing the determination of the United States with respect to the situation in Cuba.

Whereas President James Monroe, announcing the Monroe Doctrine in 1823, declared that the United States would consider any attempt on the part of European powers "to extend their system to any portion of this hemisphere as dangerous to our peace and safety"; and

Whereas in the Rio Treaty of 1947 the parties agreed that "an armed attack by any State against an American State shall be considered as an attack against all the American States, and, consequently, each one of the said contracting parties undertakes to assist in meeting the attack in the exercise of the inherent right of individual or collective self-defense recognized by article 51 of the Charter of the United Nations"; and

Whereas the Foreign Ministers of the Organization of American States at Punta del Este in January 1962 declared: "The present Government of Cuba has identified itself with the principles of Marxist-Leninist ideology, has established a political, economic, and social system based on that doctrine, and accepts military assistance from extracontinental Communist powers, including even the threat of military intervention in America on the part of the Soviet Union"; and

Whereas the international Communist movement has increasingly extended into Cuba its political, economic, and military sphere of influence; Now, therefore, be it

Source: United States Statutes at Large, 1962, Vol. 76, p. 697.

    <u>Resolved by the Senate and the House of
Representatives of the United States of America
in Congress assembled</u>, That the United States is
determined-
    (a) to prevent by whatever means may be
necessary, including the use of arms, the
Marxist-Leninist regime in Cuba from extending,
by force or the threat of force, its aggressive
or subversive activities to any part of this
hemisphere;
    (b) to prevent in Cuba the creation or use
of an externally supported military capability
endangering the security of the United States;
and
    (c) to work with the Organization of
American States and with freedom-loving Cubans
to support the aspirations of the Cuban people
for self-determination.

Radio and Television Report to the American
People on the Soviet Arms Buildup in Cuba
October 22, 1962

    This Government, as promised, has
maintained the closest surveillance of the
Soviet military buildup on the island of Cuba.
Within the past week, unmistakable evidence has
established the fact that a series of offensive
missile sites is now in preparation on that
imprisoned island. The purpose of these bases
can be none other than to provide a nuclear
strike capability against the Western
Hemisphere.
    Upon receiving the first preliminary hard
information of this nature last Tuesday morning
at 9 a.m., I directed that our surveillance be
stepped up. And having now confirmed and
completed our evaluation of the evidence and our
decision on a course of action, this Government
feels obliged to report this new crisis to you
in fullest detail.
    The characteristics of these new missile
sites indicate two distinct types of
installations. Several of them include medium-
range ballistic missiles, capable of carrying a

Source: <u>Public Papers of the Presidents</u>, John F.
Kennedy, 1962, pp. 806-809.

nuclear warhead for a distance of more than 1,000 nautical miles. Each of these missiles, in short, is capable of striking Washington, D.C., the Panama Canal, Cape Canaveral, Mexico City, or any other city in the southeastern part of the United States, in Central America, or in the Caribbean area.

Additional sites not yet completed appear to be designed for intermediate-range ballistic missiles--capable of traveling more than twice as far--and thus capable of striking most of the major cities in the Western Hemisphere, ranging as far north as Hudson Bay, Canada, and as far south as Lima, Peru. In addition, jet bombers, capable of carrying nuclear weapons, are now being uncrated and assembled in Cuba, while the necessary air bases are being prepared.

This urgent transformation of Cuba into an important strategic base--by the presence of these large, long-range, and clearly offensive weapons of sudden mass destruction--constitutes an explicit threat to the peace and security of all the Americas, in flagrant and deliberate defiance of the Rio Pact of 1947, the traditions of this Nation and hemisphere, the joint resolution of the 87th Congress, the Charter of the United Nations, and my own public warnings to the Soviets on September 4 and 13. This action also contradicts the repeated assurances of Soviet spokesmen, both publicly and privately delivered, that the arms buildup in Cuba would retain its original defensive character, and that the Soviet Union had no need or desire to station strategic missiles on the territory of any other nation.

The size of this undertaking makes clear that it has been planned for some months. Yet only last month, after I had made clear the distinction between any introduction of ground-to-ground missiles and the existence of defensive antiaircraft missiles, the Soviet Government publicly stated on September 11 that, and I quote, "the armaments and military equipment sent to Cuba are designed exclusively for defensive purposes," that, and I quote the Soviet Government, "there is no need for the Soviet Government to shift its weapons...for a retaliatory blow to any other country, for instance Cuba," and that, and I quote their government, "the Soviet Union has so powerful rockets to carry these nuclear warheads that there is no need to search for sites for them beyond the boundaries of the Soviet Union." That statement was false.

Only last Thursday, as evidence of this rapid offensive buildup was already in my hand, Soviet Foreign Minister Gromyko told me in my office that he was instructed to make it clear once again, as he said his government had already done, that Soviet assistance to Cuba was, and I quote, "pursued solely for the purpose of contributing to the defense capabilities of Cuba," that, and I quote him, "training by Soviet specialists of Cuban nationals in handling defensive armaments was by no means offensive, and if it were otherwise," Mr. Gromyko went on, "the Soviet Government would never become involved in rendering such assistance." That statement also was false.

Neither the United States of America nor the world community of nations can tolerate deliberate deception and offensive threats on the part of any nation, large or small. We no longer live in a world where only the actual firing of weapons represents a sufficient challenge to a nation's security to constitute maximum peril. Nuclear weapons are so destructive and ballistic missiles are so swift, that any substantial increased possibility of their use or any sudden change in their deployment may well be regarded as a definite threat to peace.

For many years, both the Soviet Union and the United States, recognizing this fact, have deployed strategic nuclear weapons with great care, never upsetting the precarious status quo which insured that these weapons would not be used in the absence of some vital challenge. Our own strategic missiles have never been transferred to the territory of another nation under the cloak of secrecy and deception; and our history--unlike that of the Soviets since the end of World War II--demonstrates that we have no desire to dominate or conquer any other nation or impose our system upon its people. Nevertheless, American citizens have become adjusted to living daily on the bulls-eye of Soviet missiles located inside the U.S.S.R. or in submarines.

In that sense, missiles in Cuba add to an already clear and present danger--although it should be noted the nations of Latin America have never previously been subjected to a potential nuclear threat.

But this secret, swift, and extraordinary buildup of Communist missiles--in an area well known to have a special and historical relationship to the United States and the nations of the Western Hemisphere, in violation of Soviet assurances, and in defiance of American and hemispheric policy--this sudden, clandestine decision to station strategic weapons for the first time outside of Soviet soil--is a deliberately provocative and unjustified change in the status quo which cannot be accepted by this country, if our courage and our commitments are ever to be trusted again by either friend or foe.

The 1930's taught us a clear lesson: aggressive conduct, if allowed to go unchecked and unchallenged, ultimately leads to war. This nation is opposed to war. We are also true to our word. Our unswerving objective, therefore, must be to prevent the use of these missiles against this or any other country, and to secure their withdrawal or elimination from the Western Hemisphere.

Our policy has been one of patience and restraint, as befits a peaceful and powerful nation, which leads a worldwide alliance. We have been determined not to be diverted from our central concerns by mere irritants and fanatics. But now further action is required--and it is under way; and these actions may only be the beginning. We will not prematurely or unnecessarily risk the costs of worldwide nuclear war in which even the fruits of victory would be ashes in our mouth--but neither will we shrink from that risk at any time it must be faced.

Acting, therefore, in the defense of our own security and of the entire Western Hemisphere, and under the authority entrusted to me by the Constitution as endorsed by the resolution of the Congress, I have directed that the following <u>initial</u> steps be taken immediately:

<u>First</u>: To halt this offensive buildup, a strict quarantine on all offensive military equipment under shipment to Cuba is being initiated. All ships of any kind bound for Cuba from whatever nation or port will, if found to contain cargoes of offensive weapons, be turned back. This quarantine will be extended, if needed, to other types of cargo and carriers. We are not at this time, however, denying the necessities of life as the Soviets attempted to do in their Berlin blockade of 1948.

<u>Second</u>: I have directed the continued and increased close surveillance of Cuba and its military buildup. The foreign ministers of the OAS, in their communique of October 6, rejected secrecy on such matters in this hemisphere. Should these offensive military preparations continue, thus increasing the threat to the hemisphere, further action will be justified. I have directed the Armed Forces to prepare for any eventualties; and I trust that in the interest of both the Cuban people and the Soviet technicians at the sites, the hazards to all concerned of continuing this threat will be recognized.

<u>Third</u>: It shall be the policy of this Nation to regard any nuclear missile launched from Cuba against any nation in the Western Hemisphere as an attack by the Soviet Union on the United States, requiring a full retaliatory response upon the Soviet Union.

<u>Fourth</u>: As a necessary military precaution, I have reinforced our base at Guantanamo, evacuated today the dependents of our personnel there, and ordered additional military units to be on a standby alert basis.

<u>Fifth</u>: We are calling tonight for an immediate meeting of the Organ of Consultation under the Organization of American States, to consider this threat to hemispheric security and to invoke articles 6 and 8 of the Rio Treaty in support of all necessary action. The United Nations Charter allows for regional security arrangements--and the nations of this hemisphere decided long ago against the military presence

of outside powers. Our other allies around the world have also been alerted.

Sixth: Under the Charter of the United Nations, we are asking tonight that an emergency meeting of the Security Council be convoked without delay to take action against this latest Soviet threat to world peace. Our resolution will call for the prompt dismantling and withdrawal of all offensive weapons in Cuba, under the supervision of U.N. observers, before the quarantine can be lifted.

Seventh and finally: I call upon Chairman Khrushchev to halt and eliminate this clandestine, reckless, and provocative threat to world peace and stable relations between our two nations. I call upon him further to abandon this course of world domination, and to join in an historic effort to end the perilous arms race and to transform the history of man. He has an opportunity now to move the world back from the abyss of destruction--by returning to his government's own words that it had no need to station missiles outside its own territory, and withdrawing these weapons from Cuba--by refraining from any action which will widen or deepen the present crisis--and then by participating in a search for peaceful and permanent solutions.

This Nation is prepared to present its case against the Soviet threat to peace, and our own proposals for a peaceful world, at any time and in any forum--in the OAS, in the United Nations, or in any other meeting that could be useful--without limiting our freedom of action. We have in the past made strenuous efforts to limit the spread of nuclear weapons. We have proposed the elimination of all arms and military bases in a fair and effective disarmament treaty. We are prepared to discuss new proposals for the removal of tensions on both sides--including the possibilities of a genuinely independent Cuba, free to determine its own destiny. We have no wish to war with the Soviet Union--for we are a peaceful people who desire to live in peace with all other peoples.

But it is difficult to settle or even discuss these problems in an atmosphere of intimidation. That is why this latest Soviet threat--or any other threat which is made either independently or in response to our actions this week--must and will be met with determination. Any hostile move anywhere in the world against the safety and freedom of peoples to whom we are committed--including in particular the brave people of West Berlin--will be met by whatever action is needed.

Finally, I want to say a few words to the captive people of Cuba, to whom this speech is being directly carried by special radio facilities. I speak to you as a friend, as one who knows of your deep attachment to your fatherland, as one who shares your aspirations for liberty and justice for all. And I have watched and the American people have watched with deep sorrow how your nationalist revolution was betrayed--and how your fatherland fell under foreign domination. Now your leaders are no longer Cuban leaders inspired by Cuban ideals. They are puppets and agents of an international conspiracy which has turned Cuba against your friends and neighbors in the Americas--and turned it into the first Latin American country to become a target for nuclear war--the first Latin American country to have these weapons on its soil.

These new weapons are not in your interest. They contribute nothing to your peace and well-being. They can only undermine it. But this country has no wish to cause you to suffer or to impose any system upon you. We know that your lives and land are being used as pawns by those who deny your freedom.

Many times in the past, the Cuban people have risen to throw out tyrants who destroyed their liberty. And I have no doubt that most Cubans today look forward to the time when they will be truly free--free from foreign domination, free to choose their own leaders, free to select their own system, free to own their own land, free to speak and write and worship without fear or degradation. And then shall Cuba be welcomed back to the society of free nations and to the associations of this hemisphere.

My fellow citizens: let no one doubt that this is a difficult and dangerous effort on which we have set out. No one can foresee precisely what course it will take or what costs or casualties will be incurred. Many months of sacrifice and self-discipline lie ahead--months in which both our patience and our will will be tested--months in which many threats and denunciations will keep us aware of our dangers. But the greatest danger of all would be to do nothing.

The path we have chosen for the present is full of hazards, as all paths are--but it is the one most consistent with our character and courage as a nation and our commitments around the world. The cost of freedom is always high-- but Americans have always paid it. And one path we shall never choose, and that is the path of surrender or submission.

Our goal is not victory of might, but the vindication of right--not peace at the expense of freedom, but both peace and freedom, here in this hemisphere, and, we hope, around the world. God willing, that goal will be achieved.

Message to Chairman Khrushchev Calling for
Removal of Soviet Missiles from Cuba
October 27, 1962

Dear Mr. Chairman:

I have read your letter of October 26th with great care and welcomed the statement of your desire to seek a prompt solution to the problem. The first thing that needs to be done, however, is for work to cease on offensive missile bases in Cuba and for all weapons systems in Cuba capable of offensive use to be rendered inoperable, under effective United Nations arrangements. Assuming this is done promptly, I have given my representatives in New York instructions that will permit them to work out this weekend--in cooperation with the Acting Secretary General and your representative--an arrangement for a permanent solution to the Cuban problem along the lines suggested in your letter of October 26th. As I read your letter, the key elements of your proposals--which seem

Source: Public Papers of the Presidents, John F. Kennedy, 1962, pp. 813-814.

generally acceptable as I understand them--are
as follows:

1. You would agree to remove these weapons
systems from Cuba under appropriate United
Nations observation and supervision; and
undertake, with suitable safeguards, to halt
further introduction of such weapons systems
into Cuba.

2. We, on our part, would agree--upon the
establishment of adequate arrangements through
the United Nations to ensure the carrying out
and continuation of these commitments--(a) to
remove promptly the quarantine measures now in
effect and (b) to give assurances against an
invasion of Cuba. I am confident that other
nations of the Western Hemisphere would be
prepared to do likewise.

If you will give your representative
similar instructions, there is no reason why we
should not be able to complete these
arrangements and announce them to the world
within a couple of days. The effect of such a
settlement on easing world tensions would enable
us to work toward a more general arrangement
regarding "other armaments," as proposed in your
second letter which you made public. I would
like to say again that the United States is very
much interested in reducing tensions and halting
the arms race; and if your letter signifies that
you are prepared to discuss a detente affecting
NATO and the Warsaw Pact, we are quite prepared
to consider with our allies any useful
proposals.

But the first ingredient, let me
emphasize, is the cessation of work on missile
sites in Cuba and measures to render such
weapons inoperable, under effective
international guarantees. The continuation of
this threat, or a prolonging of this discussion
concerning Cuba by linking these problems to the
broader questions of European and world
security, would surely lead to an
intensification of the Cuban crisis and a grave
risk to the peace of the world. For this reason
I hope we can quickly agree along the lines
outlined in this letter and in your letter of
October 26th.

Statement by the President Following the Soviet
Decision to Withdraw Missiles from Cuba
October 28, 1962

I welcome Chairman Khrushchev's
statesmanlike decision to stop building bases in
Cuba, dismantling offensive weapons and
returning them to the Soviet Union under United
Nations verification. This is an important and
constructive contribution to peace.

We shall be in touch with the Secretary
General of the United Nations with respect to
reciprocal measures to assure peace in the
Caribbean area.

It is my earnest hope that the governments
of the world can, with a solution of the Cuban
crisis, turn their urgent attention to the
compelling necessity for ending the arms race
and reducing world tensions. This applies to the
military confrontation between the Warsaw Pact
and NATO countries as well as to other
situations in other parts of the world where
tensions lead to the wasteful diversion of
resources to weapons of war.

THE BERLIN CRISIS

President Kennedy: Remarks in the Rudolph
Wilde Platz, Berlin
June 26, 1963

I am proud to come to this city as the
guest of your distinguished Mayor, who has
symbolized throughout the world the fighting
spirit of West Berlin. And I am proud to visit
the Federal Republic with your distinguished
Chancellor who for so many years has committed
Germany to democracy and freedom and progress,
and to come here in the company of my fellow
American, General Clay, who has been in this
city during its great moments of crisis and will
come again if needed.

Two thousand years ago the proudest boast
was "civis Romanus sum." Today, in the world of

Sources: Public Papers of the Presidents, John
F. Kennedy, 1962, p. 815; Ibid, 1963, pp. 524-
525.

freedom, the proudest boast is "Ich bin ein Berliner."

I appreciate my interpreter translating my German!

There are many people in the world who really don't understand, or say they don't, what is the great issue between the free world and the Communist world. Let them come to Berlin. There are some who say that communism is the wave of the future. Let them come to Berlin. And there are some who say in Europe and elsewhere we can work with the Communists. Let them come to Berlin. And there are even a few who say that it is true that communism is an evil system, but it permits us to make economic progress. Lass'sie nach Berlin kommen. Let them come to Berlin.

Freedom has many difficulties and democracy is not perfect, but we have never had to put a wall up to keep our people in, to prevent them from leaving us. I want to say, on behalf of my countrymen, who live many miles away on the other side of the Atlantic, who are far distant from you, that they take the greatest pride that they have been able to share with you, even from a distance, the story of the last 18 years. I know of no town, no city, that has been besieged for 18 years that still lives with the vitality and the force, and the hope and the determination of the city of West Berlin. While the wall is the most obvious and vivid demonstration of the failures of the Communist system, for all the world to see, we take no satisfaction in it, for it is, as your Mayor has said, an offense not only against history but an offense against humanity, separating families, dividing husbands and wives and brothers and sisters, and dividing a people who wish to be joined together.

What is true of this city is true of Germany--real, lasting peace in Europe can never be assured as long as one German out of four is denied the elementary right of free men, and that is to make a free choice. In 18 years of peace and good faith, this generation of Germans has earned the right to be free, including the right to unite their families and their nation in lasting peace, with good will to all people.

You live in a defended island of freedom, but your life is part of the main. So let me ask you, as I close, to lift your eyes beyond the dangers of today, to the hopes of tomorrow, beyond the freedom merely of this city of Berlin, or your country of Germany, to the advance of freedom everywhere, beyond the wall to the day of peace with justice, beyond yourselves and ourselves to all mankind.

Freedom is indivisible, and when one man is enslaved, all are not free. When all are free, then we can look forward to that day when this city will be joined as one and this country and this great Continent of Europe in a peaceful and hopeful globe. When that day finally comes, as it will, the people of West Berlin can take sober satisfaction in the fact that they were in the front lines for almost two decades.

All free men, wherever they may live, are citizens of Berlin, and, therefore, as a free man, I take pride in the words "Ich bin ein Berliner."

President Kennedy: Radio and Television Report
to the American People on the Berlin Crisis
July 25, 1961

Seven weeks ago tonight I returned from Europe to report on my meeting with Premier Khrushchev and the others. His grim warnings about the future of the world, his aide memoire on Berlin, his subsequent speeches and threats which he and his agents have launched, and the increase in the Soviet military budget that he has announced, have all prompted a series of discussions by the Administration and a series of consultations with the members of the NATO organization. In Berlin, as you recall, he intends to bring to an end, through a stroke of the pen, first our legal rights to be in West Berlin--and secondly our ability to make good our commitment to the two million free people of that city. That we cannot permit.

We are clear about what must be done--and we intend to do it. I want to talk frankly with

Source: Public Papers of the Presidents, John F. Kennedy, 1961, pp. 533-537.

you tonight about the first steps that we shall
take. These actions will require sacrifice on
the part of many of our citizens. More will be
required in the future. They will require, from
all of us, courage and perseverance in the
years to come. But if we and our allies act out
of strength and unity of purpose--with calm
determination and steady nerves--using restraint
in our words as well as our weapons--I am
hopeful that both peace and freedom will be
sustained.

The immediate threat to free men is in
West Berlin. But that isolated outpost is not an
isolated problem. The threat is worldwide. Our
effort must be equally wide and strong, and not
be obsessed by any single manufactured crisis.
We face a challenge in Berlin, but there is also
a challenge in Southeast Asia, where the borders
are less guarded, the enemy harder to find, and
the dangers of communism less apparent to those
who have so little. We face a challenge in our
own hemisphere, and indeed wherever else the
freedom of human beings is at stake....

We are there [West Berlin] as a result of
our victory over Nazi Germany--and our basic
rights to be there, deriving from that victory,
include both our presence in West Berlin and the
enjoyment of access across East Germany. These
rights have been repeatedly confirmed and
recognized in special agreements with the Soviet
Union. Berlin is not part of East Germany, but a
separate territory under the control of the
allied powers. Thus our rights there are clear
and deep-rooted. But in addition to these rights
is our commitment to sustain--and defend, if
need be--the opportunity for more than two
million people to determine their own future and
choose their own way of life....

Thus, our presence in West Berlin, and our
access thereto, cannot be ended by any act of
the Soviet government. The NATO shield was long
ago extended to cover West Berlin--and we have
given our word that an attack upon that city
will be regarded as an attack upon us all.

For West Berlin--lying exposed 110 miles
inside East Germany, surrounded by Soviet troops
and close to Soviet supply lines, has many
roles. It is more than a showcase of liberty, a

symbol, and island of freedom in a Communist sea. It is even more than a link with the Free World, a beacon of hope behind the Iron Curtain, an escape hatch for refugees.

West Berlin is all of that. But above all it has now become--as never before--the great testing place of Western courage and will, a focal point where our solemn commitments stretching back over the years since 1945, and Soviet ambitions now meet in basic confrontation.

It would be a mistake for others to look upon Berlin, because of its location, as a tempting target. The United States is there; the United Kingdom and France are there; the pledge of NATO is there--and the people of Berlin are there. It is as secure, in that sense, as the rest of us--for we cannot separate its safety from our own.

I hear it said that West Berlin is militarily untenable. And so was Bastogne. And so, in fact, was Stalingrad. Any dangerous spot is tenable if men--brave men--will make it so.

We do not want to fight--but we have fought before. And others in earlier times have made the same dangerous mistake of assuming that the West was too selfish and too soft and too divided to resist invasions of freedom in other lands. Those who threaten to unleash the forces of war on a dispute over West Berlin should recall the words of the ancient philosopher: " A man who causes fear cannot be free from fear."

We cannot and will not permit the Communists to drive us out of Berlin, either gradually or by force. For the fulfillment of our pledge to that city is essential to the morale and security of Western Germany, to the unity of Western Europe, and to the faith of the entire Free World. Soviet strategy has long been aimed, not merely at Berlin, but at dividing and neutralizing all of Europe, forcing us back to our shores. We must meet our oft-stated pledge to the free peoples of West Berlin--and maintain our rights and their safety, even in the face of force--in order to maintain the confidence of other free peoples in our word and our resolve. The strength of the alliance on which our security depends is dependent in turn on our willingness to meet our commitments to them....

As signers of the UN Charter, we shall always be prepared to discuss international problems with any and all nations that are willing to talk--and listen--with reason. If they have proposals--not demands--we shall hear them. If they seek genuine understanding--not concessions of our rights--we shall meet them. We have previously indicated our readiness to remove any actual irritants in West Berlin, but the freedom of the city is not negotiable. We cannot negotiate with those who say "What's mine is mine and what's yours is negotiable." But we are willing to consider any arrangement or treaty in Germany consistent with the maintenance of peace and freedom, and with the legitimate security interests of all nations.

We recognize the Soviet Union's historical concern about their security in Central and Eastern Europe, after a series of ravaging invasions, and we believe arrangements can be worked out which will help to meet those concerns, and make it possible for both security and freedom to exist in this troubled area.

For it is not the freedom of West Berlin which is "abnormal" in Germany today, but the situation in that entire divided country. If anyone doubts the legality of our rights in Berlin, we are ready to have it submitted to international adjudication. If anyone doubts the extent to which our presence is desired by the people of West Berlin, compared to East German feelings about their regime, we are ready to have that question submitted to a free vote in Berlin and, if possible, among all the German people. And let us hear at that time from the two and one-half million refugees who have fled the Communist regime in East Germany--voting for Western-type freedom with their feet.

The world is not deceived by the Communist attempt to label Berlin as a hot-bed of war. There is peace in Berlin today. The source of world trouble and tension is Moscow, not Berlin. And if war begins, it will have begun in Moscow and not Berlin.

For the choice of peace or war is largely theirs, not ours. It is the Soviets who have stirred up this crisis. It is they who are

trying to force a change. It is they who have
opposed free elections. It is they who have
rejected an all-German peace treaty, and the
rulings of international law. And as Americans
know from our history on our own old frontier,
gun battles are caused by outlaws, and not by
officers of the peace.

In short, while we are ready to defend our
interests, we shall also be ready to search for
peace--in quiet exploratory talks--in formal or
informal meetings. We do not want military
considerations to dominate the thinking of
either East or West. And Mr. Khrushchev may find
that his invitation to other nations to join in
a meaningless treaty may lead to their inviting
him to join in the community of peaceful men, in
abandoning the use of force, and in respecting
the sanctity of agreements....

To sum it all up: we seek peace--but we
shall not surrender. That is the central meaning
of this crisis, and the meaning of your
government's policy.

With your help, and the help of other free
men, this crisis can be surmounted. Freedom can
prevail--and peace can endure.

U.S. Note to Soviet Ministry of Foreign Affairs
August 17, 1961

On August 13, East German authorities put
into effect several measures regulating movement
at the boundary of the western sectors and the
Soviet sector of the city of Berlin. These
measures have the effect of limiting, to a
degree approaching complete prohibition, passage
from the Soviet sector to western sectors of the
city. These measures were accompanied by the
closing of the sector boundary by a sizable
deployment of police forces and by military
detachments brought into Berlin for this
purpose.

All this is a flagrant, and particularly
serious, violation of the quadripartite status
of Berlin. Freedom of movement with respect to
Berlin was reaffirmed by the quadripartite

Source: Department of State Bulletin, September
4, 1961, p. 397.

agreement of New York of May 4, 1949, and by
the decision taken at Paris on June 20, 1949, by
the Council of the Ministers of Foreign Affairs
of the Four Powers. The United States Government
has never accepted that limitations can be
imposed on freedom of movement within Berlin.
The boundary between the Soviet sector and the
Western sectors of Berlin is not a state
frontier. The United States Government considers
that the measures which the East German
authorities have taken are illegal. It
reiterates that it does not accept the
pretension that the sector of Berlin forms a
part of the so-called German Democratic Republic
and that Berlin is situated on its territory.
Such a pretension is in itself a vow of the
solemnly pledged word of the U.S.S.R. in the
Agreement on the Zones of Occupation in Germany
and the administration of Greater Berlin.
Moreover, the United States Government cannot
admit the right of the East German authorities
to authorize their armed forces to enter the
Soviet sector of Berlin.

By the very admission of the East German
authorities, the measures which have just been
taken are motivated by the fact that an ever
increasing number of inhabitants of East Germany
wish to leave this territory. The reasons for
this exodus are known. They are simply the
internal difficulties in East Germany.

To judge by the terms of a declaration of
the Warsaw Pact powers published on August 13,
the measures in question are supposed to have
been recommended to the East German authorities
by those powers. The United States Government
notes that the powers which associated
themselves with the U.S.S.R. by signing the
Warsaw Pact are thus intervening in a domain in
which they have no competence.

It is to be noted that this declaration
states that the measures taken by the East
German authorities are "in the interests of the
German peoples themselves." It is difficult to
see any basis for this statement, or to
understand why it should be for the members of
the Warsaw Pact to decide what are the interests
of the German people. It is evident that no
Germans, particularly those whose freedom of

movement is being forcibly restrained, think
this is so. This would become abundantly clear
if all Germans were allowed a free choice, and
the principle of self-determination were also
applied in the Soviet sector of Berlin and in
East Germany.

The United States Government solemnly
protests against the measures referred to above,
for which it holds the Soviet Government
responsible. The United States Government
expects the Soviet Government to put an end to
these illegal measures. This unilateral
infringement of the quadripartite status of
Berlin can only increase existing tension and
dangers.

5

Vietnam: From Assistance to Major Actor

INTRODUCTION

The period from President Kennedy's death to the end of
the Johnson Administration in 1968 was dominated by the
events in Southeast Asia. Although these events began to
unfold in the early 1960s, their most visible form
emerged in 1964 with the passage of the Gulf of Tonkin
Resolution by Congress. Initially however, important
events took place in American politics that seemed to
overshadow national security issues.

Lyndon Johnson won the presidency in his own right
in 1964 when Republican candidate Barry Goldwater was
overwhelmed at the polls. Basing his appeal on the
Kennedy legacy, President Johnson's legislative agenda
included civil rights and the Great Society. The Civil
Rights Movement, fed by demonstrations throughout the
country, emerged as one major pillar of domestic
politics. The second pillar, the Great Society, was the
basis for passing a great deal of legislation intended to
alleviate poverty and a variety of social ills.

Even though the main focus of this initial period
was on domestic politics and a domestic agenda, events
were also taking place in the Middle East and Europe that
were shaping the international security environment. In
the Six Day War in 1967, Israel, in a lightning stroke,
achieved a complete military victory over four Arab
states. The Soviet Union responded by a flurry of
diplomatic activity, warnings, and propaganda aimed at
Israel. The United States, as the defender of Israel, was
placed in a difficult position, with the prospect of
becoming engulfed in the Middle East and confronting the

Soviet Union. Fortunately, the war ended quickly with the U.S. and the USSR avoiding serious confrontations.

In Europe, the Warsaw Pact forces numbering 650,000 invaded Czechoslovakia in 1967, crushing its attempt to disentangle itself from the Soviet Union. This became the basis for the so-called Brezhnev Doctrine--a doctrine based on the premise that it was the right of the Soviet Union to crush any resistance within the Socialist camp. The implicit acceptance by the West of the Warsaw Pact invasion of Czechoslovakia seemed to give legitimacy to the doctrine.

NATO was undergoing some internal changes with President De Gaulle of France disengaging his nation from the organization. At the same time NATO members were engaged in discussing burden-sharing in order to share the costs of maintaining U.S. troops in Europe.

Closer to home, the United States intervened in the Dominican Republic in 1965 in order to avert chaos and save American lives there. Additionally, it was felt by the Johnson Administration that the country was ripe for a Communist takeover. Over 21,000 U.S. military personnel eventually landed in Santo Domingo. They were later withdrawn as the threat subsided.

Even though there were confrontations between the Soviet Union and the United States, arms negotiations progressed leading to the Nonproliferation Treaty (NPT) which was intended to prevent the proliferation of nuclear weapons. Since the signing of the Partial Test-Ban Treaty in 1963, both the U.S. and the USSR were concerned about the proliferation of nuclear weapons. The hope was that the NPT would either slow down the proliferation or preclude it entirely. The NPT agreement also set the stage for initial discussions on Strategic Arms Limitation Talks (SALT).

Regardless of these domestic and foreign issues and events, the Johnson Administration soon became preoccupied with South Vietnam. But the involvement in Southeast Asia did not begin with the Johnson presidency. The U.S. involvement can be traced back to the Geneva Declaration which established two Vietnams (albeit temporarily), after the defeat of the French Forces in the North. This declaration, for all practical purposes, spelled the end of French involvement in Southeast Asia.

As part of the policy to establish a "global containment" the Eisenhower Administration placed its support behind President Diem of South Vietnam. The United States followed with the first contingent of U.S. military advisors and economic assistance. From this point on, the U.S. involvement grew almost imperceptibly. By the time of the Johnson presidency in 1964, there were thousands of U.S. advisors in South Vietnam. From here, it was a short step to the Gulf of Tonkin Resolution and military operations against the North Vietnamese, including air strikes against selected targets. The commitment of U.S. combat troops to the defense of South Vietnam in 1965 was the turning point and opened the door to the "Americanization" of the conflict and to all of the problems and dilemmas inherent with involvement in an unconventional conflict.

By the latter part of the 1960s, particularly in the aftermath of the Tet Offensive in 1968, it became clear to many Americans that the war was unwinnable. Anti-war demonstrations throughout the country became commonplace, with both the "left" and the "right" against the war, albeit for different reasons. Regardless of the efforts of President Johnson to focus attention on the Great Society, by 1967 the Vietnam War dominated virtually everything the administration attempted. Public perceptions of the Vietnam War became increasingly pessimistic, assisted in no small way by media interpretations and, in a number of instances, media distortions of the U.S. role and military operations. The war became a millstone around the neck of the Johnson presidency. In March 1968, Lyndon Johnson declared that he was not a candidate nor would he accept his party's nomination for the presidency. A large part of his decision was the realization that he, the President, had become the symbol of America's involvement in Vietnam. Thus, what had begun as a presidency with high hopes for the improvement of the American quality of life became mired in Vietnam, leaving Americans frustrated and the country divided.

DOCUMENTS

FINAL DECLARATION ON INDOCHINA: The Geneva
Conference, July 25, 1954

Final Declaration, dated 21st July, 1954, of the Geneva Conference on the problem of restoring peace in Indo-China, in which the representatives of Cambodia, the Democratic

Source: Foreign Relations of the United States, 1952-1954, vol. XVI, pp. 1540-1542 (complete document).

Republic of Viet-Nam, France, Laos, the
People's Republic of China, the State of Viet-
Nam, the Union of Soviet Socialist Republics,
the United Kingdom, and the United States of
America took part.

1. The Conference takes note of the
agreements ending hostilities in Cambodia, Laos,
and Viet-Nam and organizing international
control and the supervision of the execution of
the provisions of these agreements.

2. The Conference expresses satisfaction at
the ending of hostilities in Cambodia, Laos and
Vietnam; the Conference expresses its conviction
that the execution of the provisions set out in
the present declaration and in the agreements on
the cessation of hostilities will permit
Cambodia, Laos, and Viet-Nam henceforth to play
their part, in full independence and
sovereignty, in the peaceful community of
nations.

3. The Conference takes note of the
declarations made by the Governments of Cambodia
and of Laos of their intention to adopt measures
permitting all citizens to take their place in
the national community, in particular by
participating in the next general elections,
which, in conformity with the constitution of
each of these countries, shall take place in the
course of the year 1955, by secret ballot and in
conditions of respect for fundamental freedoms.

4. The Conference takes note of the clauses
in the agreement on the cessation of hostilities
in Viet-Nam prohibiting the introduction into
Viet-Nam of foreign troops and military
personnel as well as of all kinds of arms and
munitions. The Conference also takes note of the
declarations made by the Governments of Cambodia
and Laos of their resolution not to request
foreign aid, whether in war material, in
personnel or in instructors except for the
purpose of the effective defence of their
territory and, in the case of Laos, to the
extent defined by the agreements on the
cessation of hostilities in Laos.

5. The Conference takes note of the clauses
in the agreement on the cessation of hostilities
in Viet-Nam to the effect that no military base
under the control of a foreign State may be

established in the regrouping zones of the two parties, the latter having the obligation to see that the zones allotted to them shall not constitute part of any military alliance and shall not be utilized for the resumption of hostilities or in the service of an aggressive policy. The Conference also takes note of the declarations of the Governments of Cambodia and Laos to the effect that they will not join in any agreement with other States if this agreement includes the obligation to participate in a military alliance not in conformity with the principles of the Charter of the United Nations or, in the case of Laos, with the principles of the agreement on the cessation of hostilities in Laos or, so long as their security is not threatened, the obligation to establish bases on Cambodian or Laotian territory for the military forces of foreign Powers.

6. The Conference recognizes that the essential purpose of the agreement relating to Viet-Nam is to settle military questions with a view to ending hostilities and that the military demarcation line is provisional and should not in any way be interpreted as constituting a political or territorial boundary. The Conference expresses its conviction that the execution of the provisions set out in the present declaration and in the agreement on the cessation of hostilities creates the necessary basis for the achievement in the near future of a political settlement in Viet-Nam.

7. The Conference declares that, so far as Viet-Nam is concerned, the settlement of political problems, effected on the basis of respect for the principles of independence, unity and territorial integrity, shall permit the Viet-Namese people to enjoy the fundamental freedoms, guaranteed by democratic institutions established as a result of free general elections by secret ballot. In order to ensure that sufficient progress in the restoration of peace has been made, and that all the necessary conditions obtain for free expression of the national will, general elections shall be held in July 1956, under the supervision of an international commission composed of

representatives of the Member States of the International Supervisory Commission, referred to in the agreement on the cessation of hostilities. Consultations will be held on this subject between the competent representative authorities of the two zones from 20 July 1955 onwards.

8. The provisions of the agreements on the cessation of hostilities intended to ensure the protection of individuals and of property must be most strictly applied and must, in particular, allow everyone in Viet-Nam to decide freely in which zone he wishes to live.

9. The competent representative authorities of the Northern and Southern zones of Viet-Nam, as well as the authorities of Laos and Cambodia, must not permit any individual or collective reprisals against persons who have collaborated in any way with one of the parties during the war, or against members of such persons' families.

10. The Conference takes note of the declaration of the Government of the French Republic to the effect that it is ready to withdraw its troops from the territory of Cambodia, Laos and Viet-Nam, at the request of the governments concerned and within periods which shall be fixed by agreement between the parties except in the cases where, by agreement between the two parties, a certain mumber of French troops shall remain at specified points and for a specified time.

11. The Conference takes note of the declaration of the French Government to the effect that for the settlement of all the problems connected with the re-establishment and consolidation of peace in Cambodia, Laos and Viet-Nam, the French Government will proceed from the principle of respect for the independence and sovereignty, unity and territorial integrity of Cambodia, Laos and Viet-Nam.

12. In their relations with Cambodia, Laos and Viet-Nam, each member of the Geneva Conference undertakes to respect the sovereignty, the independence, the unity and the territorial integrity of the above-mentioned states, and to refrain from any interference in

their internal affairs.

13. The members of the Conference agree to consult one another on any question which may be referred to them by the International Supervisory Commission, in order to study such measures as may prove necessary to ensure that the agreements on the cessation of hostilities in Cambodia, Laos and Viet-Nam are respected.

LETTER FROM PRESIDENT EISENHOWER
to PRESIDENT DIEM
October 1, 1954

Dear Mr. President:

I have been following with great interest the course of developments in Vietnam, particularly since the conclusion of the conference at Geneva. The implications of the agreement concerning Vietnam have caused grave concern regarding the future of a country temporarily divided by an artificial military grouping, weakened by a long and exhausting war and faced with enemies without and by their subversive collaborators within.

Your recent requests for aid to assist in the formidable project of the movement of several hundred thousand loyal Vietnamese citizens away from areas which are passing under a de facto rule and political ideology which they abhor, are being fulfilled. I am glad that the United States is able to assist in this humanitarian effort.

We have been exploring ways and means to permit our aid to Vietnam to be more effective and to make a greater contribution to the welfare and stability of the Government of Vietnam. I am, accordingly, instructing the American Ambassador to Vietnam to examine with you in your capacity as Chief of Government, how an intelligent program of American aid given directly to your Government can serve to assist Vietnam in its present hour of trial, provided that your Government is prepared to give assur-

Source: Public Papers of the Presidents, Dwight D. Eisenhower, 1954, pp. 948-949 (cmplete document).

ances as to the standards of performance it
would be able to maintain in the event such aid
were supplied.

The purpose of this offer is to assist the
Government of Vietnam in developing and
maintaining a strong, viable state, capable of
resisting attempted subversion or aggression
through military means. The Government of the
United States expects that this aid will be met
by performance on the part of the Government of
Vietnam in undertaking needed reforms.   It
hopes that such aid, combined with your own
continuing efforts, will contribute effectively
toward an independent Vietnam endowed with a
strong government. Such a government would, I
hope, be so responsive to the nationalist
aspirations of its people, so enlightened in
purpose and effective in performance, that it
will be respected both at home and abroad and
discourage any who might wish to impose a
foreign ideology on your free people.

MEMORANDUM FROM THE CHIEF OF THE NATIONAL
SECURITY DIVISION
Training Relations Instruction Mission
(Lansdale)
To the Special Representative in Vietnam
(Collins)

Saigon, January 3, 1955

* * * * *

2. As a start, it is worth taking a look
at the real value of the chips given to you by
President Eisenhower for the game we are
playing here. The chips are our direct aid to
the Vietnamese. To most Americans, they mean
money, material, and technical (advisory)
manpower. In the eyes of the world, and
especially Asia, they mean something more. In
this view, the value of the chips becomes Asia
itself and parts of the Middle East.

3. The Asian view is that "direct aid"
means that Communism's strongest enemy, the

Source: Foreign Relations of the United States,
1952-1954, vol. XVI, pp. 948-949.

United States, is now in close support of the Free Vietnamese against the Communists. Certainly each of the free nations which has a pact with the United States, in which we will give them close support against the Communists, sees a bit of itself in the situation of the Vietnamese. And each of those nations, in varying degree, will be measuring what our support actually means. Thus, if we lose here or withdraw however gracefully, politically powerful people in those nations will read their own futures into our action. This means that the do-business-with-China folks of Japan, the anti-American-bases folks of the Philippines, and so on, will find their arguments strengthened locally to the critical straining point for the United States in places we now find difficult enough under neutralist and Communist political pressures. This is far beyond the usual observation of the loss of Vietnam opening Southeast Asia to the impact of Communist dynamism, which is dangerous enough in itself.

4. Thus, I feel that we have too much to lose to consider loosing [sic] or withdrawing. We have no other choice but to win here or face an increasingly grim future, a heritage which none of us wants to pass along to our offspring.

5. What will it take to win? It is going to take everything we are now doing and planning to do, plus more--and I believe that the "more" now exists here as a potential awaiting proper employment.

6. I have narrowed down the elements we need for winning the present struggle here to three, which is perhaps over-simplifying. I believe that if we can make these three elements a reality here, the initiative will pass to us and we will start winning. I feel, further, that we must have clear evidence by June 1955 that we can make the three elements a reality. They are:

a. Successful teamwork

b. Strengthen the Free Vietnamese

c. Make the bulk of the population willing to risk all for freedom.

7. <u>Successful teamwork</u>. The enemy is enjoying considerable success in his teamwork, among the Vietminh, between Vietminh and supporting population and between Chinese

advisors and Vietminh. We have a distance to go before we can match this teamwork, even among us Americans here, for several reasons (including the slower progress of our type of discipline as compared to the "iron discipline" of the Communists). Competent friendly observers have told me of dangerous frictions existing among key members of the U.S. team here; perhaps the root cause of such friction is that we still are not in agreement on exactly what the U.S. wants to achieve here regardless of risk, exactly how to achieve such result, and exactly who will undertake specific parts of the whole mission. This root cause undoubtedly is fertilized by any personal antipathies arising out of the strains we have all been under in trying so hard to solve problems here. Most of these frictions can be eased through the mechanisms you have established already....

9. A great deal of thought and effort has been given to our teamwork with the Vietnamese. However, there still seems to be some confusion on our part between partisanship and desired objectives, capabilities of the Vietnamese, and the most rewarding methods of doing business with them. There seems to be an increasing suspicion of our good intentions and ability to help successfully, which if it grows unchecked can endanger our whole effort here; an intensification of personal contacts all down the line of the American team with individual Vietnamese, on a footing of equality, and with patient explanation of reasons for requests or advice, would help. We must hold and extend our friendships among the Vietnamese, in order to give successful meaning to our aid, since we are now looked upon as the only strong true friend of Vietnam (other than China and the Soviets) and probably are the only catalysts who can induce the Vietnamese on our side to unify.

10. Teamwork among the Free Vietnamese has progressed slowly. There is still too much partisanship, distrust, and obstructive jealousy. Prominent among the remedies for this complex trouble are: growth of effective people-government-army cooperation, hope of establishment of some form of representative government which the people and factions of

people feel honestly represents [them], and, perhaps, development of political techniques among leaders (apt bestowal of praise, interest in indivudal welfare, informing the people adequately of the state of the nation with emphasis on plus factors, and so on).

11. <u>Strengthening Vietnamese</u>. I am concerned about whether all our aid and efforts here will strengthen the Vietnamese or merely make them more dependent upon us. Certainly none of us who must justify actions eventually at home would desire to place the U.S. in the position of continuing major help here for endless years, on the basis that if our aid were lessened then the enemy would win. Certainly the responsible Americans here would like to see the Vietnamese capably assuming an increasing share of their own burdens in all fields of national life.

12. Thus, I would like to see our efforts here geared as completely as possible to the operating philosophy of helping the Vietnamese to help themselves, not only Vietnamese government or army, but the people themselves....

13. <u>Willingness to risk all for freedom</u>. Mao Tse-tung once clearly expressed a basic fact in the type of struggle we are now engaged in here by stating: "There is no possibility for it (he was speaking of guerrilla warfare) to survive and develop once it is cut loose from the people or fails to attract the participation and co-operation of the broad masses." The Vietminh have learned this lesson well, applied it in their military guerilla warfare prior to the Cease-Fire, and are now applying it south of the 17th Parallel in their political guerrilla warfare. Our defeat is certain unless we learn and apply this same lesson of today's warfare, and do so more effectively than the enemy. We must face up to the fact that our side was "cut loose from the people" in too many areas we must now win back, and our method of winning them back must be to attract their participation and co-operation in what we free people do and cherish, not force, scare or coerce, but attract....

15. If the entire team on our side makes

the right approach to the people, we will have taken the first major step in attracting people to our side. We must then set about convincing, and accomplishment is most convincing, the people that their own future (and that of their children and children's children) will be more rewarding under our system than under Communism--more rewarding politically or socially, economically, and spiritually. When the hope of such a rewarding future is raised within the people, coupled with hope of its possible attainment (which includes military means to protect the attainment), then the first big cleavage between the Communists and the bulk of the population will start taking place.

16. Much of the program you outlined soon after your arrival here as Ambassador is intended to establish and protect a rewarding future for the Free Vietnamese. However, a critical piece appears to be missing: giving the people a truly representative government....

17. Along with moving as rapidly as possible towards a Constitution, the Free Vietnamese must establish government and the benefits of government as rapidly as possible throughout Vietnam south of the 17th Parallel. This is what we have termed "national action" of which military "pacification" is an integral part. It is the approach to the people and the first means of raising hopes within them, as mentioned in paragraph 15 before. Neither Vietnamese government operations currently on "national action," nor U.S. actions to help are too well coordinated today.

PROMOTING THE SECURITY OF THE UNITED STATES
AND THE FREE WORLD

Excerpts from the President's Budget Message
January 17, 1955

To the Congress of the United States:

I am transmitting to you today the Budget of the United States Government for the fiscal

Source: <u>Department of State Bulletin</u>, January 31, 1955, pp. 163 and 169.

year 1956, which begins July 1, 1955....
     In Asia, active warfare has only recently
ceased and the free countries of this continent
continue to face the threat of Communist
subversion and external aggression. We therefore
have been furnishing support to several
countries including Korea, Formosa, Vietnam,
and propose to continue to furnish the defense
of Laos and Cambodia. Some assistance in
economic development has been extended in India.
Unless such support is provided, we may expect
economic deterioration and dangerous reductions
in the military defenses of the free world.
Moreover, without such assistance, these
countries, most of which border on Russia and
Communist China, will not achieve the economic
progress which is necessary to meet the threat
of Communist subversion. The loss of northern
Vietnam makes this support more imperative than
ever.

OBJECTIVES of the MUTUAL SECURITY PROGRAM in ASIA

Statement by Walter S. Robertson
Assistant Secretary of State for Far Eastern
Affairs
Made before the Committee on Foreign Affairs of
the House of Representatives, April 11, 1956

     The primary objective of our policy in the
Far East can be stated quite simply. It is to
strengthen the free world and to curb the power
and prevent the expansion of communism. The
mutual security program is an increasingly
essential factor in the attainment of that
objective.
     The people of these countries have
aspirations for a better life which they are
determined to fulfill. This program, through
technical and economic-development assistance,
is helping them to achieve these objectives. The
military assistance part of the program is
assisting them in maintaining internal order and
security and in creating a first line of defense

Source: <u>Department of State Bulletin</u>, April 30,
1956, pp. 723-727.

against aggression while they build up in a nonmilitary sense internally. But it is the success or failure of this mutual security program, in giving these nations hope that they will be more secure and better off tomorrow than they are today, that will determine whether they succumb to the blandishments of communism. This hope, if it is to last, must be firmly grounded in their own experience that progress is being made; that they are, in fact better off today than they were yesterday; and that, when tomorrow becomes today, the same thing will be true.

As Secretary Dulles said upon his return from his recent trip to the Far East:

The day is past when the peoples of Asia will tolerate leadership which keeps them on a dead center economically and socially, and when each generation merely ekes out a bare subsistence, with a brief life expectancy, and passes on to the next generation only the same bleak prospect.

As you know, I had the privilege of accompanying Secretary Dulles on his recent trip. The situation in this part of the world is still serious; there are still many points if tension; but there is general improvement in free-world competence to deal with these tensions. Doubtless there will be setbacks from time to time, but the general course is one of progress.

The Asia leaders whom we saw uniformly desired to preserve the independence of their countries. They too recognized that political independence of itself is not enough. Eight out of ten countries we visited were anti-Communist. Those two which call themselves neutrals, however, were also appreciative of United States aid and the help that United States policy affords them in preserving their independence. Faith and hope are the stuff of which free nations are made. Our aid programs are assisting the governments of free Asian countries in making such faith and hope possible.

For well over a year, the forces of armed aggression in the area have been held in check. This fact, and the radical change in Soviet tactics in recent months, are, in my opinion, evidence of the effectiveness of the courses of action we have been following. Millions of free Asians have, in consequence, enjoyed a measure of peace even though living under the constant threat of a renewal of armed aggression. That threat remains deadly serious throughout the region as it did a year ago....

It is clear that there is much to be done. It is also true that much has been done and that genuine progress has been made in the last year.

A little less than a year ago, when the aid program for fiscal year 1956 was presented before this committee, you were informed of the tremendous odds against which the newly independent Government of Viet-Nam was fighting. It was faced with the military and subversion threat of the Communists to the north of the 17th parallel; it was confronted with internal strife. There was the ominous challenge to the government's control posed by the armed, self-seeking, political-religious sects; there was the urgent necessity for resettling hundreds of thousands of refugees who had fled Communist domination following the military partition. The problems were well-nigh overwhelming. The program you approved at that time has made possible our continued support of this new republic in the economic and military sphere. We can, I believe, take great satisfaction in the remarkable improvement in the situation which without our contribution, we believe, would have been impossible.

We now find a firmly entrenched nationalist government under the leadership of President Diem. This government has proved its capacity not only to survive in the face of Communist subversive efforts but to assume the responsibilities of independence. The Diem government has achieved a decisive victory in the recent elections for the Assembly, which is now meeting to ratify a constitution for free Viet-Nam.

Our own efforts in Viet-Nam are directed in the first place toward helping to strengthen internal security forces. These consist of a regular army of about 150,000 men, a mobile civil guard of about 45,000, and local defense

units which are being formed to give protection
against subversion on the village level. We are
providing budgetary support and equipment for
these forces and have a mission assisting in the
training of the army. We are also helping to
organize, train, and equip the Vietnamese police
forces. Some 600,000 refugees who fled to South
Viet-Nam to escape the Viet Minh are being
resettled on productive lands with the
assistance of funds made available by our aid
program. In various ways under "defense support"
our program also provides assistance to the
Vietnamese Government designed to strengthen the
economy and provide a better future for the
peoples in that area....

On the whole, I believe we can all derive
genuine satisfaction from the collective
strength that the free nations of Asia have been
able, with our help, to achieve. The job is by
no means finished, however, nor have the threats
to security lessened. In our own interest, as
well as theirs, we must continue our help to
them at a rate and in a manner adequate to the
needs of the developing situation.

VIETNAM COMMITMENTS, 1961

A Staff Study
Committee on Foreign Relations
United States Senate
March 20, 1972

Escalation of the U.S.-Vietnam Involvement

On April 29 President Kennedy approved
the limited military proposals of the Task Force
Report but did not act on the recommendations of
the Laos Annex. The President authorized a 100
man increase in the size of the Military
Assistance Advisory Group, bringing the total to
785 men. Despite the fact that this exceeded the
685-man ceiling imposed by the Geneva settlement
of 1954, the increase was deemed necessary to
train the already authorized 20,000-man addition

Source: U.S. Senate, Committee on Foreign
Relations, A Staff Study, Vietnam Commitments,
1961, p. 2.

to the 150,000-man Vietnamese Army. The
President also approved 1) an increase in the
responsibilities of the Military Assistance
Advisory Group to include support and advice for
the 40,000 man Self Defense Corps and 2) an
expansion of the Military Assistance Program to
include support for the 68,000-man Civil Guard
(an addition of support for 36,000 men) and
training of South Vietnam's Junk Force.

          . . . .

National Security Action Memorandum No. 52
              May 11, 1961

To: The Secretary of State.

     The President today reviewed the report of
the Vietnam Task Force, entitled "Program of
Action to Prevent Communist Domination of South
Vietnam." Subject to amendments or revisions
which he may wish to make after providing
opportunity for a further discussion at the next
meeting of the National Security Council now
scheduled for May 19, the President has made the
following decisions on the basis of this report:
     1. The U.S. objective and concept of
operations stated in the report are approved: to
prevent Communist domination of South Vietnam;
to create in that country a viable and
increasingly democratic society; and to
initiate, on an accelerated basis, a series of
mutually supporting actions of a military,
political, economic, psychological and covert
character designed to achieve this objective.
     2. The approval given for specific
military actions by the President at the
National Security Council meeting on April 29,
1961, is confirmed.
     3. Additional actions...are authorized,
with the objective of meeting the increased
security threat resulting from the new situation
along the frontier between Laos and Vietnam. In
particular, the President directs an assessment

Source: U.S. Senate, Committee on Foreign
Relations, A Staff Study, Vietnam Commitments,
1961, pp. 32-34 for this and National Security
Memorandum No. 104 (complete document).

of the military utility of a further increase in G.V.N. forces from 170,000 to 200,000, together with an assessment of the parallel political and fiscal implications.

4. The President directs full examination by the Defense Department, <u>under the guidance of the director</u> of the continuing Task Force on Vietnam, of the size and composition of forces which would be desirable in the case of a possible commitment of U.S. forces to Vietnam. The diplomatic setting within which this action might be taken should also be examined.

5. The U.S. will seek to increase the confidence of President Diem and his government in the United States by a series of actions and messages relating to the trip of Vice President Johnson. The U.S. will attempt to strengthen President Diem's popular support within Vietnam by reappraisal and negotiation, under the direction of Ambassador Nolting. Ambassador Nolting is also requested to recommend any necessary reorganization of the Country Team for these purposes.

6. The U.S. will negotiate in appropriate ways to improve Vietnam's relationship with other countries, especially Cambodia, and its standing in world opinion.

7. The Ambassador is authorized to begin negotiations looking toward a new bilateral arrangement with Vietnam, but no firm commitment will be made to such an arrangement without further review by the President.

8. The U.S. will undertake economic programs in Vietnam with a view to both short term immediate impact and a contribution to the longer range economic viability of the country....

9. The U.S. will strengthen its efforts in the psychological field....

10. The program for covert actions...is approved....

12. Finally, the President approved the continuation of a special Task Force on Vietnam, established in and directed by the Department of State under Sterling J. Cottrell as Director, and Chalmers B. Wood as Executive Officer.

National Security Action Memorandum
No. 104

October 13, 1961

TO: The Secretary of State
      The Secretary of Defense
      The Director of Central Intelligence

Subject: Southeast Asia.

The President on October 11, 1961, directed that the following actions be taken:

1. Make preparations for the publication of the white paper on North Vietnamese aggression against South Viet Nam which is now being drafted in the Department of State.

2. Develop plans for possible action in the Viet Nam ICC based upon the white paper, preliminary to possible action under paragraph 3 below.

3. Develop plans for presentation of the Viet Nam case in the United Nations.

4. Subject to agreement with the Government of Viet Nam which is now being sought, introduce the Air Force Jungle Jim Squadron into Viet Nam for the initial purpose of training Vietnamese forces.

5. Initiate guerrilla ground action, including use of U.S. advisers if necessary, against Communist aerial resupply missions in the Tchepone area.

6. General Taylor should undertake a mission to Saigon to explore ways in which assistance of all types might be more effective.

The President also agreed that certain other actions developed by the Task Force and concurred in by the agencies concerned, but which do not require specific Presidential approval, should be undertaken on an urgent basis.

US CONGRESS, TONKIN GULF RESOLUTION
August 7, 1964

To Promote the Maintenance of International Peace and Security in Southeast Asia

<u>Whereas</u> naval units of the Communist regime in Vietnam, in violation of the principles of the Charter of the United Nations and of international law, have deliberately and repeatedly attacked United States naval vessels lawfully present in international waters, and have thereby created a serious threat to international peace; and

<u>Whereas</u> these attacks are part of a deliberate and systematic campaign of aggression that the Communist regime in North Vietnam has been waging against its neighbors and the nations joined with them in the collective defense of their freedom; and

<u>Whereas</u> the United States is assisting the peoples of Southeast Asia to protect their freedom and has no territorial, military or political ambitions in that area, but desires only that these people should be left in peace to work out their own destinies in their own way; Now therefore, be it

<u>Resolved by the Senate and House of Representatives of the United States of America in Congress assembled</u>,

That the Congress approves and supports the determination of the President, as Commander in Chief, to take all necessary measures to repel any armed attack against the forces of the United States and to prevent further aggression.

SEC. 2. The United States regards as vital to its national interest and to world peace the maintenance of international peace and security in Southeast Asia. Consonant with the Constitution of the United States and the Charter of the United Nations and in accordance with its obligations under the Southeast Asia Collective Defense Treaty, the United States is, therefore, prepared, as the President determines, to take all necessary steps,

Source: <u>Department of State Bulletin</u>, August 24, 1964 (complete document).

including the use of armed force, to assist any member or protocol state of the Southeast Asia Collective Defense Treaty requesting assistance in defense of its freedom.

SEC. 3. This resolution shall expire when the President shall determine that the peace and security of the area is reasonably assured by international conditions created by action of the United Nations or otherwise, except that it may be terminated earlier by concurrent resolution of the Congress.

INITIAL BOMBINGS
Statement by the President Upon Ordering
Withdrawal of American dependents from South
Viet-Nam, February 7, 1965

Following meetings with the National Security Council, I have directed the orderly withdrawal of American dependents from South Viet-Nam.

It has become clear that Hanoi has undertaken a more aggressive course of action against both South Vietnamese and American installations, and against Americans who are in South Viet-Nam assisting the people of that country to defend their freedom. We have no choice now but to clear the decks and make absolutely clear our continued determination to back South Viet-Nam in its fight to maintain its independence.

In addition to this action, I have ordered the deployment to South Viet-Nam of a Hawk air defense battalion. Other reinforcements, in units and individuals, may follow....

United States and South Vietnamese Forces
Launch Retaliatory Attacks Against
North Viet-Nam
White House Statement, February 7, 1965

On February 7, U.S. and South Vietnamese air elements were directed to launch retaliatory attacks against barracks and staging

Sources: Public Papers of the Presidents, Lyndon B. Johnson, 1965, p. 153; Department of State Bulletin, February 22, 1965, pp. 238-239.

areas in the southern area of North Viet-Nam
which intelligence has shown to be actively used
by Hanoi for training and infiltration of Viet
Cong personnel into South Viet-Nam.

Results of the attack and further
operational details will be announced as soon as
they are reported from the field.

Today's action by the U.S. and South
Vietnamese Governments was in response to
provocations ordered and directed by the Hanoi
regime.

Commencing at 2 a.m. on February 7th,
Saigon time (1 p.m. yesterday, eastern standard
time) two South Vietnamese airfields, two U.S.
barracks areas, several villages, and one town
in South Viet-Nam were subjected to deliberate
surprise attacks. Substantial casualties
resulted.

Our intelligence has indicated and this
action confirms, that Hanoi has ordered a more
aggressive course of action against both South
Vietnamese and American installations.

Moveover, these attacks were only made
possible by the continuing infiltration of
personnel and equipment from North Viet-Nam.
This infiltration markedly increased during 1964
and continues to increase.

To meet these attacks, the Government of
South Viet-Nam and the U.S. Government agreed to
appropriate reprisal action against North
Vietnamese targets. The President's approval of
this action was given after the action was
discussed with and recommended by the National
Security Council last night [February 6].

Today's joint response was carefully
limited to military areas which are supplying
men and arms for attacks in South Viet-Nam. As
in the case of the North Vietnamese attacks in
the Gulf of Tonkin last August, the response is
apropriate and fitting.

As the U.S. Governmment has frequently
stated, we seek no wider war. Whether or not
this course can be maintained lies with the
North Vietnamese aggressors. The key to the
situation remains the cessation of infiltration
from North Viet-Nam and the clear indication by
the Hanoi regime that it is prepared to cease
aggression against its neighbors.

VIETNAM: INITIAL US TROOP DEPLOYMENT
Department of Defense Telegram
Deployment of Marine Expeditionary Battalion
to Danang, February 24, 1965

* * * * *

3. COMUSMACV comments further on the security situation in South Vietnam and indicated his priority for deployment of US combat forces, indicating that Danang was the first priority. Second priority was Saigon/Bien Hoa/Vung Tau Complex. Third priority was Nha Trang/Cam Ranh Bay.

4. CINCPAC concurred with COMUSMACV's assessment of the security situation in RVN and with his recommendation that the MEB should be deployed to Danang now. Further stated that in view of the vulnerability of Danang, consider it important that we act rather than react and indicated the deterrent effect upon the VC that would result from a MEB in place at Danang....

6. AMB discussed pros and cons of deploying MEB to Danang. The AMB comments on the difficulty of providing complete assurance of security from surprise mortar fire even with the whole of a MEB. This is true and consequently, what we are obliged to do here is to reduce within the limits of our capability the hazards to our people. I believe that the vulnerability of the U.S. investment in Danang is as apparent to the VC/DRV as it is to us. With a strong mobile force in the area providing a tight defense of the airfield complex and good security of U.S. outlying installation, I believe that two ancillary benefits will emerge. First, the RVNAF will be encouraged to use the forces thus freed for patrol and security operations, and second, the VC/DRV will be obliged to regard Danang as a tougher target. Finally the AMB rejects the usefulness of U.S. ground elements in a counter-guerrilla role because of our color, armament, equipment and training. This stands athwart past performance in this function. The marines have a

Source: Department of Defense, National Command Center, February 24, 1965. Housed at the Lyndon Baines Johnson Presidential Library.

distinguished record in counter-guerrilla warfare....

8. ... It is apparent that our present posture is a reactive one, it gives no defense against a VC hit-and-run attack against the U.S. installation in Danang. The marines will be ashore after the damage has been done and the enemy has withdrawn.

9. My appraisal of the whole matter...is still regarded as sound. I consider the landing of the MEB in Danang to be an act of prudence which we should take before and not after another tragedy occurs....

OUTGOING TELEGRAM FROM THE DEPARTMENT OF STATE
February 26, 1965
Action: Amembassy Saigon

Subject to consultations described below, it has been decided to proceed to land at once MEB command and control element, surface BLT, and one helicopter squadron, and thereafter build up by air and surface movement Marine force by adding second BLT, all in Da Nang area, under terms of reference as indicated in MACV recommendation with primary mission of providing security for Da Nang airfield. Execute order will await following consultations.

You should consult urgently with Quat, describing proposed deployment and its purposes, and seek his approval and ascertain whether he sees any serious problem. If Quat approves, believe we should also have full understanding and acceptance of Minister of Defense, Chief of Staff, and perhaps most important Thi as Corps commander. All should clearly understand mission, and arrangements with military and particularly Thi should clearly provide for cooperation with local military, leaving them in no doubt this is deployment for a limited purpose and that GVN must continue have full responsibility in pacification program.

Since assuming GVN concurrence all levels, this will be first U.S. ground deployment of

Source: Department of State, Outgoing Telegram, February 25, 1965. Housed at the Lyndon Baines Johnson Presidential Library.

such a unit, request your recommendation as to timing of deployment and form of announcement.

Reference to general security duties seems to us best approach, since we do not wish on one hand to give impression pacification mission or on other hand to indicate we alarmed over Da Nang security.

We are considering further recommendations for Composite Marine Air Group, third BLT, and remaining elements of tailored MEB, but are deferring decision on those for present.

VIET-NAM ACTION CALLED "COLLECTIVE DEFENSE
AGAINST ARMED AGGRESSION"
March 4, 1965

The fact that military hostilities have been taking place in Southeast Asia does not bring about the existence of a state of war, which is a legal characterization of a situation rather than a factual description. What we have in Viet-Nam is armed aggression from the North against the Republic of Viet-Nam. Pursuant to a South Vietnamese request and consultations between our two Governments, South Viet-Nam and the United States are engaged in collective defense against that armed aggression. The inherent right of individual and collective self-defense is recognized in article 51 of the United Nations Charter.

If the question is intended to raise the issue of legal authority to conduct the actions which have been taken, there can be no doubt that these actions fall within the constitutional powers of the President and within the congressional resolution of August 1964.

STATEMENT by the PRESIDENT on VIET-NAM
March 25, 1965

1. It is importnat for us all to keep a cool and clear view of the situation in Viet-

Sources: Department of State Bulletin, March 22, 1965, p. 403; Public Papers of the Presidents, Lyndon B. Johnson, 1965, p. 319 (complete documents).

Nam.

2. The central cause of the danger there is aggression by Communists against a brave and independent people. There are other difficulties in Viet-Nam, of course, but if that aggression is stopped, the people and government of South Viet-Nam will be free to settle their own future, and the need for supporting American military action there will end.

3. The people who are suffering from this Communist aggression are Vietnamese. This is no struggle of white men against Asians. It is aggression by Communist totalitarians against their independent neighbors. The main burden of resistance has fallen on the people and soldiers of South Viet-Nam. We Americans have lost hundreds of our own men there, and we mourn them. But the free Vietnamese have lost tens of thousands, and the aggressors and their dupes have lost still more. These are the cruel costs of the conspiracy directed from the North. This is what has to be stopped.

4. The United States still seeks no wider war. We threaten no regime and covet no territory. We have worked and will continue to work for a reduction of tensions, on the great stage of the world. But the aggression from the North must be stopped. That is the road to peace in Asia.

5. The United States looks forward to the day when the people and governments of all Southeast Asia may be free from terror, subversion, and assassination--when they will need not military support and assistance against aggression, but only economic and social cooperation for progress in peace. Even now, in Viet-Nam and elsewhere, there are major programs of development which have the cooperation and support of the United States. Wider and bolder programs can be expected in the future from Asian leaders and Asian councils--and in such programs we would want to help. This is the proper business of our future cooperation.

6. The United States will never be second in seeking a settlement in Viet-Nam that is based on an end of Communist aggression. As I have said in every part of the Union, I am ready to go anywhere at any time, and meet with anyone

whenever there is promise of progress toward an honorable peace. We have said many times--to all who are interested in our principles for honorable negotiation--that we seek no more than a return to the essentials of the Agreements of 1954--a reliable arrangement to guarantee the independence and security of all in Southeast Asia. At present the Communist aggressors have given no sign of any willingness to move in this direction, but as they recognize the costs of their present course, and their own true interest in peace, there may come a change--if we all remain united.

Meanwhile, as I said last year and again last week, "it is and will remain the policy of the United States to furnish assistance to support South Viet-Nam for as long as is required to bring Communist aggression and terrorism under control." The military actions of the United States will be such, and only such, as serve that purpose--at the lowest possible cost in human life to our allies, to our own men, and to our adversaries, too.

BUILDUP of FORCES

A Report to the Congress by the Commander
of U.S. Military Forces in Viet-Nam

General William C. Westmoreland
Address before a joint session of Congress,

April 28, 1967

The Republic of Viet-Nam is fighting to build a strong nation while aggression--organized, directed, and supported from without--attempts to engulf it. This is an unprecedented challenge for a small nation. But it is a challenge which will confront any nation that is marked as a target for the Communist stratagem called "war of national liberation." I can assure you here and now that militarily this stratagem will not succeed in Viet-Nam.

In 3 years of close study and daily

Source: Department of State Bulletin, May 15, 1967, pp. 738-741.

observation, I have seen no evidence that this
is an internal insurrection. I have seen
evidence to the contrary--documented by the
enemy himself--that it is aggression from the
North.

Since 1954, when the Geneva accords were
signed, the North Vietnamese have been sending
leaders, political organizers, technicians, and
experts on terrorism and sabotage into the
South. Clandestinely directed from the North,
they and their Hanoi-trained southern
counterparts have controlled the entire course
of the attack against the Republic of South
Viet-Nam.

More than 2 years ago, North Vietnamese
divisions began to arrive, and the control was
no longer clandestine. Since then, the buildup
of enemy forces has been formidable. During the
past 22 months, the number of enemy combat
battalions in the South has increased
significantly, and nearly half of them are North
Vietnamese. In the same period overall enemy
strength has nearly doubled in spite of large
combat losses.

Enemy commanders are skilled
professionals. In general, their troops are
indoctrinated, well trained, aggressive, and
under tight control.

The enemy's logistic system is primitive
in many ways. Forced to transport most of his
supplies down through southeastern Laos, he uses
a combination of trucks, bicycles, men and
animals. But he does this with surprising
effectiveness. In South Viet-Nam the system is
also well organized. Many of the caches we have
found and destroyed have been stocked with
enough supplies and equipment to support months
of future operations.

The enemy emphasizes what he calls
strategic mobility, although his tactics are
based on foot mobility, relatively modest
firepower, and often primitive means of
communications. However, his operational
planning is meticulous. He gathers intelligence,
makes careful plans, assigns specific tasks in
detail and then rehearses the plan of attack
until he believes it cannot fail. Local peasants
are forced to provide food, shelter, and porters

to carry supplies and equipment for combat units and to evacuate the dead and wounded from the battlefield.

When all is ready he moves his large military formations covertly from concealed bases into the operational area. His intent is to launch a surprise attack designed to achieve quick victory by shock action. This tactic has failed because of our courageous men, our firepower, and our spoiling attacks.

For months now we have been successful in destroying a number of main-force units. We will continue to seek out the enemy, catch him off guard, and punish him at every opportunity.

But success against his main forces alone is not enough to insure a swift and decisive end to the conflict.

This enemy also uses terror--murder, mutilation, abduction, and the deliberate shelling of innocent men, women, and children--to exercise control through fear. Terror, which he employs daily, is much harder to counter than his best conventional moves.

A typical day in Viet-Nam was last Sunday. Terrorists near Saigon assassinated a 39-year-old village chief. The same day in the delta, they kidnapped 26 civilians assisting in arranging for local elections. The next day the Viet Cong attacked a group of Revolutionary Development workers, killing 1 and wounding 12 with grenades and machinegun fire in one area, and in another they opened fire on a small civilian bus and killed 3 and wounded 4 of its passengers. These are cases of calculated enemy attack on civilians to extend by fear that which they cannot gain by persuasion.

One hears little of this brutality at home. What we do hear about is our own aerial bombings against North Viet-Nam and I would like to address this for a moment.

For years the enemy has been blowing up bridges, interrupting traffic, cutting roads, sabotaging power stations, blocking canals, and attacking airfields in the South, and he continues to do so. This is a daily occurrence. Bombing in the North has been centered on precisely these same kinds of targets and for the same military purposes--to reduce the supply, interdict the movement and impair the effectivensss of enemy military forces.

Within his capabilities, the enemy in Viet-Nam is waging total war all day, every day, everywhere. He believes in force, and his intensification of violence is limited only by his resources and not by any moral inhibitions.

To us a cease-fire means "cease fire." Our observance of past truces has been open and subject to public scrutiny. The enemy permits no such observation in the North or the South. He traditionally has exploited cease-fire periods when the bombing has been suspended to increase his resupply and infiltration activity.

This is the enemy; this has been the challenge. The only strategy which can defeat such an organization is one of unrelenting but discriminating military, political, and psychological pressure on his whole structure at all levels....

Given the nature of the enemy, it seems to me that the strategy we are following at this time is the proper one and that it is producing results. While he obviously is far from quitting, there are signs that his morale and his military structure are beginning to deteriorate. Their rate of decline will be in proportion to the pressure directed against him.

Faced with this prospect, it is gratifying to note that our forces and those of the other free-world allies have grown in strength and profited from experience. In this connection it is well to remember that Korea, Australia, New Zealand, Thailand, and the Philippines all have military forces fighting and working with the Vietnamese and Americans in Viet-Nam. It also is worthy of note that 30 other nations are providing noncombat support. All of these free-world forces are doing well, whether in combat or in support of nation-building. Their exploits deserve recognition, not only for their direct contributions to the overall effort but for their symbolic reminder that the whole of free Asia opposes Communist expansion....

Our President and the representatives of the people of the United States, the Congress, have seen to it that our troops in the field have been well supplied and equipped. When a field commander does not have to look over his shoulder to see whether he is being supported, he can concentrate on the battlefield with much greater assurance of success. I speak for my troops when I say: We are thankful for this unprecedented material support.

As I have said before, in evaluating the enemy strategy, it is evident to me that he believes our Achilles' heel is our resolve. Your continued strong support is vital to the success of our mission.

Our soldiers, sailors, airmen, marines and coastguardsmen in Viet-Nam are the finest ever fielded by our nation. And in this assessment I include Americans of all races, creeds, and colors. Your servicemen in Viet-Nam are intelligent, skilled, dedicated, and courageous. In these qualities no unit, no service, no ethnic group, and no national origin can claim priority.

These men understand the confict and their complex roles as fighters and builders. They believe in what they are doing. They are determined to provide the shield of security behind which the Republic of Viet-Nam can develop and prosper for its own sake and for the future and freedom of all Southeast Asia.

Backed at home by resolve, confidence, patience, determination, and continued support, we will prevail in Viet-Nam over Communist aggression.

Mr. President, Mr. Speaker, Members of Congress, I am sure you are as proud to represent our men serving their country and the free world in Viet-Nam as I am to command them.

THE TET OFFENSIVE
Report of the Chairman, JCS, on Situation in
Vietnam and MACV Requirements
February 27, 1968

.... The Chairman, JCS and party visited SVN on 23, 24 and 25 February. This report summarizes the impressions and facts developed

Source: The Senator Gravel Edition, The Pentagon Papers, vol. IV (Boston: Beacon Press, 1971), pp. 238-239 and 546-549.

through conversations and briefings at MACV and with senior commanders throughout the country...

--The current situation in Vietnam is still developing and fraught with opportunities as well as dangers.

--There is no question in the mind of MACV that the enemy went all out for a general offensive and general uprising and apparently believed that he would succeed in bringing the war to an early successful conclusion.

--The enemy failed to achieve his initial objective but is continuing his effort. Although many of his units were badly hurt the judgment is that he has the will and the capability to continue.

--Enemy losses have been heavy; he has failed to achieve his prime objectives of mass uprisings and capture of a large number of the capital cities and towns. Morale in enemy units which were badly mauled or where the men were oversold the idea of a decisive victory at TET probably has suffered severely. However, with replacements, his indoctrination system would seem capable of maintaining morale at a generally adequate level. His determination appears to be unshaken.

--The enemy is operating with relative freedom in the countryside, probably recruiting heavily and no doubt infiltrating NVA units and personnel. His recovery is likely to be rapid; his supplies are adequate; and he is trying to maintain the momentum of his winter-spring offensive.

--The structure of the GVN held up but its effectiveness has suffered.

--The RVNAF held up against the initial assault with gratifying, and in a way, surprising strength and fortitude. However, RVNAF is now in a defensive posture around towns and cities and there is concern about how well they will bear up under sustained pressure.

--The initial attack nearly succeeded in a dozen places, and defeat in those places was only averted by the timely reaction of U.S. forces. In short, it was a very near thing.

--There is no doubt that the RD program has suffered a severe setback.

--RVNAF was not badly hurt physically--

they should recover strength and equipment
rather quickly (equipment in 2-3 months--
strength in 3-6 months). Their problems are more
psychological than physical.
        --U.S. forces have lost none of their pre-
TET capability.

        MACV has three principal problems.
First,logistic support north of Danang is
marginal owing to weather, enemy interdiction
and harassment and the massive deployment of
U.S. forces into the DMZ/Hue area. Opening Route
1 will alleviate this problem but takes a
substantial troop commitment. Second, the
defensive posture of ARVN is permitting the VC
to make rapid inroads in the formerly pacified
countryside. ARVN, in its own words, is in a
dilemma as it cannot afford another enemy thrust
into the cities and towns and yet if it remains
in a defensive posture against this contingency,
the countryside goes by default. MACV is forced
to devote much of its troop strength to this
problem. Third, MACV has been forced to deploy
50% of all U.S. maneuver battalions into I
Corps, to met the threat there, while stripping
the rest of the country of adequate reserves.
If the enemy synchronizes an attack against Khe
Sanh/Hue-Quang Tri with an offensive in the
Highlands and around Saigon while keeping the
pressure on throughout the remainder of the
country, MACV will be hard pressed to meet
adequately all threats. Under these
circumstances, we must be prepared to accept
some reverses.
        --For these reasons, General Westmoreland
has asked for a 3 division-15 tactical fighter
squadron force. This force would provide him
with a theater reserve and an offensive
capability which he does not now have.

3. THE SITUATION AS IT STANDS TODAY:

a. Enemy capabilities.
        (1) The enemy has been hurt badly in the
populated lowlands, is practically intact
elsewhere. He committed over 67,000 combat
maneuver forces plus perhaps 25% or 17,000 more
impressed men and boys, for a total of about

84,000. He lost 40,000 killed, at least 3,000 captured, and perhaps 5,000 disabled or died of wounds. He had peaked his force to about 240,000 just before TET by hard recruiting, infiltration, civilian impressment, and drawdowns on service and guerrilla personnel. So he has lost about one fifth of his total strength. About two-thirds of his trained, organized unit strength can continue offensive action. He is probably infiltrating and recruiting heavily in the countryside while allied forces are securing the urban areas....

d. GVN Strength and Effectiveness:

(1) Psychological--the people in South Vietnam were handed a psychological blow, particularly in the urban areas where the feeling of security had been strong. There is a fear of further attacks.

(2) The structure of the Government was not shattered and continues to function but at greatly reduced effectiveness.

(3) In many places, the RD program has been set back badly. In other places the program was untouched in the initial stage of the offensive. MACV reports that of the 555 RD cadre groups, 278 remain in hamlets, 245 are in district and province towns on security duty, while 32 are unaccounted for. It is not clear as to when, or even whether, it will be possible to return to the RD program in its earlier form. As long as the VC prowl the countryside it will be impossible, in many places, even to tell exactly what has happened to the program.

(4) Refugees--An additional 470,000 refugees were generated during the offensive. A breakdown of refugees is at Enclosure (7). The problem of caring for refugees is part of the larger problem of reconstruction in the cities and towns. It is anticipated that the care and reestablishment of the 250,000 persons or 50,000 family units who have lost their homes will require from GVN forces the expenditure of 500 million piasters for their temporary care and resettlement plus an estimated 30,000 metric tons of rice. From U.S. sources, there is a requirement to supply aluminum and cement for 40,000 refugee families being reestablished under the Ministry of Social Welfare and Refugee

self-help program. Additionally, the GVN/Public Works City Rebuilding Plan will require the provision of 400,000 double sheets of aluminum, plus 20,000 tons [words illegible].

4. WHAT DOES the FUTURE HOLD

a. Probable enemy strategy....
We see the enemy pursuing a reinforced offensive to enlarge his control throughout the country and keep pressures on the government and the allies. We expect him to maintain strong threats in the DMZ area, at Khe Sanh, in the highlands, and at Saigon, and to attack in force when conditions seem favorable. He is likely to try to gain control of the country's northern provinces. He will continue efforts to encircle cities and province capitals to isolate and disrupt normal activities, and infiltrate them to create chaos. He will seek maximum attrition of RVNAF elements. Against U.S. forces, he will emphasize attacks by fire on airfields and installations, using assaults and ambushes selectively. His central objective continues to be the destruction of the Government of SVN and its armed forces. As a minimum he hopes to seize sufficient territory and gain control of enough people to support establishment of the groups and committees he proposes for participation in an NLF dominated government.

b. MACV Strategy:
1) MACV believes that the central thrust of our strategy now must be to defeat the enemy offensive and that if this is done well, the situation overall will be greatly improved over the pre-TET condition.
(2) MACV accepts the fact that its first priority must be the security of the Government of Vietnam in Saigon and provincial capitals. MACV describes its objectives as:
--First, to counter the enemy offensive and to destroy or eject the NVA invasion force in the north.
--Second, to restore security in the cities and towns.
--Third, to restore security in the heavily populated areas of the countryside.

--Fourth, to regain the initiative through offensive operations....

5.   FORCE REQUIREMENTS
....

A. Forces currently assigned to MACV, plus the residual Program Five forces yet to be delivered, are inadequate in numbers to carry out the strategy and to accomplish the tasks described above in the proper priority. To contend with, and defeat, the new enemy threat, MACV has stated requirements for forces over the 525,000 ceiling imposed by Program Five. The add-on requested totals of 206,756 spaces for a proposed ceiling of 731,756, with all forces being deployed into the country by the end of CY 68. Principal forces included in the add-on are three division equivalents, 15 tactical fighter squadrons and augmentation for current Navy programs.

The President's Address to the Nation
Announcing Steps to Limit the War in Vietnam
and Reporting His Decision Not
to Seek Re-election

March 31, 1968

Now let me give you my estimate of the chances for peace:
--the peace that will one day stop the bloodshed in South Vietnam,
--that will permit all the Vietnamese people to rebuild and develop their land,
--that will permit us to turn more fully to our own tasks here at home.
I cananot promise that the initiative that I have announced will be completely successful in achieving peace any more than the 30 others that we have undertaken and agreed to in recent years.
But it is our fervent hope that North Vietnam, after years of fighting that have left the issue unresolved, will now cease its efforts

Source: Public Papers of the Presidents, Lyndon B. Johnson, 1968, pp. 473-476.

to achieve a military victory and will join with us in moving toward the peace table.

And there may come a time when South Vietnamese--on both sides--are able to work out a way to settle their own differences by free political choice rather than by war.

As Hanoi considers its course, it should be in no doubt of intentions. It must not miscalculate the pressures within our democracy in this election year.

We have no intention of widening this war.

But the United States will never accept a fake solution to this long and arduous struggle and call it peace.

No one can foretell the precise terms of an eventual settlement.

Our objective in South Vietnam has never been the annihilation of the enemy. It has been to bring about a recognition in Hanoi that its objective--taking over the South by force--could not be achieved.

We think that peace can be based on the Geneva Accords of 1954--under political conditions that permit the South Vietnamese--all the South Vietnamese--to chart their course free of any outside domination or interference, from us or from anyone else.

So tonight I reaffirm the pledge that we made at Manila--that we are prepared to withdraw our forces from South Vietnam as the other side withdraws its forces to the north, stops the infiltration, and the level of violence thus subsides.

Our goal of peace and self-determination in Vietnam is directly related to the future of all of Southeast Asia--where much has happened to inspire confidence during the past 10 years. We have done all that we knew how to do to contribute and to help build that confidence....

One day, my fellow citizens, there will be peace in Southeast Asia.

It will come because the people of Southeast Asia want it--those whose armies are at war tonight, and those who, though threatened, have thus far been spared.

Peace will come because Asians were willing to work for it--and to sacrifice for it--and to die by the thousands for it.

But let it never be forgotten: Peace will come also because America sent her sons to help secure it.

It has not been easy--far from it. During the past 4-1/2 years, it has been my fate and my responsibility to be Commander in Chief. I have lived--daily and nightly--with the cost of this war. I know the pain that it has inflicted. I know, perhaps better than anyone, the misgivings that it has aroused.

Throughout this entire, long period, I have been sustained by a single principle: that what we are doing now, in Vietnam, is vital not only to the security of Southeast Asia, but it is vital to the security of every American....

...the heart of our involvement in South Vietnam--under three different Presidents, three separate administrations--has always been America's own security.

And the larger purpose of our involvement has always been to help the nations of Southeast Asia become independent and stand alone, self-sustaining, as members of a great world community--at peace with themselves, and at peace with all others.

With such an Asia, our country--and the world--will be far more secure than it is tonight....

Yet, I believe that now, no less than when the decade began, this generation of Americans is willing to "pay any price, bear any burden, meet any hardship, support any friend, oppose any foe to assure the survival and the success of liberty."

Since those words were spoken by John F. Kennedy, the people of America have kept that compact with mankind's noblest cause. And we shall continue to keep it.

Yet, I believe that we must always be mindful of this one thing, whatever the trials and the tests ahead. The ultimate strength of our country and our cause will lie not in powerful weapons or infinite resources or boundless wealth, but will lie in the unity of our people.

This I believe very deeply....

There is division in the American house now. There is divisiveness among us all tonight.

And holding the trust that is mine, as President of all the people, I cannot disregard the peril to the progress of the American people and the hope and the prospect of peace for all peoples.

So I would ask all Americans, whatever their personal interests or concern, to guard against divisiveness and all its ugly consequences....

Believing this as I do, I have concluded that I should not permit the Presidency to become involved in the partisan divisions that are developing in this political year.

With America's sons in the fields far away, with America's future under challenge right here at home, with our hopes and the world's hopes for peace in the balance every day, I do not believe that I should devote an hour or a day of my time to any personal partisan causes or to any duties other than the awesome duties of this office--the Presidency of your country.

Accordingly, I shall not seek, and I will not accept, the nomination of my party for another term as your President.

But let men everywhere know, however, that a strong, a confident, and a vigilant America stands ready tonight to seek an honorable peace--and stands ready tonight to defend an honored cause--whatever the sacrifice that duty may require.

Thank you for listening.

Good night and God bless all of you.

6

Vietnam: Disengagement, Withdrawal, and Aftermath

INTRODUCTION

The war in Vietnam continued to dominate U.S. national security concerns throughout the 1960s and well into the 1970s. The newly elected President Richard Nixon was committed to finding an end to the war. One result was a change in strategy from direct American participation to "Vietnamization"--the idea that most of the combat duties would be turned over to the Vietnamese military. By the end of President Nixon's first term, the peace process was in place leading to an agreement between the U.S. and North Vietnam for withdrawal of U.S. forces. At the same time, the Nixon Doctrine seemed to signal a change in U.S. strategy: a strategy that shifted the burden of security to the indigenous government, supported by U.S. assistance.

Applied to South Vietnam, this meant the withdrawal of the bulk of American combat forces while simultaneously providing the necessary economic and military assistance to the South Vietnamese government to respond to the threats of the North Vietnamese and the Viet Cong. However, Congress ended all aid and within one year of American withdrawal, the South Vietnamese were defeated. The war ended with the fall of Saigon in 1975.

The preoccupation with Vietnam did not prevent other major diplomatic efforts. It was during the Nixon Administration that an opening to China was created. Attempts were also made to normalize relations with the Soviet Union, even though these efforts broadened the American involvement with perceived "adversaries." The U.S. also made efforts to strengthen its alliances.

Renewed efforts at arms control (SALT I) also characterized this period, primarily in response to the increasing nuclear arsenal possessed by the Soviet Union.

In brief, on the one hand, the U.S. was seen as retreating from external involvement with its withdrawal from Vietnam. On the other hand, serious efforts were undertaken to develop links with China and place relationships with the Soviet Union on a more friendly basis.

Regardless of the efforts to broaden U.S. influence in various security areas, domestic reaction and events eroded U.S. credibility in the eyes of many foreign states. Many Americans saw Vietnam as a debacle. Congress reacted by passing the War Powers Resolution, thereby, according to many, infringing upon presidential authority. Nonetheless, this was the first clear sign of the emerging congressional reassertion in foreign policy and national security issues. In the external world, the Southeast Asia Treaty Organization (SEATO) was dissolved.

Perhaps the most damaging domestic event was the Watergate affair. Revelations by the media and by Congress of the activities and conduct of President Nixon seemed to indicate a serious problem of presidential credibility, eventually leading to the resignation of Richard Nixon. The preoccupation with this affair turned the attention of the President and Congress away from external events. A number of foreign states, particularly allies, hesitated to become involved with a president who seemed to have lost a considerable amount of power and credibility. U.S. national security efforts suffered accordingly.

One of the important structural and process developments was the increased power and prominence of the National Security Council and the National Security Advisor. The National Security Advisor and his staff became directly involved in the policy process. The fact that Henry Kissinger was Nixon's National Security Advisor had much to do with the expansion of the power of the office. Kissinger's _realpolitik_ view of the world and his leadership style resulted in developing a national security structure that included a series of interdepartmental committees chaired by him. Additionally, his view of the world coincided to a great extent with the President's. This gave Kissinger an impact on the national security policy process unknown by previous national security advisors. In the main, it was President Nixon's own view of the functioning of the office that allowed Kissinger to shape the national security staff and develop the policy process in accord with his own preferences.

President Gerald Ford assumed office upon Richard Nixon's resignation in the aftermath of Watergate. One of the first military issues, aside from the fall of Vietnam, was the <u>Mayaguez</u> incident. Complying with the War Powers Act, the President made a formal report to Congress. Subsequently, the fall of Saigon marked the end of an era. It also coincided with a shift in American attitudes regarding the role of the U.S. in external affairs.

One result of the domestic opposition to U.S. involvement in Vietnam was the end of selective service and the shift to an all-volunteer military system. The process was started during the first part of the Nixon presidency. By the middle of the 1970s, U.S. military manpower was on an all-volunteer basis. The initial impact was a decrease in the quality of military manpower leading to a decrease in military efffectiveness. This was to become a serious problem during the latter part of the 1970s.

In sum, the Vietnam era, which began for the U.S. with high hopes of saving South Vietnam for democracy, ended in failure. Increasing domestic opposition to the war, combined with difficulties in achieving a "military" victory and continuing weekly U.S. casualties, created an environment compelling the U.S. to seek peace at almost any price. The situation was made even more untenable as the drama of Watergate unfolded. The U.S. appeared to be frustrated in Vietnam and its credibility eroded at home. The entire period ended with the resignation of President Nixon and the defeat of South Vietnam. It is no wonder that some scholars identified this period as America's "retreat from power."

DOCUMENTS

THE NIXON DOCTRINE
The Meeting of President Nixon and
President Thieu at Midway Island, June 8, 1969

President Thieu informed me that the progress of the training program and the equipping program for South Vietnamese forces had been so successful that he could now

Source: <u>Department of State Bulletin</u>, June 30, 1969, pp. 549-550.

recommend that the United States begin to replace U.S. combat forces with Vietnamese forces. This same assessment was made by General [Creighton W.] Adams when he reported to me last night and this morning.

As a consequence of the recommendation by the President and the assessment of our own commander in the field, I have decided to order the immediate redeployment from Viet-Nam of a division equivalent of approximately 25,000 men.

This troop replacement will begin within the next 30 days and will be completed by the end of August. During the month of August and at regular intervals thereafter, we shall review the situation, having in mind the three criteria that I have previously mentioned with regard to troop replacement: first, the progress insofar as the training and equipping of South Vietnamese forces; second, progress in the Paris peace talks; and third, the level of enemy activity.

I will announce plans for further replacements as decisions are made. As replacement of U.S. forces begins, I want to emphasize two fundamental principles: No actions will be taken which threaten the safety of our troops and the troops of our allies; and second, no action will be taken which endangers the attainment of our objective--the right of self-determination for the people of South Viet-Nam.

It is significant to note that it was just 27 years ago that the Battle of Midway, which history records as one of the major turning points in World War II, came to a conclusion. I believe that the decision made at Midway today, and which we are announcing at this time, marks a significant step forward in achieving our goal of protecting the right of self-determination for the people of South Viet-Nam and in bringing lasting peace to the Pacific.

President Thieu, I know that the members of the press would like to hear your views on our discussions as well.

President Thieu

Thank you, Mr. President.

... in the past months the strengthening of the Vietnamese armed forces through general mobilization and the rapid progress on the pacification and the rural development have made it possible for me to inform President Nixon to start the process of the replacement of the American forces.

And the equivalent of one U.S. combat division will be replaced by Vietnamese troops. That first replacement will start in July and will be completed the end of August. Further replacements of American troops will be considered at regular intervals in the light of the three criteria that President Nixon has decided: That means the progress in training and equipment of Vietnamese armed forces; secondly, the level of Communist hostility; and thirdly, the progress which can be made in Paris talks.

Ladies and gentlemen, on this occasion I would like once again, in the name of the Vietnamese people to express our deep gratitude for the sacrifice generously accepted by the American people in joining us in the defense of freedom in Viet-Nam.

President Nixon: Informal Remarks in Guam with Newsmen

July 25, 1969

* * * * *

I am convinced that the way to avoid becoming involved in another war in Asia is for the United States to continue to play a significant role.

I think the way that we could become involved would be to attempt withdrawal, because, whether we like it or not, geography makes us a Pacific power. And when we consider, for example, that Indonesia at its closest point is only 14 miles from the Philippines, when we consider that Guam, where we are presently standing, of course, is in the heart of Asia, when we consider the interests of the whole Pacific as they relate to Alaska and Hawaii, we can all realize this.

Also, as we look over the historical perspective, while World War II began in Europe, for the United States it began in the Pacific. It came from Asia. The Korean war came from Asia. The Vietnamese war came from Asia.

So, as we consider our past history, the United States involvement in war so often has

Source: Public Papers of the Presidents, Richard Nixon, 1969, pp. 546-548.

been tied to our Pacific policy, or our lack of a Pacific policy, as the case might be.

As we look at Asia today, we see that the major world power which adopts a very aggressive attitude and a belligerent attitude in its foreign policy, Communist China, of course, is in Asia, and we find that the two minor world powers--minor, although they do have significant strength as we have learned--that most greatly threaten the peace of the world, that adopt the most belligerent foreign policy, are in Asia: North Korea, and of course, North Vietnam.

When we consider those factors we, I think, realize that if we are thinking down the road, down the long road--not just 4 years, 5 years, but 10, 15 or 20--that if we are going to have peace in the world, that potentially the greatest threat to that peace will be in the Pacific....

As we look at Asia, it poses, in my view, over the long haul, looking down to the end of the century, the greatest threat to the peace of the world, and, for that reason the United States should continue to play a significant role. It also poses, it seems to me, the greatest hope for progress in the world-- progress in the world because of the ability, the resources, the ability of the people, the resources physically that are available in this part of the world. And for these reasons, I think we need policies that will see that we play a part and a part that is appropriate to the conditions that we will find.

Now, one other point I would make very briefly is that in terms of this situation as far as the role we should play, we must recognize that there are two great, new factors which you will see, incidentally, particularly when you arrive in the Philippines--something you will see there that we didn't see in 1953, to show you how quickly it has changed: a very great growth of nationalism, nationalism even in the Philippines, vis-a-vis the United States as well as other countries in the world. And, also, at the same time that national pride is becoming a major factor, regional pride is becoming a major factor.

The second factor is one that is going to, I believe, have a major impact on the future of Asia, and it is something that we must take into account. Asians will say in every country that from the outside, Asia for the Asians. And that is what we want, and that is the role we should play. We should assist, but we should not dictate.

At this time, the political and economic plans that they are gradually developing are very hopeful. We will give assistance to those plans. We, of course, will keep the treaty commitments that we have.

But as far as our role is concerned, we must avoid that kind of policy that will make countries in Asia so dependent upon us that we are dragged into conflicts such as the one that we have in Vietnam....

PRESIDENT NIXON HAILS SAIGON PROPOSALS for POLITICAL SETTLEMENT in SOUTH VIET-NAM

July 11, 1969

President Thieu has put forward a comprehensive, statesmanlike, and eminently fair proposal for a political settlement in South Viet-Nam. It deserves the support of all who seek peace in that tortured land.

President Thieu's proposal would establish a set of procedures and guarantees to ensure that the political future of South Viet-Nam would reflect, as accurately and as fairly as possible, the will of the people of South Viet-Nam--including those whose allegiance is to the other side as well as those whose allegiance is to his own government.

In my television address of May 14 I said:

What the United States wants for South Viet-Nam is not the important thing. What North Viet-Nam wants for South Viet-Nam is not the important thing. What is important is what the people of South Viet-Nam want for South Viet-Nam.

I believe President Thieu's proposal is in this spirit and that it would genuinely give the people of South Viet-Nam--all of them--the opportunity to determine their own fate for themselves. If the other side is prepared for serious negotiations and willing to abide by the free choice of the South Vietnamese people, this

Source: Department of State Bulletin, July 28, 1969, pp. 61-62.

should open the way at last for a rapid
settlement of the confict.

President Thieu has proposed elections in
which all political parties and groups can
participate specifically including the National
Liberation Front. He has offered to set up
special guarantees to ensure fairness:

--Establishment of an election commission,
on which the NLF and all other parties would be
represented.

--Empowering this commission to assure all
candidates equal opportunity to campaign and all
parties equal opportunity to participate in
watching the polls and in supervising the
counting of ballots.

--Establishment of an international body
to supervise the elections.

Beyond this President Thieu has indicated
his willingness to discuss with the other side
the timetable and details of these elections.
He has declared that his government will abide
by the results of such elections and has asked
that the other side do the same. He also has
renewed his offer of private talks with the NLF
without preconditions.

President Thieu's offer marks the
culmination of a long series of steps by the
South Vietnamese and American Governments, all
of which together demonstrate clearly the
sincere desire of our two Governments to
negotiate an honorable and rapid settlement of
the war.

Let us look at the record:

Prior to January 20 the United States had
halted the bombing of North Viet-Nam and agreed
to sit down at the conference table with the
NLF, as well as with the Governments of Hanoi
and Saigon. We have remained at that table and
refrained from a resumption of the bombing,
despite Hanoi's shelling of South Viet-Nam's
major cities, its violation of the demilitarized
zone, and its refusal to deal with the Saigon
Government.

On March 25 President Thieu offered to
meet with the NLF for private talks without preconditions on a political settlement. This was
refused.

On May 14, with the full support of
President Thieu, I put forward an eight-point
plan for peace. In this plan I renounced
reliance on a military solution. I offered a

months. I suggested placing the process of mutual withdrawal under international guarantees. I said that we sought no military bases and no military ties, but only to secure the right of the people of South Viet-Nam to determine their own future without outside interference.

On June 8 at Midway, with the agreement of President Thieu, I announced the withdrawal of 25,000 American troops. The fact that the troops being withdrawn are actual combat forces, not logistical units, should underscore the fact that our desire is to reduce violence and achieve a negotiated peace. The program of replacing U.S. forces with South Vietnamese will be reviewed again in August.

At that same Midway meeting President Thieu and I declared our readiness to accept any political outcome which is arrived at through free elections.

President Thieu has now offered a concrete program by which free elections can be held and the will of the South Vietnamese people can be determined. He has challenged the other side to test its claims to popular support at the polls. He has offered means by which the other side can participate in developing election procedures and by which the elections themselves can take place under international supervision.

If the other side genuinely wants peace, it now has a comprehensive set of offers which permit a fair and reasonable settlement. If it approaches us in this spirit, it will find us reasonable. Hanoi has nothing to gain by waiting.

I also want to repeat to the American people what I said in my speech of May 14:

> Nothing could have a greater effect in convincing the enemy that he should negotiate in good faith than to see the American people united behind a generous and reasonable peace offer.

We and the South Vietnamese Government have made such an offer.

I call upon the leaders of the other side to respond in a spirit of peace and let the political issues be resolved by the political process.

VIETNAM PEACE ACCORDS
Dr. Kissinger Discusses Status of Negotiations
Toward Viet-Nam Peace
News Conference, October 26, 1972

We believe that peace is at hand. We believe that an agreement is within sight based on the May 8 proposals of the President and some adaptations of our January 25 proposal which is just to all parties. It is inevitable that in a war of such complexity there should be occasional difficulties in reaching a final solution, but we believe that by far the longest part of the road has been traversed and what stands in the way of an agreement now are issues that are relatively less important than those that have already been settled....

As you know, we have been negotiating in these private sessions with the North Vietnamese for nearly four years. We resumed the discussions on July 19 of this year. Up to now, the negotiations had always foundered on the North Vietnamese insistence that a political settlement be arrived at before a military solution be discussed and on the companion demand of the North Vietnamese that the political settlement make arrangements which, in our view, would have predetermined the political outcome.

We had taken the view, from the earliest private meetings that rapid progress could be made only if the political and military issues were separated; that is to say, if the North Vietnamese and we would negotiate about methods to end the war and if the political solution of the war were left to the Vietnamese parties to discuss among themselves. During the summer, through many long private meetings, these positions remained essentially unchanged.

As Radio Hanoi correctly stated today, on October 8 the North Vietnamese for the first time made a proposal which enabled us to accelerate the negotiations. Indeed, for the first time they made a proposal which made it possible to negotiate concretely at all. This

Source: <u>Department of State Bulletin</u>, November 13, 1972, pp. 549-554.

proposal has been correctly summarized in the statements from Hanoi; that is to say, it proposed that the United States and Hanoi, in the first instance, concentrate on bringing an end to the military aspects of the war, that they agree on some very general principles within which the South Vietnamese parties could then determine the political evolution of South Viet-Nam--which was exactly the position which we had always taken.

They dropped their demand for a coalition which would absorb all existing authority. They dropped their demand for a veto over the personalities and the structure of the existing government.

They agreed for the first time to a formula which permitted a simultaneous discussion of Laos and Cambodia. In short, we had for the first time a framework where, rather than exchange general propositions and measuring our progress by whether dependent clauses of particular sentences had been minutely altered, we could examine concretely and precisely where we stood and what each side was prepared to give....

I would like to stress that my instructions from the President were exactly those that were stated by him at a press conference; that is to say, that we should make a settlement that was right, independent of any arbitrary deadlines that were established by our own domestic processes....

The principal provisions were and are that a cease-fire would be observed in South Viet-Nam at a time to be mutually agreed upon--it would be a cease-fire-in-place; that U.S. forces would be withdrawn within 60 days of the signing of the agreement; that there would be a total prohibition on the reinforcement of troops; that is to say, that infiltration into South Viet-Nam from whatever area, and from whatever country, would be prohibited. Existing miitary equipment within South Viet-Nam could be replaced on a one-to-one basis by weapons of the same characteristics, and of similar characteristics and properties, under international supervision.

The agreement provides that all captured military personnel and foreign civilians be repatriated within the same time period as the withdrawal; that is to say, there will be a return of all American prisoners, military or civilian, within 60 days after the agreement comes into force....

With respect to the political provisions, there is an affirmation of general principles guaranteeing the right of self-determination of the South Vietnamese people and that the South Vietnamese people should decide their political future through free and democratic elections under international supervision.

As was pointed out by Radio Hanoi, the existing authorities with respect to both internal and external policies would remain in office; the two parties in Viet-Nam would negotiate about the timing of elections, the nature of the elections, and the offices for which these elections were to be held.

There would be created an institution called the National Council of National Reconciliation and Concord whose general task would be to help promote the maintenance of the cease-fire and to supervise the elections on which the parties might agree. That Council would be formed by appointment, and it would operate on the basis of unanimity....

There are provisions that the unification of Viet-Nam also be achieved by negotiation among the parties without military pressure and without foreign interference, without coercion and without annexation.

There is, finally, a section on Cambodia and Laos in which the parties to the agreement agree to respect and recognize the independence and sovereignty of Cambodia and Laos, in which they agree to refrain from using the territory of Cambodia and the territory of Laos to encroach on the sovereignty and security of other countries. There is an agreement that foreign countries shall withdraw their forces from Laos and Cambodia.

And there is a general section about the future relationship between the United States and the Democratic Republic of Viet-Nam in which both sides express their conviction that this agreement will usher in a new period of reconciliation between the two countries and in which the United States expresses its view that it will in the postwar period contribute to the reconstruction of Indochina and that both countries will develop their relationships on a basis of mutual respect and noninterference in each other's affairs and that they will move from hostility to normalcy.

With respect to Hanoi, we understand its disappointment that a schedule toward the realization of which it had made serious efforts could not be met for reasons beyond the control of any party, but they know, or they should know and they certainly must know now, that peace is within reach in a matter of weeks, or less, dependent on when the meeting takes place, and that once peace is achieved we will move from hostility to normalcy and from normalcy to cooperation with the same seriousness with which we have conducted our previous less fortunate relationships with them.

As far as Saigon is concerned it is, of course, entitled to participate in the settlement of a war fought on its territory. Its people have suffered much, and they will remain there after we leave. Their views deserve great respect. In order to accelerate negotiations, we had presented them with conclusions which obviously could not be fully settled in a matter of four days that I spent in Saigon. But we are confident that our consultations with Saigon will produce agreement within the same time frame that I have indicated is required to complete the agreement with Hanoi and that the negotiations can continue on the schedule that I have outlined.

With respect to the American people, we have talked to you ladies and gentlemen here very often about the negotiations with respect to the peace, and we have been very conscious of the division and the anguish that the war has caused in this country. One reason why the President has been so concerned with ending the war by negotiation, and ending it in a manner that is consistent with our principles, is because of the hope that the act of making peace could restore the unity that had sometimes been lost at certain periods during the war and so that the agreement could be an act of healing rather than a source of new division. This remains our policy.

We will not be stampeded into an agreement until its provisions are right. We will not be deflected from an agreement when its provisions are right. And with this attitude, and with some cooperation from the other side, we believe that we can restore both peace and unity to America very soon.

President Nixon: "A Look to the Future"
Address Made to the Nation on Television and Radio

November 2, 1972

As you know, we have now made a major breakthrough toward achieving our goal of peace with honor in Viet-Nam. We have reached substantial agreement on most of the terms of a settlement. The settlement we are ready to conclude would accomplish the basic objectives that I laid down in my television speech to the Nation on May 8 of this year:

--The return of all our prisoners of war and an accounting for all of those missing in action;
--A cease-fire throughout Indochina; and
--For the 17 million people of South Viet-Nam, the right to determine their own future without having a Communist government or a coalition government imposed upon them against their will.

However, there are still some issues to be resolved. There are still some provisions of the agreement which must be clarified so that all ambiguities will be removed. I have insisted that these be settled before we sign the final agreement. That is why we refused to be stampeded into meeting the arbitrary deadline of October 31.

Now, there are some who say: "Why worry about the details? Just get the war over!"

Well my answer is this: My study of

Source: <u>Department of State Bulletin</u>, November 20, 1972, pp. 605-606.

history convinces me that the details can make
the difference between an agreement that
collapses and an agreement that lasts--and
equally crucial is a clear understanding by all
of the parties of what those details are.

We are not going to repeat the mistake of
1968, when the bombing-halt agreement was rushed
into just before an election without pinning
down the details.

We want peace, peace with honor, a peace
fair to all, and a peace that will last. That
is why I am insisting that the central points be
clearly settled, so that there will be no
misunderstandings which could lead to a
breakdown of the settlement and a resumption of
the war.

I am confident that we will soon achieve
that goal.

But we are not going to allow an election
deadline or any other kind of deadline to force
us into an agreement which would be only a
temporary truce and not a lasting peace. We are
going to sign the agreement when the agreement
is right, not one day before; and when the
agreement is right, we are going to sign,
without one day's delay....

In these past four years we have also been
moving toward lasting peace in the world at
large.

We have signed more agreements with the
Soviet Union than were negotiated in all the
previous years since World War II. We have
established the basis for a new relationship
with the People's Republic of China, where one-
fourth of all the people of the world live. Our
vigorous diplomacy has advanced the prospects
for a stable peace in the Middle East.

All around the world we are opening doors
to peace, doors that were previously closed. We
are developing areas of common interest where
there have been previously only antagonisms.
All this is a beginning. It can be the
beginning of a generation of peace, of a world
in which our children can be the first
generation in this century to escape the scourge
of war.

These next four years will set the course
on which we begin our third century as a nation.

What will that course be? Will it have us
turning inward, retreating from the
responsibilities not only of a great power but
of a great people, of a nation that embodies the
ideals man has dreamed of and fought for through
the centuries?

We cannot retreat from those
responsibilities. If we did, America would cease
to be a great nation, and peace and freedom
would be in deadly jeopardy throughout the
world.

Ours is a great and a free nation today
because past generations of Americans met their
responsibilities. And we shall meet ours.

We have made progress toward peace in the
world--toward a new relationship with the Soviet
Union and the People's Republic of China, not
through naive sentimental assumptions that good
will is all that matters or that we can reduce
our military strength because we have no
intention of making war and we therefore assume
other nations would have no such intention. We
have achieved progress through peace for
precisely the opposite reasons: because we
demonstrated that we would not let ourselves be
surpassed in military strength and because we
bargained with other nations on the basis of
their national interest and ours.

As we look at the real world, it is clear
that we will not in our lifetimes have a world
free of danger. Anyone who reads history knows
that danger has always been part of the common
lot of mankind. Anyone who knows the world
today knows that nations have not all been
suddenly overtaken by some new and unprecedented
wave of pure good will and benign intentions.
But we can lessen the danger. We can contain
it. We can forge a network of relationships and
of interdependencies that restrain aggression
and that take the profit out of war.

We cannot make all nations the same, and
it would be wrong to try. We cannot make all of
the world's people love each other. But we can
establish conditions in which they will be more
likely to live in peace with one another.
Tonight I ask for your support as we continue to
work toward that great goal.

Agreement on Ending the War and Restoring Peace
in Viet-Nam
Entered into Force January 27, 1973

The Parties participating in the Paris Conference on Viet-Nam,

With a view to ending the war and restoring peace in Viet-Nam on the basis of respect for the Vietnamese people's fundamental national rights and the South Vietnamese people's right to self-determination, and to contributing to the consolidation of peace in Asia, and the world,

Have agreed on the following provisions and undertake to respect and to implement them:

Chapter I

THE VIETNAMESE PEOPLE'S
FUNDAMENTAL NATIONAL RIGHTS

Article 1

The United States and all other countries respect the independence, sovereignty, unity, and territorial integrity of Viet-Nam as recognized by the 1954 Geneva Agreements on Viet-Nam.

Chapter II

CESSATION of HOSTILITIES--WITHDRAWAL OF TROOPS

Article 2

A cease-fire shall be observed throughout South Viet-Nam as of 2400 hours G.M.T., on January 27,1973.

At the same hour, the United States will stop all its military activities against the territory of the Democratic Republic of Viet-Nam by ground, air and naval forces, wherever they may be based, and end the mining of the territorial waters, ports, harbors, and

Source: United States Treaties and Other International Agreements, vol. 24, part 1, 1973-1974, pp. 14-23.

waterways of the Democratic Republic of Viet-
Nam. The United States will remove, permanently
deactivate or destroy all the mines in the
territorial waters, ports, harbors, and
waterways of North Viet-Nam as soon as this
Agreement goes into effect.

The complete cessation of hostilities
mentioned in this Article shall be durable and
without limit of time.

Article 3
....

(c) The regular forces of all services and
arms and the irregular forces of the parties in
South Viet-Nam shall stop all offensive
activities against each other and shall strictly
abide by the following stipulations:

All acts of force on the ground, in the
air, and on the sea shall be prohibited;

All hostile acts, terrorism and reprisals
by both sides will be banned.

Article 4

The United States will not continue its
military involvement or intervene in the
internal affairs of South Viet-Nam.

Article 5

Within sixty days of the signing of this
Agreement, there will be a total withdrawal from
South Viet-Nam of troops, military advisers, and
military personnel, including technical military
personnel and military personnel associated with
the pacification program, armaments, munitions,
and war material of the United States and those
of the other foreign countries....

Article 6

The dismantlement of all military bases in
South Viet-Nam of the United States and of the
other foreign countries...shall be completed
within sixty days of the signing of this
Agreement.

Article 7

From the enforcement of the cease-fire to the formation of the government provided for in Articles 9 (b) and 14 of this Agreement, the two South Vietnamese parties shall not accept the introduction of troops, military advisers, and military personnel including technical military personnel, armaments, munitions, and war material into South Viet-Nam.

The two South Vietnamese parties shall be permitted to make periodical replacement of armaments, munitions and war material which have been destroyed, damaged, worn out or used up after the cease-fire, on the basis of piece-for-piece, of the same characteristics and properties, under the supervision of the Joint Military Commission of the two South Vietnamese parties and of the International Commission of Control and Supervision.

Chapter III

THE RETURN of CAPTURED MILITARY PERSONNEL and FOREIGN CIVILIANS, and CAPTURED AND DETAINED VIETNAMESE CIVILIAN PERSONNEL

Article 8

(a) The return of captured military personnel and foreign civilians of the parties shall be carried out simultaneously with and completed not later than the same day as the troop withdrawal mentioned in Article 5....

Chapter IV

THE EXERCISE of the SOUTH VIETNAMESE PEOPLE'S RIGHT to SELF-DETERMINATION

Article 9

The Government of the United States of America and the Government of the Democratic Republic of Viet-Nam undertake to respect the following principles for the exercise of the South Vietnamese people's right to self-determination:

(a) The South Vietnamese people's right to self-determination is sacred, inalienable, and shall be respected by all countries.

(b) The South Vietnamese people shall decide themselves the political future of South Viet-Nam through genuinely free and democratic general elections under international supervision.

(c) Foreign countries shall not impose any political tendency or personality on the South Vietnamese people.

Article 10

The two South Vietnamese parties undertake to respect the cease-fire and maintain peace in South Viet-Nam, settle all matters of contention through negotiations, and avoid all armed conflict....

Article 12

(b) The National Council of National Reconciliation and Concord shall have the task of promoting the two South Vietnamese parties' implementation of this Agreement, achievement of national reconciliation and concord and ensurance of democratic liberties. The National Council of National Reconciliation and Concord will organize the free and democratic general elections provided for in Article 9 (b) and decide the procedures and modalities of these general elections.

Chapter V

THE REUNIFICATION of VIET-NAM and the RELATIONSHIP BETWEEN NORTH and SOUTH VIET-NAM

Article 15

The reunification of Viet-Nam shall be carried out step by step through peaceful means on the basis of discussions and agreements between North and South Viet-Nam, without coercion or annexation by either party, and without foreign interference.

Chapter VI

THE JOINT MILITARY COMMISSIONS,
THE INTERNATIONAL COMMISSION
of CONTROL and SUPERVISION,

THE INTERNATIONAL CONFERENCE

Article 16

(a) The Parties participating in the Paris Conference on Viet-Nam shall immediately designate representatives to form a Four-Party Joint Military Commission....
(b) The Four-Party Joint Military Commission shall operate in accordance with the principle of consultations and unanimity. Disagreements shall be referred to the International Commission of Control and Supervision.

Article 18

(a) After the signing of this Agreement, an International Commission of Control and Supervision shall be established immediately.
....
(d) The International Commission of Control and Supervision shall be composed of representatives of four countries: Canada, Hungary, Indonesia and Poland. The chairmanship of this Commission will rotate among the members for specific periods to be determined by the Commission.
(e) The International Commission of Control and Supervision shall carry out its tasks in accordance with the principle of respect for the sovereignty of South Viet-Nam.
(f) The International Commission of Control and Supervision shall operate in accordance with the principle of consultations and unanimity. ....

Chapter VIII

THE RELATIONSHIP BETWEEN the UNITED STATES
and the DEMOCRATIC REPUBLIC of VIET-NAM

Article 21

The United States anticipates that this Agreement will usher in an era of reconciliation with the Democratic Republic of Viet-Nam as with all the peoples of Indochina. In pursuance of its traditional policy, the United States will contribute to healing the wounds of war and to postwar reconstruction of the Democratic Republic of Viet-Nam throughout Indochina.

FOR the GOVERNMENT of the UNITED STATES of AMERICA

FOR the GOVERNMENT of the REPUBLIC of VIET-NAM

William P. Rogers
Secretary of State

Tran Van Lam
  Minister for Foreign Affairs

FOR the GOVERNMENT of the DEMOCRATIC REPUBLIC OF VIET-NAM

FOR the PROVISIONAL
  REVOLUTIONARY
  GOVERNMENT
of the
THE REPUBLIC OF
SOUTH VIET-NAM

Nguyen Duy Trinh
Minister for Foreign Affairs

Nguyen Thi Binh
  Minister for Foreign Affairs

THE FALL of SAIGON

President Ford's Statement Following Evacuation of United States Personnel from the Republic of Vietnam

April 29, 1975

During the past week, I had ordered the reduction of American personnel in the United States mission in Saigon to levels that could be quickly evacuated during an emergency, while enabling that mission to continue to fulfill its duties.

During the day on Monday, Washington time,

Source: <u>Public Papers of the Presidents</u>, Gerald R. Ford, 1975, p. 605.

the airport at Saigon came under persistent
rocket as well as artillery fire and was
effectively closed. The military situation in
the area deteriorated rapidly.

I therefore ordered the evacuation of all
American personnel remaining in South Vietnam.

The evacuation has been completed. I
commend the personnel of the Armed Forces who
accomplished it as well as Ambassador Graham
Martin and the staff of his mission, who served
so well under difficult conditions.

This action closes a chapter in the
American experience. I ask all Americans to
close ranks, to avoid recrimination about the
past, to look ahead to the many goals we share,
and to work together on the great tasks that
remain to be accomplished.

Secretary of Defense Schlesinger Commends Efforts of Armed Forces

April 29, 1975

As the last withdrawal of Americans from
Viet-Nam takes place, it is my special
responsibility to address to you, the men and
women of our Armed Forces, a few words of
appreciation on behalf of the American people.

For many of you, the tragedy of Southeast
Asia is more than a distant and abstract event.
You have fought there; you have lost comrades
there; you have suffered there. In this hour of
pain and reflection, you may feel that your
efforts and sacrifices have gone for naught.

That is not the case. When the passions
have muted and the history is written, Americans
will recall that their Armed Forces served them
well. Under circumstances more difficult than
ever before faced by our military services, you
accomplished the mission assigned to you by
higher authority. In combat you were victorious,
and you left the field with honor.

Though you have done all that was asked of
you, it will be stated that the war itself was
futile. In some sense, such may be said of any

Source: <u>Department of State Bulletin</u>, May 19,
1975, p. 633.

national effort that ultimately fails. Yet our
involvement was not purposeless. It was intended
to assist a small nation to preserve its
independence in the face of external attack and
to provide at least a reasonable chance to
survive. That Viet-Nam succumbed to powerful
external forces vitiates neither the explicit
purpose behind our involvement nor the impulse
of generosity toward those under attack that has
long infused American policy.

Your record of duty performed under
difficult conditions remains unmatched. I
salute you for it. Beyond any question you are
entitled to the nation's respect, admiration,
and gratitude.

Secretary Kissinger's News Conference,
April 29, 1975

* * * * *

Our priorities were as follows: We sought
to save the American lives still in Viet-Nam. We
tried to rescue as many South Vietnamese that
had worked with the United States for 15 years
in reliance on our commitments as we possibly
could. And we sought to bring about as humane
an outcome as was achievable under the
conditions that existed.

Over the past two weeks, the American
personnel in Viet-Nam have been progressively
reduced. Our objective was to reduce at a rate
that was significant enough so that we would
finally be able to evacuate rapidly but which
would not produce a panic which might prevent
anybody from getting out.

Our objective was also to fulfill the
human obligation which we felt to the tens of
thousands of South Vietnamese who had worked
with us for over a decade.

Finally, we sought, through various
intermediaries, to bring about as humane a
political evolution as we could.

By Sunday evening [April 27], the
personnel in our mission had been reduced to 950

Source: <u>Department of State Bulletin</u>, May 19,
1975, pp. 625-626.

and there were 8,000 South Vietnamese to be
considered in a particularly high-risk category-
-between 5,000 and 8,000. We do not know the
exact number.

On Monday evening, Washington time, around
5 o'clock which was Tuesday morning in Saigon,
the airport in Tan Son Nhut was rocketed and
received artillery fire.

The shelling did stop early in the morning
on Tuesday, Saigon time, or about 9 p.m. last
night, Washington time. We then attempted to
land C-130's but found that the population at
the airport had got out of control and had
flooded the runways. It proved impossible to
land any more fixed-wing aircraft.

The President thereupon ordered that the
DAO personnel, together with those civilians
that had been made ready to be evacuated, be
moved to the DAO compound, which is near Tan Son
Nhut Airport; and at about 11:00 last night, he
ordered the evacuation of all Americans from Tan
Son Nhut and from the Embassy as well.

This operation has been going on all day,
which of course is night in Saigon, and under
difficult circumstances, and the total number of
those evacuated numbers about 6,500--we will
have the exact figures for you tomorrow--of
which about 1,000 are Americans.

Our Ambassador has left, and the
evacuation can be said to be completed....

We succeeded in evacuating something on
the order of 55,000 South Vietnamese. And we
hope we have contributed to a political
evolution that may spare the South Vietnamese
some of the more drastic consequences of a
political change, but this remains to be seen.
This last point remains to be seen.

As far as the Administration is concerned,
I can only underline the point made by the
President. We do not believe that this is a time
for recrimination. It is a time to heal wounds,
to look at our international obligations, and to
remember that peace and progress in the world
has depended importantly on American commitment
and American conviction and that the peace and
progress of our own people is closely tied to
that of the rest of the world.

THE MAYAGUEZ
Statement by White House Press Secretary
May 14, 1975

In further pursuit of our efforts to obtain the release of the S.S. _Mayaguez_ and its crew, the President has directed the following military measures, starting this evening Washington time:
--U.S. marines to board the S.S. _Mayaguez_.
--U.S. marines to land on Koh Tang Island in order to rescue any crew members as may be on the island.
--Aircraft from the carrier _Coral Sea_ to undertake associated military operations in the area in order to protect and support the operations to regain the vessel and members of the crew.

Message to the Cambodian Authorities from the
U.S. Government

May 14, 1975

We have heard radio broadcast that you are prepared to release the S.S. _Mayaguez_. We welcome this development, if true.
As you know, we have seized the ship. As soon as you issue a statement that you are prepared to release the crew members you hold unconditionally and immediately, we will promptly cease military operations.

U.S. Letter to U.N. Security Council President;
John Scali, U.S. Representative
to the United Nations
May 14, 1975

My Government has instructed me to inform you and the Members of the Security Council of the grave and dangerous situation brought about by the illegal and unprovoked seizure by Cambodian authorities of a United States merchant vessel, the S.S. _Mayaguez_, in international waters in the Gulf of Siam.

Sources: _Department of State Bulletin_, June 2, 1975, pp. 720-721.

The S.S. _Mayaguez_, an unarmed commercial vessel owned by the Sea-Land Corporation of Menlo Park, New Jersey, was fired upon and halted by Cambodian gunboats and forcibly boarded at 9:16 p.m. (Eastern Daylight Time) on May 12. The boarding took place at 09 degrees, 48 minutes north latitude, 102 degrees, 53 minutes east longitude. The vessel has a crew of about 40, all of whom are United States citizens. At the time of seizure, the S.S. _Mayaguez_ was en route from Hong Kong to Thailand and was some 52 nautical miles from the Cambodian coast. It was some 7 nautical miles from the Islands of Poulo Wai which, my Government understands, are claimed by both Cambodia and South Viet-Nam.

The vessel was on the high seas, in international shipping lanes commonly used by ships calling at the various ports of Southeast Asia. Even if, in the view of others, the ship were considered to be within Cambodian territorial waters, it would clearly have been engaged in innocent passage to the port of another country. Hence, its seizure was unlawful and involved a clear-cut illegal use of force.
. . . .

Letter to the Speaker of the House
and the President Pro Tempore of the Senate
Reporting on United States Actions in the
Recovery of the S.S. _Mayaguez_

May 15, 1975

On 12 May 1975, I was advised that the S.S. Mayaguez, a merchant vessel of United States registry en route from Hong Kong to Thailand with a U.S. citizen crew, was fired upon, stopped, boarded, and seized by Cambodian naval patrol boats of the Armed Forces of Cambodia in international waters in the vicinity of Poulo Wai Island. The seized vessel was then forced to proceed to Koh Tang Island where it was required to anchor. This hostile act was in clear violation of international law.

Source: _Public Papers of the Presidents_, Gerald R. Ford, 1975, pp. 669-670.

In view of this illegal and dangerous
act, I ordered, as you have been previously
advised, United States military forces to
conduct the necessary reconnaissance and to be
ready to respond if diplomatic efforts to secure
the return of the vessel and its personnel were
not successful. Two United States reconnaissance
aircraft in the course of locating the Mayaguez
sustained minimal damage from small firearms.
Appropriate demands for the return of the
Mayaguez and its crew were made, both publicly
and privately, without success.

In accordance with my desire that the
Congress be informed on this matter and taking
note of Section 4(a) (1) of the War Powers
Resolution, I wish to report to you that at
about 6:20 a.m., 13 May, pursuant to my
instructions to prevent the movement of the
Mayaguez into a mainland port, U.S. aircraft
fired warning shots across the bow of the ship
and gave visual signals to small craft
approaching the ship. Subsequently, in order to
stabilize the situation and in an attempt to
preclude removal of the American crew of the
Mayaguez to the mainland, where their rescue
would be more difficult, I directed the United
States Armed Forces to isolate the island and
interdict any movement between the ship or the
island and the mainland, and to prevent movement
of this ship itself, while still taking all
possible care to prevent loss of life or injury
to the U.S. captives. During the evening of 13
May, a Cambodian patrol boat attempting to leave
the island disregarded aircraft warnings and was
sunk. Thereafter, two other Cambodian patrol
craft were destroyed and four others were
damaged and immobilized. One boat, suspect of
having some U.S. captives aboard, succeeded in
reaching Kompong Som after efforts to turn it
around without injury to the passengers failed.

Our continued objective in this operation
was the rescue of the captured American crew
along with the retaking of the ship Mayaguez.
For that purpose, I ordered late this afternoon
[May 14] an assault by United States Marines on
the island of Koh Tang to search out and rescue
such Americans as might still be held there, and
I ordered retaking of the Mayaguez by other

Marines boarding from the destroyer escort <u>Holt</u>.
In addition to continued fighter and gunship
coverage of the Koh Tang area, these Marine
activities were supported by tactical aircraft
from the <u>Coral Sea</u>, striking the military
airfield at Ream and other military targets in
the area of Kompong Som in order to prevent
reinforcement or support from the mainland of
the Cambodian forces detaining the American
vessel and crew.

At approximately 9:00 p.m. EDT on 14 May,
the <u>Mayaguez</u> was retaken by United States
forces. At approximately 11:30 p.m., the entire
crew of the <u>Mayaguez</u> was taken aboard the
<u>Wilson</u>. U.S. forces have begun the process of
disengagement and withdrawal.

This operation was ordered and conducted
pursuant to the President's constitutional
Executive power and his authority as Commander-
in-Chief of the United States Armed Forces.

President Ford

Remarks to the Nation Following Recovery of the
S.S. <u>Mayaguez</u>

May 15, 1975

At my direction, United States forces
tonight boarded the American merchant ship S.S.
<u>Mayaguez</u> and landed at the Island of Koh Tang
for the purpose of rescuing the crew and the
ship, which had been illegally seized by
Cambodian forces. They also conducted supporting
strikes against nearby military installations.

I have now received information that the
vessel has been recovered intact and the entire
crew has been rescued. The forces that have
successfully accomplished this mission are still
under hostile fire, but are preparing to
disengage.

I wish to express my deep appreciation and
that of the entire Nation to the units and the
men who participated in these operations for
their valor and for their sacrifice.

Source: <u>Public Papers of the Presidents</u>, Gerald
R. Ford, 1975, p. 668.

SEATO DISSOLUTION

Annual Meeting of the SEATO Council

Held at New York

September 24, 1975

1. The Council of the South-East Asia Treaty Organization (SEATO), comprising Ministerial Representatives of Australia, New Zealand, the Philippines, Thailand, the United Kingdom and the United States, held their Twentieth Annual Meeting in New York on 24 September.

2. The Council reviewed events in the Treaty Area in the year since they had last met. They considered the role of SEATO in light of the new situation in the South-East Asian region. While noting that the Organization had over the years made a useful contribution to stability and development in the region, they decided that in view of the changing circumstances it should now be phased out.

3. The Council accordingly instructed the Secretary-General to prepare a detailed plan for the phasing out process to be conducted in an orderly and systematic manner. Recognizing that many of the projects and activities in which the Organization had been engaged were of substantial value and might be continued under other auspices, possibly with bilateral or multilateral technical and economic support, the Council requested the Secretary-General and the Negotiating Bodies to explore this subject further.

4. The Council expressed its appreciation to the Government of Thailand for having been the host to SEATO during its existence and for all the facilities accorded by the Government of Thailand to the Organization.

Source: Department of State Bulletin, October 13, 1975, p. 575.

ALL-VOLUNTEER MILITARY FORCE
Public Law 92-129, An Act
September 28, 1971

To amend the Military Selective Service Act of 1967; to increase military pay; to authorize military active duty strengths for fiscal year 1972; and for other purposes.

Be it enacted by the Senate and House of Representatives of the United States of America in Congress assembled,

TITLE I--AMENDMENTS TO THE MILITARY SELECTIVE
SERVICE ACT of 1967; RELATED PROVISIONS

SEC. 101. (a) The Military Selective Service Act of 1967, as amended, is amended as follows:

(1) Section 1 (a) is amended to read as follows:

"(a) This Act may be cited as the 'Military Selective Service Act'".

(2) Section 3 is amended to read as follows:

"SEC. 3. Except as otherwise provided in this title, it shall be the duty of every male citizen of the United States, and every other male person residing in the United States, who, on the day or days fixed for the first or any subsequent registration, is between the ages of eighteen and twenty-six to present himself for and submit to registration at such time or times and place or places, and in such manner, as shall be determined by proclamation of the President and by rules and regulations prescribed hereunder....

(9)(e) Notwithstanding any other provision of this Act, not more than 130,000 persons may be inducted into the Armed Forces under this Act in the fiscal year ending June 30, 1972, and not more than 140,000 in the fiscal year ending June 30, 1973, unless a number greater than that authorized in this subsection for such fiscal year or years is authorized by a law enacted

Source: United States Statutes at Large, 1971, vol. 85, pp. 348-349, 353.

after the date of enactment of this subsection.
        (35) Section 17 (c) is amended by striking
out "July 1, 1971" and inserting in place
thereof "July 1, 1973". The amendment made by
the preceding sentence shall take effect July 2,
1971. [Editor's note: Induction authority was
allowed to run out without renewal on 1 July
1973.]

        President Nixon's Statement about Progress
Toward Establishment of an All-Volunteer Armed
                        Force

                  August 28, 1972

Based on the report submitted to me this morning
by Secretary Laird, and provided the Congress
enacts pending legislation I have recommended,
we will be able, as planned, to eliminate
entirely by July 1973 any need for peacetime
conscription into the armed forces.
        Four years ago I pledged that if elected I
would work toward ending the military draft and
establishing in its place an all-volunteer armed
force--and that during such time, as the need
for a draft continued, I would seek to make its
working more equitable and less capricious in
its effect on the lives of young Americans.
Immediately on taking office, my Administration
began its fulfillment of that pledge--and I take
deep and special satisfaction in the progress
that has been made.
        Within 18 months, the old, outmoded
draftee selection process, with its inequitable
system of deferments, was replaced by an even-
handed lottery system based on random
selection.
        The uncertainty created by the draft was
further minimized by reducing the period of
draft vulnerability from 7 years to one. As a
result of these and other reforms, confidence in
the fairness of the Selective Service System has
been restored.
        Meanwhile, we have also been working
toward the all-volunteer force.

Source: Public Papers of the Presidents, Richard
Nixon, 1972, pp. 825-826.

Secretary Laird today delivered to me an encouraging report detailing the substantial progress we have made in reducing dependence on the draft to meet military manpower needs. The experience of the past 3 years, as indicated in this report, seems to show that sufficient numbers of volunteers can be attracted to the armed forces to meet peacetime manpower needs, and that ending all dependence on the draft will be consistent with maintaining the force level and degree of readiness necessary to meet our vital long-term national security needs.

This remarkable record of progress in reducing our dependence on the draft is a direct result of the strong support given by Secretary Laird, by the Service Secretaries, by the Service Chiefs, and by the entire Defense Department. They can all be justifiably proud of the record:

--Draft calls have been reduced from 299,000 in 1968 to 50,000 in 1972--one-sixth of the previous level.

--The proportion of enlistees who are "true volunteers"--that is, who enlist out of their own free will and not because of pressure from the draft--has increased from 59 percent to 75 percent in the last year alone.

--The quality of enlistees has remained high, even improving slightly, while the economic and racial profile of the enlistees has not been significantly changed.

--Our military readiness has not suffered.

Some problems, however, remain to be overcome, and doing so will require the full support of the Department of Defense, the Congress, and the public. These problems include:

--Avoiding potential manpower shortages which will occur unless legislation currently pending before the Congress is passed, so as to bolster vigorous Service efforts already underway to improve manpower utilization enlistments and retention;

--Providing sufficient numbers of doctors and other highly trained specialists in critical skills;

--Maintaining Guard and Reserve force manning, which will remain below congressionally mandated strength unless pending legislation is passed.

I am confident that these problems can and will be overcome

--assuming prompt action by the Congress on the necessary pending legislation and assuming continued public and Service support. In particular:

--The benefit and worth of a military career must be more effectively communicated to the American people, while all four Services continue to improve their personnel management and manpower utilization procedures. Military careerists deserve the respect and the gratitude of the public they serve.

--The Congress must assist through timely passage of pending legislation--particularly the Uniformed Services Special Pay Act of 1972, which will provide needed bonus authority to help fill projected shortages in critical skills and other possible shortages in the number of enlistees available under a zero draft.

Given this kind of support, we will no longer need conscription to fill manpower requirements after July 1973. This means that it will not be necessary to require from the Congress an extension of induction authority of the Selective Service Act past July of 1973; further authority to conscript thereafter would rest with the Congress.

In reaching this goal, we will finally--28 years after the end of World War II--have done what I said in 1968 that we should do: that we should "show our commitment to freedom by preparing to assure our young people theirs."

7

The Post-Vietnam Era: New Environment and New Initiatives

INTRODUCTION

The U.S. national security posture took on a new dimension in the latter part of the 1970s, coinciding with the inauguration of President Jimmy Carter. Apparently frustrated and disenchanted with the U.S. role in Vietnam, Americans reacted by prefering a less visible American role throughout the world. The new President seemed to reflect this new view of the United States. Shifting from a balance-of-power world politics to one of world order and human rights, the new administration attempted to place the U.S. on the moral high ground, while limiting the role of the military as a policy instrument. An underlying theme was trilateralism, a view that gave prominence to the linkage between Europe, the United States, and Japan. Although some steps were taken in this direction, the prevailing foreign view of the United States precluded serious changes in U.S. relations with the external world.

The momentum of the Helsinki Accords and the opening of China under the Nixon and Ford Administrations, carried over into the Carter Administration. Expanding on these matters, the new administration proclaimed "human rights" as the basis of its relationships with foreign states. Further, efforts at arms control intensified.

These new efforts and attempts to project U.S. influence on a moral basis, soon became tarnished, however, by what many saw as a lack of U.S. military power and lack of resolve. The all-volunteer military system was being shaped by manpower that was considerably low in mental aptitude and lacked the most modern weaponry. Pay scales for the military were not competitive with the civilian sector. Additionally, as a result of Vietnam, the military was not held in the highest esteem. All of these led to an exodus of skilled military men. Indeed, the U.S. Army's highest ranking general called it a "hollow army."

Nonetheless, important peacemaking efforts took place including the Camp David Accords between Israel and Egypt. Additionally, the U.S. and Panama agreed on the return of the Canal to Panama. Further, the commitment to human rights did have some impact on relationships with the Third World. Human rights activists lauded the U.S. for its commitment. One of the most important events was the SALT II agreement between the U.S. and the Soviet Union, pending ratification by the Senate.

Soon, however, U.S. national security interests were being challenged in various parts of the world. The U.S. response seemed feeble and ineffective. Major crises erupted in the Middle East, Southwest Asia, and various parts of the Third World. The U.S. response seemed to be primarily rhetorical. Indeed, the U.S. military appeared incapable of responding effectively to many of these crises. The overthrow of the Shah in Iran and the subsequent seizure of American hostages plagued the Carter Administration through its last two years. Many felt that the U.S. was caught completely unaware by the events in Iran.

The invasion of Afghanistan by Soviet forces in 1979 added to the national security troubles of the Carter Administration. Condemnation of the Soviets and an embargo on grain were part of the U.S. response. President Carter also withdrew the SALT II treaty from the ratification proceedings in the Senate, killing the treaty for all practical purposes.

Closer to home, the Somoza regime in Nicaragua was overthrown. The Sandinista government taking office on the pledge of national reconciliation and openness soon reverted to the more characteristic form of dictatorship of a Marxist-Leninist variety. Nicaragua has posed a national security issue for the U.S. since that time, particularly with the emergence of anti-Marxist revolutionaries fighting against the Sandinista regime.

During the same period of time, the Soviet Union and its surrogates and proxies became extremely active in Black Africa. Marxist-Leninist regimes were established in Ethiopia, Angola, and Mozambique. Cuban troops were (and are in 1988) particularly active in Angola where they number about 20,000. Anti-Marxist revolutionaries emerged in all of these states and have become the focus of U.S. security policy in the 1980s.

Some important steps were taken by the U.S. in the last years of the Carter Administration to try to counter some of the most serious threats. The Carter Doctrine aimed primarily at the Persian Gulf, proclaimed the commitment of the U.S. to open and free navigation—it was an attempt to deter the Soviet Union from becoming a dominant power in the region. The Doctrine reinforced the the view that the Soviet Union remained an external threat to the United States. To reinforce the deterrent policy, the U.S. also expanded its nuclear strategy with a countervailing strategy aimed at the political structure of the Soviet Union.

The Carter Administration carried on the precedent of a strong National Security Advisor. Zbigniew Brzezinski replaced Henry Kissinger in that position and proved just as resolute. Conflicts between the National Security Advisor and the Secretary of State were bound to occur as they had in the past. Ultimately, this resulted in the resignation of Secretary of State Vance. The realpolitik view of Brzezinski was difficult to reconcile with the popular image of the human rights approach of Jimmy Carter.

By the end of the 1970s, the U.S. still seemed to lack the military capability and will to implement national security policy. While the idea of human rights was morally laudable, its implementation was hardly convincing. Further, the problems with the volunteer military and the American self-flagellation over Vietnam seemed to have sapped American energy to engage effectively in security issues. At the same time, a number of events took place that set into motion political dynamics that changed U.S. relations in many parts of the world, especially with respect to Iran.

DOCUMENTS

U.S.-CHINA RELATIONS
President Nixon: Remarks to the Nation Announcing Acceptance of an Invitation to Visit the People's Republic of China, July 15, 1971

I have requested this television time to-

Source: Public Papers of the Presidents, Richard Nixon, 1971, pp. 819-820.

night to announce a major development in our efforts to build a lasting peace in the world.

As I have pointed out on a number of occasions over the past 3 years, there can be no stable and enduring peace without the participation of the People's Republic of China and its 750 million people. That is why I have undertaken initiatives in several areas to open the door for more normal relations between our two countries.

In pursuance of that goal, I sent Dr. Kissinger, my Assistant for National Security Affairs to Peking during his recent world tour for the purpose of having talks with Premier Chou En-lai.

The announcement I shall now read is being issued simultaneously in Peking and in the United States:

Premier Chou En-lai and Dr. Henry Kissinger, President Nixon's Assistant for National Security Affairs, held talks in Peking from July 9 to 11, 1971. Knowing of President Nixon's expressed desire to visit the People's Republic of China, Premier Chou En-lai, on behalf of the Government of the People's Republic of China has extended an invitation to President Nixon to visit China at an appropriate date before May, 1972. President Nixon has accepted the invitation with pleasure.

The meeting between the leaders of China and the United States is to seek the normalization of relations between the two countries and also to exchange views on questions of concern to the two sides.

In anticipation of the inevitable speculation which will follow this announcement, I want to put our policy in the clearest possible context.

Our action in seeking a new relationship with the People's Republic of China will not be at the expense of our old friends. It is not directed against any other nation. We seek friendly relations with all nations. Any nation can be our friend without being another nation's enemy.

I have taken this action because of my profound conviction that all nations will gain from a reduction of tensions and a better relationship between the United States and the People's Republic of China.

It is in this spirit that I will undertake what I deeply hope will become a journey for peace, peace not just for our generation but for future generations on this earth we share together.

NOTE: This is the initial Nixon announcement of the opening of China. Formal recognition of the PRC occurred on 1 January 1979 under Carter.

President Carter: Diplomatic Relations Between the United States and the People's Republic of China

December 15, 1978

I would like to read a joint communique which is being simultaneously issued in Peking at this very moment by the leaders of the People's Republic of China:

JOINT COMMUNIQUE on the ESTABLISHMENT of DIPLOMATIC RELATIONS BETWEEN the UNITED STATES of AMERICA and the PEOPLE'S REPUBLIC of CHINA

January 1, 1979

The United States of America and the People's Republic of China have agreed to recognize each other and to establish diplomatic relations as of January 1, 1979.

The United States of America recognizes the Government of the People's Republic of China as the sole legal Government of China. Within this context, the people of the United States will maintain cultural, commercial, and other unofficial relations with the people of Taiwan.

The United States of America and the People's Republic of China reaffirm the principles agreed on by the two sides in the Shanghai Communique and emphasize once again that:

Source: Public Papers of the Presidents, Administration of Jimmy Carter, 1979, pp. 2264-2266.

--Both wish to reduce the danger of international military conflict.

--Neither should seek hegemony in the Asia-Pacific region or in any other region of the world and each is opposed to efforts by any other country or group of countries to establish such hegemony.

--Neither is prepared to negotiate on behalf of any third party or to enter into agreements or understandings with the other directed at other states.

--The Government of the United States of America acknowledges the Chinese position that there is but one China and Taiwan is part of China.

--Both believe that normalization of Sino-American relations is not only in the interest of the Chinese and American peoples but also contributes to the cause of peace in Asia and the world.

The United States of America and the People's Republic of China will exchange Ambassadors and establish Embassies on March 1, 1979.

Yesterday, our country and the People's Republic of China reached this final historic agreement. On January 1, 1979, a little more than 2 weeks from now, our two governments will implement full normalization of diplomatic relations.

As a nation of gifted people who comprise abut one-fourth of the total population of the Earth, China plays, already, an important role in world affairs, a role that can only grow more important in the years ahead.

We do not undertake this important step for transient tactical or expedient reasons. In recognizing the People's Republic of China, we are recognizing simple reality. But far more is involved in this decision than just the recognition of a fact....

The change that I'm announcing tonight will be of great long-term benefit to the peoples of both our country and China--and, I believe, to all the peoples of the world. Normalization--and the expanded commercial and cultural relations that it will bring--will contribute to the well-being of our own Nation,

to our own national interest, and it will also
enhance the stability of Asia. These more
positive relations with China can beneficially
affect the world in which we live and the world
in which our children will live....

As the United States asserted in the
Shanghai Communique of 1972, issued on
President Nixon's historic visit, we will
continue to have an interest in the peaceful
resolution of the Taiwan issue. I have paid
special attention to ensuring that normalization
of relations between our country and the
People's Republic will not jeopardize the well-
being of the people of Taiwan. The people of our
country will maintain our current commercial,
cultural, trade and other relations with Taiwan
through nongovernmental means. Many other
countries in the world are already successfully
doing this.

These decisions and these actions open a
new and important chapter in our country's
history and also in world affairs....

These events are the final result of long
and serious negotiations begun by President
Nixon in 1972, and continued under the
leadership of President Ford. The results bear
witness to the steady, determined, bipartisan
effort of our own country to build a world in
which peace will be the goal and the
responsibility of all nations.

The normalization of relations between the
United States and China has no other purpose
than this: the advancement of peace. It is in
this spirit, at this season of peace, that I
take special pride in sharing this good news
with you tonight.

Taiwan Relations Act
Public Law 96-8

April 10, 1979

To help maintain peace, security, and stability
in the Western Pacific and to promote the
foreign policy of the United States by authoriz-

Source: United States Statutes at Large, 1979,
vol. 93, pp. 14-21.

ing the continuation of commercial, cultural, and other relations between the people of the United States and the people on Taiwan, and for other purposes.

Be it enacted by the Senate and House of Representatives of the United States of America in Congress assembled,

SHORT TITLE

Section 1. This Act may be cited as the "Taiwan Relations Act."

FINDINGS And DECLARATION Of POLICY

Sec. 2. (a) The President having terminated governmental relations between the United States and the governing authorities on Taiwan recognized by the United States as the Republic of China prior to January 1, 1979, the Congress finds that the enactment of this Act is necessary--

(1) to help maintain peace, security, and stability in the Western Pacific; and
(2) to promote the foreign policy of the United States by authorizing the continuation of commercial, cultural, and other relations between the people of the United States and the people on Taiwan.

(b) It is the policy of the United States-

(1) to preserve and promote extensive, close, and friendly commercial, cultural, and other relations between the people of the United States and the people on Taiwan, as well as the people on the China mainland and all other peoples of the Western Pacific area;
(2) to declare that peace and stability in the area are in the political, security, and economic interests of the United States, and are matters of international concern;
(3) to make clear that the United States decision to establish diplomatic relations

with the People's Republic of China rests upon the expectation that the future of Taiwan will be determined by peaceful means;

(4) to consider any effort to determine the future of Taiwan by other than peaceful means, including by boycotts or embargoes, a threat to the peace and security of the Western Pacific area and of grave concern to the United States;

(5) to provide Taiwan with arms of a defensive character; and

(6) to maintain the capacity of the United States to resist any resort to force or other forms of coercion that would jeopardize the security, or the social or economic system, of the people on Taiwan.

(c) Nothing contained in this Act shall contravene the interest of the United States in human rights, especially with respect to the human rights of all the approximately eighteen million inhabitants of Taiwan. The preservation and enhancement of the human rights of all the people of Taiwan are hereby reaffirmed as objectives of the United States.

IMPLEMENTATION of UNITED STATES POLICY with REGARD to TAIWAN

Sec. 3. (a) In furtherance of the policy set forth in section 2 of this Act, the United States will make available to Taiwan such defense articles and defense services in such quantity as may be necessary to enable Taiwan to maintain a sufficient self-defense capability.

(b) The President and the Congress shall determine the nature and quantity of such defense articles and services based solely upon their judgment of the needs of Taiwan, in accordance with procedures established by law. Such determination of Taiwan's defense needs shall include review by United States military authorities in connection with recommendations to the President and the Congress.

(c) The President is directed to inform the Congress promptly of any threat to the security or the social or economic system of the people on Taiwan and any danger to the interests of the United States arising therefrom. The President and the Congress shall determine, in accordance with constitutional processes, appropriate action by the United States in response to any such danger....

THE AMERICAN INSTITUTE of TAIWAN

Sec 6.(a) Programs, transactions, and other relations conducted or carried out by the President or any agency of the United States Government with respect to Taiwan shall, in the manner and to the extent directed by the President, be conducted and carried out by or through--

(1) The American Institute in Taiwan, a nonprofit corporation incorporated under the laws of the District of Columbia, or
(2) such comparable successor nongovernmental entity as the President may designate,
(hereinafter in this Act referred to as the "Institute").

(b) Whenever the President or any agency of the United States Government is authorized or required by or pursuant to the laws of the United States to enter into, perform, enforce, or have in force an agreement or transaction relative to Taiwan, such agreement or transaction shall be entered into, performed, and enforced, in the manner and to the extent directed by the President, by or through the Institute....

TAIWAN INSTRUMENTALITY

Sec. 10. (a) Whenever the President or any agency of the United States Government is authorized or required by or pursuant to the laws of the United States to render or provide to or receive or accept from Taiwan, any performance, communication, assurance, undertaking, or other action, such action shall, in the manner and to the extent directed by the President, be rendered or provided to, or

received or accepted from, an instrumentality
established by Taiwan which the President
determines has the necessary authority under the
laws applied by the people on Taiwan to provide
assurances and take other actions on behalf of
Taiwan in accordance with this Act.

(b) The President is requested to extend
to the instrumentality established by Taiwan the
same number of offices and complement of
personnel as were previously operated in the
United States by the governing authorities on
behalf of Taiwan in accordance with this Act.

(c) Upon the granting by Taiwan of
comparable privileges and immunities with
respect to the Institute and its appropriate
personnel, the President is authorized to extend
with respect to the Taiwan instrumentality and
its appropriate personnel, such privileges and
immunities (subject to appropriate conditions
and obligations) as may be necessary for the
effective performance of their functions.

HELSINKI ACCORDS

Conference on Security and Cooperation in Europe
Final Act

August 1, 1975

The Conference on Security and Cooperation
in Europe, which opened in Helsinki on 3 July
1973 and continued at Geneva from 18 September
1973 to 21 July 1975, was concluded at Helsinki
on 1 August 1975 by the High Representatives of
Austria, Belgium, Bulgaria, Canada, Cyprus,
Czechoslovakia, Denmark, Finland, the Federal
Republic of Germany, the German Democratic
Republic, Greece, the Holy See, Hungary,
Iceland, Ireland, Italy, Liechtenstein,
Luxembourg, Malta, Monaco, the Netherlands,
Norway, Poland, Portugal, Romania, San Marino,
Spain, Sweden, Switzerland, Turkey, the Union of
Soviet Socialist Republics, the United Kingdom,
the United States of America and Yugoslavia....

Source: Department of State Bulletin, September
1, 1975, pp. 323-350.

The High Representatives of the participating States have solemnly adopted the following: ...

I. <u>Sovereign equality, respect for the rights inherent in sovereignty</u>

The participating States will respect each other's sovereign equality and individuality as well as all the rights inherent in and encompassed by its sovereignty, including in particular the right of every State to juridical equality, to territorial freedom and political independence. They will also respect each other's right freely to choose and develop its political, social, economic and cultural systems as well as its right to determine its laws and regulations.

Within the framework of international law, all the participating States have equal rights and duties. They will respect each other's right to define and conduct as it wishes its relations with other States in accordance with international law and in the spirit of the present Declaration. They consider that their frontiers can be changed, in accordance with international law, by peaceful means and by agreement. They also have the right to belong or not to belong to international organizations, to be or not to be a party to bilateral or multilateral treaties including the right to be or not to be a party to treaties of alliance; they also have the right to neutrality.

II. <u>Refraining from the threat or use of force</u>

The participating States will refrain in their mutual relations, as well as in their international relations in general, from the threat or use of force against the territorial integrity or political independence of any State, or in any other manner inconsistent with the purposes of the United Nations and with the present Declaration. No consideration may be invoked to serve to warrant resort to the threat or use of force in contravention of this principle.

Accordingly, the participating States will

refrain from any acts constituting a threat of force or direct or indirect use of force against another participating State. Likewise they will refrain from any manifestation of force for the purpose of inducing another participating State to renounce the full exercise of its sovereign rights.   Likewise they will also refrain in their mutual relations from any act of reprisal by force.

No such threat or use of force will be employed as a means of settling disputes, or questions likely to give rise to disputes, between them.

III. Inviolability of frontiers

The participating States regard as inviolable all one another's frontiers as well as the frontiers of all States in Europe and therefore they will refrain now and in the future from assaulting these frontiers.

Accordingly, they will also refrain from any demand for, or act of, seizure and usurpation of part or all of the territory of any participating State....

VI. Non-intervention in internal affairs

The participating States will refrain from any intervention, direct or indirect, individual or collective, in the internal or external affairs falling within the domestic jurisdiction of another participating State, regardless of their mutual relations.

They will accordingly refrain from any form of armed intervention or threat of such intervention against another participating State.

They will likewise in all circumstances refrain from any other act of military, or of political, economic or other coercion designed to subordinate to their own interest the exercise by another participating State of the rights inherent in its sovereignty and thus to secure advantages of any kind.

Accordingly, they will, inter alia, refrain from direct or indirect assistance to terrorist activities, or to subversive or other

activities directed towards the violent
overthrow of the regime of another participating
State....

VII. <u>Respect for human rights and fundamental freedoms, including freedom of thought, conscience, religion or belief</u>

The participating States will respect
human rights and fundamental freedoms, including
the freedom of thought, conscience, religion or
belief, for all without distinction as to race,
sex, language or religion.

They will promote and encourage the
effective exercise of civil, political,
economic, social, cultural and other rights and
freedoms all of which derive from the inherent
dignity of the human person and are essential
for his free and full development.

Within this framework the participating
States will recognize and respect the freedom of
the individual to profess and practice, alone or
in community with others, religion or belief
acting in accordance with the dictates of his
own conscience.

The participating States on whose
territory national minorities exist will respect
the right of persons belonging to such
minorities to equality before the law, will
afford them the full opportunity for the actual
enjoyment of human rights and fundamental
freedoms and will, in this manner, protect their
legitimate interests in this sphere.

The participating States recognize the
universal significance of human rights and
fundamental freedoms, respect for which is an
essential factor for the peace, justice and
well-being necessary to ensure the development
of friendly relations and co-operation among
themselves as among all States.

They will constantly respect these rights
and freedoms in their mutual relations and will
endeavour jointly and separately, including in
co-operation with the United Nations, to promote
universal and effective respect for them.

They confirm the right of the individual
to know and act upon his rights and duties in
this field.

In the field of human rights and
fundamental freedoms, the participating States
will act in conformity with the purposes and
principles of the Charter of the United Nations
and with the Universal Declaration of Human
Rights.   They will also fulfill their
obligations as set forth in the international
declarations and agreements in this field,
including inter alia the International Covenants
on Human Rights, by which they may be bound....

* * * * *

Document on confidence-building measures
and certain aspects of security and disarmament

I

Prior notification of major military movements

In accordance with the Final
Recommendations of the Helsinki Consultations
the participating States studied the question of
prior notification of major military movements
as a measure to strengthen confidence.
Accordingly, the participating States
recognize that they may, at their own discretion
and with a view to contributing to confidence-
building notify their major military movements.
In the same spirit, further consideration
will be given by the States participating in the
Conference on Security and Co-operation in
Europe to the question of prior notification of
major military movements, bearing in mind, in
particular, the experience gained by the
implementation of the measures which are set
forth in this document....

II

Questions relating to disarmament

The participating States recognize the
interest of all of them in efforts aimed at
lessening military confrontation and promoting
disarmament which are designed to complement
political detente in Europe and to strengthen
their security. They are convinced of the

necessity to take effective measures in these
fields which by their scope and by their nature
constitute steps towards the ultimate
achievement of general and complete disarmament
under strict and effective international
control, which should result in strengthening
peace and security throughout the world.

President Ford: Address in Helsinki
Before the Conference on Security
and Cooperation in Europe
August 1, 1975

* * * * *

We are bound together by the most powerful
of all ties, our fervent love for freedom and
independence, which knows no homeland but the
human heart. It is a sentiment as enduring as
the granite rock on which this city stands and
as moving as the music of Sibelius.

Our visit here, though short, has brought
us a deeper appreciation of the pride, industry,
and friendliness which Americans always
associate with the Finnish nation.

The nations assembled here have kept the
general peace in Europe for 30 years. Yet there
have been too many narrow escapes from major
conflict. There remains, to this day, the
urgent issue of how to construct a just and
lasting peace for all peoples.

I have not come across the Atlantic to say
what all of us already know--that nations now
have the capacity to destroy civilization and,
therefore, all our foreign policies must have
as their one supreme objective the prevention of
a thermonuclear war. Nor have I come to dwell
upon the hard realities of continuing
ideological differences, political rivalries,
and military competition that persist among us.

I have come to Helsinki as a spokesman for
a nation whose vision has always been forward,
whose people have always demanded that the
future be brighter than the past, and whose
united will and purpose at this hour is to work

Source: Public Papers of the Presidents, Gerald
R. Ford, 1975, pp. 1074-1081.

diligently to promote peace and progress not only for ourselves but for all mankind.

I am simply here to say to my colleagues: We owe it to our children, to the children of all continents, not to miss any opportunity, not to malinger for one minute, not to spare ourselves or allow others to shirk in the monumental task of building a better and a safer world.

The American people, like the people of Europe, know well that mere assertions of good will, passing changes in the political mood of governments, laudable declarations of principles are not enough. But if we proceed with care, with commitment to real progress, there is now an opportunity to turn our peoples' hopes into realities.

In recent years, nations represented here have sought to ease potential conflicts. But much more remains to be done before we prematurely congratulate ourselves.

Military competition must be controlled. Political competition must be restrained. Crises must not be manipulated or exploited for unilateral advantages that could lead us again to the brink of war. The process of negotiation must be sustained, not at a snail's pace but with demonstrated enthusiasm and visible progress.

Nowhere are the challenges and the opportunities greater and more evident than in Europe. That is why this Conference brings us all together. Conflict in Europe shakes the world. Twice in this century we have paid dearly for this lesson; at other times, we have come perilously close to calamity. We dare not forget the tragedy and the terror of those times.

Peace is not a piece of paper.

But lasting peace is at least possible today because we have learned from the experiences of the last 30 years that peace is a process requiring mutual restraint and practical arrangements.

This Conference is a part of that process --a challenge, not a conclusion. We face unresolved problems of military security in Europe; we face them with very real differences

in values and in aims. But if we deal with them
with careful preparation, if we focus on
concrete issues, if we maintain forward
movement, we have the right to expect real
progress.

The era of confrontation that has divided
Europe since the end of the Second World War may
now be ending. There is a new perception and a
shared perception of a change for the better,
away from confrontation and toward new
possibilities for secure and mutually beneficial
cooperation. That is what we all have been
saying here. I welcome and I share these hopes
for the future.

The postwar policy of the United States
has been consistently directed toward the
rebuilding of Europe and the rebirth of Europe's
historic identity. The nations of the west have
worked together for peace and progress
throughout Europe. From the very start, we have
taken the initiative by stating clear goals and
areas for negotiation.

We have sought a structure of European
relations, tempering rivalry with restraint,
power with moderation, building upon the
traditional bonds that link us with old friends
and reaching out to forge new ties with former
and potential adversaries....

Participation in the work of detente and
participation in the benefits of detente must be
everybody's business--in Europe and elsewhere.
But detente can succeed only if everybody
understands what detente actually is.

First detente is an evolutionary process,
not a static condition. Many formidable
challenges yet remain.

Second, the success of detente, of the
process of detente, depends on new behavior
patterns that give life to all our solemn
declarations. The goals we are stating today
are the yardstick by which our performance will
be measured.

The people of all Europe and, I assure
you, the people of North America are thoroughly
tired of having their hopes raised and then
shattered by empty words and unfulfilled
pledges. We had better say what we mean and
mean what we say, or we will have the anger of

our citizens to answer.

While we must not expect miracles, we can and we do expect steady progress that comes in steps--steps that are related to each other that link our actions with words in various areas of our relations.

Finally, there must be an acceptance of mutual obligation. Detente, as I have often said, must be a two-way street. Tensions cannot be eased by one side alone. Both sides must want detente and work to achieve it. Both sides must benefit from it. ...

The documents produced here represent compromises, like all international negotiations, but these principles we have agreed upon are more than the lowest common denominator of governmental positions.

They affirm the most fundamental human rights: liberty of thought, conscience, and faith; the exercise of civil and political rights; the rights of minorities.

They call for a freer flow of information, ideas, and people; greater scope for the press, cultural and educational exchange, family reunification, the right to travel and to marriage between nationals of different states; and for the protection of the priceless heritage of our diverse cultures.

They offer wide areas for greater cooperation: trade, industrial production, science and technology, the environment, transportation, health, space, and the oceans.

They reaffirm the basic principles of relations between states: nonintervention, sovereign equality, self-determination, territorial integrity, inviolability of frontiers, and the possibility of change by peaceful means.

The United States gladly subscribes to this document because we subscribe to every one of these principles....

When two centuries ago the United States of America issued a declaration of high principles, the cynics and doubters of that day jeered and scoffed. Yet 11 long years later, our independence was won and the stability of our Republic was really achieved through the incorporation of the same principles in our

Constitution.

But those principles, though they are still being perfected, remain the guiding lights of an American policy. And the American people are still dedicated, as they were then, to a decent respect for the opinions of mankind and to life, liberty, and the pursuit of happiness for all peoples everywhere.

To our fellow participants in this Conference: My presence here symbolizes my country's vital interest in Europe's future. Our future is bound with yours. Our economic well-being, as well as our security, is linked increasingly with yours. The distance of geography is bridged by our common heritage and our common destiny. The United States, therefore, intends to participate fully in the affairs of Europe and in turning the results of this Conference into a living reality.

To America's allies: We in the West must vigorously pursue the course upon which we have embarked together, reinforced by one another's strength and mutual confidence. Stability in Europe requires equilibrium in Europe. Therefore, I assure you that my country will continue to be a concerned and reliable partner. Our partnership is far more than a matter of formal agreements. It is a reflection of beliefs, traditions, and ties that are of deep significance to the American people. We are proud that these values are expressed in this document.

To the countries of the East: The United States considers that the principles on which this Conference has agreed are a part of the great heritage of European civilization, which we all hold in trust for all mankind. To my country, they are not cliches or empty phrases. We take this work and these words very seriously. We will spare no effort to ease tensions and to solve problems between us. But it is important that you recognize the deep devotion of the American people and their Government to human rights and fundamental freedoms and thus to the pledges that this Conference has made regarding the freer movement of people, ideas, information.

In building a political relationship

between East and West, we face many challenges.
...
     Our people want a better future. Their
expectations have been raised by the very real
steps that have already been taken--in arms
control, political negotiations, and expansion
of contacts and economic relations. Our
presence here offers them further hope. We must
not let them down.
     If the Soviet Union and the United States
can reach agreement so that our astronauts can
fit together the most intricate scientific
equipment, work together, and shake hands 137
miles out in space, we as statesmen have an
obligation to do as well on Earth.
     History will judge this Conference not by
what we say here today, but by what we do
tomorrow--not by the promises we make, but by
the promises we keep.

Public Law 94-304
June 3, 1976

An Act

To Establish a Commission on Security and
Cooperation in Europe

Be it enacted by the Senate and House of
Representatives of the United States of America
in Congress Assembled, That there is established
the Commission on Security and Cooperation in
Europe (hereafter in this Act referred to as the
"Commission").

     SEC. 2. The Commission is authorized and
directed to monitor the acts of the signatories
which reflect compliance with or violation of
the articles of the Final Act of the Conference
on Security and Cooperation in Europe, with
particular regard to the provisions relating to
cooperation in Humanitarian Fields. The
Commission is further authorized and directed to
monitor and encourage the development of
programs and activities of the United States

Source: United States Statutes at Large, 1976,
vol. 90, pp. 661-662.

Government and private organizations with a
view toward taking advantage of the provisions
of the Final Act to expand East-West economic
cooperation and a greater interchange of people
and ideas between East and West.

SEC. 3. The Commission shall be composed
of fifteen members as follows:

(1) Six Members of the House of
Representatives appointed by the Speaker of the
House of Representatives. Four members shall be
selected from the majority party and two shall
be selected, after consultation with the
minority leader of the House, from the minority
party. The Speaker shall designate one of the
House Members as chairman.

(2) Six Members of the Senate appointed by
the President of the Senate. Four members shall
be selected from the majority party and two
shall be selected, after consultation with the
minority leader of the Senate, from the minority
party.

(3) One member of the Department of State
appointed by the President of the United States.

(4) One member of the Defense Department
appointed by the President of the United States.

(5) One member of the Commerce Department
appointed by the President of the United States.
. . . .

SEC. 5. In order to assist the Commission
in carrying out its duties, the President shall
submit to the Commission a semiannual report,
the first one to be submitted six months after
the date of enactment of this Act, which shall
include (1) a detailed survey of actions by the
signatories of the Final Act reflecting
compliance with or violation of the provisions
of the Final Act, and (2) a listing and
description of present or planned programs and
activities of the appropriate agencies of the
executive branch and private organizations aimed
at taking advantage of the provisions of the
Final Act to expand East-West economic
cooperation and to promote a greater
interchange of people and ideas between East and
West. . . .

PEACEMAKING and HUMAN RIGHTS

President Carter: Commencement Address at the
University of Notre Dame

May 22, 1977

* * * * *

I want to speak to you today about the strands that connect our actions overseas with our essential character as a nation. I believe we can have a foreign policy that is democratic, based on fundamental values, and that uses power and influence, which we have, for humane purposes. We can also have a foreign policy that the American people both support and, for a change, know about and understand.

I have a quiet confidence in our own political system. Because we know that democracy works, we can reject the arguments of those rulers who deny human rights to their people.

We are confident that the democratic example will be compelling, and so we seek to bring that example closer to those from whom in the past few years we have been separated and who are not yet convinced about the advantages of our kind of life.

We are confident that the democratic methods are the most effective, and so we are not tempted to employ improper tactics here at home or abroad.

We are confident of our own strength, so we can seek substantial mutual reductions in the nuclear arms race.

And we are confident of the good sense of the American people, and so we let them share in the process of making foreign policy decisions. We can thus speak with the voices of 215 million, and not just of an isolated handful.

Democracy's great recent successes--in India, Portugal, Spain, Greece--show that confidence in this system is not misplaced.

Source: <u>Public Papers of the Presidents</u>, Administration of Jimmy Carter, 1977, pp. 954-962.

Being confident of our own future, we are now free of that inordinate fear of communism which once led us to embrace any dictator who joined us in that fear. I'm glad that that's being changed.

For too many years, we've been willing to adopt the flawed and erroneous principles and tactics of our adversaries, sometimes abandoning our own values for theirs. We've fought fire with fire, never thinking that fire is better quenched with water. This approach failed, with Vietnam the best example of its intellectual and moral poverty. But through failure we have now found our way back to our own principles and values, and we have regained our lost confidence.

By the measure of history, our Nation's 200 years are very brief, and our rise to world eminence is briefer still. It dates from 1945, when Europe and the old international order lay in ruins. Before then, America was largely on the periphery of world affairs. But since then, we have inescapably been at the center of world affairs.

Our policy during this period was guided by two principles: a belief that Soviet expansion was almost inevitable but that it must be contained, and the corresponding belief in the importance of an almost exclusive alliance among non-Communist nations on both sides of the Atlantic. That system could not last forever unchanged. Historical trends have weakened its foundation. The unifying threat of conflict with the Soviet Union has become less intensive, even though the competition has become more extensive....

The world is still divided by ideological disputes, dominated by regional conflicts, and threatened by the danger that we will not resolve the differences of race and wealth without violence or without drawing into combat the major military powers. We can no longer separate the traditional issues of war and peace from the new global questions of justice, equity, and human rights.

It is a new world, but America should not fear it. It is a new world, and we should help to shape it. It is a new world that calls for a new American foreign policy--a policy based on constant decency in its values and an optimism in our historical vision.

We can no longer have a policy solely for the industrial nations as the foundation of global stability, but we must respond to the new reality of a politically awakening world.

We can no longer expect that the other 150 nations will follow the dictates of the powerful, but we must continue--confidently--our efforts to inspire, to persuade, and to lead.

Our policy must reflect our belief that the world can hope for more than simple survival and our belief that dignity and freedom are fundamental spiritual requirements. Our policy must shape an international system that will last longer than secret deals.

We cannot make this kind of policy by manipulation. Our policy must be open; it must be candid; it must be one of constructive global involvement, resting on five cardinal principles.

I've tried to make these premises clear to the American people since last January. Let me review what we have been doing and discuss what we intend to do.

First, we have reaffirmed America's commitment to human rights as a fundamental tenet of our foreign policy. In ancestry, religion, color, place of origin, and cultural background, we Americans are as diverse a nation as the world has ever seen. No common mystique of blood or soil unites us. What draws us together, perhaps more than anything else, is a belief in human freedom. We want the world to know that our nation stands for more than financial prosperity.

This does not mean that we can conduct our foreign policy by rigid moral maxims. We live in a world that is imperfect and which will always be imperfect--a world that is complex and confused and which will always be complex and confused.

I understand fully the limits of moral suasion. We have no illusion that changes will come easily or soon. But I also believe that it is a mistake to undervalue the power of words and of the ideas that words embody. In our own

history, that power has ranged from Thomas
Paine's "Common Sense" to Martin Luther King,
Jr.'s "I have a Dream."

In the life of the human spirit, words <u>are</u>
action, much more so than many of us may realize
who live in countries where freedom of
expression is taken for granted. The leaders of
totalitarian nations understand this very well.
The proof is that words are precisely the action
for which dissidents in those countries are
being persecuted.

Nonetheless, we can already see dramatic,
worldwide advances in the protection of the
individual from the arbitrary power of the
state. For us to ignore this trend would be to
lose influence and moral authority in the world.
To lead it will be to regain the moral stature
that we once had.

The great democracies are not free because
we are strong and prosperous. I believe we are
strong and influential and prosperous because we
are free.

Throughout the world today, in free
nations and in totalitarian countries as well,
there is a preoccupation with the subject of
human freedom, human rights. And I believe it
is incumbent on us in this country to keep that
discussion, that debate, that contention alive.
No other country is as well-qualified as we to
set an example. We have our own shortcomings
and faults, and we should strive constantly and
with courage to make sure that we are
legitimately proud of what we have.

Second, we've moved deliberately to
reinforce the bonds among our democracies....

Third, we've moved to engage the Soviet
Union in a joint effort to halt the strategic
arms race. This race is not only dangerous,
it's morally deplorable. We must put an end to
it....

Fourth, we are taking deliberate steps to
improve the chances of lasting peace in the
Middle East. Through wide-ranging consultation
with leaders of the countries involved--
Israel, Syria, Jordan, and Egypt--we have found
some areas of agreement and some movement toward
consensus. The negotiations must continue....

And fifth, we are attempting, even at the

risk of some friction with our friends, to reduce the danger of nuclear proliferation and the world-wide spread of conventional weapons....

But all of this that I've described is just the beginning. It's a beginning aimed towards a clear goal: to create a wider framework of international cooperation suited to the new and rapidly changing historical circumstances.

We will cooperate more closely with the newly influential countries in Latin America, Africa, and Asia. We need their friendship and cooperation in a common effort as the structure of world power changes.

More than 100 years ago, Abraham Lincoln said that our Nation could not exist half slave and half free. We know a peaceful world cannot long exist one-third rich and two-thirds hungry.

Most nations share our faith that, in the long run, expanded and equitable trade will best help the developing countries to help themselves. But the immediate problems of hunger, disease, illiteracy, and repression are here now.

The Western democracies, the OPEC nations, and the developed Communist countries can cooperate through existing international institutions in providing more effective aid. This is an excellent alternative to war.

We have a special need for cooperation and consultation with other nations in this hemisphere--to the north and to the south. We do not need another slogan. Although these are our close friends and neighbors, our links with them are the same links of equality that we forge for the rest of the world. We will be dealing with them as part of a new, world-wide mosaic of global, regional, and bilateral relations.

It's important that we make progress toward normalizing relations with the People's Republic of China....

Finally, let me say that we are committed to a peaceful resolution of the crisis in southern Africa. The time has come for the principle of majority rule to be the basis for

political order, recognizing that in a
democratic system, the rights of the minority
must also be protected....
        Let me conclude by summarizing: Our
policy is based on an historical vision of
America's role. Our policy is derived from a
larger view of global change. Our policy is
rooted in our moral values, which never change.
Our policy is reinforced by our material wealth
and by our military power. Our policy is
designed to serve mankind. And it is a policy
that I hope will make you proud to be Americans.
....

                Panama Canal Treaty
                September 7, 1977

        The United States of America and the
Republic of Panama,
        Acting in the spirit of the Joint
Declaration of April 3, 1964, by the
Representatives of the Governments of the United
States of America and the Republic of Panama,
and of the Joint Statement of Principles of
February 7, 1974, initialed by the Secretary of
State of the United States of America and the
Foreign Minister of the Republic of Panama, and
        Acknowledging the Republic of Panama's
sovereignty over its territory,
        Have decided to terminate the prior
Treaties pertaining to the Panama Canal and to
conclude a new Treaty to serve as the basis for
a new relationship between them and accordingly,
have agreed upon the following:...
        2. In accordance with the terms of this
Treaty and related agreements, the Republic of
Panama, as territorial sovereign, grants to the
United States of America, for the duration of
this Treaty, the rights necessary to regulate
the transit of ships through the Panama Canal,
and to manage, operate, maintain, improve,
protect and defend the Canal. The Republic of
Panama guarantees to the United States of
America the peaceful use of the land and water
areas which it has been granted the rights to

Source: Department of State Bulletin, October
17, 1977, pp. 483-493.

use for such purposes pursuant to this Treaty and related agreements.

    3. The Republic of Panama shall participate increasingly in the management and protection and defense of the Canal, as provided in this Treaty.

    4. In view of the special relationship established by this Treaty, the United States of America and the Republic of Panama shall cooperate to assure the uninterrupted and efficient operation of the Panama Canal.

ARTICLE IV

PROTECTION and DEFENSE

    1. The United States of America and the Republic of Panama commit themselves to protect and defend the Panama Canal. Each Party shall act, in accordance with its constitutional processes, to meet the danger resulting from an armed attack or other actions which threaten the security of the Panama Canal or of ships transiting it.

    2. For the duration of this Treaty, the United States of America shall have primary responsibility to protect and defend the Canal. The rights of the United States of America to station, train, and move military forces within the Republic of Panama are described in the Agreement in Implementation of this Article, signed this date. The use of areas and installations and the legal status of the armed forces of the United States of America in the Republic of Panama shall be governed by the aforesaid Agreement.

    3. In order to facilitate the participation and cooperation of the armed forces of both Parties in the protection and defense of the Canal, the United States of America and the Republic of Panama shall establish a Combined Board comprised of an equal number of senior military representatives of each Party. These representatives shall be charged by their respective governments with consulting and cooperating on all matters pertaining to the protection and defense of the Canal, and with planning for actions to be taken

in concert for that purpose. Such combined protection and defense arrangements shall not inhibit the identity or lines of authority of the armed forces of the United States of America or the Republic of Panama. The Combined Board shall provide for coordination and cooperation concerning such matters as:

(a) The preparation of contingency plans for the protection and defense of the Canal based upon the cooperative efforts of the armed forces of both Parties;

(b) The planning and conduct of combined military exercises; and

(c) The conduct of United States and Panamanian military operations with respect to the protection and defense of the Canal.

4. The Combined Board shall, at five-year intervals throughout the duration of this Treaty, review the resources being made available by the two Parties for the protection and defense of the Canal. Also, the Combined Board shall make appropriate recommendations to the two Governments respecting projected requirements, the efficient utilization of available resources of the two Parties, and other matters of mutual interest with respect to the protection and defense of the Canal.

5. To the extent possible consistent with its primary responsibility for the protection and defense of the Panama Canal, the United States of America will endeavor to maintain its armed forces in the Republic of Panama in normal times at a level not in excess of that of the armed forces of the United States of America in the territory of the former Canal Zone immediately prior to the entry into force of this Treaty.

ARTICLE V

PRINCIPLE of NON-INTERVENTION

Employees of the Panama Canal Commission, their dependents and designated contractors of the Panama Canal Commission, who are nationals of the United States of America, shall respect the laws of the Republic of Panama and shall abstain from any activity incompatible with the spirit of this Treaty. Accordingly, they shall abstain from any political activity in the Republic of Panama as well as from any intervention in the internal affairs of the Republic of Panama. The United States of America shall take all measures within its authority to ensure that the provisions of this Article are fulfilled.

President Carter: Remarks at the Annual Convention of the American Legion

August 21, 1980

* * * * *

The surest guarantee of...peace today is an American military force strong enough for now and for tomorrow. All of us--myself, the American Congress, you, and other citizens--are making the hard and sometimes costly choices that ensure that American strength remains not only unsurpassed for the present but equal to all our needs in the future.... As Commander in Chief of America's Armed Forces, working with the Congress, I have the final responsibility for making those difficult choices. They are critical choices. They are far from simple....

Our goals, simple but profound: security, honor, and peace. Those are the victories we seek for ourselves, for our children, and for our children's children. These victories can be won, but not by nostalgic nor wishful thinking, and not by bravado. They cannot be won by a futile effort either to run the world or to run away from the world. Both of these are dangerous myths that cannot be the foundation for any responsible national policy.

America requires the authority and the strength--and the moral force--to protect ourselves, to provide for the defense of our friends, and to promote the values of human dignity and well-being that have made our own Nation strong at home and respected abroad. To this end, our national security policy has

Source: <u>Public Papers of the Presidents</u>, Administration of Jimmy Carter, 1980, pp. 1549-1556.

four specific objectives.

First, to prevent war, through the assurance of our Nation's strength and our Nation's will. In this we will not fail.

Second, to share with our friends and allies the protection of industrial democracies of Europe and Asia. In this we will not fail.

Third, to safeguard and to strengthen our vital links to the nations and the resources of the Middle East. In this we will not fail.

And fourth, to defend America's vital interests if they are threatened anywhere in the world. And in this we will not fail.

All of these objectives require America's great military strength. But arms alone cannot provide the security within which our values and our interests can flourish. Our foreign policy must be directed toward greater international stability, without which there is no real prospect for a lasting peace. Thus, our strength in arms--very important--must be matched by creative, responsible, and courageous diplomacy.

We have as a nation that strength and that courage now to present clearly to potential adversaries as well as to our allies. We must continue to build wisely for a future when our patience and persistence will be taxed by challenges perhaps even more diverse and even more dangerous than those that we've seen in recent years. In planning for that future we must have the foresight to accept the reality of change. Americans have never feared change. We must prepare for what we cannot completely predict--there is no way for any nation or any person to know what might happen next--and to know with certainty the objectives that we intend to reach and to hold.

For the sake of all humanity, we must prevent nuclear war. To do so requires the most modern strategic forces based on America's superior technology. Our country has always been in the forefront of new developments, new ideas, new technology, new systems for defense. The decisions that we make today, some of them highly secret, will affect the risks of nuclear war well into the next century....

No potential enemy of the United States should anticipate for one moment a successful use of military power against our vital interest. This decision will make that prohibition and that cautionary message even more clear. In order to ensure that no adversary is even tempted, however, we must have a range of responses to potential threats or crises and an integrated plan for their use.

Equally vital for our strategic purposes is the pursuit of nuclear arms control and balanced reduction of nuclear arsenals in the world. Just as we build strategic forces equal to our needs, we seek through negotiated agreements to keep unnecessary competition from carrying us into a purposeless and dangerous nuclear arms race to the detriment of our Nations' security and to the detriment of the adequate strength of our conventional and other forces. We will continue to make every responsible effort to bring our forces and those of any potential foe under strict, balanced, and verifiable controls, both in the quantity of strategic arms and in their quality.

I want to make clear that if an unlimited nuclear arms race should be forced upon us, we will compete and compete successfully. Let no one doubt that for a moment. But to initiate such a dangerous and costly race, abandoning our efforts for nuclear weapons control, would be totally irresponsible on our part....

In the most volatile and vital area to our security, the Persian Gulf and Southwest Asia, we're taking additional steps to protect our vital interests. The security of the region and the crucial energy that it supplies to us and other nations are both now exposed to the new threat of Soviet forces in Afghanistan, which have turned that country from its former status as a buffer state into a wedge pointed at the sealanes of the Persian Gulf and to the rich oil deposits. To deter any further encroachment of Soviet power in this region, we must help to strengthen the resolve and the defenses of the countries there....

It should be clear to everyone who studies national security or defense that our work to keep America the strongest nation in the world is not finished. There are no laurels on which to rest. There are no victories which are final. There are no challenges which have disappeared magically. But we've resumed a firm and steady course of diplomacy and defense preparedness to lead our allies and our friends and ourselves with confidence toward the challenges facing the world of today and the world of tomorrow....

We've revived in this administration the policy that gives added purpose to our Nation's strength: our whole-hearted, national commitment to promote the universal standards of human rights. Freedom for ourselves is not enough. Americans want to see other people enjoy freedom also. It's an unswerving commitment of our Nation, and as long as I'm in the White House, it'll be a major part of our international policy.

We do not maintain our power in order to seize power from others. Our goal is to strengthen our own freedom and the freedom of others, to advance the dignity of the individual and the right of all people to justice, to a good life, and to a future secure from tyranny. In choosing our course in the world, America's strength must be used to serve America's values. ....

I've known America's courage by seeing it tested. I've seen it in the men who went to Iran to attempt so valiantly in an isolated desert to rescue their fellow Americans who are still held hostage there. I saw it in the families of the men who died in that effort, and I've seen it in the families with whom I've met as frequently as possible of the citizens who are still held captive in Iran. What a nation we are to produce such men and women. All Americans are thankful to them....

I know America will continue to be a nation of unmatched strength, a nation that faces the world as it is today and works with realism to bring to the world of the future freedom, peace, and justice.

THE MIDDLE EAST

Camp David Meeting on the Middle East
President Carter: Address Before a Joint Session
of Congress

September 18, 1978

Vice President Mondale, Speaker O'Neill, distinguished Members of the United States Congress, Justices of the Supreme Court, other leaders of our great Nation, ladies and gentlemen:

It's been more than 2,000 years since there was peace between Egypt and a free Jewish nation. If our present expectations are realized, this year we shall see such peace again.

The first thing I would like to do is to give tribute to the two men who made this impossible dream now become a real possibility, the two great leaders with whom I have met for the last 2 weeks at Camp David: first, President Anwar Sadat of Egypt, and the other of course, is Prime Minister Menachem Begin of the nation of Israel....

The strategic location of these countries and the resources that they possess mean that events in the Middle East directly affect people everywhere. We and our friends could not be indifferent if a hostile power were to establish domination there. In few areas of the world is there a greater risk that a local conflict could spread among other nations adjacent to them and then, perhaps, erupt into a tragic confrontation between us superpowers ourselves....

The second main issue is providing for the security of all parties involved, including of course, our friends, the Israelis, so that none of them need fear attack or military threats from one another. When implemented, the Camp David agreement, I'm glad to announce to you, will provide for such mutual security.

Third is the question of agreement on

Source: <u>Public Papers of the Presidents</u>, Administration of Jimmy Carter, 1978, pp. 1533-1537.

secure and recognized boundaries, the end of
military occupation, and the granting of self-
government or else the return to other nations
of territories which have been occupied by
Israel since the 1967 conflict. The Camp David
agreement, I'm glad to announce to you,
provides for the realization of all these goals.

And finally, there is the painful human
question of the fate of the Palestinians who
live or who have lived in these disputed
regions. The Camp David agreement guarantees
that the Palestinian people may participate in
the resolution of the Palestinian problem in all
its aspects, a commitment that Israel has made
in writing and which is supported and
appreciated, I'm sure by all the world....

When this conference began, I said that
the prospects for success were remote. Enormous
barriers of ancient history and nationalism and
suspicion would have to be overcome if we were
to meet our objectives. But President Sadat and
Prime Minister Begin have overcome these
barriers, exceeded our fondest expectations, and
have signed two agreements that hold out the
possibility of resolving issues that history had
taught us could not be resolved.

The first of these documents is entitled,
"A Framework for Peace in the Middle East Agreed
at Camp David." It deals with a comprehensive
settlement, comprehensive agreement, between
Israel and all her neighbors, as well as the
difficult question of the Palestinian people and
the future of the West Bank and the Gaza area.

The agreement provides a basis for the
resolution of issues involving the West Bank and
Gaza during the next 5 years. It outlines a
process of change which is in keeping with Arab
hopes, while also carefully respecting Israel's
vital security.

The Israeli military government over these
areas will be withdrawn and will be replaced
with a self-government of the Palestinians who
live there. And Israel has committed that this
government will have full autonomy. Prime
Minister Begin said to me several times, not
partial autonomy, but full autonomy.

Israeli forces will be withdrawn and
redeployed into specified locations to protect

Israel's security. The Palestinians will
further participate in determining their own
future through talks in which their own elected
representatives, the inhabitants of the West
Bank and Gaza, will negotiate with Egypt and
Israel and Jordan to determine the final status
of the West Bank and Gaza.

Israel has agreed, has committed
themselves, that the legitimate rights of the
Palestinian people will be recognized. After
the signing of this framework last night, and
during the negotiations concerning the
establishment of the Palestinian self-
government, no new Israeli settlements will be
established in this area. The future
settlements issue will be decided among the
negotiating parties.

The final status of the West Bank and Gaza
will be decided before the end of the 5-year
transitional period during which the
Palestinian Arabs will have their own
government, as part of a negotiation which will
produce a peace treaty between Israel and
Jordan specifying borders, withdrawal, all those
very crucial issues.

These negotiations will be based on all
the provisions and the principles of Security
Council Resolution 242, with which you all are
so familiar. The agreement on the final status
of these areas will then be submitted to a vote
by the representatives of the inhabitants of the
West Bank and Gaza, and they will have the
right for the first time in their history, the
Palestinian people, to decide how they will
govern themselves permanently.

We also believe of course, all of us, that
there should be a just settlement of the
problems of displaced persons and refugees,
which takes into account appropriate United
Nations resolutions.

Finally, this document also outlines a
variety of security arrangements to reinforce
peace between Israel and her neighbors. This is,
indeed, a comprehensive and fair framework for
peace in the Middle East, and I'm glad to report
this to you.

The second agreement is entitled, "A
Framework for the Conclusion of a Peace Treaty

Between Egypt and Israel." It returns to Egypt
its full exercise of sovereignty over the Sinai
Peninsula and establishes several security
zones, recognizing carefully that sovereignty
right for the protection of all parties. It
also provides that Egypt will extend full
diplomatic recognition to Israel at the time the
Israelis complete an interim withdrawal from
most of the Sinai, which will take place
between 3 months and 9 months after the
conclusion of the peace treaty. And the peace
treaty is to be fully negotiated and signed no
later than 3 months from last night....

Final and complete withdrawal of all
Israeli forces will take place between 2 and 3
years following the conclusion of the peace
treaty....

None of us should underestimate the
historic importance of what has already been
done. This is the first time that an Arab and an
Israeli leader have signed a comprehensive
framework for peace. It contains the seeds of a
time when the Middle East, with all its vast
potential, may be a land of human richness and
fulfillment, rather than a land of bitterness
and continued conflict. No region in the world
has greater natural and human resources than
this one, and nowhere have they been more
heavily weighed down by intense hatred and
frequent war. These agreements hold out the
real possibility that this burden might finally
be lifted....

We must also join in an effort to bring an
end to the conflict and the terrible suffering
in Lebanon. This is a subject that President
Sadat discussed with me many times while I was
in Camp David with him. And the first time that
the three of us met together, this was a subject
of heated discussion. On the way to Washington
last night in the helicopter, we mutually
committed ourselves to join with other nations,
with the Lebanese people themselves, all
factions, with President Sarkis, with Syria and
Saudi Arabia, perhaps the European countries
like France, to try to move toward a solution of
the problem in Lebanon, which is so vital to us
and to the poor people in Lebanon, who have
suffered so much....

And I would like to say, as a Christian, to these two friends of mine, the words of Jesus, "Blessed are the peacemakers, for they shall be the children of God."...

Israel: Middle East Peace Agreement Implementing the Egyptian-Israeli Peace Treaty, March 26, 1979

Letter from President Carter to Prime Minister Menachem Begin

In the event of an actual or threatened violation of the Treaty of Peace between Israel and Egypt, the United States will, on request of one or both of the Parties, consult with the Parties with respect thereto and will take such other action as it may deem appropriate and helpful to achieve compliance with the Treaty.

The United States will conduct aerial monitoring as requested by the Parties pursuant to Annex I of the Treaty.

The United States believes the Treaty provision for permanent stationing of United Nations personnel in the designated limited force zone can and should be implemented by the United Nations Security Council. The United States will exert its utmost efforts to obtain the requisite action by the Security Council. If the Security Council fails to establish and maintain the arrangements called for in the Treaty, the President will be prepared to take those steps necessary to ensure the establishment and maintenance of an acceptable alternative multinational force.

Letter from President Carter to President Mohamed Anwar El-Sadat

In the event of an actual or threatened violation of the Treaty of Peace between Egypt and Israel, the United States will, on request of one or both of the Parties, consult with the

Sources: United States Treaties and Other International Agreements, 1979-1980, vol. 32, part 2 pp. 2141-2149.

Parties with respect thereto and will take such other action as it may deem appropriate and helpful to achieve compliance with the Treaty.

The United States will conduct aerial monitoring as requested by the Parties pursuant to Annex I of the Treaty.

The United States believes the Treaty provision for permanent stationing of United Nations personnel in the designated limited force zone can and should be implemented by the United Nations Security Council. The United States will exert its utmost efforts to obtain the requisite action by the Security Council. If the Security Council fails to establish and maintain the arrangements called for in the Treaty, the President will be prepared to take those steps necessary to ensure the establishment and maintenance of an acceptable alternative multinational force.

Israel: Assurances Relating to the Middle East Peace

Memorandum of Agreement, March 26, 1979

Recognizing the significance of the conclusion of the Treaty of Peace between Israel and Egypt and considering the importance of full implementation of the Treaty of Peace to Israel's security interests and the contribution of the conclusion of the Treaty of Peace to the security and development of Israel as well as its significance to peace and stability in the region and to the maintenance of international peace and security; and

Recognizing that the withdrawal from Sinai imposes additional heavy security, military and economic burdens on israel;

The Governments of the United States of America and of the State of Israel, subject to their constitutional processes and applicable law confirm as follows:

1. In the light of the role of the United States in achieving the Treaty of Peace and the parties' desire that the United States continue its supportive efforts, the United States will take appropriate measures to promote full observanace of the Treaty of Peace.

2. Should it be demonstrated to the satisfaction of the United States that there has been a violation or threat of violation of the Treaty of Peace, the United States will consult with the parties with regard to measures to halt or prevent the violation, ensure observance of the Treaty of Peace, enhance friendly and peaceful relations between the parties and promote peace in the region, and will take such remedial measures as it deems appropriate, which may include diplomatic, economic and military measures as described below.

3. The United States will provide support it deems appropriate for proper actions taken by Israel in response to such demonstrated violations of the Treaty of Peace. In particular, if a violation of the Treaty of Peace is deemed to threaten the security of Israel, including, inter alia, a blockade of Israel's use of international waterways, a violation of the provisions of the Treaty of Peace concerning limitation of forces or an armed attack against Israel, the United States will be prepared to consider, on an urgent basis, such measures as the strengthening of the United States presence in the area, the providing of emergency supplies to Israel, and the exercise of maritime rights in order to put an end to the violation.

4. The United States will support the parties' rights to navigation and overflight for access to either country through and over the Strait of Tiran and the Gulf of Aqaba pursuant to the Treaty of Peace.

5. The United States will oppose and, if necessary, vote against any action or resolution in the United Nations which in its judgment adversely affects the Treaty of Peace.

6. Subject to Congressional authorization and appropriation, the United States will endeavor to take into account and will endeavor to be responsive to military and economic assistance requirements of Israel.

7. The United States will continue to impose restrictions on weapons supplied by it to any country which prohibit their unauthorized transfer to any third party. The United States will not supply or authorize transfer of such

weapons for use in an armed attack against Israel, and will take steps to prevent such unauthorized transfer.

THE CARTER DOCTRINE

Protecting U.S. Interests in the Persian Gulf Region

Address Before the Council on Foreign Relations in New York City by Secretary of Defense Harold Brown

March 6, 1980

The 1970s closed with the Soviet invasion of Afghanistan. The 1980s opened with the ensuing debate, both in this country and around the world, about how to respond to the invasion. At times confused, at times angry, at times profound, this debate is not yet resolved.

In my remarks today, I want to talk about U.S. interests--some of them vital--in that part of the world, about the nature of the challenge presented by the Soviet threat there, about our response to that challenge, and particularly about how our military capabilities fit into an overall security policy framework for the region and contribute to that response.

While recent events in Afghanistan are of critical significance, they are by no means the entire problem. Any discussion of the appropriate U.S. response must begin by placing these specific events--the invasion and its consequences--in the broader context of historical and possible or likely future developments.

The full context of the Soviet invasion includes historical Russian ambitions in that region, a 20-year buildup of Soviet military forces, the more recent development of Soviet power projection capabilities, and the very recent upheavals in the Islamic world.

Interpretations of the reasons for the Soviet invasion vary. The simple fact is that

Source: <u>Department of State Bulletin</u>, May 1980, pp. 63-67.

their motives are very likely to be mixed, and we don't know the exact mixture. But policymakers cannot avoid dealing with both the specific incident-invasion and the longer-range question of how to deter such actions in the future. Reflecting this, the U.S. response since the December invasion has been on two levels:

- Extracting a real price from the Soviets for this specific case of outright aggression, and

- Continuing to design a strategy and to develop a set of economic, political, diplomatic, and military measures to deter or defeat similar Soviet moves in the future--moves that could more directly threaten U.S. interests.

U.S. Interests

U.S. interests related to the Persian Gulf-Southwest Asian region, certainly in the short term, focus on the safe and speedy release of the Americans held hostage in Tehran. For the longer term, our interests can be stated quite simply:

- To insure access to adequate oil supplies;

- To resist Soviet expansion;

- To promote stability in the region; and

- To advance the Middle East peace process, while insuring--and, indeed, in order to help insure--the continued security of the State of Israel.

Let us look more closely at each of these in turn.

Oil is the lifeblood of modern industrial societies. Sixty percent of the world's imported petroleum comes from this region: about 13% of the oil consumed in the United States and much higher percentages for our allies--45% for Germany and 75% for France and for Japan.

The loss of this oil to the economies of the West and the industrialized Far East would be a blow of catastrophic proportions.

Even given success in the much needed effort to reduce American dependence on imported oil, the loss of Persian Gulf supplies would do irreparable damage to our allies and friends. In fact, Soviet control of this area would make virtual economic vassals of much of both the industrialized and the less developed worlds. The U.S.S.R. would not even need actually to interrupt the flow of oil.

Russian dreams and schemes of expansion and dominion in this region go back to Tsarist days. But our long term interests, and those of the area, are best served if the countries of that region are free to develop in their own ways not subject to foreign pressure of domination. Putting Soviet power astride vast oil resources would, for the first time, give the Soviet state international economic leverage on a par with its military might....

As we seek to advance these four interests, our determination to respond to any threat to them is clear. As President Carter said in his State of the Union speech: "An attempt by any outside force to gain control of the Persian Gulf region will be regarded as an assault on the vital interests of the United States of America, and such an assault will be repelled by any means necessary, including military force."...

Military Components of Deterrence

...In our military planning for the Persian Gulf and Southwest Asia--as indeed across the board--our first objective is to deter; that is, we seek to make clear that there will be major risks and penalties associated with aggression. We must be able, if need be, to defeat aggression at various levels. Without question, such an ability and the will to use it constitute the most effective deterrent.

Before I move on to discuss the kinds of force that are necessary to carry out this objective, let me make four general observations about the military components of our response.

First, while the terms "rapid deployment forces" and "power projection" are relatively new additions to the jargon, the military missions they signify are not new at all. The United States has been in the rapid deployment

and power projection business for a long time.
...

Second, I reject altogether the proposition that we should not develop the capability to use military forces effectively because we might then be tempted to use them unwisely. I believe the American people and their political and military leaders are wise enough--and, one might add, experienced enough--to understand and accept a few simple truths.

- Military forces alone cannot solve all the world's problems.

- Their commitment is a very serious business.

- Such forces and the will to use them when necessary are essential to the defense of our vital interests.

- Those interests must be carefully defined.

We must be guided by the lessons of history and not haunted by its ghosts.

Third, there have been some press reports of alleged U.S. reliance on a "trip wire" strategy, in which we would, by preference or necessity, quickly resort to theater nuclear weapons to defend against Soviet attack in the area. Several points need to be made. Any direct conflict between American and Soviet forces carries the risk of intensification and geographical spread of the conflict. We cannot concede to the Soviets full choice of the arena or the actions.

But that by no means implies that escalation to the use of nuclear weapons will be the consequence of a U.S.-Soviet clash in Southwest Asia. In part to make such a result less likely, a major portion of our effort in the region is devoted to improving the conventional strength we can bring to bear there. ...

My fourth general observation is that this overall response is, and must be, a multilateral one, involving local forces, U.S. forces, and those of other countries outside the region. For example, we are working with several countries

in the region for increased U.S. access to local
facilities. We are talking with both potential
contributors and potential recipients concerning
programs of economic support and security
assistance--which are necessary complements to
our other efforts. And we are consulting with
countries both in the region and outside
concerning military cooperation there.

Despite the complexities inherent in
multilateral action by independent nations, on
the whole we have been quite successful in our
endeavors, and we expect this to continue. I
should note that in many instances, we seek not
formal, public guarantees and agreements but
rather the establishment of a pattern of quiet
consultation and parallel pursuit of common
security goals.

Meeting the objective of deterrence will
require a combination of local forces for self-
defense, U.S. forces present in the area, and,
as appropriate, U.S. and other forces capable
of rapid deployment to reinforce threatened
areas....What is important is the ability to
rapidly move forces into the region with the
numbers, mobility, and firepower to preclude
initial adversary forces from reaching vital
points. It is not necessary for our initial
units to be able to defeat the whole force an
adversary might eventually have in place. It is
also not necessary for us to await the firing of
the first shot or the prior arrival of hostile
forces; many of our forces can be moved upon
strategic warning and some upon receipt of even
very early and ambiguous indications.

An effective U.S. response to aggression
in this or other troublespots consists of
several ingredients. The first--an enhanced
continuing peacetime presence--will involve
primarily naval forces. Our current naval power
in the region is greatly superior to that of the
Soviet Union in the area. It provides us with
an immediate tactical air capability. I might
add that the French also have a powerful naval
force in the Indian Ocean. Further, we are
continuing to make improvements, begun several
years ago, in the facilities on Diego Garcia. We
will have a permanent presence in the region
that is much greater than it was a year ago.

Prepositioning of equipment is the vital second ingredient. We have begun a program to procure a number of maritime prepositioning ships, which will give us greater flexibility and avoid the problems of large, permanent U.S. bases overseas in sensitive areas....

Mobility--especially air and sealift capabilities--is the third ingredient....

Fourth is the access and transit rights which I alluded to earlier. We are intensively--and I judge successfully--negotiating increased access to port, airfield, and other facilities to improve our ability to sustain naval and aircraft deployments.

Let me again emphasize the difference between seeking access and seeking permanent bases. Essentially, we are asking various countries in the area to enable us to come more effectively to their assistance if and when they need and want us. This is far different from asking them to host permanent U.S. garrisons.

Frequent deployment and exercises in the area comprise another key ingredient. We have increased the scale and pace of our periodic naval task force deployments in the region....

Conclusion

The policies and the approach I have outlined are not steps toward war. They are designed to build strength and to prevent war. What we are doing constitutes a necessary and reasonable response to real needs. The massive growth of Soviet military capabilities is a fact. Their willingness to use surrogates and, indeed, units of the Red Army to assert military and political power outside the borders of the Soviet Union has been demonstrated. The United States and the nations to which we have the closest ties are now, and will be for a long time, linked by a highly vulnerable lifeline to the Middle East and the Persian Gulf.

Perhaps the Soviets will never move to threaten that lifeline. Perhaps the more "benign" interpretations of their invasion of Afghanistan--if the word "benign" can be used at all--are correct. But, as policymakers and as responsible citizens and world leaders, we

cannot safely assume that it is. Indeed, the
actions that we must take to guard against the
consequences of the immediate threat posed by
recent aggressive Soviet behavior are probably
the most effective way to moderate future Soviet
actions over the long term.

We are not saying to the Soviet Union that
competition is the only path between us. We
remain willing to cooperate in those areas where
our interests overlap, as in the case of SALT.
But where they threaten our interests, we will
meet them on that ground as well.

We must demonstrate to the Soviet Union
that:

- The invasion of Afghanistan is seen,
throughout that part of the world that is not
ruled from Moscow, as a callous violation of the
norms of international behavior;

- Their stated justification for it is
universally regarded as a transparent
misrepresentation; and

- The international community believes
that similar steps in the future carry the
gravest dangers for the Soviets as well as for
the rest of us.

For the United States to assume its proper
role in deterring such aggression in the future,
we must have adequate military capability and
the will to use it if necessary. If we intend
to remain a major world power, and to preserve
our own pluralistic and economic systems, then
we must engage over the long haul in an economic
rebuilding, a program to reduce our dependence
on imported energy, and not least, an
enhancement of our military capability,
including an ability to deploy forces rapidly to
areas far from but vital to us, in a security
framework that helps to stabilize such regions.

These tasks will not be easy. They cannot
be done as a one-time crash program. They will
not be inexpensive. But if we fail to carry
them out, the 21st century will be a dangerous
one indeed for our ideals, for our society, and
for our children.

Carter Doctrine: The State of the Union
Address to the Congress

January 16, 1981

* * * * *

The Persian Gulf has been a vital
crossroads for trade between Europe and Asia at
many key moments in history. It has become
essential in recent years for its supply of oil
to the United States, our allies, and our
friends. We have taken effective measures to
control our own consumption of imported fuel,
working in cooperation with the other key
industrial nations of the world. However, there
is little doubt that the healthy growth of our
American and world economies will depend for
many years on continued safe access to the
Persian Gulf's oil production. The denial of
these oil supplies would threaten not only our
own but world security.

The potent new threat from an advancing
Soviet Union, against the background of regional
instability of which it can take advantage,
requires that we reinforce our ability to defend
our regional friends and to protect the flow of
oil. We are continuing to build on the strong
political, economic, social and humanitarian
ties which bind this government and the American
people to friendly governments and peoples of
the Persian Gulf.

We have also embarked on a course to
reinforce the trust and confidence our regional
friends have in our ability to come to their
assistance rapidly with American military force
if needed. We have increased our naval presence
in the Indian Ocean. We have created a Rapid
Deployment Force which can move quickly to the
Gulf--or indeed any other area of the world
where outside aggression threatens. We have
concluded several agreements with countries
which are prepared to let us use their airports
and naval facilities in an emergency. We have
met requests for reasonable amounts of American

Source: Public Papers of the Presidents,
Administration of Jimmy Carter, 1981, p. 2985.

weaponry from regional countries which are anxious to defend themselves. And we are discussing with a number of our friends further ways we can help to improve their security and ours, both for the short and the longer term.

The Rapid Deployment Joint Task Force

The RDJTF Command Decision, April 24, 1981

The Secretary of Defense announced today that over a period of three to five years the Rapid Deployment Joint Task Force (RDJTF) should evolve into a separate unified command--with its own geographic responsibilities, Service components, forces, intelligence, communications, logistics facilities and other support elements.

During the short time of the RDJTF's existence, considerable progress has been made in improving our strategic posture in Southwest Asia: detailed, joint contingency planning has been undertaken; Service force and support requirements have been identified; joint exercises of rapid deployment forces of all four of our military Services have been conducted-- some in combination with the forces of other nations in the region; and significant equipment has been pre-positioned to increase the speed with which we can deploy forces.

But more is needed to increase its power projection capability, including enhanced sealift and airlift, further pre-positioning, improved facilities, and greater sustaining capability. The Administration's recent force- structuring initiatives represent significant steps toward speeding our progress.

As our capabilities grow, however, the structure of the RDJTF must grow to keep pace. The first change the Secretary of Defense will direct in the RDJTF's organization will be the assignment of XVIII Airborne Corps and, shortly, other units to strengthen the RDJTF, its Service components and combat units. This will permit

Source: Office of the Assistant Secretary of Defense (Public Affairs), News Release, April 24, 1981.

better deployability and sustainability of forces in Southwest Asia. Other changes will come later as additional resources become available for the command.

For the time being, relationships among the present unified commands will not change, and the RDJTF headquarters will continue to be located at MacDill Air Force Base in Florida. Nor will its mission change. The RDJTF will continue to have a potential for world-wide deployment, but its major focus will remain on Southwest Asia.

Formation of the United States Central Command (USCENTCOM) Announced December 8, 1982

Secretary of Defense Caspar W. Weinberger announced today that the President has decided to activate a new unified command for Southwest Asia on January 1, 1983. Following a review of the situation in Southwest Asia in 1981, it was decided that the Rapid Deployment Joint Task Force (RDJTF), currently charged with operational planning for the region, should evolve into a separate unified command. The decision was announced by Secretary Weinberger on April 24, 1981, and was outlined in the Secretary's Annual Report to Congress on February 8, 1982.

The new unified command, which will be named the United States Central Command (USCENTCOM), will better serve U.S. interests and the security concerns of friendly regional states and demonstrate U.S. resolve to come to the defense of our friends in the region. USCENTCOM will comprise the Southwest Asia/Horn of Africa/Persian Gulf area and is being established to improve U.S. response capabilities.

Army, Air Force and Naval component headquarters will be assigned to USCENTCOM. U.S. forces operating in or deployed to USCENTCOM's area of responsibility will be

Source: Office of Assistant Secretary of Defense (Public Affairs), News Release, December 8, 1982.

placed under the operational command of the Commander in Chief, USCENTCOM. These will include such forces as the Middle East Force in the Persian Gulf and Red Sea area. When required and authorized, USCENTCOM can also draw upon the reservoir of rapidly deployable forces that are located primarily in the United States.

CRISES
Iranian Hostages
White House Statement
November 9, 1979

The seizure of more than 60 Americans in our Embassy in Tehran has provoked strong feelings here at home. There is outrage. There is frustration. And there is deep anger.

There is also pride in the courage of those who are in danger and sympathy for them and for their families. But the most important concern for all Americans at this moment is the safety of our fellow citizens held in Tehran.

The President shares these feelings. He is pursuing every possible avenue in a situation that is extremely volatile and difficult. His efforts involve many countries and individuals. Many of these efforts must of necessity be conducted without publicity, and all require the calmest possible atmosphere.

The President knows that no matter how deeply we may feel, none of us would want to do anything that would worsen the danger in which our fellow Americans have been placed.

He calls on all Americans, public officials and private citizens alike, to exercise restraint, and to keep the safety of their countrymen uppermost in their minds and hearts. Members of the families of the American hostages with whom the President met this morning have asked to join with him in this appeal. The President expects every American to refrain from any action that might increase the danger to the American hostages in Tehran.

Source: <u>Public Papers of the Presidents</u>, Administration of Jimmy Carter, 1979, pp. 2102-2103.

Rescue Attempt of American Hostages in Iran:
The President's Address to the Nation

April 25, 1980

Late yesterday, I cancelled a carefully planned operation which was underway in Iran to position our rescue team for later withdrawal of American hostages who have been held captive there since November 4. Equipment failure in the rescue helicopters made it necessary to end the mission.

As our team was withdrawing, after my order to do so, two of our American aircraft collided on the ground following a refueling operation in a remote desert location in Iran. Other information about this rescue mission will be made available to the American people when it is appropriate to do so.

There was no fighting; there was no combat. But to my deep regret, eight of the crewmen of the two aircraft which collided were killed, and several other Americans were hurt in the accident. Our people were immediately airlifted from Iran. Those who were injured have gotten medical treatment, and all of them are expected to recover.

No knowledge of this operation by any Iranian officials or authorities was evident to us until several hours after all Americans were withdrawn from Iran.

Our rescue team knew and I knew that the operation was certain to be difficult and it was certain to be dangerous. We were all convinced that if and when the rescue operation had been commenced that it had an excellent chance of success. They were all volunteers; they were all highly trained. I met with their leaders before they went on this operation. They knew then what hopes of mine and of all Americans they carried with them.

To the families of those who died and were wounded, I want to express the admiration I feel for the courage of their loved ones and the

Source; Public Papers of the Presidents, Administration of Jimmy Carter, 1980, pp. 772-773.

sorrow that I feel personally for their sacrifice.

The mission on which they were embarked was a humanitarian mission. It was not directed against Iran; it was not directed against the people of Iran. It was not undertaken with any feeling of hostility toward Iran or its people. It has caused no Iranian casualties.

Planning for this rescue effort began shortly after our Embassy was seized, but for a number of reasons, I waited until now to put those rescue plans into effect. To be feasible, this complex operation had to be the product of intensive planning and intensive training and repeated rehearsal. However, a resolution of this crisis through negotiations and with voluntary action on the part of the Iranian officials was obviously then, has been, and will be preferable.

This rescue attempt had to await my judgment that the Iranian authorities could not or would not resolve this crisis on their own initiative. With the steady unraveling of authority in Iran and the mounting dangers that were posed to the safety of the hostages themselves and the growing realization that their early release was highly unlikely, I made a decision to commence the rescue operation plans.

This attempt became a necessity and a duty. The readiness of our team to undertake the rescue made it completely practicable. Accordingly, I made the decision to set our long-developed plans into operation. I ordered this rescue mission prepared in order to safeguard American lives, to protect America's national interests, and to reduce the tensions in the world that have been caused among many nations as this crisis has continued.

It was my decision to attempt the rescue operation. It was my decision to cancel it when problems developed in the placement of our rescue team for a future rescue operation. The responsibility is fully my own.

In the aftermath of the attempt, we continue to hold the Government of Iran responsible for the safety and for the early release of the American hostages, who have been held so long. The United States remains determined to bring about their safe release at the earliest date possible.

As President, I know that our entire Nation feels the deep gratitude I feel for the brave men who were prepared to rescue their fellow Americans from captivity. And as President, I also know that the Nation shares not only my disappointment that the rescue effort could not be mounted, because of mechanical difficulties, but also my determination to persevere and to bring all of our hostages home to freedom.

We have been disappointed before. We will not give up in our efforts. Throughout this extraordinarily difficult period, we have pursued and will continue to pursue every possible avenue to secure the release of the hostages. In these efforts, the support of the American people and of our friends throughout the world has been a most crucial element. That support of other nations is even more important now.

We will seek to continue, along with other nations and with the officials of Iran, a prompt resolution of the crisis without any loss of life and through peaceful and diplomatic means.

Rescue Attempt for American Hostages in Iran
Letter to the Speaker of the House and the
President Pro Tempore of the Senate
Reporting on the Operation

April 26, 1980

Because of my desire that Congress be informed on this matter and consistent with the reporting provisions of the War Powers Resolution of 1973 (Public Law 93-148), I submit this report.

On April 24, 1980, elements of the United States Armed Forces under my direction commenced the positioning stage of a rescue operation which was designed, if the subsequent stages had been executed, to effect the rescue of the

Source: Public Papers of the Presidents, Administration of Jimmy Carter, 1980, pp. 777-779 (complete document).

American hostages who have been held captive in Iran since November 4, 1979, in clear violation of international law and the norms of civilized conduct among nations. The subsequent phases of the operation were not executed. Instead, for the reasons described below, all these elements were withdrawn from Iran and no hostilities occurred.

The sole objective of the operation that actually occurred was to position the rescue team for the subsequent effort to withdraw the American hostages. The rescue team was under my overall command and control and required my approval before executing the subsequent phases of the operation designed to effect the rescue itself. No such approval was requested or given because, as described below, the mission was aborted.

Beginning approximately 10:30 AM EST the six transports and six of the eight helicopters landed at a remote desert site in Iran approximately 200 miles from Tehran where they disembarked the rescue team, commenced refueling operations and began to prepare for the subsequent phases.

During the flight to the remote desert site, two of the eight helicopters developed operating difficulties. One was forced to return to the carrier _Nimitz_; the second was forced to land in the desert, but its crew was taken aboard another of the helicopters and proceeded on to the landing site. Of the six helicopters which landed at the remote desert site, one developed a serious hydraulic problem and was unable to continue with the mission. The operational plans called for a minimum of six helicopters in good operational condition able to proceed from the desert site. Eight helicopters had been included in the force to provide sufficient redundancy without imposing excessive strains on the refueling and exit requirements of the operation. When the number of helicopters available to continue dropped to five, it was determined that the operation could not proceed as planned. Therefore, on the recommendation of the force commander and my military advisers, I decided to cancel the mission and ordered the United States Armed

Forces involved to return from Iran.

During the process of withdrawal, one of the helicopters accidentally collided with one of the C-130 aircraft, which was preparing to take off, resulting in the death of eight personnel and the injury of several others. At this point, the decision was made to load all surviving personnel aboard the remaining C-130 aircraft and to abandon the remaining helicopters at the landing site. Altogether, the United States Armed Forces remained on the ground for a total of approximately three hours. The five remaining aircraft took off about 5:45 PM EST and departed from Iran airspace without further incident at about 8:00 PM EST on April 24. No United States Armed Forces remain in Iran.

The remote desert area was selected to conceal this phase of the mission from discovery. At no time during the temporary presence of United States Armed Forces in Iran did they encounter Iranian forces of any type. We believe, in fact, that no Iranian military forces were in the desert area, and that the Iranian forces were unaware of the presence of United States Armed Forces until after their departure from Iran. As planned, no hostilities occurred during this phase of the mission--the only phase that was executed.

At one point during the period in which United States Armed Forces elements were on the ground at the desert landing site a bus containing forty-four Iranian civilians happened to pass along a nearby road. The bus was stopped and then disabled. Its occupants were detained by United States Armed Forces until their departure, and then released unharmed. One truck closely followed by a second vehicle also passed by while United States Armed Forces elements were on the ground. These elements stopped the truck by a shot into its headlights. The driver ran to the second vehicle which then escaped across the desert. Neither of these incidents affected the subsequent decision to terminate the mission.

Our rescue team knew, and I knew, that the operation was certain to be dangerous. We were all convinced that if and when the rescue phase of the operation had been commenced, it had an excellent chance of success. They were all volunteers; they were all highly trained. I met with their leaders before they went on this operation. They knew then what hopes of mine and of all Americans they carried with them. I share with the nation the highest respect and appreciation for the ability and bravery of all who participated in the mission.

To the families of those who died and who were injured, I have expressed the admiration I feel for the courage of their loved ones and the sorrow that I feel personally for their sacrifice.

The mission on which they were embarked was a humanitarian mission. It was not directed against Iran. It was not directed against the people of Iran. It caused no Iranian casualties.

This operation was ordered and conducted pursuant to the President's powers under the Constitution as Chief Executive and as Commander-in-Chief of the United States Armed Forces, expressly recognized in Section 8(d)(1) of the War Powers Resolution. In carrying out this operation, the United States was acting wholly within its right, in accordance with Article 51 of the United Nations Charter, to protect and rescue its citizens where the government of the territory in which they are located is unable or unwilling to protect them.

Agreement on the Release
of the American Hostages

President Carter's Announcement
January 19, 1981

I know you've been up all night with me and I appreciate that very much.

We have now reached an agreement with Iran which will result, I believe, in the freedom of our American hostages. The last documents have now been signed in Algiers following the signing of the documents in Iran which will result in this agreement. We still have a few documents to

Source: Department of State Bulletin, February 1981, pp. 1-2.

sign before the money is actually transferred and the hostages are released.

The essence of the agreement is that following the release of our hostages then we will unfreeze and transfer to the Iranians a major part of the assets which were frozen by me when the Iranians seized our embassy compound and took our hostages.

We have also reached complete agreement on the arbitration procedures between ourselves and Iran with the help of the Algerians which will resolve the claims that exist between residents of our nation and Iran and vice-versa.

DECLARATION of the GOVERNMENT
of the DEMOCRATIC and POPULAR REPUBLIC
of ALGERIA

The Government of the Democratic and Popular Republic of Algeria, having been requested by the Governments of the Islamic Republic of Iran and the United States of America to serve as an intermediary in seeking a mutually acceptable resolution of the crisis in their relations arising out of the detention of the 52 United States nationals in Iran, has consulted extensively with the two governments as to the commitments which each is willing to make in order to resolve the crisis within the framework of the four points stated in the resolution of November 2, 1980, of the Islamic Consultative Assembly of Iran. On the basis of formal adherences received from Iran and the United States, the Government of Algeria now declares that the following interdependent commitments have been made by the two governments:

GENERAL PRINCIPLES

The undertakings reflected in this Declaration are based on the following general principles:

A. Within the framework of and pursuant to the provisions of the two Declarations of the Government of the Democratic and Popular Republic of Algeria, the United States will restore the financial position of Iran, in so

far as possible, to that which existed prior to
November 14, 1979. In this context, the United
States commits itself to ensure the mobility and
free transfer of all Iranian assets within its
jurisdiction....
        B.   It is the purpose of both parties,
within the framework and pursuant to the
provisions of the two Declarations of the
Government of the Democratic and Popular
Republic of Algeria, to terminate all litigation
as between the government of each party and the
nationals of the other, and to bring about the
settlement and termination of all such claims
through binding arbitration.   Through the
procedures provided in the Declaration, relating
to the Claims Settlement Agreement, the United
States agrees to terminate all legal proceedings
in United States courts involving claims of
United States persons and institutions against
Iran and its state enterprises, to nullify all
attachments and judgments obtained therein, to
prohibit all further litigation based on such
claims, and to bring about the termination of
such claims through binding arbitration....The
United States pledges that it is and from now on
will be the policy of the United States not to
intervene, directly or indirectly, politically
or militarily, in Iran's internal affairs....

        Iran   and   the   United   States....will
imediately select a mutually agreeable central
bank....to act, under the instructions of the
Government of Algeria and the Central Bank of
Algeria....as depositary of the escrow and
security funds hereinafter precribed....All
funds placed in escrow with the Central Bank
pursuant to this declaration shall be held in an
account in the name of the Algerian Central
Bank....
        The depositary arrangements shall provide
thta, in the event that the Government of
Algeria certifies to the Algerian Central Bank
that the 52 U.S. nationals have safely departed
from Iran, the Algerian Central Bank will
thereupon instruct the Central Bank to transfer
immediately all monies or other assets in escrow
with the Central Bank pursuant to this
declaration....

Iranian Hostages
President Reagan-Welcoming Ceremony
The White House

January 27, 1981

You are home, and believe me, you're welcome. If my remarks were a sermon, my text would be lines from the 126th Psalm, "We are like those who dreamed. Now our mouth is filled with laughter and our tongue with shouts of joy. The Lord has done great things for us. We are glad." You've come home to a people who for 444 days suffered the pain of your imprisonment, prayed for your safety, and most importantly, shared your determination that the spirit of free men and women is not a fit subject for barter.

You've represented under great stress the highest traditions of public service. Your conduct is symbolic of the millions of professional diplomats, military personnel, and others who have rendered service to their country.

We're now aware of the conditions under which you were imprisoned. Though now is not the time to review every abhorrent detail of your cruel confinement, believe me, we know what happened. Truth may be a rare commodity today in Iran; it's alive and well in America.

By no choice of your own, you've entered the ranks of those who throughout our history have undergone the ordeal of imprisonment: the crew of the Pueblo, the prisoners in two World Wars and in Korea and Vietnam. And like those others, you are special to us. You fulfilled your duty as you saw it, and now like the others, thank God you're home, and our hearts are full of gratitude....

Let terrorists be aware that when the rules of international behavior are violated, our policy will be one of swift and effective retribution. We hear it said that we live in an era of limit to our powers. Well, let it also be understood, there are limits to our patience.

Source: Department of State Bulletin, February 1981, p. 19.

AFGHANISTAN
Soviet Invasion
President Carter's Address to the Nation

January 4, 1980

I come to you this evening to discuss the extremely important and rapidly changing circumstances in Southwest Asia.

I continue to share with all of you the sense of outrage and impatience because of the kidnaping of innocent American hostages and the holding of them by militant terrorists with the support and the approval of Iranian officials. Our purposes continue to be the protection of the long-range interests of our Nation and the safety of the American hostages. We are attempting to secure the release of the Americans through the International Court of Justice, through the United Nations and through public and private diplomatic efforts. We are determined to achieve this goal. We hope to do so without bloodshed and without any further danger to the lives of our 50 fellow Americans. In these efforts, we continue to have the strong support of the world community. The unity and the common sense of the American people under such trying circumstances are essential to the success of our efforts.

Recently, there has been another very serious development which threatens the maintenance of the peace in Southwest Asia. Massive Soviet military forces have invaded the small, nonaligned, sovereign nation of Afghanistan, which had hitherto not been an occupied satellite of the Soviet Union.

Fifty thousand heavily armed Soviet troops have crossed the border and are now dispersed throughout Afghanistan, attempting to conquer the fiercely independent Muslim people of that country.

The Soviets claim, falsely, that they were invited into Afghanistan to help protect that country from some unnamed outside threat. But

Source: Public Papers of the Presidents, Administration of Jimmy Carter, 1980, pp. 21-24 (complete document).

the President, who had been the leader of
Afghanistan before the Soviet invasion, was
assassinated--along with several members of his
family--after the Soviets gained control of the
capital city of Kabul. Only several days later
was the new puppet leader even brought into
Afghanistan by the Soviets.

This invasion is an extremely serious
threat to peace because of the threat of further
Soviet expansion into neighboring countries in
Southwest Asia and also because such an
aggressive military policy is unsettling to
other peoples throughout the world.

This is a callous violation of
international law and the United Nations
Charter. It is a deliberate effort of a
powerful atheistic government to subjugate an
independent Islamic people.

We must recognize the strategic importance
of Afghanistan to stability and peace. A
Soviet-occupied Afghanistan threatens both Iran
and Pakistan and is a steppingstone to possible
control over much of the world's oil supplies.

The United States wants all nations in the
region to be free and to be independent. If the
Soviets are encouraged in this invasion by
eventual success, and if they maintain their
dominance over Afghanistan and then extend their
control to adjacent countries, the stable,
strategic, and peaceful balance of the entire
world will be changed. This would threaten the
security of all nations including, of course,
the United States, our allies, and our friends.

Therefore, the world simply cannot stand
by and permit the Soviet Union to commit this
act with impunity. Fifty nations have petitioned
the United Nations Security Council to condemn
the Soviet Union and to demand the immediate
withdrawal of all Soviet troops from
Afghanistan. We realize that under the United
Nations Charter the Soviet Union and other
permanent members may veto action of the
Security Council. If the will of the Security
Council should be thwarted in this manner, then
immediate action would be appropriate in the
General Assembly of the United Nations where no
Soviet veto exists.

In the meantime, neither the United States

nor any other nation which is committed to world peace and stability can continue to do business as usual with the Soviet Union.

I have already recalled the United States Ambassador from Moscow back to Washington. He's working with me and with my other senior advisers in an immediate and comprehensive evaluation of the whole range of our relations with the Soviet Union.

The successful negotiation of the SALT II treaty has been a major goal and a major achievement of this administration, and we Americans, the people of the Soviet Union, and indeed the entire world will benefit from the successful control of strategic nuclear weapons through the implementation of this carefully negotiated treaty.

However, because of the Soviet aggression, I have asked the United States Senate to defer further consideration of the SALT II treaty so that the Congress and I can assess Soviet actions and intentions and devote our primary attention to the legislative and other measures required to respond to this crisis. As circumstances change in the future, we will, of course, keep the ratification of SALT II under active review in consultation with the leaders of the Senate.

The Soviets must understand our deep concern. We will delay opening of any new American or Soviet consular facilities, and most of the cultural and economic exchanges currently under consideration will be deferred. Trade with the Soviet Union will be severely restricted.

I have decided to halt or to reduce exports to the Soviet Union in three areas that are particularly important to them. These new policies are being and will be coordinated with those of our allies.

I've directed that no high technology or other strategic items will be licensed for sale to the Soviet Union until further notice, while we revise our licensing policy.

Fishing privileges for the Soviet Union in United States waters will be severely curtailed.

The 17 million tons of grain ordered by the Soviet Union in excess of that amount which we are committed to sell will not be delivered. This grain was not intended for human consumption but was to be used for building up Soviet livestock herds.

I am determined to minimize any adverse impact on the American farmer from this action. The undelivered grain will be removed from the market through storage and price support programs and through purchases at market prices. We will also increase amounts of grain devoted to the alleviation of hunger in poor countries, and we'll have a massive increase of the use of grain for gasohol production here at home.

After consultation with other principal grain-exporting nations, I am confident that they will not replace these quantities of grain by additional shipments on their part to the Soviet Union.

These actions will require some sacrifice on the part of all Americans, but there is absolutely no doubt that these actions are in the interest of world peace and in the interest of the security of our own Nation, and they are also compatible with actions being taken by our own major trading partners and others who share our deep concern about this new Soviet threat to world stability.

Although the United States would prefer not to withdraw from the Olympic games scheduled in Moscow this summer, the Soviet Union must realize that its continued aggressive actions will endanger both the participation of athletes and the travel to Moscow by spectators who would normally wish to attend the Olympic games.

Along with other countries, we will provide military equipment, food, and other assistance to help Pakistan defend its independence and its national security against the seriously increased threat it now faces from the north. The United States also stands ready to help other nations in the region in similar ways.

Neither our allies nor our potential adversaries should have the slightest doubt about our willingness, our determination, and our capacity to take the measures I have outlined tonight. I have consulted with leaders of the Congress, and I am confident they will support legislation that may be required to carry out these measures.

History teaches, perhaps very few clear lessons. But surely one such lesson learned by the world at great cost is that aggression, unopposed, becomes a contagious disease.

The response of the international community to the Soviet attempt to crush Afghanistan must match the gravity of the Soviet action.

With the support of the American people and working with other nations, we will deter aggression, we will protect our Nation's security, and we will preserve the peace. The United States will meet its responsibilities.

General Assembly Resolution A/Res/ES-6/2

January 14, 1980

The General Assembly,

Taking note of Security Council Resolution 462 (1980) of 9 January 1980, calling for an emergency Special Session of the General Assembly to examine the question contained in document S/Agenda/2185,

Gravely concerned at the recent developments in Afghanistan and their implications for international peace and security,

Reaffirming the inalienable right of all peoples to determine their own future and to choose their own form of government free from outside interference,

Mindful of the obligations of all states to refrain in their international relations from the threat or use of force against the sovereignty, territorial integrity and political independence of any State, or in any other manner inconsistent with the purposes and principles of the Charter of the United Nations,

Recognizing the urgent need for immediate termination of foreign armed intervention in Afghanistan so as to enable its people to deter-

Source: Department of State Bulletin, February 1980, pp. 73-74 (complete document).

mine their own destiny without outside
interference or coercion,
    <u>Noting</u> with profound concern the large
outflow of refugees from Afghanistan,
    <u>Recalling</u> its resolutions on the
strengthening of international security, on the
inadmissibility of intervention in the domestic
affairs of States and the protection of their
independence and sovereignty and on the
principles of international law concerning
friendly relations and co-operation among States
in accordance with the Charter of the United
Nations,
    <u>Expressing</u> its deep concern at the dangerous
escalation of tension, intensification of
rivalry and increased recourse to military
intervention and interference in the internal
affairs of States, which are detrimental to the
interests of all nations, particularly the non-
aligned countries.
    <u>Mindful</u> of the purposes and principles of the
Charter and of the responsibility of the General
Assembly under the relevant provisions of the
Charter and of Assembly Resolution 377A(V) of 3
November 1950
    1. Reaffirms that respect for the
sovereignty, territorial integrity and political
independence of every state is a fundamental
principle of the Charter of the United Nations,
any violation of which on any pretext whatsoever
is contrary to its aims and purposes;
    2. Strongly deplores the recent armed
intervention in Afghanistan, which is
inconsistent with that principle;
    3. Appeals to all States to respect the
sovereignty, territorial integrity, political
independence and non-aligned character of
Afghanistan and to refrain from any interference
in the internal affairs of that country;
    4. Calls for the immediate, unconditional
and total withdrawal of the foreign troops from
Afghanistan in order to enable its people to
determine their own form of government and
choose their economic, political and social
systems free from outside intervention,
subversion or coercion or constraint of any
kind whatsoever;
    5. Urges all Parties concerned to assist

in bringing about, speedily and in accordance
with the purposes and principles of the Charter,
conditions necessary for the voluntary return of
the Afghan refugees to their homes;
      6. Appeals to all States and national and
international organizations to extend
humanitarian relief assistance with a view to
alleviating the hardship of the Afghan refugees
in coordination with the United Nations High
Commissioner for Refugees;
      7. Requests the Secretary-General to keep
Member States and the Security Council promptly
and concurrently informed on the progress
towards the implementation of the present
resolution;
      8. Calls upon the Security Council to
consider ways and means which could assist in
the implementation of this resolution.
Vote on Resolution, January 14, 1980
      Of the 152 members of the United Nations,
140 participated in the special session vote on
General Assembly Resolution A/RES/ES-6/2 on
January 14 as follows:
For (104)   Against (18)   Abstain (18)   Absent
(12)

            Afghanistan: 18 Months of Occupation
                       August 1981

After 1-1/2 years of Soviet occupation, the
Soviets and the Democratic Republic of
Afghanistan (DRA) have not been able to make
headway in establishing the authority of the
Babrak regime. Indeed they appear to be losing
ground to the guerrilla freedom fighters
(mujahidin), who are maintaining impressive
momentum.
      On the other hand, the Soviets show no
signs of abandoning their long-term objective of
legitimizing a pro-Soviet government in
Afghanistan and suppressing the resistance. They
acknowledge that it will take longer than
originally anticipated but seem to believe time
is on their side....
      A combination of political restraints and

Source: Department of State, Special Report No.
86, August 1981.

operational realities is the principal obstacle
to the success of Moscow's military policy in
Afghanistan. The fact that the Soviets have not
increased their troop strength beyond 85,000, in
spite of the continuing military standoff, may
reflect concern about the political cost both in
the international arena and in the effort to
enhance Babrak's image with the Afghan populace.
A massive military effort would doom the
political strategy and undercut the Soviets'
primary military goal of maintaining adequate
stability while building up the Afghan forces to
fight the mujahidin.

This policy has failed badly. The
situation has become progressively more
unstable, and the Afghan forces are increasingly
unreliable. Aggressive resistance tactics have
forced the Soviets to involve themselves in
military operations throughout the country on a
daily basis. Suffering from excessive concern
with bureaucratic procedures and from a lack of
zeal, Soviet forces have not been able to deal
decisively with guerrilla ambush operations
along all major roads and with expanded
guerrilla operations against military and
government targets.

Soviet offensives to take important
resistance strongholds and to penetrate into
territory held by the resistance have failed
repeatedly. The most striking recent example is
the mid-July effort to drive resistance
guerrillas out of the Paghman mountains, only 12
miles northwest of Kabul. Heavy casualties were
sustained by both sides, including hundreds of
villagers in the area, but the combined Soviet-
Afghan force was forced to retreat. It was
impossible for the authorities to cover up this
defeat so close to Kabul, particularly as the
dead included at least 70 military school
cadets.

Other instances of the failure of Soviet
offensives include repeated attempts to
penetrate the Panjshir Valley, an important
resistance stronghold that gives access to the
main north-south road in the strategic Salang
Pass area, and an unsuccessful attempt in June
to take a key guerrilla redoubt in the western
province of Nangarhar. Furthermore, most of the

central uplands of Afghanistan, the area known
as the Hazarajat, remain inaccessible to Soviet
troops.

Even though Soviet forces have not been
very effective against the insurgents, Soviet
casualties probably are not heavy enough by
themselves to induce the Soviets to seek a
negotiated withdrawal of their forces. Soviet
casualty figures are not known, but it is
evident that they have lost a considerable
number of men and many tanks and helicopters.

That the Soviets are aware of the need to
improve their performance is reflected in the
measures they have taken to reorganize and
tailor their forces to guerrilla warfare. It is
unlikely, however, that they will be able to
deal satisfactorily with sagging morale. The
Soviet soldier whose father fought heroically at
Stalingrad does not have a cause in Afghanistan,
but his opponent is fighting a holy war.

Efforts to build up the Afghan forces have
had even less success. Defections continue, and
the morale of those who remain is extremely low.
The government's refusal to release soldiers
who have completed their extended tours of duty
is causing particular unhappiness. The
seriousness of the military manpower shortage
has been made abundantly clear in many ways;
party members have been ordered to the "hot"
fronts, forced conscription continues throughout
the country, and militia and regular units are
suffering unnecessarily heavy casualties
because of inadequate training.

Resistance

The mujahidin forces are active everywhere
in Afghanistan. Drawn from all tribes and
ethnic groups, most of them follow local leaders
and fight in their own areas. Others, however,
are affiliated with the political groups in
Peshawar. Rivalries between organizations have
led to some major clashes in recent months
between mujahidin bands over territorial rights,
but there have also been many instances of joint
operations and sharing of equipment and
resources. When word spreads that a mujahidin
unit is threatened, many others will converge on
the area to render assistance.

The resistance fighters recently have been particularly active in the areas north of Kabul and even in the Kabul suburbs. The most dramatic operation occurred in early June when large quantities of ammunition and petroleum stores were blown up at Bagram airbase near Kabul. There have been many other instances of mujahidin aggressiveness in recent months along major supply and convoy routes and against government held provincial and district centers. During the spring and early summer, the government has been forced to abandon additional districts to resistance control. Although the mujahidin still cannot take and hold a major city or provincial capital, they have made life increasingly dangerous for government sympathizers in all urban centers.

Mujahidin mobility generally serves to protect them from heavy casualties, although occasionally they are trapped and must stand and fight. There continue to be reports that the Soviets are using potent chemical agents to flush out guerrillas and make them targets for helicopter gunships. More often it is the noncombatant villager sympathizers who bear the full brunt of Soviet retaliation. The continuing heavy flow of refugees to Pakistan, totaling over 2.2 million as of late June 1981, is a constant reminder of the daily destruction, suffering, and upheaval produced by Soviet military operations.

Efforts continue to unite exile resistance groups. Representatives of the six major groups signed an agreement in Peshawar in late June to set up a coordinating council. There are already signs, however, that the council is destined to be short lived.

The guerrilla fighters inside Afghanistan, however, seem to flourish despite the competition among exile groups. Babrak and his Soviet sponsors may be counting on traditional tribal and ethnic rivalries to undermine the mujahidin. But nationalist reaction to foreign occupation and the religious fervor of a holy war have proved to be powerful forces in motivating the resistance movement.

8

Nuclear Strategy, Weaponry, and Arms Control

INTRODUCTION

By the end of the 1970s, serious questions were raised in America regarding U.S. nuclear capability, particularly in terms of deterrence and the "standoff" with the Soviet Union. The effort by the Soviet Union to equal, and, in the view of some, to surpass the U.S. in nuclear weaponry had reached serious levels. Indeed President Carter's Presidential Directive No. 59 was seen as an attempt to redress the Soviet buildup by targeting the Soviet political infrastructure.

The SALT II agreement signed by Secretary General Brezhnev and President Carter was an effort to achieve some arms control goals as well as slow the arms buildup. However, the ratification process in the U.S. Congress collapsed after the Soviet invasion of Afghanistan in 1979. This series of events refocused U.S. attention on security issues and Soviet intentions.

A new policy and strategy seemed to be put into place with the administration of President Ronald Reagan. An important part of this was efforts at modernizing the U.S. military and parts of the nuclear arsenal on the one hand, and arms control and arms reduction, on the other. Before turning to the Reagan defense buildup, it is important to review arms control developments up to the beginning of the 1980s.

Arms control treaties and issues in the post–World War II era stretch back to the 1946 Baruch Plan for the international control of nuclear technology. At that time the U.S. was the sole atomic power. The Soviets rejected the plan and pursued the development of their own atomic capability. In 1953, President Eisenhower proposed the "atoms for peace" program. The purpose of the offer was to help other countries to develop nuclear energy for peaceful purposes. It was this initiative that led to the formation of the International Atomic Energy Agency.

In the aftermath of the Cuban Missile Crisis, the Soviets seemed to make a particularly determined effort to match the U.S. in nuclear weaponry. In this sense, it was the efforts by the Soviet Union to gain nuclear parity with the U.S. and to develop the military instruments appropriate for a superpower that gave impetus to arms control efforts.

In 1963, a Limited Test Ban Treaty was concluded prohibiting nuclear testing in Earth's atmosphere. This treaty has been signed by more than 125 nations, excluding France and China. In 1967 an Outer Space Treaty prohibited the use of nuclear weapons by placing them in Earth orbit. It also prohibited the use of the moon or other outer space bodies for military purposes. This was followed by a Treaty for the Prohibition of Nuclear Weapons in Latin America, creating a nuclear-free zone.

The Treaty on the Non-Proliferation of Nuclear Weapons (NPT) was placed into effect in 1970. The purpose of the Treaty was to preclude states that possessed nuclear weapons from transferring--or otherwise assisting any state to acquire--such weapons or assisting any state to gain the technology necessary to make such weapons. In 1972, the Treaty on the Prohibition of the Emplacement of Nuclear Weapons and Other Weapons of Mass Destruction on the Seabed and the Ocean Floor and the Subsoil Thereof was signed.

The first major effort to control the nuclear arsenal in the hands of the superpowers was the Strategic Arms Limitation Treaty (SALT I) signed in 1972 by Secretary General Leonid Brezhnev and President Richard Nixon. There were two parts to the Treaty. Part One was the Antiballistic Missile Treaty; Part Two was the Interim Agreement on Strategic Offensive Weapons. The latter part provided that neither of the two powers would deploy a larger number of strategic missiles than it already had deployed or under construction. It was this part that paved the way for SALT II negotiations.

In 1979, SALT II was signed by Secretary General Brezhnev and President Jimmy Carter. This Treaty set equal limits on the aggregate number of strategic delivery systems for both sides. It also provided for future reductions in the ceilings on weapons; limited the number of warheads for each missile; and limited each side to no more than one new type of missile. Provisions were also made for verification procedures. SALT II was never ratified by the U.S. Senate, primarily as a result of the Soviet invasion of Afghanistan. Yet, both nations appeared to abide by SALT II.

President Ronald Reagan continued the initiative toward arms control by announcing a new set of premises associated with START (Strategic Arms Reduction Talks). The purpose was not simply to place ceilings on strategic weapons, but to actually reduce them. However, well into the 1980s there appeared to be little progress.

A major new dimension was added to arms control and nuclear weaponry by President Reagan's Strategic Defense Initiative (SDI), or "Star Wars" as it has been nicknamed by its critics. SDI is intended to be a defensive strategy employing an array of yet to be developed lasers, electronics, radar, and sophisticated satellites, among other things. The Soviet Union reacted with distinct displeasure, viewing SDI as an obstacle to any meaningful arms control negotations between the U.S. and the USSR.

With the coming to power in the Soviet Union of Mikhail Gorbachev, a new environment was created for U.S.-USSR relationships. SDI notwithstanding, the U.S. and the USSR signed an INF Agreement in 1987. The INF Treaty (Intermediate Nuclear Forces) reduces the number of medium-range missiles in the hands of both powers. Equally important, it sets a political tone to the relationships between the two superpowers that appears to reduce world tensions, particularly in terms of nuclear confrontation. Further, the political impact on Europe appears to be positive, in the sense of responding to European groups who seek some type of weapons reduction. In brief, for the first time, an entire class of nuclear missiles will be eliminated, in contrast to SALT I and SALT II provisions. Moreover, verification procedures are particularly stringent, with on-site inspections in both countries. The primary effort of the INF was the elimination of U.S. Pershing II and Cruise missiles in Europe and the SS-20s of the Soviet Union.

President Reagan and General Secretary Gorbachev met again in Moscow in 1988. Although no final agreements were reached, the friendly relationships that emerged gave some hope that progress on arms control would continue. At the end of 1988, it was still too early to determine what impact the INF Treaty will have on U.S. national security or how far the negotiations will proceed on strategic missiles.

DOCUMENTS

THE MISSILE GAP

The President's News Conference

February 8, 1961

Mr. President, in the past 24 hours there has arisen a somewhat hard to understand situation concerning the missile gap. An official of your administration, who was identified in some newspapers this morning as Secretary McNamara, has been quoted as saying that the missile gap which was expected and talked about so much did not exist, nor did he see prospects of it. Your press secretary, yesterday afternoon, denied this story....

The President: Mr. McNamara stated that no study had been concluded in the Defense Department which would lead to any conclusion at this time as to whether there is a missile gap or not....

So I think in answer to your question, the study has not been completed. It has not come, therefore, across my desk....

Q. Well, sir, during the campaign you seemed to feel very strongly that a serious missile gap did exist then. Do you now feel as strongly?...

The President: I hope that we will have a clearer answer to that question. Of course, it is my hope that the United States is fully secure. I will be pleased if that is the result. If it isn't I think it is important that we know about it, and I will say that we will then—I will then take on the responsibility of passing on to the Congress this collective judgment as to our position and what needs to be done.

So that without getting into the discussion of these stories this morning, I do want to say that it is my information that these studies are not complete, and therefore it would be premature to reach a judgment as to whether there is a gap or not....

Source: Public Papers of the Presidents, John F. Kennedy, 1961, pp. 66-68.

The President's News Conference, March 8, 1961

Mr. President, you told us last month that you expected to have an answer from the Defense Department about this time on whether there is or is not a missile gap. Are you able to say at this time whether there is or is not?

The President. We are concluding our review of the recommendations which the Defense Department has made for changes in the Defense budget. I am hopeful that this survey can be completed in the next few days, and then we plan to send the results of our study to the Congress. And at that time we will indicate what I believe to be the relative defensive position of the United States and other countries and what needs to be done to improve it.

PRESIDENT KENNEDY'S RADIO and TELEVISION
ADDRESS to the AMERICAN PEOPLE
on the TEST BAN TREATY
July 26, 1963

I speak to you tonight in a spirit of hope. Eighteen years ago the advent of nuclear weapons changed the course of the world as well as the war. Since that time, all mankind has been struggling to escape from the darkening prospect of mass destruction on earth....

Yesterday a shaft of light cut into the darkness....

For the first time, an agreement has been reached on bringing the forces of nuclear destruction under international control--a goal first sought in 1946 when Bernard Baruch presented a comprehensive control plan to the United Nations....

While it will not prevent this Nation from testing underground, or from being ready to conduct atmospheric tests if the acts of others so require, it gives us a concrete opportunity to extend its coverage to other nations and later to other forms of nuclear tests.

This treaty is in part the product of

Sources: Public Papers of the Presidents, John F. Kennedy, 1961, p. 153; Ibid., 1963, pp. 601-604.

Western patience and vigilance. We have made clear--most recently in Berlin and Cuba--our deep resolve to protect our security and our freedom against any form of aggression. We have also made clear our steadfast determination to limit the arms race....

...the achievement of this goal is not a victory for one side--it is a victory for mankind. It reflects no concessions either to or by the Soviet Union. It reflects simply our common recognition of the dangers in further testing.

This treaty is not the millennium. It will not resolve all conflicts, or cause the Communists to forego their ambitions, or eliminate the dangers of war. It will not reduce our need for arms or allies or programs of assistance to others. But it is an important first step--a step towards peace--a step towards reason--a step away from war....

Western policies have long been designed to persuade the Soviet Union to renounce aggression direct or indirect, so that their people and all people may live and let live in peace. The unlimited testing of new weapons of war cannot lead towards that end--but this treaty, if it can be followed by further progress, can clearly move in that direction. ...

During the next several years, in addition to the four current nuclear powers, a small but significant number of nations will have the intellectual, physical, and financial resources to produce both nuclear weapons and the means of delivering them. In time, it is estimated, many other nations will have either this capacity or other ways of obtaining nuclear warheads, even as missiles can be commercially purchased today.

I ask you to stop and think for a moment what it would mean to have nuclear weapons in so many hands, in the hands of countries large and small, stable and unstable, responsible and irresponsible, scattered throughout the world. There would be no rest for anyone then, no stability, no real security, and no chance of effective disarmament. There would only be the increased chance of accidental war, and an increased necessity for the great powers to involve themselves in what otherwise would be local conflicts....

TREATY BANNING NUCLEAR WEAPONS TESTS
in the ATMOSPHERE, in OUTER SPACE and UNDER
WATER

Moscow, August 5, 1963; Entered into Force

October 19, 1963

The Governments of the United States of America, the United Kingdom of Great Britain and Northern Ireland, and the Union of Soviet Socialist Republics,...
Seeking to achieve the discontinuance of all test explosions of nuclear weapons for all time, determined to continue negotiations to this end, and desiring to put an end to the contamination of man's environment by radioactive substances,

Have agreed as follows:

Article I

1. Each of the Parties to this Treaty undertakes to prohibit, to prevent, and not to carry out any nuclear weapon test explosion, or any other nuclear explosion, at any place under its jurisdiction or control:

(a) in the atmosphere; beyond its limits, including outer space; or underwater, including territorial waters or high seas....

2. Each of the Parties to this Treaty undertakes furthermore to refrain from causing, encouraging, or in any way participating in, the carrying out of any nuclear weapon test explosion, or any other nuclear explosion, anywhere which would take place in any of the environments described....

Source: United States Treaties and Other International Agreements, vol. 14, part 2, 1963, pp. 1316–1317.

THE NONPROLIFERATION TREATY

President Johnson's Address to the UN General Assembly

June 12, 1968

The resolution that you have just approved commends to the governments of the world for their speedy ratification the treaty for the non-proliferation of nuclear weapons.

It is the most important international agreement in the field of disarmament since the nuclear age began....

It commits the nuclear powers to redouble their efforts to end the nuclear arms race and to achieve nuclear disarmament.

It will insure the equitable sharing of the peaceful uses of nuclear energy--under effective safeguards--for the benefit of all nations....

We of the United States will carry out our responsibilities under it in full measure.

First, we shall fully and scrupulously discharge our obligations as a nuclear-weapon party:

--not to transfer nuclear weapons, or control over them, to any recipient whatsoever; and

--not to help any non-nuclear state acquire such weapons.

Second, we shall cooperate fully in bringing the treaty's safeguards into being, safeguards that will prevent the diversion of nuclear energy from peaceful uses to weapons.

Third, we shall, as the treaty requires, facilitate the fullest possible exchange of equipment, materials, scientific and technical information for the peaceful uses of nuclear energy. We shall give particular attention to the needs of the developing nations.

We shall share our technical knowledge and experience in peaceful nuclear research--fully-- and we shall share it without reservation. This will include very important new developments in

Source: Department of State Bulletin, July 1, 1968, pp. 1-2.

electrical power generation, agriculture, medicine, industry, and in the desalting of sea water.

Fourth, we shall continue our research and development into the use of nuclear explosions for peaceful purposes. We shall make available to the non-nuclear treaty parties--without delay and under the treaty's provisions--the benefits of such explosions.

Finally, in keeping with our obligations under the treaty, we shall, as a major nuclear-weapon power, promptly and vigorously pursue negotiations on effective measures to halt the nuclear arms race and to reduce existing nuclear arsenals....

We desire--yes, we urgently desire--to begin early discussions on the limitation of strategic offensive and defensive nuclear weapons systems.

We shall search for an agreement that will not only avoid another costly and futile escalation of the arms race but will deescalate it....

From this ground that we have won here together, let us press forward

--to halt and reverse the buildup of nuclear arsenals;

--to find new ways to eliminate the threat of conventional conflicts that might grow into nuclear disaster....

Treaty on Non-Proliferation of Nuclear Weapons
July 1, 1968
Entered into Force March 5, 1970

ARTICLE I

Each nuclear-weapon State Party to the Treaty undertakes not to transfer to any recipient whatsoever nuclear weapons or other nuclear explosive devices or control over such weapons or explosive devices, directly or indirectly; and not in any way to assist, encourage, or induce any non-nuclear-weapon

Source: United States Treaties and Other International Agreements, vol. 21, part 1, 1970, pp. 487-488, 493-494.

State to manufacture or otherwise acquire nuclear weapons or other nuclear explosive devices or control over such weapons or explosive devices.

ARTICLE II

Each non-nuclear weapon State Party to the Treaty undertakes not to receive the transfer from any transferor whatsoever of nuclear weapons or other nuclear explosive devices or of control over such weapons or explosive devices, directly or indirectly; not to manufacture or otherwise acquire nuclear weapons or other nuclear explosive devices; and not to seek or receive any assistance in the manufacture of nuclear weapons or other nuclear explosive devices.

ARTICLE III

1. Each non-nuclear-weapon State Party to the Treaty undertakes to accept safeguards, as set forth in an agreement to be negotiated and concluded with the International Atomic Energy Agency in accordance with the Statute of the International Atomic Energy Agency and the Agency's safeguards system, for the exclusive purpose of verification of the fulfillment of its obligations assumed under this Treaty with a view to preventing diversion of nuclear energy from peaceful uses to nuclear weapons or other nuclear explosive devices. Procedures for the safeguards required by this article shall be followed with respect to source or special fissionable material whether it is being produced, processed or used in any principal nuclear facility or is outside any such facility. The safeguards required by this article shall be applied on all source or special fissionable material in all peaceful nuclear activities within the territory of such State, under its jurisdiction, or carried out under its control anywhere.

2. Each State Party to the Treaty undertakes not to provide: (a) source or special fissionable material, or (b) equipment or material especially designed or prepared for the

processing, use or production of special fissionable material, to any non-nuclear-weapon State for peaceful purposes, unless the source or special fissionable material shall be subject to the safeguards required by this article....

ARTICLE X

1. Each Party shall in exercising its national sovereignty have the right to withdraw from the Treaty if it decides that extraordinary events, related to the subject matter of this Treaty, have jeopardized the supreme interests of its country. It shall give notice of such withdrawal to all other Parties to the Treaty and to the United Nations Security Council three months in advance. Such notice shall include a statement of the extraordinary events it regards as having jeopardized its supreme interests.

2. Twenty-five years after the entry into force of the Treaty, a conference shall be convened to decide whether the Treaty shall continue in force indefinitely, or shall be extended for an additional fixed period or periods. This decision shall be taken by a majority of the Parties to the Treaty....

SALT I
Interim Agreement
Moscow, May 26, 1972

Entered into Force, October 3, 1972

Interim Agreement between the United States of America and the Union of Soviet Socialist Republics on Certain Measures with Respect to the Limitation of Strategic Offensive Arms.

Article I
The Parties undertake not to start construction of additional fixed land-based intercontinental ballistic missile (ICBM) launchers after July 1, 1972.

Source: United States Treaties and Other International Agreements, vol. 23, part 4, 1972, pp. 3462-3482.

Article II

The Parties undertake not to convert land-based launchers for light ICBMs or for ICBMs of older types deployed prior to 1964, into land-based launchers for heavy ICBMs of types deployed after that time.

Article III

The Parties undertake to limit submarine-launched ballistic missile (SLBM) launchers and modern ballistic missile submarines to the numbers operational and under construction on the date of signature of this Interim Agreement, and in addition to launchers and submarines constructed under procedures established by the Parties as replacements for an equal number of ICBM launchers of older types deployed prior to 1964 or for launchers on older submarines.

Article IV

Subject to the provisions of this Interim Agreement, modernization and replacement of strategic offensive ballistic missiles and launchers covered by this Interim Agreement may be undertaken....

Protocol to the Interim Agreement
May 26, 1972

The Parties understand that, under Article III of the Interim Agreement, for the period during which that Agreement remains in force:

The US may have no more than 710 ballistic missile launchers on submarines (SLBMs) and no more than 44 modern ballistic missile submarines. The Soviet Union may have no more than 950 ballistic missile launchers on submarines and no more than 62 modern ballistic missile submarines.

Additional ballistic missile launchers on submarines up to the above-mentioned levels, in the U.S.--over 656 ballistic missile launchers on nuclear-powered submarines, and in the U.S.S.R.--over 740 ballistic missile launchers on nuclear-powered submarines, operational and under construction, may become operational as replacements for equal numbers of ballistic missile launchers of older types deployed prior to 1964 or of ballistic missile launchers on older submarines.

The deployment of modern SLBMs on any submarine, regardless of type, will be counted against the total level of SLBMs permitted for the U.S. and the U.S.S.R....

(b) <u>Common Understandings</u>--Common understanding of the Parties on the following matters was reached during the negotiations:

A. Increase in ICBM Silo Dimensions

Ambassador Smith made the following statement on May 26, 1972:
> The Parties agree that the term "significantly increased" means that an increase will not be greater than 10-15 percent of the present dimensions of land-based ICBM silo launchers.

Minister Semenov replied that this statement corresponded to the Soviet understanding....

C. Standstill

On May 6, 1972, Minister Semenov made the following statement:
> In an effort to accommodate the wishes of the U.S. side, the Soviet Delegation is prepared to proceed on the basis that the two sides will in fact observe the obligations of both the Interim Agreement and the ABM Treaty beginning from the date of signature of these two documents.

In reply, the U.S. Delegation made the following statement on May 20, 1972:
> The U.S. agrees in principle with the Soviet statement made on May 6 concerning observance of obligations beginning from date of signature but we would like to make clear our understanding that this means that, pending ratification and acceptance, neither side would take any action prohibited by the agreements after they had entered into force. This understanding would continue to apply in

the absence of notification by either
signatory of its intention not to proceed
with ratification or approval.

The Soviet Delegation indicated agreement
with the U.S. statement.

2. Unilateral Statements

(a) The following noteworthy unilateral
statements were made during the negotiations by
the United States Delegation:

A. Withdrawal from the ABM Treaty

On May 9, 1972, Ambassador Smith made the
following statement:

> The U.S. Delegation has stressed the
> importance the U.S. government attaches to
> achieving agreement on more complete
> limitations on strategic offensive
> arms,following agreement on an ABM Treaty
> and on an Interim Agreement on certain
> measures with respect to the limitation
> of strategic offensive arms. The U.S.
> Delegation believes that an objective of
> the follow-on negotiations should be to
> constrain and reduce on a long-term basis
> threats to the survivability of our
> respective strategic retaliatory forces.
> The USSR Delegation has also indicated
> that the objectives of SALT would remain
> unfulfilled without the achievement of an
> agreement providing for more complete
> limitations on strategic offensive arms.
> Both sides recognize that the initial
> agreements would be steps toward the
> achievement of more complete limitations
> on strategic arms. If an agreement
> providing for more complete strategic
> offensive arms limitations were not
> achieved within five years, U.S. supreme
> interests could be jeopardized. Should
> that occur, it would constitute a basis
> for withdrawal from the ABM Treaty. The
> U.S. does not wish to see such a
> situation occur, nor do we believe that
> the USSR does. It is because we wish to

prevent such a situation that we emphasize
the importance the U.S. Government
attaches to achievement of more complete
limitations on strategic offensive arms.
The U.S. Executive will inform the
Congress, in connection with Congressional
consideration of the ABM Treaty and the
Interim Agreement, of this statement of
the U.S. position.

B. Land-Mobile ICBM Launchers

The U.S. Delegation made the following
statement on May 20, 1972:
In connection with the important subject
of land-mobile ICBM launchers, in the
interest of concluding the Interim
Agreement the U.S. Delegation now
withdraws its proposal that Article I or
an agreed statement explicitly prohibit
the deployment of mobile land-based ICBM
launchers. I have been instructed to
inform you that, while agreeing to defer
the question of limitation of operational
land-mobile ICBM launchers to the
subsequent negotiations on more complete
limitations on strategic offensive arms,
the U.S. would consider the deployment of
operational land-mobile ICBM launchers
during the period of the Interim Agreement
as inconsistent with the objectives of
that Agreement....

D. Heavy ICBM'S

The U.S. Delegation made the following
statement on May 26, 1972:
The U.S. Delegation regrets that the
Soviet delegation has not been willing to
agree on a common definition of a heavy
missile. Under these circumstances, the
U.S. Delegation believes it necessary to
state the following: The United States
would consider any ICBM having volume
significantly greater than that of the
largest light ICBM now operational on
either side to be a heavy ICBM. The U.S.
proceeds on the premise that the Soviet

side will give due account to this
consideration.

(b) The following noteworthy unilateral
statement was made by the Delegation of the USSR
and is shown here with the U.S. reply:

On May 17, 1972, Minister Semenov made the
following unilateral "Statement of the Soviet
Side":

Taking into account that modern ballistic
missile submarines are presently in the
possession of not only the U.S. but also
of its NATO allies, the Soviet Union
agrees that for the period of
effectiveness of the Interim 'Freeze'
Agreement the U.S. and its NATO allies
have up to 50 such submarines with a total
of up to 800 ballistic missile launchers
thereon (including 41 U.S. submarines with
656 ballistic missile launchers).
However, if during the period of
effectiveness of the Agreement U.S. allies
in NATO should increase the number of
their modern submarines to exceed the
numbers of submarines they would have
operational or under construction on the
date of signature of the Agreement, the
Soviet Union will have the right to a
corresponding increase in the number of
its submarines. In the opinion of the
Soviet side, the solution of the question
of modern ballistic missile submarines
provided for in the Interim Agreement only
partially compensates for the strategic
imbalance in the deployment of the
nuclear-powered missile submarines of the
USSR and the U.S. Therefore, the Soviet
side believes that this whole question,
and above all the question of liquidating
the American missile submarine bases
outside the U.S., will be appropriately
resolved in the course of follow-on
negotiations.

On May 24, Ambassador Smith made the
following reply to Minister Semenov:

The United States side has studied the
"statement made by the Soviet side" of May

17 concerning compensation for submarine basing and SLBM submarines belonging to third countries. The United States does not accept the validity of the considerations in that statement.

On May 26 Minister Semenov repeated the unilateral statement made on May 24. Ambassador Smith also repeated the U.S. rejection on May 26.

ABM TREATY
Limitation of Anti-Ballistic Missile Systems (ABM) Treaty
Moscow, May 26, 1972
Entered into Force October 3, 1972

Treaty Between the United States of America And the Union of Soviet Socialist Republics on the Limitation of Anti-Ballistic Missile Systems

Article I
2. Each Party undertakes not to deploy ABM systems for a defense of the territory of its country and not to provide a base for such a defense, and not to deploy ABM systems for defense of an individual region except as provided for in Article III of this Treaty.

Article II
1. For the purposes of this Treaty an ABM system is a system to counter strategic ballistic missiles or their elements in flight trajectory, currently consisting of:
    (a) ABM interceptor missiles, which are interceptor missiles constructed and deployed for an ABM role, or of a type tested in an ABM mode;
    (b) ABM launchers, which are launchers constructed and deployed for launching ABM interceptor missiles; and
    (c) ABM radars, which are radars structed and deployed for an ABM role, or of a type test-

Source: United States Treaties and Other International Agreements, vol. 23, part 4, 1972, pp. 3435-3461.

ed in an ABM mode.

2. The ABM system components listed in paragraph 1 of this Article include those which are:

(a) operational;

(b) under construction;

(c) undergoing testing;

(d) undergoing overhaul, repair or conversion; or

(e) mothballed.

Article III

Each Party undertakes not to deploy ABM systems or their components except that:

(a) within one ABM system deployment area having a radius of one hundred and fifty kilometers and centered on the Party's national capital, a Party may deploy: (1) no more than one hundred ABM launchers and no more than one hundred ABM interceptor missiles at launch sites, and (2) ABM radars within no more than six ABM radar complexes, the area of each complex being circular and having a diameter of no more than three kilometers; and

(b) within one ABM system deployment area having a radius of one hundred and fifty kilometers and containing ICBM silo launchers, a Party may deploy: (1) no more than one hundred ABM launchers and no more than one hundred ABM interceptor missiles at launch sites, (2) two large-phased-array ABM radars comparable in potential to corresponding ABM radars operational or under construction on the date of signature of the Treaty in an ABM system deployment area containing ICBM silo launchers, and (3) no more than eighteen ABM radars each having a potential less than the potential of the smaller of the above-mentioned two large-phased-array ABM radars....

Article V

1. Each Party undertakes not to develop, test, or deploy ABM systems or components which are sea-based, air-based, space-based, or mobile

land-based....

Article VII

Subject to the provisions of this Treaty, modernization and replacement of ABM systems or their components may be carried out....

Agreed Interpretations, Common Understandings, and Unilateral Statements

1. Agreed Interpretations

(a) <u>Initialed Statements</u>.--The document set forth below was agreed upon and initialed by the Heads of the Delegations on May 26, 1972:

Agreed Statements regarding the Treaty between the United States of America and the Union of Soviet Socialist Republics on the Limitation of Anti-Ballistic Missile Systems

[A]

The Parties understand that, in addition to the ABM radars which may be deployed in accordance with subparagraph (a) of Article III of the Treaty, those non-phased-array ABM radars operational on the date of signature of the Treaty within the ABM system deployment area for defense of the national capital may be retained.

[B]

The Parties understand that the potential (the product of mean emitted power in watts and antenna area in square meters) of the smaller of the two large-phased-array ABM radars referred to in subparagraph (b) of Article III of the Treaty is considered for purposes of the Treaty to be three million.

[C]

The Parties understand that the center of the ABM system deployment area centered on the national capital and the center of the ABM system deployment area containing ICBM silo

launchers for each Party shall be separated by
no less than thirteen hundred kilometers.

[D]

In order to insure fulfillment of the
obligation not to deploy ABM systems and their
components except as provided in Article III of
the Treaty, the Parties agree that in the event
ABM systems based on other physical principles
and including components capable of substituting
for ABM interceptor missiles, ABM launchers, or
ABM radars are created in the future, specific
limitations on such systems and their components
would be subject to discussion in accordance
with Article XIII and agreement in accordance
with Article XIV of the Treaty.

[E]

The Parties understand that Article V of
the Treaty includes obligations not to develop,
test or deploy ABM interceptor missiles for the
delivery by each ABM interceptor missile of more
than one independently guided warhead.

[F]

The Parties agree not to deploy phased-
array-radars having a potential (the product of
mean emitted power in watts and antenna area in
square meters) exceeding three million, except
as provided for in Articles III, IV and VI of
the Treaty, or except for the purposes of
tracking objects in outer space or for use as
national technical means of verification.

[G]

The Parties understand that Article IX of
the Treaty includes the obligation of the U.S.
and the USSR not to provide to other States
technical descriptions or blueprints specially
worked out for the construction of ABM systems
and their components limited by the Treaty.

Common understandings.--Common
understanding of the Parties on the following

matters was reached during the negotiations:

A. Location of ICBM Defenses

The U.S. Delegation made the following statement on May 26, 1972:

> Article III of the ABM Treaty provides for each side one ABM system deployment area centered on its national capital and one ABM system deployment area containing ICBM silo launchers. The two sides have registered agreement on the following statement: "The Parties understand that the center of the ABM system deployment area centered on the national capital and the center of the ABM system deployment area containing ICBM silo launchers for each Party shall be separated by no less than thirteen hundred kilometers." In this connection, the U.S. side notes that its ABM system deployment area for defense of ICBM silo launchers, located west of the Mississippi River, will be centered in the Grand Forks ICBM silo launcher deployment area. (See Initialed Statement [C].)...

C. Mobile ABM Systems

On January 28, 1972, the U.S. Delegation made the following statement:

> Article V(1) of the Joint Draft Text of the ABM Treaty includes an undertaking not to develop, test, or deploy mobile land-based ABM systems and their components. On May 5, 1971, the U.S. side indicated that, in its view, a prohibition on deployment of mobile ABM systems and components would rule out the deployment of ABM launchers and radars which were not permanent fixed types. At that time, we asked for the Soviet view of this interpretation. Does the Soviet side agree with the U.S. side's interpretation put forward on May 5, 1971?

On April 13, 1972, the Soviet Delegation said there is a general common understanding on this matter....

E. Standstill

On May 6, 1972, Minister Semenov made the following statement:
> In an effort to accommodate the wishes of the U.S. side, the Soviet Delegation is prepared to proceed on the basis that the two sides will in fact observe the obligations of both the Interim Agreement and the ABM Treaty beginning from the date of signature of these two documents.

In reply, the U.S. Delegation made the following statement on May 20, 1972:
> The U.S. agrees in principle with the Soviet statement made on May 6 concerning observance of obligations beginning from date of signature but we would like to make clear our understanding that this means that, pending ratification and acceptance, neither side would take any action prohibited by the agreements after they had entered into force. This understanding would continue to apply in the absence of notification by either signatory of its intention not to proceed with ratification or approval.

The Soviet Delegation indicated agreement with the U.S. statement.

2. Unilateral Statements

(a) The following noteworthy unilateral statements were made during the negotiations by the United States Delegation:

A. Withdrawal from the ABM Treaty

On May 9, 1972, Ambassador Smith made the following statement:
> The U.S. Delegation has stressed the importance the U.S. Government attaches to achieving agreement on more complete

limitations on strategic offensive arms, following agreement on an ABM treaty and on an Interim Agreement on certain measures with respect to the limitation of strategic offensive arms. The U.S. Delegation believes that an objective of the follow-on negotiations should be to constrain and reduce on a long-term basis threats to the survivability of our respective strategic retaliatory forces. The USSR Delegation has also indicated that the objectives of SALT would remain unfulfilled without the achievement of an agreement providing for more complete limitations on strategic offensive arms. Both sides recognize that the initial agreements would be steps toward the achievement of more complete limitations on strategic arms. If an agreement providing for more complete strategic offensive arms limitations were not achieved within five years U.S. supreme interests could be jeopardized... It is because we wish to prevent such a situation that we emphasize the importance the U.S. Government attaches to achievement of more complete limitations on strategic offensive arms. The U.S. Executive will inform the Congress, in connection with Congressional consideration of the ABM Treaty and the Interim Agreement, of this statement of the U.S. position.

ABM Protocol
Protocol to the Treaty
Between the United States of America
And the Union of Soviet Socialist Republics
On the Limitation of Anti-Ballistic Missile
Systems Moscow, July 3, 1974
Entered into Force May 24, 1976

Article I
1. Each Party shall be limited at any one

Source: United States Treaties and Other International Agreements, vol. 27, part 2, 1976, pp. 1645-1650.

time to a single area out of the two provided
in Article III of the Treaty for deployment of
anti-ballistic missile (ABM) systems or their
components and accordingly shall not exercise
its right to deploy an ABM system or its
components in the second of the two ABM system
deployment areas permitted by Article III of the
Treaty, except as an exchange of one permitted
area for the other in accordance with Article II
of this Protocol.

   2. Accordingly, except as permitted by
Article II of this Protocol: the United States
of America shall not deploy an ABM system or its
components in the area centered on its capital,
as permitted by Article III (a) of the Treaty,
and the Soviet Union shall not deploy an ABM
system or its components in the deployment area
of intercontinental ballistic missile (ICBM)
silo launchers as permitted by Article III (b)
of the Treaty.

SALT I AND ABM TREATY

Address by President Richard Nixon to
Joint Session of Congress
June 1, 1972

The final achievement of the Moscow conference
was the signing of a landmark declaration
entitled Basic Principles of Mutual Relations
Between the United States and the U.S.S.R. As
these 12 basic principles are put into practice,
they can provide a solid framework for the
future development of better American-Soviet
relations.

   They begin with the recognition that two
nuclear nations, each of which has the power to
destroy humanity, have no alternative but to
coexist peacefully because in a nuclear war
there would be no winners, only losers.

   The basic principles commit both sides to
avoid direct military confrontation and to
exercise constructive leadership and restraint
with respect to smaller conflicts in other parts
of the world which could drag the major powers

Source: <u>Department of State Bulletin</u>, June 26,
1972, pp. 858-859.

into war.

They disavow any intention to create spheres of influence or to conspire against the interests of any other nation--a point I would underscore by saying once again tonight that America values its ties with all nations, from our oldest allies in Europe and Asia, as I emphasized by my visit to Iran, to our good friends in the Third World, and to our new relationship with the People's Republic of China.

However, we must remember that Soviet ideology still proclaims hostility to some of America's most basic values. The Soviet leaders remain committed to that ideology. Like the nation they lead, they are, and they will continue to be, totally dedicated competitors of the United States of America.

As we shape our policies for the period ahead, therefore, we must maintain our defenses at an adequate level until there is mutual agreement to limit forces. The time-tested policies of vigilance and firmness which have brought us to this summit are the only ones that can safely carry us forward to further progress in reaching agreements to reduce the danger of war.

By the same token, we must stand steadfastly with our NATO partners if negotiations leading to a new detente and a mutual reduction of forces in Europe are to be productive. Maintaining the strength, integrity, and steadfastness of our free-world alliances is the foundation on which all of our other initiatives for peace and security in the world must rest. As we seek better relations with those who have been our adversaries, we will not let down our friends and allies around the world.

For decades, America has been locked in hostile confrontation with the two great Communist powers, the Soviet Union and the People's Republic of China. We were engaged with the one at many points and almost totally isolated from the other, but our relationships with both had reached a deadly impasse. All three countries were victims of the kind of bondage about which George Washington long ago

warned in these words: The nation which
indulges toward another an habitual hatred is a
slave to its own animosity.

But now in the brief space of 4 months,
these journeys to Peking and Moscow have begun
to free us from perpetual confrontation. We
have moved toward better understanding, mutual
respect, and point-by-point settlement of
differences with both the major Communist
powers.

This one series of meetings has not
rendered an imperfect world suddenly perfect.
There still are deep philosophical differences;
there still are parts of the world in which age-
old hatreds persist. The threat of war has not
been eliminated--it has been reduced. We are
making progress toward a world in which leaders
of nations will settle their differences by
negotiation, not by force, and in which they
learn to live with their differences so that
their sons will not have to die for those
differences.

THE VLADIVOSTOK SUMMIT
Joint U.S.-Soviet Statement, November 24, 1974

During their working meeting in the area
of Vladivostok on November 23-24, 1974, the
President of the U.S.A. Gerald R. Ford, and
General Secretary of the Central Committee of
the CPSU L.I.Brezhnev discussed in detail the
question of further limitations of strategic
offensive arms....

Having noted the value of previous
agreements on this question, including the
Interim Agreement of May 26, 1972, they reaffirm
the intention to conclude a new agreement on the
limitation of strategic offensive arms, to last
through 1985....

.... further negotiations will be based on
the following provisions.

1. The new agreement will incorporate the
relevant provisions of the Interim Agreement of
May 26, 1972, which will remain in force until
October 1977.

Source: Department of State Bulletin, December
23, 1974, p. 879.

2. The new agreement will cover the period from October 1977 through December 31, 1985.

Based on the principle of equality and equal security, the new agreement will include the following limitations:

a. Both sides will be entitled to have a certain agreed aggregate number of strategic delivery vehicles;

b. Both sides will be entitled to have a certain agreed aggregate number of ICBMS and SLBMs [intercontinental ballistic missiles; submarine-launched ballistic missiles] equipped with multiple independently targetable warheads (MIRVS).

SALT II
Announcement by Secretaries Vance and Brown
May 9, 1979

With this treaty, we will take an essential step toward a safer America and a safer world. Our overriding purpose in these negotiations has been to strengthen our nation's security and that of our allies through practical and verifiable restraints on the nuclear arms race. Today we are on the threshold of signing a strategic arms agreement that achieves our purpose.

The treaty will enhance the security of the United States and our allies. It will restrain the nuclear arms race. It will lessen the likelihood of nuclear war. The treaty will serve these essential interests of the American people in several concrete ways. It will establish equal ceilings on the strategic
forces of the Soviet Union and the United States. It will begin the process of actually reducing the level of nuclear weapons, and it will limit not only the quantitative but also the qualitative race in nuclear arms.

As a result, this treaty will limit the strategic challenges we would otherwise have to meet. It will hold down the expense we would have to bear to meet those challenges. And it will avoid much of much of the uncertainty about Soviet arms that would otherwise prevail.

Source: <u>Department of State Bulletin</u>, June 1979, p. 23.

There will be a limit on the number of strategic launchers. Each side can have 2,250. With SALT the Soviets will have to make some reductions. Without SALT, the Soviets could, by continuing at their present rates of deployment of new systems, have a third more than this by 1985.

There will also be sublimits on the numbers of launchers for missiles with independently targetable multiple warheads, that is, MIRVs. With the SALT II agreement, the Soviet launchers will be limited to 820 for MIRV'ed intercontinental ballistic missiles, the most threatening part of their force. This is fewer than we believe they planned. Without the SALT II agreement, they could have many more than that by 1985.

In addition, there will be limits on the introduction of new intercontinental ballistic systems and on the number of warheads they can carry. With a SALT II agreement, the Soviets can have, for example, 10 warheads on their largest missile. Without the SALT II agreement, they could have 20, perhaps 40.

Finally, there will be a ban on interfering with national technical means of verification, and there will be other provisions to make verification easier.

We now have highly capable monitoring systems in place. They will be bolstered by measures we are taking to replace expeditiously the capability lost in the Iranian stations.

We will be able to detect any Soviet violation in ample time to protect our military security. With a SALT II agreement, we will be able to verify the agreement from the outset. Without the SALT II agreement, we could be faced with concealment, countermeasures, and so-called cheating of all sorts, because without SALT, all of these actions would be permitted.

Even with SALT, we will need to expand our defense efforts, including specifically our efforts devoted to strategic nuclear forces.

...the limit on warhead numbers will make more survivable the mobile missiles whose deployment we're considering as an answer to the growing vulnerability of our Minuteman ICBM's....

...we will be able to work with our allies
on both force modernization and on arms control
in response to the problems posed by the Soviet
buildup of theater nuclear forces.

Treaty on the Limitation of Strategic
Offensive Arms

June 18, 1979

* * * * *

Article IV

1. Each Party undertakes not to start
construction of additional fixed ICBM laucnhers.
2. Each Party undertakes not to relocate
fixed ICBM launchers.
3. Each Party undertakes not to convert
launchers of light ICBMs, or of ICBMs of older
types deployed prior to 1964, into launchers of
heavy ICBMs of types deployed after that time.
4. Each Party undertakes in the process of
modernization and replacement of ICBM silo
launchers not to increase the original internal
volume of an ICBM silo launcher by more than
thirty-two percent. Within this limit each Party
has the right to determine whether such an
increase will be made through an increase in the
original diameter or in the original depth of an
ICBM silo launcher, or in both of these
dimensions.

Article VII

1. The limitations provided for in Article
III shall not apply to ICBM and SLBM test and
training launchers for exploration and use of
outer space. ICBM and SLBM test and training
launchers are ICBM and SLBM launchers used only
for testing and training.

Common Understanding. The term "testing"
as used in Article VII of the Treaty, includes
research and development.

_____
Source: Department of State Bulletin, July 1979,
pp. 29, 36-38, 44-45.

2. The Parties agree that:

(a) there shall be no significant increase in the number of ICBM or SLBM test and training launchers or in the number of such launchers of heavy ICBMs;

(b) construction or conversion of ICBM launchers at test ranges shall be undertaken only for purposes of testing and training;

(c) there shall be no conversion of ICBM test and training launchers or of space vehicle launchers into ICBM launchers subject to the limitations provided for in Article III.

Article VIII

1. Each Party undertakes not to flight-test cruise missiles capable of a range in excess of 600 kilometers or ASBMs from aircraft other than bombers or to convert such aircraft into aircraft equipped for such missiles.

Article IX

1. Each Party undertakes not to develop, test, or deploy:

(a) ballistic missiles capable of a range in excess of 600 kilometers for installation on waterborne vehicles other than submarines, or launchers of such missiles;

(b) fixed ballistic or cruise missile launchers for emplacement on the ocean floor, on the seabed, or on the beds of internal waters and inland waters, or in the subsoil thereof, or mobile launchers of such missiles, which move only in contact with the ocean floor, the seabed, or the beds of internal waters and inland waters, or missiles for such launchers;

(c) systems for placing into Earth orbit nuclear weapons or any other kind of weapons of mass destruction, including fractional orbital missiles;

(d) mobile launchers of heavy ICBMs;

(e) SLBMs which have a launch-weight greater or a throw-weight greater than that of the heaviest, in terms of either launch-weight or throw-weight, respectively, of the light ICBMs deployed by either Party as of the date of signature of this Treaty, or launchers of such SLBMs; or

(f) ASBMs which have a launch-weight greater or a throw-weight greater than that of the heaviest, in terms of either launch-weight or throw-weight, respectively, of the light ICBMs deployed by either party as of the date of signature of this Treaty.

2. Each Party undertakes not to flight-test from aircraft cruise missiles capable of a range in excess of 600 kilometers which are equipped with multiple independently targetable warheads and not to deploy such cruise missiles on aircraft.

Protocol to the Treaty on the Limitation of Strategic Offensive Arms
June 18, 1979

The United States of America and the Union of Soviet Socialist Republics, hereinafter referred to as the Parties,

Having agreed on limitations on strategic offensive arms in the Treaty,

Have agreed on additional limitations for the period during which this Protocol remains in force, as follows:

Article I

Each Party undertakes not to deploy mobile ICBM launchers or to flight-test ICBMs from such launchers.

Article II

1. Each Party undertakes not to deploy cruise missiles capable of a range in excess of 600 kilometers on sea-based launchers or on land-based launchers.

2. Each Party undertakes not to flight-test cruise missiles capable of a range in excess of 600 kilometers which are equipped with multiple independently targetable warheads from sea-based launchers or from land-based launchers.

3. For the purposes of this Protocol, cruise missiles are unmanned, self-propelled, guided,

weapon-delivery vehicles which sustain flight through the use of aerodynamic lift over most of their flight path and which are flight-tested from or deployed on sea-based or land-based launchers, that is sea-launched cruise missiles and ground-launched cruise missiles, respectively....

Article III

Each Party undertakes not to flight-test or deploy ASBMs.

President Carter Reports to the Congress
on the SALT II Treaty
Address to a Joint Session of Congress
June 18, 1979

...SALT II does not end the arms competition, but it does make that competition safer and more predictable, with clear rules and verifiable limits where otherwise there would be no rules and there would be no limits.

It's in our interest because it slows down--it even reverses--the momentum of the Soviet arms buildup that has been of such great concern to all of us.

Under this new treaty, the Soviet Union will be held to a third fewer strategic missile launchers and bombers by 1985 than they would have--simply by continuing to build at their present rate.

With SALT II, the numbers of warheads on missiles, their throw-weight, and the qualitative development of new missiles will all be limited. The Soviet Union will have to destroy or dismantle some 250 strategic missile systems--systems such as nuclear submarines armed with relatively new missiles, built in the early 1970s, and aircraft will have to be destroyed by the Soviet Union carrying their largest multimegaton bomb. Once dismantled, under the provisions of SALT II, these systems cannot be replaced.

By contrast, no operational U.S. forces

Source: Department of State Bulletin, July 1979, pp. 1-3.

will have to be reduced. For one Soviet missile alone--the SS 18--the SALT II limits will mean that some 6,000 fewer Soviet nuclear warheads can be built and aimed at our country.

SALT II limits severely for the first time the number of warheads that can be mounted on these very large missiles of the Soviet Union, cutting down their actual potential by 6,000.

With or without SALT II, we must modernize and strengthen our own strategic forces, and we are doing so, but SALT II will make this task easier, surer, and less expensive. The agreement constrains none of the reasonable programs we've planned to improve our own defenses. Moreover, it helps us to respond more effectively to our most pressing strategic problem--the prospective vulnerability in the 1980's of our land-based silo missile. The M-X missile, which has been so highly publicized, is permitted under SALT II, yet its verifiable mobile development system will enhance stability as it deprives an attacker of the confidence that a successful first-strike could be launched against the United States ICBMs, or intercontinental ballistic missiles.

Without the SALT II limits, the Soviet Union could build so many warheads that any land-based system, fixed or mobile, could be jeopardized.

With SALT II, we can concentrate more effort on preserving the balance in our own conventional and NATO forces. Without the SALT II treaty, we would be forced to spend extra billions and billions of dollars each year in a dangerous, destabilizing, unnecessary nuclear arms race.

Verification of SALT II

As I have said many times, SALT II is not based on trust. Compliance will be assured by our own nation's means of verification, including extremely sophisticated satellites, powerful electronic systems, and a vast intelligence network. Were the Soviet Union to take the enormous risk of trying to violate this treaty in any way that might affect the strategic balance, there is no doubt that we would discover it in time to respond fully and effectively.

It is the SALT II agreement itself which forbids concealment measures, many of them for the first time, forbids interference with our monitoring, and forbids the encryption or the encoding of crucial missile test information. A violation of this part of the agreement--which we would quickly detect--would be just as serious as a violation of the limits on strategic weapons themselves.

Letter to the Majority Leader of the Senate
Requesting a Delay in Senate Consideration
of the Treaty
January 3, 1980

In light of the Soviet invasion of Afghanistan, I request that you delay consideration of the SALT II Treaty on the Senate floor.

The purpose of this request is not to withdraw the Treaty from consideration, but to defer the debate so that the Congress and I as President can assess Soviet actions and intentions, and devote our primary attention to the legislative and other measures required to respond to this crisis.

As you know, I continue to share your view that the SALT II Treaty is in the national security interest of the United States and the entire world, and that it should be taken up by the Senate as soon as these more urgent issues have been addressed.

[The Honorable Robert Byrd, Majority Leader of the United States Senate, Washington, D.C.]

CRUISE And PERSHING MISSILE DEPLOYMENT In EUROPE
Statement by Secretary Vance
NATO Special Meeting
December 12, 1979

The Atlantic alliance is committed to a reduction of tensions between East and West.

Sources: <u>Weekly Compilation of Presidential Documents</u>, Administration of Jimmy Carter, 1980, p. 12; <u>Department of State Bulletin</u>, February 1980, pp. 15-16.

But our pursuit of detente, including balanced arms control agreements, must rest on a firm foundation of military security. Relaxation of tensions is possible only when each side has confidence in its own strength. Serious negotiations can only proceed when neither side doubts the will and capacities of the other. Steps to consolidate and strengthen NATO's collective defense thus are central not only to a secure deterrence of military threats; they also provide a basis for broader efforts to find a relaxation of tensions.

In a political as well as military sense, defense modernization and the pursuit of detente are twin paths along the road of security. In recent years, the Soviet Union has improved significantly its nuclear forces in Europe. The Soviet deployment of modern MIRVed SS-20s, and the Backfire bomber, threatens to provide the Soviets with nuclear preponderance in the European theater. In response, the alliance has developed parallel programs of modernization and arms control.

In deciding to deploy new long-range nuclear forces in Europe and to support the United States in its pursuit of a serious arms control agreement involving theater nuclear forces, the alliance is giving new meaning and force to its policy of deterrence, defense, and detente. Our deployment decision gives evidence of the continued vitality and cohesiveness of the alliance. This decision has strengthened our spirit as well as our forces, and it has conveyed the clear message that we define detente as a search for mutual and balanced, rather than unilateral, advantage.

In this context, we are prepared to enter into serious negotiations on long-range theater nuclear forces, within the framework of SALT III. Any agreement reached must--like SALT II-- be balanced and adequately verifiable. We will not entertain any notion of a freeze which would confirm a Soviet preponderance in long-range nuclear forces in this theater. But we are prepared to negotiate an equitable agreement on U.S. and Soviet deployments of these systems at reduced levels. This would mean a reduction of the Soviet threat and a reduction in NATO's deployment program.

The modernization decision that we have made here also makes it possible for us to withdraw 1,000 nuclear warheads from Europe. In addition to this reduction, for each of these weapons we deploy, we will withdraw one existing weapon from Europe. Thus, far from increasing NATO's reliance on nuclear weapons, our decisions will result in a significant reduction in the size of NATO's overall nuclear stockpile in Europe.

Our willingness to enter into negotiations on theater nuclear forces in the SALT framework is but one of a comprehensive set of arms control initiatives which the alliance is now developing. Mutual and balanced force reductions and the Conference on Security and Cooperation in Europe are other negotiations which the alliance members are pursuing with equal vigor.

The political effects of the decisions taken here today are considerable. Faced with a real challenge to the security of Western Europe, the alliance has reacted decisively, prudently, and in a way that invites the pursuit of arms control initiatives. I believe that our governments can be proud of this memorable achievement, and that the free peoples of the alliance will show overwhelming support for the decisions made here today.

NATO Communique, December 12, 1979

1. At a Special Meeting of Foreign and Defense Ministers in Brussels on 12 December 1979:

2. Ministers recalled the May 1978 Summit where governments expressed the political resolve to meet the challenges to their security posed by the continuing momentum of the Warsaw Pact military build-up.

3. The Warsaw Pact has over the years developed a large and growing capability in nuclear systems that directly threaten Western Europe and have a strategic significance for the Alliance in Europe. This situation has been especially aggravated over the last few years by

Soviet decisions to implement programs modernizing and expanding their long-range nuclear capability substantially. In particular, they have deployed the SS-20 missile, which offers significant improvements over previous systems in providing greater accuracy, more mobility, and greater range, as well as having multiple warheads, and the Backfire bomber, which has a much better performance than other Soviet aircraft deployed hitherto in a theater role. During this period, while the Soviet Union has been reinforcing its superiority in LRTNF [long-range theater nuclear forces] both quantitatively and qualitatively, Western capabilities have remained static. Indeed these forces are increasing in age and vulnerability and do not include land-based, long-range theater nuclear missile systems.

4. At the same time, the Soviets have also undertaken a modernization and expansion of their shorter-range TNF [theater nuclear forces] and greatly improved the overall quality of their conventional forces. These developments took place against the background of increasing Soviet inter-continental capabilities and achievement of parity in inter-continental capability with the United States....

6. Ministers noted that these recent developments require concrete actions on the part of the Alliance if NATO's strategy of flexible response is to remain credible. After intensive considerations, including the merits of alternative approaches, and after taking note of the positions of certain members, Ministers concluded that the overall interest of the Alliance would best be served by pursuing two parallel and complementary approaches of TNF modernization and arms control.

7. Accordingly Ministers have decided to modernize NATO's LRTNF by the deployment in Europe of U.S. ground-launched systems comprising 108 Pershing II launchers, which would replace existing U.S. Pershing I-A, and 464 GLCM [ground-launched cruise missiles], all with single warheads. All the nations currently

participating in the integrated defense structure will participate in the program: the missiles will be stationed in selected countries, and certain support costs will be met through NATO's existing common funding arrangements. The program will not increase NATO's reliance upon nuclear weapons.

8. Ministers attach great importance to the role of arms control in contributing to a more stable military relationship between East and West and in advancing the process of detente. This is reflected in a broad set of initiatives being examined within the Alliance to further the course of arms control and detente in the 1980's. They regard arms control as an integral part of the Alliance's efforts to assure the undiminished security of its member states and to make the strategic situation between East and West more stable, more predictable, and more manageable at lower levels of armaments on both sides. In this regard they welcome the contribution which the SALT II treaty makes towards achieving these objectives.

President Reagan's Radio Address to the Nation
October 29, 1983

My Fellow Americans:
   ...I'd like to talk about a very important decision that was made Thursday by the Defense Ministers of the North Atlantic Treaty Organization, or NATO, as it's commonly called. This decision has great importance for us and for the NATO alliance as a whole, because it addressess the future size and composition of our shorter-range nuclear forces in Europe.
   As you know, we're negotiating with the Soviets in Geneva on the longer-range missiles. The current imbalance on those systems is over 350 to 1 in their favor. But with regard to the shorter range missiles, the tactical missiles, I think you'll be very pleased with today's news. But first, a little background.

Source: Weekly Compilation of Presidential Documents, Administration of Ronald Reagan, 1983, pp. 1507-1508.

The nuclear forces in Europe are fundamental to our overall strategy of deterrence and to protecting our allies and ourselves. The weapons strengthen NATO and protect the peace because they show that the alliance is committed to sharing the risks and the benefits of mutual defense. Just by being there, these weapons deter others from aggression and, thereby, serve the cause of peace. Unfortunately, we must keep them there until we can convince the Soviets and others that the best thing would be a world in which there is no further need for nuclear weapons at all.

The alliance's goal, as General Rogers, NATO's Supreme Allied Commander for Europe, has so often said, is to maintain no more military forces than are absolutely necessary for deterrence and defense.

In December of 1979, NATO reached a decision to reduce immediately the number of shorter-range nuclear weapons stationed in Europe. In 1980 we carried out that decision by removing 1,000 of these weapons. The same decision also committed the alliance to a further review of the remaining systems of this category, and that brings us to our decision of Thursday.

Drawing on the recommendation put forward by a special, high-level study group, the NATO Defense Ministers decided that in addition to the 1,000 nuclear weapons which we withdrew in 1980, the overall size of the NATO nuclear stockpile could be reduced by an additional 1,400 weapons.

When these 2,400 weapons have been withdrawn, the United States will have reduced its nuclear weapons in Europe by over one-third from 1979 levels, and NATO will have the lowest number of nuclear weapons in 20 years. What this means is that the alliance will have removed at least five nuclear weapons for every new missile warhead we will deploy if the negotiations in Geneva don't lead to an agreement.

This step, taken by the alliance as a whole, stands in stark contrast to the actions of the Soviet Union. The Soviet leaders have so

far refused to negotiate in good faith at the
Geneva talks. Since our 1979 decision to reduce
nuclear forces, the Soviet Union has added over
600 SS-20 warheads to their arsenal.

Coupled with this, they offer threats and
the acceleration of previous plans, which they
now call counter-measures, if NATO carries
through with its deployment plan intended to
restore the balance.

The comparison of Soviet actions with
NATO's reductions and restraint clearly
illustrates once again that the so-called arms
race has only one participant--the Soviet Union.

On Thursday NATO took a dramatic and far-
reaching decision, a decision that puts us a
giant step along the path toward increased
stability in Europe and around the world. As we
reduce our nuclear warheads in Europe and, of
equal importance, take the necessary actions to
maintain the effectiveness of the resulting
force, we will continue in the future what we've
accomplished so well in the past--to deter
Soviet aggression. We seek peace and we seek
security, and the NATO decision serves both.

PRESIDENTIAL DIRECTIVE No. 59
President Carter's Address Before the Annual
Convention of the American Legion in Boston

August 21, 1980

* * * * *

Recently there's been a great deal of
press and public attention paid to a
Presidential Directive that I have issued, known
as PD-59. As a new President charged with great
responsibilities for the defense of this
nation, I decided that our nation must have
flexibility in responding to a possible nuclear
attack--in responding to a possible nuclear
attack. Beginning very early in my term, working
with the Secretaries of State and Defense and
with my own national security advisers, we have
been evolving such an improved capability. It's

Source: Department of State Bulletin, October
1980, p. 9.

been recently revealed to the public in outline form by Secretary of Defense Harold Brown. It's a carefully considered, logical, and evolutionary improvement in our nation's defense capability and will contribute to the prevention of a nuclear conflict.

No potential enemy of the United States should anticipate for one moment a successful use of military power against our vital interest. This decision will make that prohibition and that cautionary message even more clear. In order to insure that no adversary is even tempted, however, we must have a range of responses to potential threats or crises and an integrated plan for their use....

Statement by Secretary of Defense Harold Brown
Before the Senate Foreign Relations Committee
September 16, 1980

* * * * *

The principal objective of our strategic nuclear forces is to deter nuclear war. Deterrence requires stability, and to achieve strategic nuclear stability, three requirements must be met:

First, we must have strategic nuclear forces that can absorb a Soviet first strike and still retaliate with devastating effects.

Second, we must meet our security requirements and maintain an overall strategic balance at the lowest and most stable levels made possible by our own force planning and by arms control agreements.

Third, we must have a doctrine and plans for the use of our forces (if they are needed) that make clear to the Soviets the hard reality that, by any course leading to nuclear war and in any course a nuclear war might take, they could never gain an advantage that would outweigh the unacceptable price they would have to pay.

The United States has never had a doctrine based simply and solely on reflexive, massive

Source: Office of the Secretary of Defense, September 16, 1980 (mimeographed).

attacks on Soviet cities and population. We have always planned both more selectively (options limiting urban-industrial damage) and more comprehensively (a range of military targets). Previous administrations, going back almost two decades, recognized the inadequacy of a strategic doctrine that would give us too narrow a range of options....

The fundamental premises of our countervailing strategy today are a natural evolution of the conceptual foundations built over a generation by men like Robert McNamara and James Schlesinger.

Our countervailing strategy is fully consistent with NATO's flexible response, and it indicates our determination to carry out that alliance strategy....

On July 25, 1980, President Carter signed an implementing directive--Presidential Directive No. 59--codifying our restated doctrine, and giving guidance for further evolution in our planning and systems acquisition.

PD 59 is not a new strategic doctrine; it is not a radical departure from U.S. strategic policy over the past decade or so. It is, more precisely, a refinement, a re-codification of previous statements of our strategic policy....

PD 59 does not assume that we can "win" a limited nuclear war, nor does it intend or pretend to enable us to do so. It does seek both to prevent the Soviets from being able to win such a war and to convince them that they could not. I do not believe that either side could "win" a limited nuclear war; I want to ensure as best we can that the Soviets do not believe so either.

PD 59 does not assume that a nuclear war will necessarily be protracted over a period of many weeks or even months, because we are not at all convinced that it would be, or even could be. PD 59 does take into account Soviet literature which considers such a scenario to be a real possibility....

PD 59 also does not assume that a nuclear exchange could remain limited, and I, for one, have very serious doubts that one could. PD 59 does, however, reconfirm and refine our ability

to be able to respond to a limited Soviet
nuclear strike--should one occur--other than by
a single, massive, all-out retaliation against
Soviet cities, population, and industry.

PD 59 does <u>not</u> substitute primarily
military for primarily civilian targets. It
<u>does</u> increase the number and the variety of
options available to the President in the event
of Soviet attack, at any level....

PD 59 is <u>not</u> a first strike strategy. It
<u>is</u> a strategy of deterrence, which deals with
what we could and (depending on the nature of a
Soviet attack) would do <u>in response to</u> a Soviet
attack....

STRATEGIC ARMS REDUCTION TALKS (START)

President Reagan's Address at Commencement
Exercises

Eureka College in Illinois, May 9, 1982

* * * * *

The main threat to peace posed by nuclear
weapons today is the growing instability of the
nuclear balance. This is due to the
increasingly destructive potential of the
massive Soviet buildup in its ballistic missile
force.

Therefore, our goal is to enhance
deterrence and achieve stability through
significant reductions in the most
destabilizing nuclear systems, ballistic
missiles, and especially the giant
intercontinental ballistic missiles, while
maintaining a nuclear capability sufficient to
deter conflict, to underwrite our national
security, and to meet our commitment to allies
and friends.

For the immediate future, I'm asking my
START--and START really means--we've given up on
SALT--START means "Strategic Arms Reduction
Talks," and that negotiating team to propose to

Source: <u>Public Papers of the Presidents</u>,
Administration of Ronald Reagan, 1982, pp. 584-
585.

their Soviet counterparts a practical, phased reduction plan. The focus of our efforts will be to reduce significantly the most destabilizing systems, the ballistic missiles, the number of warheads they carry, and their overall destructive potential.

At the first phase, or the end of the first phase of START, I expect ballistic missile warheads, the most serious threat we face, to be reduced to equal levels, equal ceilings, at least a third below the current levels. To enhance stability, I would ask that no more than half of those warheads be land-based....

In a second phase, we'll seek to achieve an equal ceiling on other elements of our strategic nuclear forces, including limits on the ballistic missile throw-weight at less than current American levels. In both phases, we shall insist on verification procedures to ensure compliance with the agreement....

The President's News Conference
May 13, 1982

Today the United States and the Soviet Union each have about 7,500 nuclear warheads poised on missiles that can reach their targets in a matter of minutes. In the first phase of negotiations, we want to focus on lessening this imminent threat. We seek to reduce the number of ballistic missile warheads to about 5,000--one-third less than today's levels--limit the number of warheads on land-based missiles to half that number, and cut the total number of all ballistic missiles to an equal level--about one-half that of the current U.S. level.

In the second phase, we'll seek reductions to equal levels of throwweight, a critical indicator of overall destructive potential of missiles. To be acceptable, a new arms agreement with the Soviets must be balanced, equal, and verifiable. And most important, it must increase stability and the prospects of peace.

Source: <u>Public Papers of the Presidents</u>, Adminstration of Ronad Reagan, 1982, p. 618.

THE STRATEGIC DEFENSE INITIATIVE (SDI)
President Reagan's Address to the Nation
on Defense and National Security
March 23, 1983

* * * * *

My predecessors in the Oval Office have appeared before you on other occasions to describe the threat posed by Soviet power and have proposed steps to address that threat. But since the advent of nuclear weapons, those steps have been increasingly directed toward deterrence of aggression through the promise of retaliation.

This approach to stability through offensive threat has worked. We and our allies have succeeded in preventing nuclear war for more than three decades. In recent months, however, my advisers, including in particular the Joint Chiefs of Staff, have underscored the necessity to break out of a future that relies solely on offensive retaliation for our security.

After careful consultation with my advisers, including the Joint Chiefs of Staff, I believe there is a way. Let me share with you a vision of the future which offers hope. It is that we embark on a program to counter the awesome Soviet missile threat with measures that are defensive. Let us turn to the very strengths in technology that spawned our great industrial base and that have given us the quality of life we enjoy today.

What if free people could live secure in the knowledge that their security did not rest upon the threat of instant U.S. retaliation to deter a Soviet attack, that we could intercept and destroy strategic ballistic missiles before they reached our own soil or that of our allies?

I know this is a formidable, technical task, one that may not be accomplished before the end of this century. Yet, current technology

Source: <u>Public Papers of the Presidents</u>, Administration of Ronald Reagan, 1983, pp. 442-443.

has attained a level of sophistication where it's reasonable for us to begin this effort. It will take years, probably decades of effort on many fronts. There will be failures and setbacks, just as there will be successes and breakthroughs. And as we proceed, we must remain constant in preserving the nuclear deterrent and maintaining a solid capability for flexible response. But isn't it worth every investment necessary to free the world from the threat of nuclear war? We know it is....

I clearly recognize that defensive systems have limitations and raise certain problems and ambiguities. If paired with offensive systems, they can be viewed as fostering an aggressive policy, and no one wants that. But with these considerations firmly in mind, I call upon the scientific community in our country, those who gave us nuclear weapons, to turn their great talents now to the cause of mankind and world peace, to give us the means of rendering these nuclear weapons impotent and obsolete.

Tonight, consistent with our obligations of the ABM treaty and recognizing the need for closer consultation with our allies, I'm taking an important first step. I am directing a comprehensive and intensive effort to define a long-term research and development program to begin to achieve our ultimate goal of eliminating the threat posed by strategic nuclear missiles. This could pave the way for arms control measures to eliminate the weapons themselves. We seek neither military superiority nor political advantage. Our only purpose--one all people share--is to search for ways to reduce the danger of nuclear war....

The Strategic Defense Initiative
Special Report, June 1985

* * * * *

Scientific developments and several emerging technologies now do offer the possibility of defenses that did not exist and

Source: Department of State, Special Report No. 129, The Strategic Defense Initiative, June 1985, pp. 2-4.

could hardly have been conceived earlier. The state of the art of defense has now progressed to the point where it is reasonable to investigate whether new technologies can yield options, especially non-nuclear options, which could permit us to turn to defense not only to enhance deterrence but to allow us to move to a more secure and more stable long-term basis for deterrence....

...we must now also take steps to provide future options for ensuring deterrence and stability over the long term, and we must do so in a way that allows us both to negate the destabilizing growth of Soviet offensive forces and to channel longstanding Soviet propensities for defenses toward more stabilizing and mutually beneficial ends. The Strategic Defense Initiative is specifically aimed toward these goals. In the near term, the SDI program also responds directly to the ongoing and extensive Soviet antiballistic missile effort, including the existing Soviet deployments permitted under the ABM Treaty. The SDI research program provides a necessary and powerful deterrent to any near-term Soviet decision to expand rapidly its antiballistic missile capability beyond that contemplated by the ABM Treaty. This, in itself, is a critical task. However, the overriding, long-term importance of SDI is that it offers the possibility of reversing the dangerous military trends cited above by moving to a better, more stable basis for deterrence and by providing new and compelling incentives to the Soviet Union for seriously negotiating reductions in existing offensive nuclear arsenals.

The Soviet Union recognizes the potential of advanced defense concepts--especially those involving boost, postboost, and mid-course defenses--to change the strategic situation. In our investigation of the potential these systems offer, we do not seek superiority or to establish a unilateral advantage. However, if the promise of SDI technologies is proven, the de-stabilizing Soviet advantage can be redressed. And, in the process, deterrence will be strengthened significantly and placed on a foundation made more stable by reducing the role

of ballistic missile weapons and by placing
greater reliance on defenses which threaten no
one.

...the SDI research program is and will be
conducted in full compliance with the ABM
Treaty. If the research yields positive
results, we will consult with our allies about
the potential next steps. We would then consult
and negotiate, as appropriate, with the Soviet
Union, pursuant to the terms of the ABM treaty,
which provide for such consultations, on how
deterrence might be strengthened through the
phased introduction of defensive systems into
the force structures of both sides. This
commitment does not mean that we would give the
Soviets a veto over the outcome anymore than the
Soviets have a veto over our current strategic
and intermediate-range programs. Our commitment
in this regard reflects our recognition that, if
our research yields appropriate results, we
should seek to move forward in a stable way. We
have already begun the process of bilateral
discussion in Geneva needed to lay the
foundation for the stable integration of
advanced defenses into the forces of both sides
at such time as the state of the art and other
considerations make it desirable to do so.

Following are a dozen key points that
capture the direction and scope of the program:

1. The aim of SDI is not to seek
superiority but to maintain the strategic
balance and thereby assure stable deterrence.

2. Research will last for some years. We
intend to adhere strictly to ABM Treaty
limitations and will insist that the Soviets do
so as well.

3. We do not have any preconceived notions
about the defensive options the research may
generate. We will not proceed to development
and deployment unless the research indicates
that defenses meet strict criteria.

4. Within the SDI research program, we
will judge defenses to be desirable only if they
are survivable and cost effective at the margin.

5. It is too early in our research program
to speculate on the kinds of defensive systems--
whether ground-based or space-based and with
what capabilities--that might prove feasible and

desirable to develop and deploy.

6. The purpose of the defensive options we seek is clear--to find a means to destroy attacking ballistic missiles before they can reach any of their potential targets.

7. U.S. and allied security remains indivisible. The SDI program is designed to enhance allied security as well as U.S. security. We will continue to work closely with our allies to ensure that, as our research progresses, allied views are carefully considered.

8. If and when our research criteria are met, and following close consultation with our allies, we intend to consult and negotiate, as appropriate, with the Soviets pursuant to the terms of the ABM Treaty, which provide for such consultations, on how deterrence could be enhanced through a greater reliance by both sides on new defensive systems.

9. It is our intention and our hope that, if new defensive technologies prove feasible, we (in close and continuing consultation with our allies) and the Soviets will jointly manage a transition to a more defense-reliant balance.

10. SDI represents no change in our commitment to deterring war and enhancing stability.

11. For the foreseeable future, offensive nuclear forces and the prospect of nuclear retaliation will remain the key element of deterrence. Therefore, we must maintain modern, flexible, and credible strategic nuclear forces.

12. Our ultimate goal is to eliminate nuclear weapons entirely. By necessity, this is a very long-term goal, which requires, as we pursue our SDI research, equally energetic efforts to diminish the threat posed by conventional arms imbalances, both through conventional force improvements and the negotiation of arms reductions and confidence-building measures.

9

The Reagan Reassertion

INTRODUCTION

The U.S. began a defense buildup in the first part of the 1980s. President Reagan, campaigning on the need to build America's strength, came into office with a popular mandate. This was reinforced by the return of the American hostages held by Iran. Most Americans credited the new administration for this. All of this, combined with a Republican-controlled Senate for the first time in over 30 years, gave President Reagan the political power to push through a far ranging defense policy and large defense budget. Defense spending was aimed at upgrading the quality of military manpower and modernizing the armed forces. This included renewed efforts at counterinsurgency capability. All of these efforts were an attempt to renew U.S. national security credibility and to develop U.S. staying power.

The presumed weakness of the U.S. intelligence establishment that emerged under the previous administration was also strengthened. At the same time, the Reagan Administration showed its willingness to use military force to achieve national security goals. The U.S. intervened in Grenada in 1983, deposing a Marxist-Leninist regime supported by Cuba. Further, it took steps to support the Duarte regime in El Salvador, which was locked in a struggle with the FMLN being supported by the Nicaraguan Sandinista regime. In this respect, problems in Central America became an important national security issue in the early 1980s. The emergence of the Nicaraguan Freedom Fighters combined with the struggle in El Salvador highlighted the Central American issue.

Early during the first Reagan Administration, the President made it clear that the USSR was the major U.S. adversary. His "evil empire" speech set the tone. The focus on the Soviet Union and the defense buildup was part of the strategic direction that differed in many respects from the previous administration. For many Americans, this appeared to be a fresh and welcomed change from the frustrations of the 1970s and the debacle of Vietnam. What made it even more welcome to many was the change in attitudes towards the Vietnam War and the Vietnam veterans signaled by President Reagan's honoring of Vietnam veterans and his view that the U.S. involvement in Vietnam was a noble cause.

The strategic underpinning for the U.S. national security posture continued to be deterrence combined with the Reagan Doctrine. This Doctrine held that the U.S. would support revolutions against established Marxist-Leninist regimes and support established non-Marxist-Leninist systems struggling against Marxist-Leninist revolutions. The focus was primarily on the Third World, with particular attention to Central America.

Part of this strategic underpinning also rested with SDI as an option beyond deterrence. Not only did this trigger controversy in the United States, but it caused considerable problems in the Soviet Union. The Soviets feared that SDI could be converted into an offensive system.

Military reform, which began in the late 1970s, became an important factor in the defense buildup during the Reagan presidency. Military reform movements have periodically emerged in the United States since the end of World War II. The latest movement was sparked by the view that U.S. military effectiveness had been reduced dramatically in the post-Vietnam era. This view was reinforced by the concern over the increasing USSR capability in nuclear weaponry. Composed mainly of civilians, the reform movement focused not only on the quality and effectiveness of U.S. military forces but on military policy. While it is not clear what impact this movement has had on U.S. national security policy, it has had some impact on congressional views. Further, it seems clear that a number of questions have been raised by the military reform debate regarding defense expenditures, U.S. security strategy, and military doctrine. In 1988, the revelations about insider information and bribery associated with defense contractors and consultants reinforced the view about military reform. These remained major issues as the Reagan presidency came to an end.

Major controversies emerged with respect to the Reagan Doctrine. Aid to the Nicaraguan Freedom Fighters (Contras) was an on-again, off-again matter with Congress. In any case, it was hotly debated and opposed in many quarters, particularly by those groups in the U.S. linked with Nicaragua. Indeed, the issue became a matter of congressional restriction with the passage of the Boland Amendment and a variety of Boland revisions regarding U.S. intelligence activities in Central America, with particular attention to Nicaragua. The confusing language of the legislation left many in the dark as to the real purpose and impact of the Boland Amendment. This Amendment took on added importance and controversy with the Iran-Contra affair in 1987.

Intelligence authorization acts and budget amendments also focused on U.S. activities in Central America. In the main, congressional intent appeared to be restriction of official U.S. intelligence involvement in Central America, particularly with respect to Nicaragua.

Responding to the regional problems of Central America, President Reagan appointed a commission to explore U.S. policy options in response to regional needs. The Kissinger Commission designed the Caribbean Basin Initiative, which was an attempt to develop a policy for the long haul, primarily addressing economic and social issues. At the same time, the problems of security were addressed. Congressional reaction was lukewarm and few of the recommended programs were put into place.

The Reagan Doctrine was also aimed at the anti-Marxist revolutionaries in Angola, where Jonas Savimbi and his forces (UNITA) appeared to have brought the Angolan government and its Cuban forces to a standstill. With some U.S. support in the form of ground-to-air weapons, among other things, UNITA was even able to take the offensive on a number of occasions.

Crises developed in other parts of the world. The killing of 240 U.S. Marines in Lebanon who were on a peacekeeping mission did much to increase criticism of U.S. security policy. Combined with the perceived increase in international terrorism and the taking of a number of American hostages by terrorists in Lebanon, the Reagan Administration was under increasing pressure for some sort of response, particularly in light of the "tough" anti-terrorist policy proclaimed by the U.S.

Two incidents revealed that the U.S. was willing to take some military measures against terrorists and states that supported terrorist activity. Terrorists involved in the hijacking of passengers aboard the <u>Achille Lauro</u> were intercepted by U.S. naval aircraft as they attempted to fly to Algeria aboard a civilian airliner. The airliner was forced down in Italian territory and the hijackers apprehended by the Italian government.

In an even more dramatic incident, U.S. warplanes bombed selected targets in Libya in response to the terrorism supported by Libya's Quaddafi. Most Americans supported the U.S. action, although some of America's European allies were critical, particularly since the bombing killed some civilians including Quaddafi's young son.

The covert operations in Central America and elsewhere and the continuing confrontations with Iran set the stage for the Iran-Contra affair in 1987. Congressional hearings followed as a result of revelations regarding U.S. secret dealings with Iranians for release of hostages which, in turn, were thought to have led to money connections between the selling of weapons to Iran and money for the Contras. The real issue seemed to be congressional reassertion into the powers of the Executive. Prior to the congressional hearings, the President appointed a commission led by former Democratic Senator John Tower. The Tower Commission report anticipated most of the issues revealed by congressional hearings.

In any case, these matters came to light in the latter part of the 1980s and are not covered in detail in this volume. The same is true with respect to the new arms control initiatives--the INF Agreement and the results of the Moscow Summit meeting between President Reagan and Secretary General Gorbachev in 1988.

In sum, the first part of the 1980s saw a strengthening of the U.S. security posture and a power projection into Central America and other parts of the world. In sharp contrast to the latter part of the 1970s, this new security posture was based on a highly capable military establishment. The increase in military pay and efforts to increase military benefits, as well as welfare and morale, combined with renewed efforts to create greater esteem for the military, helped in attracting high quality men and women into the military institution. The fading of the Vietnam War also gave the military a new vigor in pursuing its efforts in developing effectiveness against the Soviet Union, particularly through NATO.

The second term of the Reagan Administration brought with it problems in domestic social and economic matters and the Iran-Contra affair, among other things. Further, regional efforts from within Central America seemed to provide alternatives to U.S. support of the Nicaraguan Freedom Fighters. The U.S. flagging of Kuwaiti oil tankers and the commitment of over two dozen U.S. warships to the Persian Gulf brought the U.S. directly into Middle East affairs, with some fearing U.S. involvement in the Iran-Iraq war. Many of the security problems seemed to fade temporarily with the INF Agreement. But all of these matters were for the future. By the middle of the 1980s, the U.S. seemed to have regained its military strength and credibility. Most Americans felt optimistic about U.S. national security capability as President Reagan began his second term.

DOCUMENTS

THE U.S.-USSR CONFRONTATION

President Reagan's Remarks at the Annual Convention of the National Association of Evangelicals

[The "Evil Empire" Speech]
Orlando, Florida, March 8, 1983

* * * * *

During my first press conference as President, in answer to a direct question, I pointed out that, as good Marxist-Leninists, the Soviet leaders have openly and publicly declared that the only morality they recognize is that which will further their cause, which is world revolution. I think I should point out I was only quoting Lenin, their guiding spirit, who said in 1920 that they repudiate all morality that proceeds from supernatural ideas--that's their name for religion--or ideas that are outside class conceptions. Morality is entirely subordinate to the interests of class war. And everything is moral that is necessary for the annihilation of the old, exploiting social order and for uniting the proletariat.

Source: <u>Public Papers of the Presidents</u>, Administration of Ronald Reagan, 1981, pp. 359-364.

...illustrates an historical reluctance to see totalitarian powers for what they are. We saw this phenomenon in the 1930's. We see it too often today.

This doesn't mean we should isolate ourselves and refuse to seek an understanding with them. I intend to do everything I can to persuade them of our peaceful intent, to remind them that it was the West that refused to use its nuclear monopoly in the forties and fifties for territorial gain and which now proposes a 50-percent cut in strategic ballistic missiles and the elimination of an entire class of land-based, intermediate-range nuclear missiles.

At the same time, however, they must be made to understand we will never compromise our principles and standards. We will never give away our freedom. We will never abandon our belief in God. And we will never stop searching for a genuine peace....

...let us pray for the salvation of all of those who live in that totalitarian darkness--pray they will discover the joy of knowing God. But until they do, let us be aware that while they preach the supremacy of the state, declare its omnipotence over individual man, and predict its eventual domination of all peoples on the Earth, they are the focus of evil in the modern world....

...I urge you to speak out against those who would place the United States in a position of military and moral inferiority....I urge you to beware the temptation of pride--the temptation of blithely declaring yourselves above it all and label both sides equally at fault, to ignore the facts of history and the aggressive impulses of an evil empire, to simply call the arms race a giant misunderstanding and thereby remove yourself from the struggle between right and wrong and good and evil....

While America's military strength is important, let me add here that I've always maintained that the struggle now going on for the world will never be decided by bombs or rockets, by armies or military might. The real crisis we face today is a spiritual one; at root, it is a test of moral will and faith....

I believe we shall rise to the challenge.

I believe that communism is another sad, bizarre chapter in human history whose last pages even now are being written. I believe this because the source of our strength in the quest for human freedom is not material, but spiritual. And because it knows no limitation, it must terrify and ultimately triumph over those who would enslave their fellow man.

DEFENSE BUILDUP

Statement on Signing
the Department of Defense Appropriation Act,
1982
December 29, 1981

...This legislation is a significant step in this administration's commitment to enhancing the defense posture of the United States and of maintaining our responsibilities to the nations of the free world. This is just a beginning, and in the years ahead we will need to sustain the effort mandated by the American people and supported by the Congress so that we will succeed in strengthening the nation's defense.

In addition to containing funds for essential strategic programs...the legislation provides funds to support the military and civilian personnel of the Department of Defense....

Finally, I would like to take the opportunity to commend the dedicated men and women of the Armed Forces and to express, on behalf of the American people, the gratitude of us all for the dedication and sacrifice they exhibit in the defense of our Nation.

Annual Report to the Congress, FY 1985
Caspar W. Weinberger, Secretary of Defense

TO THE CONGRESS OF THE UNITED STATES

Sources: Public Papers of the Presidents, Administration of Ronald Reagan, 1981, p. 1204; Report of the Secretary of Defense Caspar W. Weinberger to the Congress, FY 1985 Defense Budget, pp. 3-9.

Three years ago a newly inaugurated
President Ronald Reagan stood at the West Front
of the Capitol and promised that "when action is
required to preserve our national security, we
will act." Recognizing that the preservation of
peace required more than just rhetoric or good
intentions, he committed his Administration to
take the steps necessary to deter aggression and
promote stability and freedom in a complex and
changing world.

For a President taking office in January
1981, this was not a pledge to be given lightly.
By the beginning of this decade, a majority of
Americans were expressing their concern, indeed
their fear, that the world had become a more
dangerous place. They recognized that we faced
a crisis of leadership, as the impression grew
both at home and abroad that the United States
was a superpower on the decline, unable to
protect its citizens or its interests against a
growing threat.

The 1980 election sent a clear signal that
the American people wanted to reverse this
dangerous slide and to restore America's
position in the world. They recognized that we
must regain the strength of our armed forces and
restore the military balance so essential for
preserving deterrence. They recognized that we
must begin again the quest for genuine arms
reductions, not settling for negotiations that
resulted in merely codifying the growth in
nuclear arsenals. We seek agreements that will
reduce armaments of all kinds to lower, equal,
and verifiable levels. Finally, they recognized
that the United States, while it could not and
should not be the world's policeman,
nevertheless needed to reassume a leadership
role recognized by our allies and friends, and
our foes and potential enemies.

The American people entrusted
responsibility for fulfilling this mandate to
Ronald Reagan, and he and his Administration
accepted that responsibility. Today, we have
firm leadership to keep us steady on our course
-- leadership that combines a realistic
understanding of the dangers and complexities of
our world with a firm commitment to do what is
necessary to preserve peace.

In this year's <u>Annual Report to the Congress</u>, we present our defense program for preserving peace in a dangerous world. We also assess this Administration's three-year stewardship of our nation's defenses, and the progress we have made toward fulfilling the mandate entrusted by the American people to Ronald Reagan in 1980.

A Realistic Approach to Peace

"A safer world," President Reagan told the American Legion last August, "will not be realized simply through honorable intentions and good will....No, the pursuit of the fundamental goals our nation seeks in world affairs--peace, human rights, economic progress, national independence, and international stability--requires a dedicated effort to support our friends and defend our interests. Our commitment as peacemaker is focused on those goals."

In making this statement, President Reagan confronted the paradox of peace--that to preserve it, the peacemaker must be prepared to use force and use it successfully. Only if we can convince any potential adversary that the cost of aggression would be far greater than any possible benefit, can we be certain that aggression will be deterred and peace preserved.

We had to begin with a hard look at the challenge facing this nation as it entered a new decade. Our alliances were being subjected to new strains, as expanding Soviet military power required greater defense efforts by all members to restore the military balance. In the Third World, we saw the reach and intensity of conflict fueled by increased Soviet support for terrorism, insurgency, and aggression. Above all, at the beginning of this decade we were confronted by a Soviet Union increasingly capable of upsetting the stability of nuclear deterrence, of projecting power well beyond its borders, and of conducting offensive operations with larger, technologically sophisticated, and increasingly flexible forces.

This renewed sense of realism about the challenges we faced only strengthened our resolve to work for peace. Indeed, by directly

facing the dangers posed by the erosion in the
military balance with the Soviet Union, and by
demonstrating in Grenada and Lebanon that the
United States would not be held hostage to
terrorism, President Reagan's leadership
enhanced deterrence by strengthening the
confidence of our friends and allies and
complicating the calculations of potential
aggressors.

Similarly, a realistic appraisal of Soviet
negotiating behavior--an appraisal that does not
rely on assumptions of Soviet good will--has
improved the prospects for arms reductions. We
recognized that the Soviets would accept
genuine, significant, verifiable arms reductions
only if they became convinced that the
alternative was not Soviet superiority, but an
American determination to maintain the strategic
balance. By demonstrating the capability and the
will to restore that balance, we are offering
the Soviets a strong incentive to join us in
reaching a negotiated "build-down" of the most
dangerous arsenal ever to threaten mankind.

Restoring America's Defenses
In facing up to the realities of a
dangerous world, we also had to confront the
serious deterioration of our own military
posture. Any one of the problems we faced-- low
levels of readiness and sustainability,
difficulty recruiting and retaining qualified
personnel, shortfalls and obsolescence of
military hardware, and higher costs from
inefficient management of defense resources--
would have required immediate attention. This
Administration had little choice but to address
them simultaneously if we were to fulfill
President Reagan's pledge and, indeed, the
American people's mandate to act to preserve our
national security. And so, with the bipartisan
support of the Congress, we started a major
effort to restore the strength of our defenses.

Readiness and Sustainability. By the
beginning of this decade, the readiness of our
forces to meet a crisis and sustain operations
had seriously eroded. In a speech from the Oval
Office last March, President Reagan recalled
from the early days of his Administration that

"I was appalled by what I found: American planes that could not fly and American ships that could not sail for lack of spare parts and trained personnel, and insufficient fuel and ammunition for essential training." Depleted stores of vital military supplies were inadequate for combat operations, encouraging potential aggressors to calculate they could outlast us in a conventional conflict.

We acted immediately to improve the readiness and sustainability of our forces. Today, three years later, 39% of our major military units are categorized as fully or substantially ready for combat. At the same time, our capability to sustain our forces in the field will have increased by almost 50% when the munitions and secondary items procured by the FY 1985 budget are delivered.

Personnel. When this Administration took office, morale in the armed forces was dangerously low, the result of a failure to give our men and women in uniform the compensation, the tools, or the respect they needed and deserved. The quality of new recruits declined, while experienced personnel left the military in droves. Fewer than ten years after its establishment, many were claiming that the All-Volunteer Armed Forces was a failed experiment, and calling for a return to conscription.

Today, people are our biggest success story. Retention and recruiting are up dramatically. The Navy and Air Force attained record high reenlistment rates last year, and all the Services are meeting their recruiting quotas. Moreover 91% of the new recruits are high school graduates, up from 68% in 1980. And these retention and recruiting successes are coming at a time when the economy is improving, a time when skeptics said young Americans would turn their backs on the military.

Conventional Modernization. This Administration also had to confront a major shortfall in weapons and equipment. Much of what we did have, moreover, was aging and increasingly obsolete compared with new Soviet hardware. The 1960s-era tanks, artillery, and armored vehicles in our ground forces were threatened with block obsolescence; the number of ships in our Navy had fallen by more than half; and our aircraft needed upgrading to counter dramatic improvements in Soviet aircraft and air defenses. Although the previous Administration had announced a new commitment to defend our access to resources in Southwest Asia, we lacked the airlift, sealift, and amphibious capabilities to move our forces quickly in time of crisis, or to support them if they became involved in combat.

It would be a heavy responsibility for any President or Secretary of Defense to have to order American troops into battle facing Soviet equipment that was known to be superior to ours. That is a responsibility the previous Administration would have had to face. We had to change that situation. Now, we can be confident that should war break out, our men will have equipment that is at least equal to, and in many cases superior to, that of the Soviets. For that very reason, it is increasingly unlikely we will have to test any of it in combat.

The FY 1982 budget and associated five-year plan of the previous Administration were not only inadequate for the rebuilding task we confronted; they were also gravely underfunded and could not have been carried out as planned. During the past three years, we have restored funding for several vitally needed programs, and are now successfully embarked on a long-term program to modernize our forces for the future.

Our ground forces are now receiving the modern weapons they need to deter quantitatively superior and increasingly sophisticated Soviet forces. The M-1 tank recently proved its tremendous capability in NATO's annual tank competition, performing better than any other U.S. tank in history. The Army's new Bradley fighting vehicle gives the infantry the mobility and firepower to fight alongside the tanks. And giving support and protection to those ground forces is the new multiple-launched rocket system (MLRS), which provides long-range artillery fire.

The Navy fleet now stands at 516 ships, as 23 modern, more capable ships were delivered in

1983. The saga of one of these ships--the battleship <u>New Jersey</u>--since she was recommissioned by President Reagan in December 1982 points out the timeliness of our naval expansion. Having left San Diego last summer on a shakedown cruise to Asia and the South Pacific, the <u>New Jersey</u> was then called back to Central America to support U.S. forces training there. She was next sent to the Eastern Mediterranean, where she remains on station supporting the multinational peacekeeping force. In her first year, the <u>New Jersey</u> put 30,000 miles under her keel.

The Marine Corps, with longer-range 155m howitzers, Ch-53E helicopters and F/A-18 fighter and attack aircraft, will have even greater mobility and greater firepower to accomplish the wide range of missions it must be prepared to undertake. We are also revitalizing our amphibious assault capability with the construction of new amphibious ships and air cushion landing craft.

Over the past ten years, the Soviets have significantly increased both the quantity and quality of their aircraft. To maintain our qualitative edge in airpower, we are now producing advanced versions of the F-15 and F-16 tactical fighters, two of the finest aircraft in the world. We have also begun a large-scale acquisition program that will increase our intertheater airlift capability by 75% by the end of the decade.

<u>Strategic Modernization</u>. Dangerous obsolescence threatened all three legs of our strategic triad in 1980, challenging the stability of deterrence. When President Reagan took office, our <u>newest</u> long-range bomber was 19 years old. Our newest strategic submarine was 15 years old and did not have missiles capable of destroying hardened Soviet targets. Our land-based missiles were increasingly threatened by huge new, accurate Soviet ICBMs, while our own lacked the accuracy and destructive force we needed for continued deterrence.

Our strategic modernization program is now strengthening all three legs of the strategic triad, as well as our strategic command, control, and communications (C^3) systems. Three successful tests of the Peacekeeper missile have now been completed. Our first new strategic bomber in more than thirty years is in production; and TRIDENT II missiles now under development will provide our submarine force the increased payload and improved accuracy needed to assure effective retaliation against hardened targets. Finally, our C^3 systems are being modernized and upgraded.

At President Reagan's behest, we are also embarking on a bold new effort to develop a reliable defense against ballistic missiles. This will require many years, during which we will assess different technological options and secure the means to adopt the best. I believe it is the most significant step we can and will take to preserve peace with freedom and to pass on to our children the legacy of a safer world. It is a program that offers the hope of rendering nuclear missiles impotent. Removing this horror from the future is one of our highest priorities.

Management Reform. Upon taking office, we also discovered that the outdated defense procurement system contained few incentives to reduce costs or improve efficiency and failed to take full advantage of competition. Likewise, as investments in ammunition, spare parts, and new weapons and equipment were canceled, postponed, or stretched out, cost-efficient production became impossible. Many businesses decided to leave defense contracting altogether, further reducing competition and limiting our ability to mobilize resources in an emergency.

This Administration undertook a wide-ranging management reform program that included a thorough and forthright audit program to identify the sources of waste and inefficiency and a comprehensive acquisition improvement program to instill sound business practices in defense procurement. The extensive procurement reforms begun in 1981 are now paying dividends.

We are aggressively combating fraud and inefficiency. In the past fiscal year alone, 657 convictions and $14 million in fines, restitutions, and recoveries resulted from DOD and Justice Department cooperation. Our auditors, likewise, identified $1.6 billion in potential savings associated with greater efficiency.

We have taken firm steps to end the spare parts pricing abuses that we uncovered and reported. These reforms include tightening contracts, challenging high prices, obtaining refunds, continuing audits, and enhancing competition. Besides taking very firm and strict measures against irresponsible contractors and negligent employees, we are also rewarding those employees who come up with ways to save the taxpayers money.

To obtain lower costs and better quality, we are stressing greater competition in defense procurement; and advocates of competition are now working in all buying commands to challenge noncompetitive purchases. Already we are seeing results; for example, competition to supply aircraft spare parts has tripled. To assure continued competition, new contracts include provisions designed to provide the data necessary to seek second sources of supply in purchasing parts.

To maintain control over costs, the Defense Department is enforcing realistic budget estimates in order to halt the past practice of over-optimistic estimates that made a weapon system appear affordable, but left a legacy of cost overruns. The Department is also making the tough decisions necessary to eliminate marginal programs and maintain high-priority programs at stable and efficient rates.

Meeting the Challenges of the Future

In 1984, we will continue our long-term defense program, all the wiser for the lessons we have learned in the past three years, and confident that we are on the right course. But let us have no illusions: the next few years will be as crucial for America's defense program as they will be difficult.

In weighing the investments we must make, we cannot forget that the costs of maintaining a strong defense are easily measured. But the benefits are not. When we spend our savings on a new car, or a new home, we have acquired a tangible good. When we spend tax dollars on food stamps or federal highways, we have

created a tangible result for all to see. But
although we can count our missiles, or our
tanks, or our men in arms, we can never really
measure how much aggression we have deterred, or
how much peace we have preserved. These are
intangibles--until they are lost.

Indeed, it is a paradox of deterrence that
the longer it succeeds, the less necessary it
appears. As time passes, the maintenance of
peace is attributed not to a strong defense, but
to a host of more facile assumptions: some
imagined new-found "peaceful intent" of the
opponent, or the spirit of detente, or growing
economic interdependency.

As the bills that we as a nation put off
too long continue to come due, it will be
tempting to search for excuses to avoid the
reckoning once more. We must not yield to that
temptation. Already the Congress has cut back
on our operations and maintenance budgets,
threatening our improvements in readiness, and
slowed down several programs, increasing the
cost of what all agree we will need--and
courting the dangers inherent in taking too long
to secure an effective deterrent. Already
critics of the defense budget are discovering a
new enthusiasm for weapons that are--
conveniently--still on the drawing boards, even
as they oppose procurement of hardware
available now to strengthen our forces.

Unfortunately, we cannot make up for a
decade of neglect in only three years of higher
defense budgets. Restoring--and then
maintaining--the military balance requires a
determined and sustained effort. If we stop in
midcourse, we will only endanger the progress we
have made in recent years, and invite
speculation by friends and adversaries alike
that the United States can sustain neither its
will nor its leadership.

By the same token, if we are allowed to
continue on the path we have set, we can look
forward to a time, only two fiscal years from
now, when defense increases can begin to slow
dramatically.

The Fiscal Year 1985 Annual Report to the
Congress presents a prudent and responsible
defense budget, and provides a thorough

rationale for that budget. It shows that we
arrived at this budget not by picking a budget
number arbitrarily, but by weighing the threats
and challenges to our interests, by refining
our strategy for meeting those threats, and by
identifying the capabilities we need to fulfill
that strategy. The report also analyzes the
resources available for acquiring those
capabilities, and describes in detail the
specific programs for which we are requesting
funds.
     Most importantly, the report is a document
to help members of Congress in this coming year
as they confront important--and difficult--
budgetary decisions that will shape America's
security through the end of this century. Over
the past three years, the Congress and this
Administration have worked together to rebuild
America's defenses and restore our leadership in
the world. We have made great progress. This
year, let us again work together to preserve our
gains and move closer to our goal of a stronger
and more secure America, which is the best
guarantee of a lasting peace.

                The United States Budget in Brief
                       Fiscal Year 1986
                        * * * * *
                      National Defense

     Defense.--Since 1981, the administration
has made important progress toward ensuring that
our defense capabilities are strong enough to
protect our national interests. The need to
sustain the progress we have already made,
combined with the relentless growth in the
threats to U.S. security, requires continuing
real growth in the resources committed to our
defense capabilities.
     Budget authority of $ 314 billion is
requested for the Department of Defense in 1986,
a 5.9% increase over 1985 in real terms (i.e.,
after adjustment for inflation). The 3-year
budget request is $ 30 billion below the current
services level....

_____

Source: The United States Budget in Brief,
Fiscal Year 1986, pp. 10-11.

Comptroller General Report to the Congress
The Defense Budget: A Look at Budgetary
Resources, Accomplishments, and Problems
April 27, 1983

THE DEFENSE BUDGET: RECENT TRENDS and GOALS
TRENDS in DEFENSE SPENDING

During the 1970s, the United States
focused less attention on peacetime national
security needs than on other domestic policy
issues. Between 1970 and 1979, the real
purchasing power of the defense budget declined
by almost 25 percent. The 1979 defense budget
was $58 billion less, after deducting for
inflation, than it was in 1969. This trend has
reversed in the 1980s as more attention was
focused on defense programs.

After nearly 10 years of decline, the
fiscal year 1980 defense budget proposals led to
real increases in total obligational authority
(TOA) of 2.2 percent. In fiscal years 1981 to
1983, TOA increased in real terms by $65.7
billion, or 36 percent, over 1980. The shift in
TOA during the last two decades for both current
and constant dollars is tracked below.
Noticeable is the contrast between the buildup
in the 1980s and the negative real growth that
persisted throughout most of the 1970s. Also
noticeable is how less inflation in fiscal year
1982 affected growth in TOA; thus, larger real
increases are recorded despite a drop in the
growth of TOA in current dollar terms....

DEFENSE PRIORITIES FOR THE 1980s
The fiscal year 1981 DOD budget emphasized
the need to modernize and strengthen both
conventional and nuclear forces. Attention was
directed to theater nuclear weapons, the Navy's
shipbuilding program, air and sea mobility, and
research and development. The fiscal year 1982
DOD budget proposal did not change these
priorities, but focused more attention on
materiel and personnel readiness problems of

Source: Report to Congress, The Comptroller
General of the United States, GAO/PLRD-83-62,
April 27, 1983, pp. 1-10.

conventional forces and nuclear modernization, and several new strategic programs were proposed.

Amendments to the fiscal years 1981 and 1982 budgets also proposed no radical changes in priorities but basically expanded funding, by adding items already on services' priority lists that could not be funded within the original budget constraints. The additional funds permitted expansion of conventional forces, including new ships and reactivation of three older ones; additional aircraft, helicopters, tanks, wheeled combat vehicles, and air defense systems; increased pay; coverage of cost growth in weapons programs and fuel; increased capability in the Persian Gulf; and additional war reserve stocks.

The fiscal year 1983 DOD budget increased funding for almost every category of defense spending. It expanded operations and maintenance (O&M) funds to improve the readiness of existing capabilities and accelerated procurement and research, development, test, and evaluation (RDT&E) to modernize the existing force structure....

LINKING MILITARY CAPABILITY TO BUDGET RESOURCES

The defense budget goals set for the early 1980s are expressed by DOD in terms of four pillars of military capability, which are defined below.

--Force structure. The number, size, and composition of the units that constitute the defense forces, such as divisions, ships and airwings.

--Readiness. The ability of forces, units, weapon systems, or equipment to deliver the outputs for which they were designed and to deploy and employ without unacceptable delays (includes materiel readiness, manpower, facilities, and other support).

--Sustainability. The ability of our forces to continue fighting in the event of a prolonged conventional war (includes replacement equipment, spare parts, ammunition, fuel and other essential consumables, and the manpower required to maintain combat strength in the course of a campaign).

--<u>Modernization</u>. The technical sophistication of forces, units, weapon systems, and equipment (includes new or improved technology and replacement equipment).

The purpose of increased defense funding is to raise our military capability to a level sufficient to meet national objectives. The Congress has long expressed an interest in the relationship between defense funding and the accomplishment of improved force structure, readiness, sustainability and modernization.

In 1977 the Congress enacted Public Law 95-79 requiring the Department of Defense to submit an annual materiel readiness report describing the effect of its appropriation requests on materiel readiness. We have evaluated this report over the years and improvements have been made.

-DOD recognizes the importance of being able to quantify the additional military capability that accrues from defense resources requested. DOD has also improved coordination with congressional committees, which has resulted in a better understanding of their informational needs. But the Congress continues to lack full visibility of how funding will improve military capability.

THE INTELLIGENCE ESTABLISHMENT
Executive Order 12333
United States Intelligence Activities
December 4, 1981

<u>Goals</u>, <u>Directions</u>, <u>Duties</u> <u>and</u> <u>Responsibilities</u> <u>with</u> <u>Respect</u> <u>to</u> <u>the</u> <u>National</u> <u>Intelligence</u> <u>Effort</u>

1.1 <u>Goals</u>. The United States intelligence effort shall provide the President and the National Security Council with the necessary information on which to base decisions concern-

Source: <u>Federal Register</u>, The President, 46 FR 59941, pp. 59941-59954.

ing the conduct and development of foreign, defense and economic policy, and the protection of United States national interests from foreign security threats. All departments and agencies shall cooperate fully to fulfill this goal....

1.2 The National Security Council.
(a) Purpose. The National Security Council (NSC) was established by the National Security Act of 1947 to advise the President with respect to the integration of domestic, foreign and military policies relating to the national security. The NSC shall act as the highest Executive Branch entity that provides review of, guidance for and direction to the conduct of all national foreign intelligence, counterintelligence, and special activities, and attendant policies and programs.
(b) Committees. The NSC shall establish such committees as may be necessary to carry out its functions and responsibilities under this Order. The NSC, or a committee established by it, shall consider and submit to the President a policy recommendation, including all dissents, on each special activity and shall review proposals for other sensitive intelligence operations. ...

2.2 Purpose. This Order is intended to enhance human and technical collection techniques, especially those undertaken abroad, and the acquisition of significant foreign intelligence, as well as the detection and countering of international terrorist activities and espionage conducted by foreign powers. Set forth below are certain general principles that, in addition to and consistent with applicable laws, are intended to achieve the proper balance between the acquisition of essential information and protection of individual interests. Nothing in this Order shall be construed to apply to or interfere with any authorized civil or criminal law enforcement responsibility of any department or agency....

2.7 Contracting. Agencies within the Intelligence Community are authorized to enter into contracts or arrangements for the provision of goods or services with private companies or institutions in the United States

and need not reveal the sponsorship of such
contracts or arrangements for authorized
intelligence purposes. Contracts or
arrangements with academic institutions may be
undertaken only with the consent of appropriate
officials of the institution....

2.11 Prohibition on Assassination. No person
employed by or acting on behalf of the United
States Government shall engage in, or conspire
to engage in, assassination.

2.12 Indirect Participation. No agency of the
Intelligence Community shall participate in or
request any person to undertake activities
forbidden by this Order.

General Provisions

3.1 Congressional Oversight. The duties and
responsibilities of the Director of Central
Intelligence and the heads of other
departments, agencies, and entities engaged in
intelligence activities to cooperate with the
Congress in the conduct of its responsibilities
for oversight of intelligence activities shall
be as provided in title 50, United States Code,
section 413. The requirements of section 662 of
the Foreign Assistance Act of 1961, as amended
(22 U.S.C. 2422), and section 501 of the
National Security Act of 1947, as amended (50
U.S.C. 413), shall apply to all special
activities as defined in this Order.

3.2 Implementation. The NSC, the Secretary of
Defense, the Attorney General, and the Director
of Central Intelligence shall issue such
appropriate directives and procedures as are
necessary to implement this Order. Heads of
agencies within the Intelligence Community shall
issue appropriate supplementary directives and
procedures consistent with this Order. The
Attorney General shall provide a statement of
reasons for not approving any procedures
established by the head of an agency in the
Intelligence Community other than the FBI. The
National Security Council may establish
procedures in instances where the agency head

and the Attorney General are unable to reach
agreement on other than constitutional or other
legal grounds....
        (e) Intelligence activities means all
activities that agencies within the Intelligence
Community are authorized to conduct pursuant to
this Order.
        (f) Intelligence Community and agencies
within the Intelligence Community refer to the
following agencies or organizations:
(1) The Central Intelligence Agency (CIA);
(2) The National Security Agency (NSA);
(3) The Defense Intelligence Agency (DIA);
(4) The offices within the Department of Defense
for the collection of specialized national
foreign intelligence and reconnaissance
programs;
(5) The Bureau of Intelligence and Research of
the Department of State;
(6) The intelligence elements of the Army, Navy,
Air Force, and Marine Corps, the Federal Bureau
of Investigation (FBI), the Department of the
Treasury, and the Department of Energy; and
(7) The staff elements of the Director of
Central Intelligence.
        (g) The National Foreign Intelligence
Program includes the programs listed below, but
its composition shall be subject to review by
the National Security Council and modification
by the President:

(1) The programs of the CIA;
(2) The Consolidated Cryptologic Program, the
General Defense Intelligence Program, and the
programs of the offices within the Department of
Defense for the collection of specialized
national foreign intelligence through
reconnaissance, except such elements as the
Director of Central Intelligence and the
Secretary of Defense agree should be excluded;
(3) Other programs of agencies within the
Intelligence Community designated jointly by the
Director of Central Intelligence and the head of
the department or by the President as national
foreign intelligence or counterintelligence
activities;
(4) Activities of the staff elements of the
Director of Central Intelligence;

(5) Activities to acquire the intelligence required for the planning and conduct of tactical operations by the United States military forces are not included in the National Foreign Intelligence Program.

(h) _Special_ _activities_ means activities conducted in support of national foreign policy objectives abroad which are planned and executed so that the role of the United States Government is not apparent or acknowledged publicly, and functions in support of such activities, but which are not intended to influence United States political processes, public opinion, policies or media and do not include diplomatic activities or the collection and production of intelligence or related support functions.

Statement by Mr. Richard L. Armitage
Assistant Secretary of Defense for
International Security Affairs

July 16, 1986

* * * * *

In 1981, the SOF [Special Operations Forces] Budget stood at $441 million. For 1987, we have requested $1.6 billion--a very real increase both in terms of dollars and the SOF share of the DOD budget. Readiness is improving, and force structure has expanded with the addition of a special forces group, a ranger battalion, a seal team, and a psychological operations battalion. Both the Seafox and the Dry Deck Shelter have entered service during this period.

We have seen the management of SOF units enhanced by the creation of the 1st Special Operations Command (SOCOM) in the Army, and the 23rd Air Force in the Air Force.

As part of the foundation for this progress, the Joint Special Operations Agency was formed in 1984 to advise the Joint Chiefs

Source: Special Operations Forces Reorganization, Statement Before the Subcommittee on Armed Services, House of Representatives, July 16, 1986, (mimeographed).

of Staff on all SOF matters. Secretary Weinberger has directed that SOF should be the topic for regular and frequent secretary's performance reviews, and both the Army and Air Force have taken steps to enhance headquarters management--the general officers steering committee and SOF panel respectively. We have charted our course in SOF master plans that are now being updated. ...

We are determined that the rest of the SOF Revitalization agenda will be realized.

That agenda includes another Special Forces Group, another seal team, 21 new MC-130 combat talons, 12 new AC-130 Spectre gunships, and 11 newly modified MH-53J Pave Low helicopters. Recognizing that the vast majority of rotary-wing aviation resides in the Army, we are also working to ensure an orderly transfer of the SOF rotary-wing mission from the Air Force to the Army through development of the MH-60X and the MH-47E aircraft....

All of us, in Congress and in the Department of Defense, are motivated by the belief that Special Operations must have an effective command and control system _and_ strong advocacy in the resource arena if they are to succeed. We all agree that too often in the past one or both of these essential ingredients has been lacking.

SOFC will correct the command and control deficiency by ensuring that SOF are maintained in the highest state of readiness and, more importantly, prepared for _joint_ deployment.

Embedded within the command will be eight-to-ten man elements immediately available to the CINCs as augmentation for their special operations commands, and reserve component elements assigned to SOFC will be specifically organized, trained, and equipped to provide the major augmentation needed in wartime.

One key aspect of the chief's proposal is that SOFC would report to the NCA through the Joint Chiefs of Staff in the same manner as the theater unified commands, thus ensuring that all military operations remain properly integrated. ...

...the Commander of SOFC will carry the same weight as the CINCs in the deliberations of the Defense Resources Board. Coupled with my responsibilities in this area, as well as those of the Assistant Secretary of Defense for C^3I [Command, Control, Communications and Intelligence] and the personal commitment of Admiral Crowe, one can start to see the extent to which SOF advocacy has become an institutional reality....

...The services retain responsibility for organizing, training, and equipping the individual elements of SOF and SOF remain integrated into the military command structure through the JCS. A variety of offices in OSD, chief among them ISA and C^3I, bring to the table varied interests and perspectives but a common goal with regard to SOF. In short, the future holds the promise of a united front within DOD that will <u>ensure</u> that special operations are ready to succeed.

Public Law 99-591
October 30, 1986
Making continuing appropriations for the
fiscal year 1987, and for other purposes

<u>Resolved by the Senate and House of Representatives of the United States of America in Congress assembled</u>, That the following sums are hereby appropriated, out of any money in the Treasury not otherwise appropriated, and out of applicable corporate or other revenues, receipts, and funds, for the several departments, agencies, corporations, and other organizational units of the Government for the fiscal year 1987, and for other purposes, namely:...

An Act
Making appropriations for the Department of Defense for the fiscal year ending September 30, 1987, and for other purposes.

* * * * *

SEC. 9115. (a) ASSISTANT SECRETARY of DEFENSE.

Source: <u>United States Statutes at Large</u>, 1986, vol. 100, p. 3341.

"(4) One of the Assistant Secretaries shall be the Assistant Secretary of Defense for Special Operations and Low Intensity Conflict. He shall have as his principal duty the overall supervision (including oversight of policy and resources) of special operations activities (as defined in section 167 (j) of this title) and low intensity conflict activities of the Department of Defense."

(b) Unified Combatant Command.

"S. 167. Unified combatant command for special operations forces
(a)   Establishment.--With   the   advice   and assistance of the Chairman of the Joint Chiefs of Staff, the President, through the Secretary of Defense, shall establish under section 161 of this title a unified combatant command for special operations forces (hereinafter in this section referred to as the 'special operations command'). The principal function of the command is to prepare special operations forces to carry out assigned missions.
"(c) Grade of Commander.--The Commander of the special operations command shall hold the grade of general, or in the case of an officer of the Navy, admiral while serving in that position, without vacating his permanent grade.   The commander of such command shall be appointed to that grade by the President, by and with the advice and consent of the Senate, for service in that position.
"(d)   Command   of   Activity   or   Mission.--(1) Unless otherwise directed by the President or Secretary of Defense, a special operations activity or mission shall be conducted under the command   of   the   commander   of   the   unified combatant command in whose geographic area the activity or mission is to be conducted.
(2)   The   commander   of   the   special operations command shall exercise command of a selected special operations mission if directed to do so by the President or the Secretary of Defense.
"(j) Special Operations Activities.--For purposes of this section, special operations activities include each of the following insofar

as it relates to special operations:

> "(1) Direct action.
> "(2) Strategic reconnaissance.
> "(3) Unconventional warfare.
> "(4) Foreign internal defense.
> "(5) Civil affairs.
> "(6) Psychological operations.
> "(7) Counterterrorism.
> "(8) Humanitarian assistance.
> "(9) Theater search and rescue.
> "(10) Such other activities as may be

specified by the President or the Secretary of Defense."

(c) Major Force Program Category.--The Secretary of Defense shall create for the special operations forces a major force program category for the Five-Year Defense Plan of the Department of Defense. The Assistant Secretary of Defense for Special Operations and Low Intensity Conflict, with the advice and assistance of the commander of the special operations command, shall provide overall supervision of the preparation and justification of program recommendations and budget proposals to be included in such major force program category.
(f) Board for Low Intensity Conflict.--Section 101 of the National Security Act of 1947 (50 U.S.C. 402) is amended by adding at the end the following new subsection:

> "(f) The President shall establish within the National Security Council a board to be known as the 'Board for Low Intensity Conflict.' The principal function of the board shall be to coordinate the policies of the United States for low intensity conflict.

> "(g) Deputy Assistant to the President for National Security Affairs for Low Intensity Conflict.--It is the sense of Congress that the President should designate within the Executive Office of the President a Deputy Assistant to the President for National Security Affairs to be the Deputy Assistant for Low Intensity Conflict...."

GRENADA

President Reagan's Address to the Nation
October 27, 1983

* * * * *

Now, another part of the world is very
much on our minds, a place much closer to our
shores: Grenada. The island is only twice the
size of the District of Columbia, with a total
population of about 110,000 people....

In 1979 trouble came to Grenada. Maurice
Bishop, a protege of Fidel Castro, staged a
military coup and overthrew the government which
had been elected under the constitution left to
the people by the British. He sought the help
of Cuba in building an airport, which he claimed
was for tourist trade, but which looked
suspiciously suitable for military aircraft,
including Soviet-built long-range bombers.

The six sovereign countries and one
remaining colony are joined together in what
they call the Organization of Eastern Caribbean
States. The six became increasingly alarmed as
Bishop built an army greater than all of theirs
combined. Obviously, it was not purely for
defense....

On October 12th, a small group in his
militia seized him [Maurice Bishop] and put him
under arrest. They were, if anything, more
radical and more devoted to Castro's Cuba than
he had been.

Several days later, a crowd of citizens
appeared before Bishop's home, freed him, and
escorted him toward the headquarters of the
military council. They were fired upon. A
number, including some children, were killed,
and Bishop was seized. He and several members
of his cabinet were subsequently executed, and a
24-hour shoot-to-kill curfew was put in effect.
Grenada was without a government, its only
authority exercised by a self-proclaimed band of
military men.

Source: Weekly Compilation of Presidential
Documents, Administration of Ronald Reagan,
1983, pp. 1500-1502.

There were then about 1,000 of our citizens on Grenada, 800 of them students in St. George's University Medical School....

Last weekend I was awakened in the early morning hours and told that six members of the Organization of Eastern Caribbean States, joined by Jamaica and Barbados, had sent an urgent request that we join them in a military operation to restore order and democracy to Grenada. They were proposing this action under the terms of a treaty, a mutual assistance pact that existed among them.

These small, peaceful nations needed our help. Three of them don't have armies at all, and the others have very limited forces. The legitimacy of their request, plus my own concern for our citizens, dictated my decision. I believe our government has a responsibility to go to the aid of its citizens, if their right to life and liberty is threatened. The nightmare of our hostages in Iran must never be repeated.

We had to assume that several hundred Cubans working on the airport could be military reserves. Well, as it turned out, the number was much larger, and they were a military force. Six hundred of them have been taken prisoner, and we have discovered a complete base with weapons and communications equipment, which makes it clear a Cuban occupation of the island had been planned....

The events in Lebanon and Grenada, though oceans apart, are closely related. Not only has Moscow assisted and encouraged the violence in both countries, but it provides direct support through a network of surrogates and terrorists....

REAGAN DOCTRINE
Central America

President Reagan's Interview with Walter Cronkite of CBS News March 3, 1981

Source: <u>Public Papers of the Presidents</u>, Administration of Ronald Reagan, 1981, pp. 191-193.

What we're actually doing is, at the request of a government in one of our neighboring countries, offering some help against the import or the export into the Western Hemisphere of terrorism of disruption. And it isn't just El Salvador. That happens to be the target at the moment. Our problem is this whole hemisphere and keeping this sort of thing out....

I don't think we're planning on having to extricate ourselves from there. But the only thing that I could see that could have brought that about is if the guerrillas had been correct in their assessment and there had been the internal disturbance. Well, then it would be a case of we're there at the behest of the present government. If that government is no longer there, we're not going there without an invitation. We're not forcing ourselves upon them, and you'd simply leave--and there aren't that many people to be extricated....

I certainly don't see any likelihood of us going in with fighting forces. I do see our continued work in the field of diplomacy with neighboring countries that are interested in Central America and South America to bring this violence to a halt and to make sure that we do not just sit passively by and let this hemisphere be invaded by outside forces.

U.S. Assistance to El Salvador
July 1981

* * * * *

Salvadoran guerrillas have received large quantities of arms and other assistance from Cuba and other Communist governments. On January 10, 1981, they launched a general offensive intended to bring down the government. Although it failed, the offensive taxed the poorly trained and ill-equipped Salvadoran Armed Forces....

We believe that Central American countries should be free to solve their internal problems

Source: Department of State Bulletin, July 1981, pp. 56-57.

without intimidation or violence supported by Cuba and other Communist governments. Our policy is to support President Napoleon Duarte's interim government as it implements reforms, moves toward free and open elections, and works to end all forms of terrorism. In addition to diplomatic support, the United States provides economic and military assistance, with economic aid more than 3 1/2 times the amount of military aid...Until the guerrillas' January offensive, the United States had earmarked $5 million for loan guarantees to help finance Salvadoran purchases of nonlethal military equipment, such as trucks, and $440,000 for military education and training. As an immediate response to the offensive, the United States leased six U.S. Army helicopters to El Salvador and made available a small number of U.S. military personnel to help with their delivery and assembly and to train Salvadorans in their use. On January 16, 1981, President Carter agreed to provide defense articles and services valued at $5 million to meet the emergency resupply needs of the Salvadoran forces. Under this authorization, the United States supplied arms and ammunition to the Salvadoran Government for the first time since 1977.

In March 1981 President Reagan authorized another $25 million in security assistance to provide for additional equipment and the assignment of additional training personnel. This increased the level of FY 1981 security assistance from $10.4 million to $35.4 million. The new U.S. assistance will provide four additional transport helicopters (bringing the total number to 10), jeeps, trucks, tents, tools, and first-aid supplies, as well as small arms, grenade-launchers, mortars, and ammunition....

The additional training personnel will consist of:

. A 5-man addition to the operational planning assistance team working with the Salvadoran high command and regional commands on communications, intelligence, and planning;

. Three 5-man army teams working outside the capital, providing small unit training,

particularly in counterinfiltration techniques,
to the Salvadoran Army's newly created quick-
reaction forces (training will be conducted
exclusively inside Salvadoran military
garrisons);
        . A 6-man naval team to instruct
Salvadoran personnel in interdiction at sea and
maintenance of patrol craft and to survey the
need for upgrading the boats and for further
training; and
        . A 14-man helicopter maintenance and
pilot training team....

        The Administration has concluded that
present circumstances do not indicate an
imminent involvement of U.S. personnel in
hostilities.
        Since January the level of hostilities has
declined. Our personnel will be stationed in
San Salvador or in carefully selected regional
military garrisons, and special precautions will
be taken to provide security for them. They
will not go on patrol or combat missions with
Salvadoran forces nor will they otherwise be
placed in situations where combat is likely.
Although U.S. personnel are authorized to carry
sidearms, they may use them only in self-defense
or to protect other Americans. They will not
serve as combat advisers. Instead they will
train Salvadoran personnel who come to the
training centers.

Public Law 97-113
International Security and Development
Cooperation Act of 1981
December 29, 1981

NICARAGUA

        Section 1. This Act may be cited as the
"International Security and Development
Cooperation Act of 1981."
        SEC. 724.(a) In furnishing assistance
under this Act to the Government of Nicaragua,
the President shall take into account the extent

Source: United States Statutes at Large, vol.
95, part one, 1982, pp. 1519-1564.

to which that Government has engaged in
violations of internationally recognized human
rights (including the right to organize and
operate labor unions free from political
oppression, the right to freedom of the press,
and the right to freedom of religion) and shall
encourage the Government of Nicaragua to respect
those rights.

(b) In furnishing assistance under this
Act to the Government of Nicaragua, the
President shall take into account the extent to
which that Government has fulfilled its pledge
of July 1979 to the member states of the
Organization of American States--

(1) to establish full respect for human
rights in Nicaragua in accordance with the
United Nations Universal Declaration of the
Rights and Duties of Man and the Charter on
Human Rights of the Organization of American
States;

(2) to allow the free movement in
Nicaragua of the Inter-American Commission on
Human Rights; and

(3) to establish the framework for free
and democratic elections so that the people of
Nicaragua may elect their representatives to
city councils, to constitutional assembly, and
to Nicaragua's highest-ranking authorities, with
such framework to include, but not be limited
to, the full and complete opportunity for
political activity of the Nicaraguan people.

(c) Assistance to the Government of
Nicaragua under this Act shall be terminated if
the President determines and reports to the
Congress that the Government of Nicaragua
cooperates with or harbors any international
terrorist organization or is aiding, abetting,
or supporting acts of violence or terrorism in
other countries, or that Soviet, Cuban, or other
foreign combat military forces are stationed or
situated within the borders of Nicaragua and the
presence of such forces constitutes a threat to
the national security of the United States or to
any Latin American ally of the United States.

ASSISTANCE to EL SALVADOR

SEC 727. (a) It is the sense of the

Congress that assistance furnished to the
Government of El Salvador, both economic and
military, should be used to encourage--
          (1) full observance of internationally
recognized human rights ...;
          (2) full respect for all other
fundamental human rights, including the right of
freedom of speech, and of the press, the right
to organize and operate free labor unions, and
the right to freedom of religion;
          (3) continued progress in implementing
essential economic and political reforms,
including land reform and support for the
private sector;
          (4) a complete and timely investigation
of the deaths of all United States citizens
killed in El Salvador since October 1979;
          (5) an end to extremist violence and the
establishment of a unified command and control
of all government security forces in this
effort;
          (6) free, fair, and open elections at
the earliest date; and
          (7) increased professional capability of
the Salvadoran Armed Forces in order to
establish a peaceful and secure environment in
which economic development and reform and the
democratic processes can be fully implemented,
thereby permitting a phased withdrawal of United
States military training and advisory personnel
at the earliest possible date.
          (b) It is the sense of the Congress that
the United States economic assistance to El
Salvador should put emphasis on revitalizing the
private sector and supporting the free market
system. The Congress recognizes that the lack
of foreign exchange to buy imported raw
materials and intermediate goods is a major
impediment to the ability of the Salvadoran
economy to provide jobs....
          SEC. 728. (a) (1) The Congress finds that
peaceful and democratic development in Central
America is in the interest of the United States
and of the community of American States
generally, that the recent civil strife in El
Salvador has caused great human suffering and
disruption to the economy of that country, and
that substantial assistance to El Salvador is

necessary to help alleviate that suffering and to promote economic recovery within a peaceful and democratic process. Moreover, the Congress recognizes that the efforts of the Government of El Salvador to achieve these goals are affected by the activities of forces beyond its control.

(2) Taking note of the substantial progress made by the Government of El Salvador in land and banking reforms, the Congress declares it should be the policy of the United States to encourage and support the Government of El Salvador in the implementation of these reforms.

(3) The United States also welcomes the continuing efforts of President Duarte and his supporters in the Government of El Salvador to establish greater control over the activities of members of the armed forces and government security forces. The Congress finds that it is in the interest of the United States to cooperate with the Duarte government in putting an end to violence in El Salvador by extremist elements among both the insurgents and the security forces, and in establishing a unified command and control of all government forces.

(4) The United States supports the holding of free, fair, and open elections in El Salvador at the earliest date. The Congress notes the progress being made by the Duarte government in this area, as evidenced by the appointment of an electoral commission....

(d) The certification required...is a certification by the President to the Speaker of the House of Representatives and to the chairman of the Committee on Foreign Relations of the Senate of a determination that the Government of El Salvador--

(1) is making a concerted and significant effort to comply with internationally recognized human rights;

(2) is achieving substantial control over all elements of its own armed forces, so as to bring to an end the indiscriminate torture and murder of Salvadoran citizens by these forces;

(3) is making continued progress in implementing essential economic and political reforms, including the land reform program;

(4) is committed to the holding of free elections at an early date and to that end has demonstrated its good faith efforts to begin discussions with all major political factions in El Salvador which have declared their willingness to find and implement an equitable political solution to the conflict, with such solution to involve a commitment to--
(A) a renouncement of further military or paramilitary activity; and
(B) the electoral process with internationally recognized observers....
(e) On making the first certification..., the President shall also certify to the Speaker of the House of Representatives and the chairman of the Committee on Foreign Relations of the Senate that he has determined that the Government of El Salvador has made good faith efforts both to investigate the murders of the six United States citizens in El Salvador in December 1980 and January 1981 and to bring to justice those responsible for those murders.

AID to the CONTRAS

Public Law 99-83, to Amend
the Foreign Assistance Act of 1961

August 8, 1985

SEC. 722. NICARAGUA....

(2) The Government of Nicaragua.--The Congress further finds that--
(A) The Government of National Reconstruction of Nicaragua formally accepted the June 23, 1979, resolution as a basis for resolving the Nicaraguan conflict in its "Plan to Achieve Peace" which was submitted to the Organization of American States on July 12, 1979;
(B) The June 23, 1979, resolution and its acceptance by the Government of National Reconstruction was the formal basis for the removal of the Somoza regime and the install-

Source: U.S. Congress, Congressional Record, July 29, 1985, pp. H 6720-H 6723.

ation of the Government of National
Reconstruction;

(C) The Government of National Reconstruction,
now known as the Government of Nicaragua and
controlled by the Frente Sandinista (the FSLN),
has flagrantly violated the provisions of the
June 23, 1979, resolution, the rights of the
Nicaraguan people, and the security of the
nations in the region, in that it--

(i) no longer includes the democratic
members of the Government of National
Reconstruction in the political process;

(ii) is not a government freely elected
under conditions of freedom of the press,
assembly, and organization, and is not
recognized as freely elected by its neighbors,
Costa Rica, Honduras, and El Salvador;

(iii) has taken significant steps
towards establishing a totalitarian Communist
dictatorship, including the formation of FSLN
neighborhood watch committees and the enactment
of laws that violate human rights and grant
undue executive power;

(iv) has committed atrocities against
its citizens as documented in reports by the
Inter-American Commission on Human Rights of the
Organization of American States;

(v) has aligned itself with the Soviet
Union and Soviet allies including the German
Democratic Republic, Bulgaria, Libya, and the
Palestine Liberation Organization;

(vi) has committed and refuses to cease
aggression in the form of armed subversion
against its neighbors in violation of the
Charter of the United Nations, the Charter of
the Organization of American States, the Inter-
American Treaty of Reciprocal Assistance, and
the 1965 United Nations General Assembly
Declaration on Intervention; and

(vii) has built up an army beyond the
needs of immediate self--defense, at the expense
of the needs of the Nicaraguan people and about
which the nations of the region have expressed
deepest concern.

(3) The Nicaraguan Democratic Opposition--The
Congress further finds that--

(A) as a result of these violations, the

Government of Nicaragua has lost the support of virtually all independent sectors of Nicaraguan society who initially supported the removal of the Somoza regime (including democratic political parties of the left, center, and right; the leadership of the Church; free unions; and the business, farmer, and professional sectors) and who still seek democracy, reject the rule of the Frente Sandinista, and seek the free elections promised in 1979;...

(5) Resolution of the Conflict.--The Congress--
    (A) condemns the Government of Nicaragua for violating its solemn commitments to the Nicaraguan people, the United States and the Organization of American States;
    (B) affirms that the Government of Nicaragua will be regarded as having achieved political legitimacy when it fulfills its 1979 commitment to the Organization of American States to implement genuinely democratic elections, under the supervision of the Organization of American States, in which all elements of the Nicaraguan resistance can peacefully participate under conditions recognizad as necessary for free elections by international bodies;...
    (D) supports the Nicaraguan democratic resistance in its efforts to peacefully resolve the Nicaraguan conflict and to achieve the fulfillment of the Government of Nicaragua's solemn commitments to the Nicaraguan people, the United States, and the Organization of American States;...
        (g) Humanitarian assistance for Nicaraguan Democratic Resistance--(1) Effective upon the date of enactment of this Act, there are authorized to be appropriated $27,000,000 for humanitarian assistance to the Nicaraguan democratic resistance. Such assistance shall be provided to such department or agency of the United States as the President shall designate, except the Central Intelligence Agency or the Department of Defense.

(2) The assistance authorized by this subsection is authorized to remain available for obligation until March 31, 1986.

International Security and Development
Cooperation Act of 1985

President's Statement on Signing S. 960 into Law
August 8, 1985

Security assistance is, quite simply, the most effective instrument we have for helping to shape a more secure international environment. And yet since the decades of the fifties and sixties, the resources committed to these programs have shrunk drastically in real terms. I invite the Congress to work with us to see how we might best go abut reinvigorating this important area. We need to strengthen our security assistance partners so as to give them the confidence and the capability to better defend our common interests.

Foreign assistance resources are essential to a successful foreign policy. One of our highest national security priorities in the years ahead must be to reinvigorate our foreign assistance program. At a time of defense reductions, we must pay particular attention to our most compelling international security needs....I believe that this bill sets forth a viable policy framework for Central America, which enjoys strong bipartisan support; it will guide our assistance programs as we seek the goals of peace, democracy, and development in that region of such great importance to the United States....

Equally important, S. 960 authorizes vital humanitarian assistance for the democratic resistance in Nicaragua. This aid is an important element in our overall efforts to assist neighboring countries in their defense against Nicaraguan attack and subversion. Unfortunately, the provision unduly and unnecessarily restricts efficient management and administration of the program. Nevertheless, I will continue to work with the Congress to carry out the program as effectively as possible and take care that the law be faithfully executed.

Source: Weekly Compilation of Presidential Documents, Administration of Ronald Reagan, 1985, pp. 972-973.

Public Law 99-88
Supplemental Appropriations Act
August 15, 1985

<u>Be it enacted by the Senate and House of
Representatives of the United States of America
in Congress assembled</u>, That the following sums
are appropriated, out of any money in the
Treasury not otherwise appropriated, to provide
supplemental appropriations for the fiscal year
ending September 30, 1985, and for other
purposes, namely:

Humanitarian Assistance
for Nicaraguan Democratic Resistance

For an additional amount for humanitarian
assistance provided to such department or agency
of the United States as the President shall
designate, except the Central Intelligence
Agency or the Department of Defense to the
Nicaraguan democratic resistance, $27,000,000 to
remain available for obligation until March 31,
1986. Notwithstanding the Impoundment Control
Act of 1974, one-third of the amount
appropriated by this paragraph shall be
available for obligation upon the enactment of
this Act, an additional one-third shall be
available for obligation upon submission of the
first report required by section 104 of this
chapter, and the remaining one-third shall be
available for obligation upon submission of the
second such report. As used in this paragraph,
the term "humanitarian assistance" means the
provision of food, clothing, medicine, and other
humanitarian assistance, and it does not include
the provision of weapons, weapon systems,
ammunition, or other equipment, vehicles or
material which can be used to inflict serious
bodily harm or death....

Sec. 103. The President is urged--
(1) to vigorously pursue the use of
diplomatic and economic steps to resolve the
conflict in Nicaragua, including negotiations

Source: <u>United States Statutes at Large</u>, vol.
99, 1985, pp. 293, 324-329.

to--

(A) implement the Contadora Document of Objectives of September 9, 1983; and

(B) at the same time, develop trade and economic measures in close consultation and cooperation with other nations which will encourage the Government of Nicaragua to take the necessary steps to resolve the conflict;

(2) to suspend military maneuvers in Honduras and off Nicaragua's coast, and to lift the embargo on trade with Nicaragua, if the Government of Nicaragua agrees to a cease-fire, to open a dialog with the Nicaraguan democratic resistance and to suspend the state of emergency; and

(3) to resume bilateral discussions with the Government of Nicaragua with a view of encouraging--

(A) a church-mediated dialog between the Government of Nicaragua and the Nicaraguan democratic resistance in support of internal reconciliation, as called for by the Contadora Document of Objectives; and

(B) a comprehensive, verifiable agreement among the nations of Central America, based on the Contadora Document of Objectives.

The President's Message to Congress
Assistance for Nicaraguan Democratic Resistance
February 25, 1986

When the Congress approved humanitarian assistance for the Nicaraguan democratic resistance last year, it assured the survival of those fighting for democracy in Nicaragua. However, this assistance has not been sufficient to bring about changes in the policies of the communist Government of Nicaragua that would make possible a peaceful resolution of the conflict in Central America and end Nicaragua's aggression against our allies there....

Negotiations based on the Contadora Document of Objectives of September 9, 1983,

Source: Weekly Compilation of Presidential Documents, Administration of Ronald Reagan, 1986, pp. 266-270.

have failed to produce an agreement, and other
trade and economic measures have failed to
resolve the conflict. At the same time, the
legislation for humanitarian assistance is about
to expire. If no further action is taken, it
is clear that the Nicaraguan communists will
steadily intensify their efforts to crush all
opposition to their tyranny, consolidating their
ability to use Nicaragua, in concert with their
Soviet-bloc patrons, as a base for further
intimidating the democratic nations of Central
America and spreading subversion and terrorism
in our hemisphere....

...Our persistent efforts to achieve a
peaceful solution have failed to resolve the
conflict because Nicaragua has continued to
reject meaningful negotiations. Communist
attempts to circumvent and subvert Contadora,
apparent from the beginning of the negotiating
process, have left a clear trail of lost
opportunities for peaceful reconciliation. In
most recent months, Nicaragua has repeatedly
frustrated negotiations aimed at producing a
final, comprehensive Contadora treaty....

The request transmitted herewith asks your
approval for the transfer of $100,000,000 from
funds already appropriated for the Department of
Defense so that those funds would be available
for assistance to the Nicaraguan democratic
resistance. I am requesting this transfer
authority, in lieu of a supplemental
appropriation, because I regard this request as
a matter of high priority for the national
security of the United States....

Of the $100,000,000, $30,000,000 will be
for a program of humanitarian assistance
administered by the present Nicaraguan
Humanitarian Assistance Office, including
$3,000,000 exclusively for strengthening the
observance and advancement of human rights. This
emphasis on human rights reflects a
determination that human rights must be
respected. As in our support for democracy
elsewhere, human rights training and assistance
can be expected to achieve significant positive
results....

In particular, I am undertaking in this
request:

--That United States policy toward Nicaragua will be based on Nicaragua's responsiveness to our well-known concerns about the Government of Nicaragua's close military and security ties to Cuba and the Soviet Union, its military buildup, its unlawful support for subversion and terrorism, its internal repression and its refusal to negotiate in good faith with its neighbors or its own people;

--That in addition to support for the democratic resistance, the United States will rely on economic, political and diplomatic measures to address these concerns....

Since the beginning of my first administration, there has been no foreign policy issue more directly affecting United States national interests than the conflict in Central America, for this conflict challenges not only our strategic position but the very principles upon which this Nation is founded. We can be justifiably proud of progress in the region to alleviate and ultimately eliminate the causes of that conflict. With strong support from the United States, freedom and democracy, the fundamental pillars of peace, have made dramatic gains. Guatemala, Honduras, and El Salvador have held free and open elections. Costa Rica continues its tradition as a vigorous democratic example. United States economic, political, and military support have strengthened the moderate center in Central America and reversed the tragic polarization on the left and right that threatened to engulf the region in endless violence. As a result, the only president in Central America who wears a military uniform today is Daniel Ortega of Nicaragua. He presides over a repressive regime, armed to the teeth by the Soviets and Cubans, which is the most immediate threat to the progress of its neighbors....

Our experience with the Sandinistas over six and a half years points unmistakably to the need to accompany diplomatic policy with substantial pressure focused on the same objectives. Without power, diplomacy lacks leverage. The Sandinistas will not take meaningful steps toward national reconciliation until they realize that opposition to the consolidation of a Marxist-Leninist regime is too strong to be repressed. Approval of this request will enable the United States to be in a position to provide assistance that permits the resistance to conduct sustained operations in Nicaragua and expand their area of operations. The resistance will be able to incorporate more of the thousands of volunteers waiting to join their forces but who cannot be accepted for lack of supplies. They will be able to establish a stronger presence among a larger segment of the Nicaraguan population, thus increasing the pressure on the Sandinistas to enter into dialogue with all opposition elements, and to negotiate seriously in the Contadora process.

The cause of the United States in Nicaragua, as in the rest of Central America, is the cause of freedom and, ultimately, our own national security.

Public Law 99-591
October 30, 1986

TITLE II

CENTRAL AMERICA

SEC.203....

(e) Notwithstanding any other provision of this title, no member of the United States Armed Forces or employee of any department, agency, or other component of the United States Government may enter Nicaragua to provide military advice, training, or logistical support to paramilitary groups operating inside that country. Nothing in this title shall be construed as authorizing any member or unit of the Armed Forces of the United States to engage in combat against the Government of Nicaragua....

SEC. 206. (a) (1) The Congress hereby approves the provision of assistance for the Nicaraguan democratic resistance in accordance with the provisions of this title.

Source: United States Statutes at Large, vol. 100, 1986, pp. 3341-3343.

(2) There are hereby transferred to the President for the purposes of this section $100,000,000 of unobligated funds from such accounts for which appropriations were made by the Department of Defense Appropriations Act, 1986 (as contained in Public Law 99-190), as the President shall designate....

SEC. 211. (a) Assistance to the Nicaraguan democratic resistance under this title shall be provided in a manner designed to encourage the Government of Nicaragua to respond favorably to the many opportunities available for achieving a negotiated settlement of the conflict in Central America. These opportunities include the following proposals:

(1) Six opposition Nicaraguan political parties on February 7, 1986 called for an immediate cease-fire, an effective general amnesty, abolition of the state of emergency, agreement on a new electoral process and general elections, effective fulfillment of international commitments for democratization, and observance of implementation of these actions and commitments by appropriate international groups and organizations;

(2) President Reagan on February 10, 1986, offered simultaneous talks between the Government of Nicaragua and all elements of the Nicaraguan democratic opposition in Nicaragua and between the Government of Nicaragua and the United States Government;

(3) President Jose Napoleon Duarte of El Salvador on March 5, 1986, offered an additional dialogue between the Government of El Salvador and the insurgents in El Salvador if the Government of Nicaragua would simultaneously engage in a dialogue with all elements of the Nicaraguan democratic opposition; and

(4) The United Nicaraguan Opposition on May 29, 1986, reiterated its support for the six-party proposal described in paragraph (1) as a means to achieve national reconciliation and democratization.

(b)(1) In furtherance of the objectives set forth in subsection (a), and except as provided in subsection (e), assistance to the Nicaraguan democratic resistance under this title shall be limited to the following:

(A) humanitarian assistance (as defined in section 722 (g)(5) of the International Security and Development Cooperation Act of 1985);

(B) logistics advice and assistance;

(C) support for democratic political and diplomatic activities;

(D) training, services, equipment and supplies for radio   c o m m u n i c a t i o n s, collection and utilization of intelligence, logistics, and small-unit skills, tactics and operations; and

(E) equipment and supplies necessary for defense against air attacks....

ANGOLA

Public Law 99-83
International Security and Development
Cooperation Act of 1985

(Repeal of the Clark Amendment)

August 8, 1985

Be it enacted by the Senate and House of Representatives of the United States of America in Congress assembled,

(a) Short Title.--This Act may be cited as the "International Security and Development Cooperation Act of 1985."

SEC. 811. Repeal of Clark Amendment.

Section 118 of the International Security and Development Cooperation Act of 1980 (prohibiting assistance for military or para-military operations in Angola) is repealed.

Source: United States Statutes at Large, vol. 99, 1985, pp. 190 and 264.

Statement by Chester Crocker
Assistant Secretary of State
for African Affairs

February 18, 1986

* * * * *

Our objectives are clear: to restore and advance U.S. influence in the region; to expand our cooperative relations with African states; and to deny to the Soviet Union the opportunity to use its influence to exacerbate already dangerous situations in Angola, South Africa, and the other countries of the area....

It is obvious...that our interest and objectives are decidedly not served by a Namibia which is not free and by an Angola which is the scene of a bloody conflict and foreign intervention. Thus, we have worked hard to bring peace to Angola and independence to Namibia. In recent years we have made progress in pursuit of our goals. Allow me to review with you the path we have followed and where we are today.

In 1981, at the start of this Administration, there was no peace process at all under way in southwestern Africa. The quest for Namibian independence was moribund; South Africa sat seemingly unmovable on its side of the Angolan-Namibian border while some 30,000 Cubans sat across on their side of the same border. UNITA [National Union for the Total Independence of Angola] was fighting an apparently endless civil war. No one was talking to anyone else.

This blocked situation posed real dangers to the region and U.S. interests there. The absence of a viable Western strategy for Namibian decolonization and the presence of a seemingly permanent Soviet-Cuban military in Angola risked heightened polarization and open-ended opportunities for Moscow to exploit African frustration over Namibia and fuel internal and regional tensions. It was essential

Source: Department of State Bulletin, April 1986, pp. 59-61.

we regain the initiative.

It took 2 years to engage Luanda and Pretoria in a real negotiation. It took another year to begin to erode the mutual mistrust and build confidence in an American role. But with the Lusaka accord of February 1984, the South Africans began the process of disengagement from their military positions in Angola in return for restraint by SWAPO [South West Africa People's Organization]. In November of the same year, the Angolans said they were ready to commit themselves to withdraw 20,000 Cuban troops over 3 years, starting with the beginning of implementation of UN Security Council Resolution 435, the internationally agreed independence plan for Namibia....

...by early 1985, we had made real progress in devising and gaining acceptance for a framework for resolving the dual question of Namibian independence and Cuban troop presence in Angola. I would emphasize that this progress in the years 1981-85 helped thwart Soviet goals of advancing its positions in southern Africa. Moscow did not encourage our efforts on Angola and has clearly been placed on the defensive there, in Mozambique, and elsewhere. However, the negotiating process has always moved in fits and starts and has been characterized by mutual suspicion among the parties to the conflict-- South Africa, the MPLA [Popular Movement for the Liberation of Angola], UNITA, and SWAPO--and by continuing efforts, sometimes more intense than others, to pursue the military options. Moscow has fueled distrust and fear among the local parties.

...after we tabled fresh compromise proposals--a synthesis of both South African and Angolan ideas on the timing and sequencing of Cuban troop withdrawal--in March 1985, each of the parties pulled back from taking the tough decisions needed to advance the process....

In recent months we have had several important meetings with both the MPLA and the South African Government in which the negotiating context has been further defined. ...

These negotiations, and the continuing warfare inside Angola and across its borders

into Namibia, represent the backdrop against
which the visit of Dr. Jonas Savimbi of UNITA
occurred.   Dr. Savimbi's visit has generated a
lot of public interest and some debate, much of
it divorced from the political and military
realities of southern Africa....

Some may perceive that the reception
Savimbi received here signals a change in U.S.
policy. It does not. Our strategy recognizes
that the scene on the ground in Angola has
changed, largely owing to Soviet actions, and
that our ability to respond diplomatically and
in other ways has been measurably increased by
the repeal of the Clark amendment, effective
October 1, 1985. However, I want to
categorically state here that the basis and
goals of our policy remain unchanged: we seek a
negotiated solution that will bring
independence to Namibia and withdrawal of Cuban
forces from Angola. Such a solution opens the
way for Angolans to reconcile and achieve
peace....

We do support UNITA; it has sustained a
long and brave fight against Soviet and Cuban
political and military designs. Our reception
of him here was an element of that support. It
sent a strong signal to Luanda and Moscow that
the United States views UNITA as a nationalist
organization with legitimate aspirations of
playing a role in the process of national
reconciliation that must come about if Angola is
eventually to achieve real peace. We intend to
be supportive of UNITA in an effective and
appropriate manner.   As the President said in
his State of the Union message, we want to
support all those fighting for freedom....

Some may perceive that the reception
Savimbi received here signals a change in U.S.
policy. It does not. Our strategy recognizes
that the scene on the ground in Angola has
changed, largely owing to Soviet actions, and
that our ability to respond diplomatically and
in other ways has been measurably increased by
the repeal of the Clark amendment, effective
October 1, 1985. However, I want to
categorically state here that the basis and
goals of our policy remain unchanged: we seek a
negotiated solution that will bring
independence to Namibia and withdrawal of Cuban
forces from Angola. Such a solution opens the
way for Angolans to reconcile and achieve
peace....

While here, Dr. Savimbi stated his view
that there is no possibility for either side in
Angola to gain an outright military victory and
that national reconciliation will have to come
about through a process of negotiation. He
emphasized that UNITA does not wish to destroy
the MPLA. UNITA, he said, seeks rather to
convince the leaders in Luanda of the need to
compromise and reach a political settlement. We
share Dr. Savimbi's belief that there are no
military solutions in Angola. And he affirmed
to us his support for our efforts, which focus

on the linked issues of Resolution 435 and Cuban troop withdrawal, to provide the political context necessary to achieve peace and reconciliation in Angola.

CARIBBEAN BASIN INITIATIVE

The President's Remarks on Central America and El Salvador at the Annual Meeting of The National Association of Manufacturers

March 10, 1983

We've been slow to understand that the defense of the Caribbean and Central America against Marxist-Leninist takeover is vital to our national security in ways we're not accustomed to thinking about.

For the past 3 years, under two Presidents, the United States has been engaged in an effort to stop the advance of communism in Central America by doing what we do best--by supporting democracy. For 3 years, our goal has been to support fundamental change in this region, to replace poverty with development and dictatorship with democracy.

These objectives are not easy to obtain. We're on the right track. Costa Rica continues to set a democratic example, even in the midst of economic crises and Nicaraguan intimidation. Honduras has gone from military rule to a freely elected civilian government. Despite incredible obstacles, the democratic center is holding in El Salvador, implementing land reform and working to replace the politics of death with a life of democracy.

So, the good news is that our new policies have begun to work. Democracy, with free elections, free labor unions, freedom of religion and respect for the integrity of the individual, is the clear choice of the overwhelming majority of Central Americans. In fact, except for Cuba and its followers, no government and no significant sector of the

Source: Public Papers of the Presidents, Administration of Ronald Reagan, 1983, pp. 373 -377.

public anywhere in this hemisphere wants to see the guerrillas seize power in El Salvador.

The bad news is that the struggle for democracy is still far from over. Despite their success in largely eliminating guerrilla political influence in populated areas, and despite some improvements in military armaments and mobility, El Salvador's people remain under strong pressure from armed guerrillas controlled by extremists with Cuban Soviet support....

Bullets are no answer to economic inequities, social tensions, or political disagreements. Democracy is what we want, and what we want is to enable Salvadorans to stop the killing and sabotage so that economic and political reforms can take root. The real solution can only be a political one....

... we must continue to help the people of El Salvador and the rest of Central America and the Caribbean to make economic progress. More than three-quarters of our assistance to this region has been economic. Because of the importance of economic development to that region, I will ask the Congress for $65 million in new moneys and the reprograming of $103 million from already appropriated worldwide funds, for a total of $168 million in increased economic assistance for Central America. And to make sure that this assistance is as productive as possible, I'll continue to work with the Congress for the urgent enactment of the long-term opportunities for trade and free initiative that are contained in the Caribbean Basin Initiative....

Public Law 98-67
Caribbean Basin Economic Recovery Act
August 5, 1983

SEC. 211. Authority to Grant Duty-Free Treatment

The President may aproclaim duty-free treatmenty for all eligible articles from any beneficiary country in accordance with the pro-

---

Source: <u>United States Statutes at Large</u>, vol. 97, pp. 384-386.

visions of this title.

SEC. 212. Beneficiary Country

(a)(1) For purposes of this title--
(A) The term "beneficiary country" means any country listed in subsection (b) with respect to which there is in effect a proclamation by the President designating such country as a beneficiary country for purposes of this title. Before the President designates any country as a beneficiary country for purposes of this title, he shall notify the House of Representatives and the Senate of his intention to make such designation, together with considerations entering into such decision.
(B) The term "entered" means entered, or withdrawn from warehouse for consumption, in the customs territory of the United States.
(C) The term "TSUS" means Tariff Schedules of the United States (19 U.S.C. 1202).
(2) If the President has designated any country as a beneficiary country for purposes of this title, he shall not terminate such designation (either by issuing a proclamation for that purpose or by issuing a proclamation which has the effect of terminating such designation) unless, at least sixty days before such termination, he has notified the House of Representatives and the Senate and has notified such country of his intention to terminate such designation, together with the considerations entering into such decision.
        ... the President shall not designate any country a beneficiary country under this title--

(1) if such country is a Communist country;
(2) if such country--
(A) has nationalized, expropriated or otherwise seized ownership or control of property owned by a United States citizen or by a corporation, partnership, or association which is 50 per centum or more beneficially owned by United States citizens,
(B) has taken steps to repudiate or nullify--

(i) any existing contract or agreement with, or

(ii) any patent, trademark, or other intellectual property of, a United States citizen or a corporation, partnership, or association which is 50 per centum or more beneficially owned by United States citizens, the effect of which is to nationalize, expropriate, or otherwise seize ownership or control of property so owned, or

(C) has imposed or enforced taxes or other exactions, restrictive maintenance or operational conditions, or other measures with respect to property so owned, the effect of which is to nationalize, expropriate, or otherwise seize ownership or control of such property, unless the President determines that--

(i) prompt, adequate, and effective compensation has been or is being made to such citizen, corporation, partnership or association,

(ii) good-faith negotiations to provide prompt, adequate and effective compensation under the applicable provisions of international law are in progress, or such country is otherwise taking steps to discharge its obligations under international law with respect to such citizen, corporation, partnership, or association, or

(iii) a dispute involving such citizen, corporation, partnership, or association, over compensation for such a seizure has been submitted to arbitration under the provisions of the Convention for the Settlement of Investment Disputes, or in another mutually agreed upon forum, and

(3) if such country fails to act in good faith in recognizing as binding or in enforcing arbitral awards in favor of United States citizens or a corporation, partnership or association which is 50 per centum or more beneficially owned by United States citizens, which have been made by arbitrators appointed for each case or by permanent arbitral bodies to which the parties involved have submitted their dispute;

(4) if such country affords preferential

treatment to the products of a developed country, other than the United States, which has, or is likely to have, a significant adverse effect on United States commerce, unless the President has received assurances satisfactory to him that such preferential treatment will be eliminated or that action will be taken to assure that there will be no such significant adverse effect, and he reports those assurances to the Congress;

(5) if a government-owned entity in such country engages in the broadcast of copyrighted material, including films or television material, belonging to United States copyright owners without their express consent;

(6) if such country does not take adequate steps to cooperate with the United States to prevent narcotic drugs and other controlled substances [as listed in the schedules in section 202 of the Comprehensive Drug Abuse Prevention and Control Act of 1970 (21 U.S.C. 812)] produced, processed, or transported in such country from entering the United States unlawfully; and

(7) unless such country is a signatory to a treaty, convention, protocol, or other agreement regarding the extradition of United States citizens.

CRISES

Events in Lebanon (Marine Casualties):
President's Address to the Nation
October 27, 1983

* * * * *

In Lebanon, we have some 1,600 marines, part of a multinational force that's trying to help the people of Lebanon restore order and stability to that troubled land. Our marines are assigned to the south of the city of Beirut, near the only airport operating in Lebanon. Just a mile or so to the north is the Italian contin-

Source: Weekly Compilation of Presidential Documents, Administration of Ronald Reagan, 1983, pp. 1497-1500.

gent and not far from them, the French and a
company of British soldiers.

This past Sunday, at 22 minutes after 6
Beirut time, with dawn just breaking, a truck,
looking like a lot of other vehicles in the
city, approached the airport on a busy, main
road. There was nothing in its appearance to
suggest it was any different from the trucks or
cars that were normally seen on and around the
airport. But this one was different. At the
wheel was a young man on a suicide mission.

The truck carried some 2,000 pounds of
explosives, but there was no way our marine
guards could know this.... The guards opened
fire, but it was too late. The truck smashed
through the doors of the headquarters building
in which our marines were sleeping and instantly
exploded. The four-story concrete building
collapsed in a pile of rubble.

More than 200 of the sleeping men were
killed in that one hideous, insane attack. Many
others suffered injury and are hospitalized here
or in Europe.

This was not the end of the horror. At
almost the same instant, another vehicle on a
suicide and murder mission crashed into the
headquarters of the French peacekeeping force,
an eight-story building, destroying it and
killing more than 50 French soldiers.

Prior to this day of horror, there had
been several tragedies for our men in the
multinational force. Attacks by snipers and
mortar fire had taken their toll....

...Lebanon is a small country, more than
five-and-a-half thousand miles from our shores
on the edge of what we call the Middle East.
But every President who has occupied this office
in recent years has recognized that peace in the
Middle East is of vital concern to our Nation,
and indeed, to our allies in Western Europe and
Japan. We've been concerned because the Middle
East is a powderkeg; four times in the last 30
years, the Arabs and Israelis have gone to war.
And each time, the world has teetered near the
edge of catastrophe.

The area is key to the economic and
political life of the West. Its strategic
importance, its energy resources, the Suez

Canal, and the well-being of the nearly 200 million people living there--all are vital to us and to world peace. If that key should fall into the hands of a power or powers hostile to the free world, there would be a direct threat to the United States and to our allies....

For several years, Lebanon has been torn by internal strife. Once a prosperous, peaceful nation, its government had become ineffective in controling the militias that warred on each other....

Syria, which makes no secret of its claim that Lebanon should be a part of a Greater Syria, was occupying a large part of Lebanon. Today, Syria has become a home for 7,000 Soviet advisers and technicians who man a massive amount of Soviet weaponry, including SS-21 ground-to-ground missiles capable of reaching vital areas of Israel.

A little over a year ago, hoping to build on the Camp David accords, which had led to peace between Israel and Egypt, I proposed a peace plan for the Middle East to end the wars between the Arab States and Israel. It was based on UN resolutions 242 and 338 and called for a fair and just solution to the Palestinian problem, as well as a fair and just settlement of issues between the Arab States and Israel.

Before the necessary negotiations could begin, it was essential to get all foreign forces out of Lebanon and to end the fighting there. So, why are we there? Well the answer is straightforward: to help bring peace to Lebanon and stability to the vital Middle East. To that end, the multinational force was created to help stabilize the situation in Lebanon until a government could be established and a Lebanese sovereignty over its own soil as the foreign forces withdrew. Israel agreed to withdraw as did Syria, but Syria then reneged on its promise. Over 10,000 Palestinians who had been bringing ruin down on Beirut, however, did leave the country.

Lebanon has formed a government under the leadership of President Gemayal, and that government, with our assistance and training, has set up its own army. In only a year's time, that army has been rebuilt. It's a good army, composed of Lebanese of all factions....

In the year that our marines have been there, Lebanon has made important steps toward stability and order. The physical presence of the marines lends support to both the Lebanese Government and its army. It allows the hard work of diplomacy to go forward. Indeed, without the peace-keepers from the U.S., France, Italy, and Britain, the efforts to find a peaceful solution in Lebanon would collapse.

United States Air Strike Against Libya: President's Address to the Nation April 14, 1986

At 7 o'clock this evening eastern time air and naval forces of the United States launched a series of strikes against the headquarters, terrorist facilities, and military assets that support Mu'ammar Qadhafi's subversive activities. The attacks were concentrated and carefully targeted to minimize casualties among the Libyan people, with whom we have no quarrel. ...

On April 5th in West Berlin a terrorist bomb exploded in a nightclub frequented by American servicemen. Sergeant Kenneth Ford and a young Turkish woman were killed and 230 others were wounded, among them some 50 American military personnel. This monstrous brutality is but the latest act in Colonel Qadhafi's reign of terror. The evidence is now conclusive that the terrorist bombing of La Belle discotheque was planned and executed under the direct orders of the Libyan regime....

Colonel Qadhafi is not only an enemy of the United States. His record of subversion and aggression against the neighboring States in Africa is well documented and well-known. He has ordered the murder of fellow Libyans in countless countries. He has sanctioned acts of terror in Africa, Europe and the Middle East, as well as the Western Hemisphere.

Today we have done what we had to do. If

Source: Weekly Compilation of Presidential Documents, Administration of Ronald Reagan, 1986, pp. 491-492.

necessary, we shall do it again. It gives me no pleasure to say that, and I wish it were otherwise....

Sometimes it is said that by imposing sanctions against Colonel Qadhafi or by striking at his terrorist installations we only magnify the man's importance, that the proper way to deal with him is to ignore him. I do not agree. Long before I came into this office, Colonel Qadhafi had engaged in acts of international terror, acts that put him outside the company of civilized men. For years, however, he suffered no economic or political or military sanction; and the atrocities mounted in number, as did the innocent dead and wounded. And for us to ignore by inaction the slaughter of American civilians and American soldiers, whether in nightclubs or airline terminals, is simply not in the American tradition. When our citizens are abused or attacked anywhere in the world on the direct orders of a hostile regime, we will respond so long as I'm in this Oval Office. Self-defense is not only our right, it is our duty. It is the purpose behind the mission undertaken tonight, a mission fully consistent with Article 51 of the United Nations Charter....

I warned that there should be no place on Earth where terrorists can rest and train and practice their deadly skills. I meant it. I said that we would act with others, if possible, and alone if necessary to ensure that terrorists have no sanctuary anywhere. Tonight, we have.

The President's Letter to the Speaker of the
House and the President Pro Tempore
of the Senate, April 16, 1986

Commencing at about 7:00 p.m. (EST) on April 14, air and naval forces of the United States conducted simultaneous bombing strikes on headquarters, terrorist facilities and military installations that support Libyan subversive activities. These strikes were completed by

Source: Weekly Compilation of Presidential Documents, Administration of Ronald Reagan, 1986, pp. 499-500.

approximately 7:30 p.m. (EST).

The United States Air Force element, which launched from bases in the United Kingdom, struck targets at Tripoli Military Air Field, Tarabulus (Aziziyah) Barracks, and Sidi Bilal Terrorist Training Camp. The United States Navy element, which launched from the USS <u>Coral Sea</u> and the USS <u>America</u> struck targets at Benina Military Air Field and Benghazi Military Barracks. One F-111 with its two crew members is missing. These targets were carefully chosen, both for their direct linkage to Libyan support of terrorist activities and for the purpose of minimizing collateral damage and injury to innocent civilians.

These strikes were conducted in the exercise of our right of self-defense under Article 51 of the United Nations Charter

This necessary and appropriate action was a pre-emptive strike, directed against the Libyan terrorist infrastructure and designed to deter acts of terrorism by Libya, such as the Libyan-ordered bombing of a discotheque in West Berlin on April 5. Libya's cowardly and murderous act resulted in the death of two innocent people--an American soldier and a young Turkish woman--and the wounding of 50 United States Armed Forces personnel and 180 other innocent persons. This was the latest in a long series of terrorist attacks against United States installations, diplomats and citizens carried out or attempted with the support and direction of Mu'ammar Qadhafi.

Should Libyan-sponsored terrorist attacks against United States citizens not cease, we will take appropriate measures necessary to protect United States citizens in the exercise of our right of self-defense.

In accordance with my desire that Congress be informed on this matter, and consistent with the War Powers Resolution, I am providing this report on the employment of the United States Armed Forces. These self-defense measures were undertaken pursuant to my authority under the Constitution, including my authority as Commander in Chief of United States Armed Forces.

Terrorism and Hostages:
The Continuing Crises

Public Report of the Vice President's
Task Force on Combatting Terrorism

February 1986

THE NATURE OF TERRORISM

Terrorism is a phenomenon that is easier to describe than define. It is the unlawful use or threat of violence against persons or property to further political or social objectives. It is generally intended to intimidate or coerce a government, individuals or groups to modify their behavior or policies. The terrorist's methods may include hostage-taking, aircraft piracy or sabotage, assassination, threats, hoaxes, indiscriminate bombings or shootings. Yet, most victims of terrorism seldom have a role in either causing or affecting the terrorist's grievances.

Some experts see terrorism as the lower end of the warfare spectrum, a form of low-intensity, unconventional aggression. Others, however, believe that referring to it as war rather than criminal activity lends dignity to terrorists and places their acts in the context of accepted international behavior.

While neither the United States nor the United Nations has adopted official definitions of terrorism, Americans readily recognize the bombing of an embassy, political hostage-taking and most hijackings of an aircraft as terrorist acts. They realize that terrorism needs an audience; that it is propaganda designed to shock and stun them; that it is behavior that is uncivilized and lacks respect for human life. They also believe that terrorism constitutes a growing danger to our system, beliefs and policies worldwide.

TASK FORCE CONCLUSIONS AND RECOMMENDATIONS

Source: Public Report of the Vice President's Task Force on Combatting Terrorism, February 1986, pp. 1-5, 19-27.

Terrorists of the '80s have machine-gunned their way through airports, bombed U.S. Embassies and military facilities, pirated airplanes and ships, and tortured and murdered hostages as if "performing" on a global theater screen. These international criminals have seized not only innocent victims but also the attention of viewers who sit helplessly before televisions around the world.

International terrorism is clearly a growing problem and priority, requiring expanded cooperation with other countries to combat it. Emphasis must be placed on increased intelligence gathering, processing and sharing, improved physical security arrangements, more effective civil aviation and maritime security, and the ratification and enforcement of treaties.

It is equally essential, however, that our defense against terrorism be enhanced domestically. For unless the trend of terrorism around the world is broken, there is great potential for increased attacks in our own backyard.

The Task Force's review of the current national program to combat terrorism found our interagency system and the Lead Agency concept for dealing with incidents to be soundly conceived. However, the system can be substantially enhanced through improved coordination and increased emphasis in such areas as intelligence gathering, communications procedures, law enforcement efforts, response option plans, and personal and physical security.

Terrorism is a bipartisan issue and one that members of Congress have jointly and judiciously addressed in recent years. Significant bills have been passed that markedly expand U.S. jurisdiction over terrorists and close prosecution loopholes.

However, there are stronger legislative proposals that are now before Congress that would further strengthen the nation's ability to combat terrorism both at home and abroad. Many of these proposals merit strong Administration support. It is also essential that the Executive Branch agencies continue to work closely with Congress in reviewing our current programs and recommending other legislative initiatives as appropriate.

Terrorism deeply troubles the American people. They feel angry, victimized, vulnerable and helpless. At the same time, they clearly want the United States Government to have a strong and consistent national antiterrorist policy. While such a policy exists, the Task Force believes that better communication is necessary to educate the public to our policy and to the ramifications of using force during a terrorist attack.

Americans also believe that terrorists take advantage of our free press to achieve their goals. News coverage of terrorism has created a dilemma for media executives: how to keep the people informed without compromising public security. Solving this problem will have to be a joint effort between media and government representatives. The government must improve its communications with the media during a terrorist attack. At the same time, the media must maintain high standards of reporting to ensure that the lives of innocent victims and national security are not jeopardized.

In December 1985, the Task Force on Combatting Terrorism completed its comprehensive examination of terrorism both internationally and domestically. It also finished its review of our nation's policy and programs for combatting terrorism.

The resultant findings emphasized the importance and appropriateness of a no-concessions position when dealing with terrorists. Some of the recommendations must remain classified, but the following unclassified Task Force recommendations are in keeping with that national policy and are intended to strengthen and streamline our current response system.

NATIONAL POLICY AND PROGRAM RECOMMENDATIONS

National Programming Document

Currently a number of agencies and departments within the Executive Branch are responsible for the elements of our national program to combat terrorism. While this is a reasonable and appropriate approach, the various elements should be compiled in a single programming document. Such a comprehensive listing would allow quick identification of agencies responsible for dealing with particular aspects of terrorism and their available resources.

The Task Force believes that such a document is necessary for the most effective coordination of the department and agency activities that comprise our national program. The NSC staff, in conjunction with OMB and the Departments of State and Justice, would maintain this national programming document.

Policy Criteria for Response to Terrorists

Because acts of terrorism vary so much in time, location, jurisdiction and motivation, consistent response is virtually impossible. However, the Interdepartmental Group on Terrorism should prepare, and submit to the NSC for approval, policy criteria for deciding when, if and how to use force....

Criteria for developing response options might include the following:
.Potential for injury to innocent victims
.Adequacy and reliability of intelligence
.Status of forces for preemption, reaction or retaliation
.Ability to identify the target
.Host country and international cooperation or opposition
.Risk and probability of success analysis
.U.S. public attitude and media reaction
.Conformance with national policy and objectives

Establish New National Security Council Position

A full-time NSC position with support staff is necessary to strengthen coordination of our national program. Working closely with the designated Lead Agencies, the position will be responsible for:

. participating in all interagency groups
. maintaining the national programming document
. assisting in coordinating research and development
. facilitating development of response options
. overseeing implementation of the Task Force recommendations

Speak with One Voice

Clear communications by appointed spokespersons and coordination of public statements during a terrorist incident are vital. Interagency working groups should provide specific guidance to all spokespersons on coordinating public statements. Without coordination, inaccurate information may result, intelligence resources may be compromised and political distress can result among friends and allies throughout the world--at a time when international cooperation can save lives.

Designation of spokespersons and response guidelines are especially important given the intense media pressure for comment during terrorist incidents. A misstatement or failure to consider legal issues before commenting to news media could jeopardize a criminal investigation or an eventual prosecution.

Review American Personnel Requirements in High-Threat Areas

Actions already have been taken to strengthen security of U.S. installations and to reduce personnel in dangerous areas. However, to date these efforts have not been fully coordinated among all agencies. The Department of State should direct Ambassadors in all designated high-threat areas to thoroughly review personnel requirements to determine if further personnel reductions are possible at U.S. facilities overseas. This review should include careful consideration of physical vulnerability of embassy-related facilities. The Department of Defense also should conduct a similar review for military commands abroad.

INTERNATIONAL COOPERATION RECOMMENDATIONS

Pursue Additional International Agreements

International cooperation is crucial to long-term deterrence of terrorism. It can be achieved through multilateral and bilateral agreements. While progress in achieving a multilateral agreement has been slow, efforts should continue to reach an agreement to show that many nations are committed to fighting terrorism as an international crime against society.

In the absence of a multilateral agreement, the Department of State should aggressively continue to seek international cooperation through:

. general resolutions or agreements, in the United Nations and in other specialized organizations, concerning civil aviation, maritime affairs and tourism

. enhanced and more widely ratified international conventions on subjects such as hijacking, hostage-taking and protection of diplomats

. less formal agreements that illustrate an international consensus to take effective action against terrorism

Close Extradition Loopholes

The United States itself is sometimes used as a safe haven for terrorists. Present extradition treaties with other countries preclude the turning over of fugitives wanted for "political offenses," an obvious loophole for terrorists. The State Department should seek extradition treaty revisions with countries with democratic and fair judicial systems to ensure that terrorists are extradited to the country with legal jurisdiction.

The process of closing these loopholes has begun with the United Kingdom in the form of proposed revisions to the US/UK Supplementary Treaty. The State Department should vigorously pursue Senate approval of this treaty and continue the revision process with other countries to ensure that terrorists are brought to justice.

Impose Sanctions Against Vienna Convention Violators

It is a fact that certain governments actively support terrorism. These states sometimes use their diplomatic missions as safe havens for terrorists or as caches for their materiel--a direct violation of the Vienna Convention. The State Department should continue working with other governments to prevent and expose violations of the Vienna Convention. A UN General Assembly resolution condemning the protection of terrorists in diplomatic missions could complement U.S. efforts to counter this abuse.

Evaluate and Strengthen Airport and Port Security

Pre-flight screening of passengers and carry-on baggage is a cornerstone of our domestic security program. Since 1972 these procedures have detected over 30,000 firearms and resulted in 13,000 arrests. However, the recent terrorist acts against international aviation and maritime interests indicate a need for continual monitoring and updated security procedures. This is especially true at ports and on board ships where there are no international or federally prescribed security measures.

The interagency Working Group on Maritime Security, chaired by the Department of Transportation, should survey security procedures and the threat potential to vessels, passengers and crew members. It also should review statutory authority. If adequate authority does not exist, recommendations should be made, in consultation with other appropriate agencies for new legislation. In addition, legislation should be pursued to allow for a criminal background investigation of individuals working in restricted areas at airports and terminals. Finally, the Department of State and the Coast Guard should continue to work through the International Maritime Organization to develop internationally agreed measures to protect ships' passengers and crews.

INTELLIGENCE RECOMMENDATIONS

Establish a Consolidated Intelligence Center on Terrorism

Intelligence gathering analysis and dissemination play a pivotal role in combatting terrorism. Currently, while several federal departments and agencies process intelligence within their own facilities, there is no consolidated center that collects and analyzes all-source information from those agencies participating in antiterrorist activities. The addition of such a central facility would improve our capability to understand and anticipate future terrorist threats, support national crisis management and provide a common data-base readily accessible to individual agencies. Potentially, this center could be the focus for developing a cadre of interagency intelligence analysts specializing in the subject of terrorism.

Increased Collection of Human Intelligence

U.S. intelligence gathered by technical means is adequate and pursued appropriately. At the same time, there is clear need for certain information that can only be gained by individuals. An increase in human intelligence gathering is essential to penetrate terrorist groups and their support systems.

Exchange of Intelligence Between Governments

The national intelligence effort relies heavily on collection and liaison arrangements that exist with many friendly governments. Such exchanges with like-minded nations and international law enforcement organizations have been highly useful and should be expanded to support our own intelligence efforts.

LEGISLATIVE RECOMMENDATIONS

Make Murder of U.S. Citizens Outside the Country a Federal Crime

Currently, it is not a crime under U.S. law to murder an American citizen outside our borders--with the exception of diplomats and some government officials. Legal protection of diplomats should be extended to include all U.S. nationals who are victims of international terrorism. The Departments of State and Justice should continue urging Congress to adopt legislation, such as the Terrorist Prosecution Act of 1985, that would accomplish this objective.

Establish the Death Penalty for Hostage Murders

While there is legislation that allows the imposition of the death penalty if a death results from the seizure of an aircraft, there is no specific legislation that would allow for the same penalty for murder of hostages in other situations. The Justice Department should pursue legislation making anyone found guilty of murdering a hostage under any circumstances subject to the death penalty.

Form a Joint Committee on Intelligence

Procedures that the Executive Branch must follow to keep the Select Intelligence Committees informed of intelligence activities need streamlining. Adoption of a Joint Resolution introduced last year by Congressman Hyde would create a Joint Committee on Intelligence. This Resolution would reduce the number of people with access to sensitive information and provide a single secure repository for classified material. The Department of Justice should lead an Administration effort to secure passage of the Hyde proposal.

Establish Additional Incentives for Terrorist Information

The 1984 Act to Combat International Terrorism authorizes payment of up to $500,000 for information in cases of domestic and international terrorism. Many feel this legislation does not go far enough.

The State Department should lead an interdepartmental push with Justice and CIA for legislation to develop a unilateral and/or bilateral program to encourage individuals to provide information about terrorists' identity or location. In addition to monetary rewards, other incentives include immunity from prosecution for previous offenses and U.S. citizenship for the individual and immediate family.

Authorized rewards should be publicized to both foreign and American audiences, and consideration should be given to raising the current $500,000 ceiling to $1 million.

Prohibit Mercenary Training Camps

The International Trafficking in Arms Regulations have been strengthened to require a license to train foreign persons in the use of certain firearms; however, mercenary/survival training camps still operate domestically within the law. Appropriate agencies should closely monitor the extent to which foreign nationals are being trained in the United States in the use of firearms and explosives and seek additional legislation if necessary.

Stop Terrorist Abuse of the Freedom of Information Act

Members of terrorist groups may have used the Freedom of Information Act to identify FBI informants, frustrate FBI investigations and tie up government resources in responding to requests. This would be a clear abuse of the Act that should be investigated by the Department of Justice and, if confirmed, addressed through legislation to close the loophole.

Study the Relationship between Terrorism and the Domestic and International Legal System

International and domestic legal systems are adequate to deal with conventional war and crime. However, on occasion, questions of jurisdiction and authority arise when it comes to terrorism. For example, there are ambiguities concerning the circumstances under which military force is appropriate in dealing with terrorism. This lack of clarity about the international law enforcement relationships and legal systems could limit governments' power to act quickly and forcefully. The Departments of State and Justice should encourage private and academic study to determine how international law might be used to hasten--rather than hamper--efforts to respond to an act of terrorism.

Determine If Certain Private Sector Activities Are Illegal

In some cases individuals and companies have paid ransoms to terrorists for the return of kidnapped employees or stolen property. Such action is in direct conflict with the national policy against making concessions or paying ransoms to terrorists. The Department of Justice should consider whether legislation could be enacted and enforced to make such payments to terrorist organizations illegal.

COMMUNICATIONS RECOMMENDATIONS

Expand Our Current Support Program for Hostage Families

Due to the intense pressure of a hostage situation, some family members of hostages have pressured the highest levels of government for information. While this is understandable, such activity has the potential to delay return of hostages by giving terrorists the media attention they seek or the belief that their demands are being considered. Further, the inadvertent disclosure of sensitive information could jeopardize efforts to gain the release of hostages.

The family liaison program, conducted by State's Bureau of Consular Affairs, should provide a broader outreach program to include

visits, hot-lines, information on private
counseling services and a personal contact for
each family for communication even when there is
nothing new to report. Such an expanded contact
program will help the families understand that
the hostages' interests are being given the
highest priority by our government.

Launch a Public Education Effort

Because of the lack of understanding and
currently available information concerning our
national program for combatting terrorism, a
broad education effort should be undertaken to
inform the American public about our policy and
proposals as well as the many ramifications of
the use of force against terrorism, including
death of innocent people, destruction of
property, alienation of allies and possible
terrorist reprisals. The education effort would
take the form of publications, such as this
report, seminars and speaking opportunities by
government officials.

Working with the Media

Terrorists deliberately manufacture
sensations to capture maximum media attention--a
ploy that often takes advantage of U.S. press
freedom. This activity can be offset by close
communication between media and government. The
U.S. Government should provide the media with
timely information during a terrorist crisis.
The media, in turn, should ensure that their
reporting meets the highest professional and
ethical standards.
Regular meetings between media and
government officials on the coverage of
terrorism could contribute to more effective
government-media relations.

10

Congressional Constraints on the Executive

INTRODUCTION

Since the end of the Vietnam War, Congress has attempted to reassert itself into the national security and foreign policy process in a way virtually unknown in previous decades. In part, this was a reaction to what some called the "imperial presidency." Also in part, this was a reaction to U.S. involvement in a variety of power projections and the use of the military instrument. Historically, however, political partisanship usually stopped at the "water's edge." Further, deference to the Executive was usually the case in national security and foreign policy matters.

The U.S. withdrawal from Vietnam and the subsequent defeat and conquest of South Vietnam precipitated a change in the relationship between Congress and the President, particularly in terms of national security policy. By the end of the 1970s, some were convinced that Congress had gone too far and was itself becoming "imperial." Indeed, there were countless charges that Congress contained 535 secretaries of state.

One of the major constraints placed on the Executive in reaction to Vietnam is the War Powers Resolution of 1973. Although it was vetoed by President Nixon, Congress was successful in overriding the veto. President Nixon based his veto on the view that such an Act is a clear encroachment on the constitutional powers of the President.

For over a decade following the enactment of the War Powers Resolution, Congress continued to inject itself into areas that had previously been almost the

exclusive preserve of the Executive. Defense budgetary
matters and various legislative acts became the means to
constrain presidential flexibility in national security
affairs.

The 1974 Hughes-Ryan Amendment to the Foreign
Assistance Act of 1947 prohibited the expenditure of
money by the Central Intelligence Agency for any
operation other than the collection of intelligence,
unless the President specifically stated that the
operation was important to U.S. national security. In
such a case, the President had to report the details of
such an operation in a timely fashion to the Congress;
Senate Foreign Relations and the House Foreign Affairs
Committees. These provisions for U.S. covert operations
created problems for U.S. intelligence agencies in the
1980s and were part of the issues raised in the Iran-
Contra hearings in 1987.

During the mid-1970s, much criticism was directed
at the activities of the CIA leading to demands for major
changes in oversight procedures and control of
intelligence activities. The Church Committee was
particularly critical in its assessment of CIA
activities. The recommendations of that committee led to
the creation of the Senate Select Committee on
Intelligence and later of the House Permanent Select
Committee on Intelligence. The purpose of these
committees is to provide Congress a stringent oversight
of intelligence activities.

It was during the same period that the Clark
Amendment was enacted (1976) as part of the Foreign
Assistance Act of 1961. It prohibited U.S. support of any
operations, including paramilitary, against the Marxist-
Leninist Angolan regime without specific approval by
Congress. This was enacted even after the massive Soviet
intervention in Angola, acknowledged in the Clark
Amendment. This was repealed in 1985.

Some of the most important acts affecting the U.S.
intelligence system were embodied in the Intelligence
Authorization Acts and congressional appropriations. The
Intelligence Oversight Act of 1980, for example, was
passed as part of the Intelligence Authorization Act for
Fiscal Year 1981, establishing procedures and obligations
on "the Director of Central Intelligence and the heads
of all departments, agencies, and other entities of the
United States involved in intelligence activities" to
keep the House and Senate Select committees fully and
currently informed of all intelligence activities...
including any significant anticipated intelligence

activity."[1] This did not mean needing congressional approval, but simply having to inform Congress.

The Iran-Contra hearings revealed the impact of the Boland Amendment and its various interpretations. While attempting to constrain and control intelligence activities, the Boland Amendment was ambiguous with respect to the role of the National Security Council and its staff. For some, the Boland Amendment was simply another attempt by Congress to infringe upon presidential authority.

In 1984 Congress used its power in budgetary issues to prohibit expenditures of appropriated funds for supporting directly or indirectly military or paramilitary operations in Nicaragua. To strengthen its position, Congress passed a "sense of the Congress" that U.S. armed forces should not be introduced into or over Nicaragua for combat.

Regardless of these various provisions, throughout the first part of the 1980s, Congress appeared to vacillate between assisting the Nicaraguan freedom fighters and denying them aid. At the same time, a number of Congressmen and-women appeared to stand firmly on the side of the Sandinista regime in Nicaragua. In any case, during the first term of the Reagan Presidency, there was a reassertion of Presidential prerogatives in the area of intelligence and national security, including covert operations and counterinsurgency efforts. While some of this was a reaction to perceived "hobbling" of the U.S. intelligence effort and the erosion of U.S. military effectiveness, much of it had to do with President Reagan's own ability to convince the American people of the need for a strong defense and for the reassertion of American power in the external environment.

Finally, the extent of attempted congressional constraints on the executive is reflected in the amount of legislation enacted. A compilation of legislation revealed that in 1964 there were about 650 pages of laws on foreign relations. By early 1980, there were three volumes, with each running about 1,000 pages.

Note

1. Standing Committee on Law and National Security, American Bar Association, Oversight and Accountability of the U.S. Intelligence Agencies: An Evaluation, 1985, pp. 11-12.

DOCUMENTS

WAR POWERS RESOLUTION
Public Law 93-148, Veto Override
November 7, 1973
Concerning the war powers of Congress and the
President.
<u>Resolved by the Senate and House of
Representatives of the United States of America
in Congress assembled</u>,

Short Title

SECTION 1.   This joint resolution may be
cited as the "War Powers Resolution."

Purpose and Policy

SEC. 2. (a) It is the purpose of this
joint resolution to   fulfill the intent of the
framers of the Constitution of the United States
and insure that the collective judgment of both
the Congress and the President will apply to the
introduction of United States Armed Forces into
hostilities, or into situations where imminent
involvement in hostilities is clearly indicated
by the circumstances, and to the continued use
of such forces in hostilities or in such
situations.
(b) Under article I, section 8, of the
Constitution, it is specifically provided that
the Congress shall have the power to make all
laws necessary and proper for carrying into
execution, not only its own powers but also all
other powers vested by the Constitution in the
Government of the United States, or in any
department or officer thereof.
(c) The constitutional powers of the
President as Commander-in-Chief to introduce
United States Armed Forces into hostilities, or
into situations where imminent involvement in
hostilities is clearly indicated by the
circumstances, are exercised only pursuant to
(1) a declaration of war, (2) specific statutory
authorization, or (3) a national emergency

Source: <u>United States Statutes at Large</u>, 1973,
vol. 87, pp. 555-560.

created by attack upon the United States, its territories or possessions, or its armed forces.

Consultation

SEC. 3. The President in every possible instance shall consult with Congress before introducing United States Armed Forces into hostilities or into situations where imminent involvement in hostilities is clearly indicated by the circumstances, and after every such introduction shall consult regularly with the Congress until United States Armed Forces are no longer engaged in hostilities or have been removed from such situations.

Reporting

SEC. 4. (a) In the absence of a declaration of war, in any case in which United States Armed Forces are introduced--

(1) into hostilities or into situations where imminent involvement in hostilities is clearly indicated by the circumstances;

(2) into the territory, airspace or waters of a foreign nation, while equipped for combat, except for deployments which relate solely to supply, replacement, repair, or training of such forces; or

(3) in numbers which substantially enlarge United States Armed Forces equipped for combat already located in a foreign nation;

the President shall submit within 48 hours to the Speaker of the House of Representatives and to the President pro tempore of the Senate a report, in writing, setting forth--

(A) the circumstances necessitating the introduction of United States Armed Forces;

(B) the constitutional and legislative authority under which such introduction took place; and

(C) the estimated scope and duration of the hostilities or involvement.

(b) the President shall provide such other information as the Congress may request in the fulfillment of its constitutional responsibilities with respect to committing the Nation to war and to the use of United States Armed Forces abroad.

(c) Whenever United States Armed Forces are introduced into hostilities or into any situation described in subsection (a) of this section, the President shall, so long as such armed forces continue to be engaged in such hostilities or situation, report to the Congress periodically on the status of such hostilities or situation as well as on the scope and duration of such hostilities or situation, but in no event shall he report to the Congress less often than once every six months.

Congressional Action

SEC. 5. (a) Each report submitted pursuant to section 4 (a) (1) shall be transmitted to the Speaker of the House of Representatives and to the President pro tempore of the Senate on the same calendar day. Each report so transmitted shall be referred to the Committee on Foreign Affairs of the House of Representatives and to the Committee on Foreign Relations of the Senate for appropriate action. If, when the report is transmitted, the Congress has adjourned sine die or has adjourned for any period in excess of three calendar days, the Speaker of the House of Representatives and the President pro tempore of the Senate, if they deem it advisable (or if petitioned by at least 30 percent of the membership of their respective Houses) shall jointly request the President to convene Congress in order that it may consider the report and take appropriate action pursuant to this section.

(b) Within sixty calendar days after a report is submitted or is required to be submitted pursuant to section 4(a)(1) whichever is earlier, the President shall terminate any use of United States Armed Forces with respect to which such report was submitted (or required to be submitted), unless the Congress (1) has declared war or has enacted a specific authorization for such use of United States Armed Forces, (2) has extended by law such sixty-day period, or (3) is physically unable to meet as a result of an armed attack upon the United States. Such sixty-day period shall be extended for not more than an additional thirty days if the President determines and certifies to the Congress in writing that unavoidable military necessity respecting the safety of United States Armed Forces requires the continued use of such armed forces in the course of bringing about a prompt removal of such forces.

(c) Notwithstanding subsection (b), at any time that United States Armed Forces are engaged in hostilities outside the territory of the United States, its possessions and territories without a declaration of war or specific statutory authorization, such forces shall be removed by the President if the Congress so directs by concurrent resolution....

Interpretation of Joint Resolution

SEC. 8. ... (c) For purposes of this joint resolution, the term "introduction of United States Armed Forces" includes the assignment of members of such armed forces to command, coordinate, participate in the movement of, or accompany the regular or irregular military forces of any foreign country or government when such military forces are engaged, or there exists an imminent threat that such forces will become engaged, in hostilities,

(d) Nothing in this joint resolution--

(1) is intended to alter the constitutional authority of the Congress or of the President, or the provisions of existing treaties; or

(2) shall be construed as granting any authority to the President with respect to the introduction of United States Armed Forces into hostilities or into situations wherein involvement in hostilities is clearly indicated by the circumstances which authority he would not have had in the absence of this joint resolution.

Veto of the War Powers Resolution
October 24, 1973

To the House of Representatives:

I hereby return without my approval House
Joint Resolution 542--the War Powers Resolution.
While I am in accord with the desire of the
Congress to assert its proper role in the
conduct of our foreign affairs, the restrictions
which this resolution would impose upon the
authority of the President are both
unconstitutional and dangerous to the best
interests of our Nation.

The proper roles of the Congress and the
Executive in the conduct of foreign affairs have
been debated since the founding of our country.
Only recently, however, has there been a serious
challenge to the wisdom of the Founding Fathers
in choosing not to draw a precise and detailed
line of demarcation between the foreign policy
powers of the two branches.

The Founding Fathers understood the
impossibility of foreseeing every contingency
that might arise in this complex area. They
acknowledged the need for flexibility in
responding to changing circumstances. They
recognized that foreign policy decisions must be
made through close cooperation between the two
branches and not through rigidly codified
procedures.

CLEARLY UNCONSTITUTIONAL

House Joint Resolution 542 would attempt
to take away, by a mere legislative act,
authorities which the President has properly
exercised under the Constitution for almost 200
years. One of its provisions would
automatically cut off certain authorities after
sixty days unless the Congress extended them.
Another would allow the Congress to eliminate
certain authorities merely by the passage of a
concurrent resolution--an action which does not
normally have the force of law, since it denies

Source: <u>Public Papers of the Presidents</u>, Richard
Nixon, 1973, pp. 893-895.

the President his constitutional role in approving legislation.

I believe that both these provisions are unconstitutional. The only way in which the constitutional powers of a branch of the Government can be altered is by amending the Constitution--and any attempt to make such alterations by legislation alone is clearly without force.

UNDERMINING OUR FOREIGN POLICY

While I firmly believe that a veto of House Joint Resolution 542 is warranted solely on constitutional grounds, I am also deeply disturbed by the practical consequences of this resolution. For it would seriously undermine this Nation's ability to act decisively and convincingly in times of international crisis. As a result, the confidence of our allies in our ability to assist them could be diminished and the respect of our adversaries for our deterrent posture could decline. A permanent and substantial element of unpredictability would be injected into the world's assessment of American behavior, further increasing the likelihood of miscalculation and war.

If this resolution had been in operation, America's effective response to a variety of challenges in recent years would have been vastly complicated or even made impossible. We may well have been unable to respond in the way we did during the Berlin crisis of 1961, the Cuban missile crisis of 1962, the Congo rescue operation in 1964, and the Jordanian crisis of 1970--to mention just a few examples. In addition, our recent actions to bring about a peaceful settlement of the hostilities in the Middle East would have been seriously impaired if this resolution had been in force.

While all the specific consequences of House Joint Resolution 542 cannot yet be predicted, it is clear that it would undercut the ability of the United States to act as an effective influence for peace. For example, the provision automatically cutting off certain authorities after 60 days unless they are extended by the Congress could work to prolong

or intensify a crisis. Until the Congress
suspended the deadline, there would be at least
a chance of United States withdrawal, and an
adversary would be tempted therefore to postpone
serious negotiations until the 60 days were up.
Only after the Congress acted would there be a
strong incentive for an adversary to negotiate.
In addition, the very existence of a deadline
could lead to an escalation of hostilities in
order to achieve certain objectives before the
60 days expired.

The measure would jeopardize our role as a
force for peace in other ways as well. It
would, for example, strike from the President's
hand a wide range of important peace-keeping
tools by eliminating his ability to exercise
quiet diplomacy backed by subtle shifts in our
military deployments. It would also cast into
doubt authorities which Presidents have used to
undertake certain humanitarian relief missions
in conflict areas, to protect fishing boats from
seizure, to deal with ship or aircraft
hijackings, and to respond to threats of attack.
Not the least of the adverse consequences of
this resolution would be the prohibition
contained in section 8 against fulfilling our
obligations under the NATO treaty as ratified by
the Senate. Finally, since the bill is somewhat
vague as to when the 60 day rule would apply, it
could lead to extreme confusion and dangerous
disagreements concerning the prerogatives of the
two branches, seriously damaging our ability to
respond to international crises.

FAILURE to REQUIRE POSITIVE CONGRESSIONAL ACTION

I am particularly disturbed by the fact
that certain of the President's constitutional
powers as Commander in Chief of the Armed Forces
would terminate automatically under this
resolution 60 days after they were invoked. No
overt Congressional action would be required to
cut off these powers--they would disappear
automatically unless the Congress extended them.
In effect, the Congress is here attempting to
increase its policy-making role through a
provision which requires it to take absolutely
no action at all....

It would give every future Congress the ability to handcuff every future President merely by doing nothing and sitting still. In my view, one cannot become a responsible partner unless one is prepared to take responsible action.

STRENGTHENING COOPERATION BETWEEN The CONGRESS
And The EXECUTIVE BRANCHES

The responsible and effective exercise of the war powers requires the fullest cooperation between the Congress and the Executive and the prudent fulfillment by each branch of its constitutional responsibilities. House Joint Resolution 542 includes certain constructive measures which would foster this process by enhancing the flow of information from the Executive branch to the Congress. Section 3, for example, calls for consultations with the Congress before and during the involvement of the United States forces in hostilities abroad. This provision is consistent with the desire of this Administration for regularized consultations with the Congress in an even wider range of circumstances....

This Administration is dedicated to strengthening cooperation between the Congress and the President in the conduct of foreign affairs and to preserving the constitutional prerogatives of both branches of our Government. I know that Congress shares that goal.

PUBLIC LAW 93-559
(Hughes-Ryan Amendment)
Limitations on Intelligence Activities
December 30, 1974

An Act

To amend the Foreign Assistance Act of 1961, and for other purposes.

Be it enacted by the Senate and House of Representatives of the United States of America

Source: United States Statutes at Large, 1974, vol. 88, part 2, pp. 1795 and 1804.

in Congress assembled, That this Act may be
cited as the "Foreign Assistance Act of 1974".

* * * * *

Intelligence Activities and Exchanges of Materials

SEC. 32. The Foreign Assistance Act of
1961 is amended by adding at the end of part
III the following new sections:

"Sec. 662. Limitation on Intelligence
Activities.--(a) No funds appropriated under the
authority of this or any other Act may be
expended by or on behalf of the Central
Intelligence Agency for operations in foreign
countries, other than activities intended solely
for obtaining necessary intelligence, unless and
until the President finds that each such
operation is important to the national security
of the United States and reports, in a timely
fashion, a description and scope of such
operation to the appropriate committees of the
Congress, including the Committee on Foreign
Relations of the United States Senate and the
Committee on Foreign Affairs of the United
States House of Representatives.
"(b) The provisions of subsection (a) of
this section shall not apply during military
operations initiated by the United States under
a declaration of war approved by the Congress or
an exercise of powers by the President under the
War Powers Resolution.

PUBLIC LAW 94-329
(Clark Amendment)
Limitations on Activities in Angola
June 30, 1976

An Act

To amend the Foreign Assistance Act of 1961 and
the Foreign Military Sales Act, and for other
purposes.

Source: United States Statutes at Large, 1976,
vol. 90, part 1, pp. 729, 757-758.

Be it enacted by the Senate and House of Representatives of the United States of America in Congress assembled, That this Act may be cited as the "International Security Assistance and Arms Export Control Act of 1976."

Limitation on Certain Assistance to and Activities in Angola

SEC. 404. (a) Notwithstanding any other provision of law, no assistance of any kind may be provided for the purpose, or which would have the effect, of promoting or augmenting, directly or indirectly, the capacity of any nation, group, organization, movement, or individual to conduct military or paramilitary operations in Angola unless and until the Congress expressly authorizes such assistance by law enacted after the date of enactment of this section.

(b) If the President determines that assistance prohibited by subsection (a) should be furnished in the national security interests of the United States, he shall submit to the Speaker of the House of Representatives and the Committee on Foreign Relations of the Senate a report containing--

(1) a description of the amounts and categories of assistance which he recommends to be authorized and the identity of the proposed recipients of such assistance; and

(2) a certification that he has determined that the furnishing of such assistance is important to the national security interests of the United States and a detailed statement, in unclassified form, of the reasons supporting such determination.

(c) The prohibition contained in subsection (a) does not apply with respect to assistance which is furnished solely for humanitarian purposes.

(d) The provisions of this section may not be waived under any other provision of law.

Soviet Intervention in Angola

SEC. 405. The Congress views the large-scale and continuing Soviet intervention in Angola, including active sponsorship and support of Cuban armed forces in Angola, as being completely inconsistent with any reasonably defined policy of detente, as well as with Articles 1 and 2 of the United Nations Charter, the principle of noninterference in the affairs of other countries agreed to at Helsinki in 1975, and with the spirit of bilateral agreements between the United States and the Union of Soviet Socialist Republics. Such intervention should be taken explicitly into account in United States foreign policy planning and negotiations.

PUBLIC LAW 96-450
CONGRESSIONAL OVERSIGHT Of INTELLIGENCE

October 14, 1980

An Act

To authorize appropriations for fiscal year 1981 for the intelligence and intelligence-related activities of the United States Government, for the Intelligence Community Staff, and for the Central Intelligence Agency Retirement and Disability System, and for other purposes.

Be it enacted by the Senate and House of Representatives of the United States of America in Congress assembled, That this Act may be cited as the "Intelligence Authorization Act for Fiscal Year 1981."

"Congressional Oversight

"SEC. 501. (a)... the Director of Central Intelligence and the heads of all departments, agencies, and other entities of the United States involved in intelligence activities shall--

"(1) keep the Select Committee on Intelligence of the Senate and the Permanent Select Committee on Intelligence

Source: United States Statutes at Large, 1980, vol. 94, part 2, pp. 1975, 1981-1982.

of the House of Representatives
(hereinafter in this section referred to
as the 'intelligence committees') fully
and currently informed of all
intelligence activities which are the
responsibility of, are engaged in by, or
are carried out for or on behalf of, any
department, agency, or entity of the
United States, including any significant
anticipated intelligence activity, except
that (A) the foregoing provision shall not
require approval of the intelligence
committees as a condition precedent to the
initiation of any such anticipated
intelligence activity, and (B) if the
President determines it is essential to
limit prior notice to meet extraordinary
circumstances affecting vital interests of
the United States, such notice shall be
limited to the chairman and ranking
minority members of the intelligence
committees, the Speaker and minority
leader of the House of Representatives,
and the majority and minority leaders of
the Senate;
"(2) furnish any information or material
concerning intelligence activities which
is in the possession, custody, or control
of any department, agency, or entity of
the United States and which is requested
by either of the intelligence committees
in order to carry out its authorized
responsibilities; and
"(3) report in a timely fashion to the
intelligence committees any illegal
intelligence activity or significant
intelligence failure and any corrective
action that has been taken or is planned
to be taken in connection with such
illegal activity or failure.

"(b) The President shall fully inform the
intelligence committees in a timely fashion of
intelligence operations in foreign countries,
other than activities intended solely for
obtaining necessary intelligence, for which
prior notice was not given under subsection (a)
and shall provide a statement of the reasons for

not giving prior notice....

"(d) ... each of the intelligence committees shall promptly call to the attention of its respective House, or to any appropriate committee or committees of its respective House, any matter relating to intelligence activities requiring the attention of such House or such committee or committees.

"(e) Nothing in this Act shall be construed as authority to withhold information from the intelligence committees on the grounds that providing the information to the intelligence committees would constitute the unauthorized disclosure of classified information or information relating to intelligence sources and methods."

THE BOLAND AMENDMENT

Limitations on CIA Activities

December 8, 1982

Department of Defense Appropriation Bill, 1983

* * * * *

Amendment Offered by Mr. Boland as a Substitute
for the Amendment Offered by Mr. Harkin

Mr.BOLAND. Mr. Chairman, I offer an amendment as a substitute for the amendment.

The Clerk read as follows:

Amendment offered by Mr. BOLAND as a substitute for the amendment offered by Mr. HARKIN. Strike the matter proposed by the Harkin amendment and insert in lieu thereof the following:

"SEC. 793. None of the funds provided in this Act may be used by the Central Intelligence Agency or the Department of Defense to furnish military equipment, military training or advice, or other support for military activities, to any

Source: U.S. Congress, Congressional Record, December 8, 1982, pp. 9158-9159, H 9123.

group or individual, not part of a country's armed forces, for the purpose of overthrowing the Government of Nicaragua or provoking a military exchange between Nicaragua and Honduras." ...

Mr. BOLAND.   Mr. Chairman, I demand a recorded vote.

A recorded vote was ordered.

The vote was taken by electronic device, and there were--ayes 411, noes 0, not voting 22,...

PUBLIC LAW 98-215
(Boland Amendment Revision)
Limitations on Covert Assistance-Nicaragua

December 9, 1983

An Act

Be it enacted by the Senate and House of Representatives of the United States of America in Congress assembled, That this Act may be cited as the "Intelligence Authorization Act for Fiscal Year 1984."....

SEC. 108. During fiscal year 1984, not more than $24,000,000 of the funds available to the Central Intelligence Agency, the Department of Defense, or any other agency or entity of the United States involved in intelligence activities may be obligated or expended for the purpose, or which would have the effect, of supporting, directly or indirectly, military or paramilitary operations in Nicaragua by any nation, group, organization, movement or individual....

SEC. 109. (a) The Congress finds that--

(1) the Government of National Reconstruction of Nicaragua has failed to keep solemn promises, made to the Organization of

Source: United States Statutes at Large, 1983, vol. 97, pp. 1473, 1475-1476.

American States in July 1979, to establish full
respect for human rights and political
liberties, hold early elections, preserve a
private sector, permit political pluralism, and
pursue a foreign policy of nonaggression and
nonintervention;

(2) by providing military support
(including arms, training, and logistical
command and control, and communications
facilities) to groups seeking to overthrow the
Government of El Salvador and other Central
American governments, the Government of National
Reconstruction of Nicaragua has violated article
18 of the Charter of the Organization of
American States which declares that no state
has the right to intervene, directly or
indirectly, for any reason whatsoever, in the
internal or external affairs of any other state;

(3) the Government of Nicaragua should
be held accountable before the Organization of
American States for activities violative of
promises made to the Organization and for
violations of the Charter of that Organization;
and

(4) working through the Organization of
American States is the proper and most effective
means of dealing with threats to the peace of
Central America, of providing for common action
in the event of aggression, and of providing the
mechanisms for peaceful resolution of disputes
among the countries of Central America.

(b) The President should seek a prompt
reconvening of the Seventeenth Meeting of
Consultation of Ministers of Foreign Affairs of
the Organization of American States for the
purpose of reevaluating the compliance by the
Government of National Reconstruction of
Nicaragua--

(1) with the commitments made by the
leaders of that Government in July 1979 to the
Organization of American States; and

(2) with the Charter of the Organization
of American States.

(c) The President should vigorously seek
actions by the Organization of American States
that would provide for a full range of effective
measures by the member states to bring about
compliance by the Government of National

Reconstruction of Nicaragua with those obligations, including verifiable agreements to halt the transfer of military equipment and to cease furnishing of military support facilities to groups seeking the violent overthrow of governments of countries in Central America.

(d) The President should use all diplomatic means at his disposal to encourage the Organization of American States to seek resolution of the conflicts in Central America based on the provisions of the Final Act of the San Jose Conference of October 1982, especially principles (d), (e), and (g), relating to nonintervention in the internal affairs of other countries, denying support for terrorist and subversive elements in other states, and international supervision of fully verifiable arrangements.

(e) The United States should support measures at the Organization of American States, as well as efforts of the Contadora Group, which seek to end support for terrorist, subversive, or other activities aimed at the violent overthrow of the governments of countries in Central America.

PUBLIC LAW 98-473
CENTRAL AMERICA

October 12, 1984

Resolved by the Senate and House of Representatives of the United States of America in Congress assembled,...

Such amounts as may be necessary for programs, projects or activities provided for in the Department of Defense Appropriation Act, 1985, at a rate of operations and to the extent and in the manner provided as follows, to be effective as if it had been enacted into law as the regular appropriation Act:

An Act

Source: United States Statutes at Large, 1984, vol. 98, pp. 1837, 1904, 1935-1936, 1942.

Making appropriations for the Department of Defense for the fiscal year ending September 30, 1985, and for other purposes.

* * * * *

SEC. 8066. (a) During fiscal year 1985, no funds available to the Central Intelligence Agency, the Department of Defense, or any other agency or entity of the United States involved in intelligence activities may be obligated or expended for the purpose or which would have the effect of supporting, directly or indirectly, military or paramilitary operations in Nicaragua by any nation, group, organization, movement, or individual.

(b) The prohibition concerning Nicaragua contained in subsection (a) shall cease to apply if, after February 28, 1985--

(1) the President submits to Congress a report--

(A) stating that the Government of Nicaragua is providing materiel or monetary support to anti-government forces engaged in military or paramilitary operations in El Salvador or other Central American countries;

(B) analyzing the military significance of such support;

(C) stating that the President has determined that assistance for military or paramilitary operations prohibited by subsection (a) is necessary;

(D) justifying the amount and type of such assistance and describing its objectives; and

(E) explaining the goals of United States policy for the Central American region and how the proposed assistance would further such goals, including theachievement of peace and security in Central America through a comprehensive, verifiable and enforceable agreement based upon the Contadora Document of Objectives; and

(2) a joint resolution approving assistance for military or paramilitary operations in Nicaragua is enacted....

SEC. 8101. (a) The Congress makes the

following findings:

(1) The President has stated that there is no need to introduce United States Armed Forces into Central America for combat and that he has no intention of doing so.

(2) The President of El Salvador has stated that there is no need for United States Armed Forces to conduct combat operations in El Salvador and that he has no intention of asking that they do so.

(3) The possibility of the introduction of United States Armed Forces into Central America for combat raises very grave concern in the Congress and the American people.

(b) It is the sense of Congress that--

(1) United States Armed Forces should not be introduced into or over the countries of Central America for combat; and

(2) if circumstances change from those present on the date of the enactment of this Act and the President believes that those changed circumstances require the introduction of United States Armed Forces into or over a country of Central America for combat, the President should consult with Congress before any decision to so introduce United States Armed Forces and any such introduction of United States Armed Forces must comply with the War Powers Resolution.

PUBLIC LAW 99-145
LIMITATIONS on U.S. ARMED FORCES-NICARAGUA

November 8, 1985

An Act

Be it enacted by the Senate and House of Representatives of the United States of America in Congress assembled,

(a) Short Title--This Act may be cited as

Source: United States Statutes at Large, 1985, vol. 99, p. 760.

the "Department of Defense Authorization Act, 1986": ...
SEC. 1451. Sense of Congress on Introduction of Armed Forces into Nicaragua for Combat

It is the sense of Congress that United States Armed Forces should not be introduced into or over Nicaragua for combat. However, nothing in this section shall be construed as affecting the authority and responsibility of the President or Congress under the Constitution, statutes, or treaties of the United States in force.

BOLAND AMENDMENT REVISION

Limitations on Intelligence Activities in Nicaragua
November 14, 1985

H.R. 2419. Intelligence Authorization Act for Fiscal Year 1986

SEC. 105. (a) Funds available to the Central Intelligence Agency, the Department of Defense, or any other agency or entity of the United States involved in intelligence activities may be obligated and expended during fiscal year 1986 to provide funds, materiel, or other assistance to the Nicaraguan democratic resistance to support military or paramilitary operations in Nicaragua only as authorized in Section 101 and as specified....
(b) Nothing in this section precludes--
(1) administration by the Nicaraguan Humanitarian Assistance Office established by Executive Order 12530, of the program of humanitarian assistance to the Nicaraguan democratic resistance provided for in the Supplemental Appropriations Act, 1985, or
(2) activities of the Department of State to solicit such humanitarian assistance for the Nicaraguan democratic resistance.

Source: U.S. Congress Congressional Record, November 14, 1985, 14, 1985, H 10201.

11

Research on U.S. National Security

Robert A. Vitas

In its research function, academia has traditionally valued the utilization of primary sources in its work, be they documents, relevant periodicals, or participant-observation. This is due to the fact that distortion can arise when secondary sources are relied upon, especially when considering that such sources are based upon even more secondary sources of information and analysis. The scholarly pursuit of truth can be hampered when dealing with perhaps skewed information. The use of primary sources, obviously, is not made in an attempt to revert to our origins, intellectual or otherwise. Indeed, the endeavor is made in the hope that our roots may be discovered, whether in terms of a particular public policy, set of events, or the development of civilization itself. This is especially important when keeping in mind that the United States is entering its fifth decade of the contemporary national security era. In order to fully understand where the country stands today in terms of its national security, it is necessary to see how it developed, and how it continues to develop.

Undoubtedly, the best primary sources to consult in the specialty of national security are documents produced by the federal government. This is the bedrock of the present volume. However, lest one come quickly to the conclusion that reliance on military publications will lead to biased views, it must be remembered that the intellectual beauty of studying national security is its pervasiveness in American society. After all, our survival depends upon it. It is not necessary to rely solely on material produced by the military establishment, for both the legislative and executive branches have been quite active in its development. In examining a wide range of government national security documents, it is possible to view the arguments and decision-making processes as they occurred. The give-and-take and pro-and-con can be viewed from a better perspective than the participants themselves possessed. Of course, public documents can give public rationales for action or inaction. For example, hawkish talk emanating from the Carter administration in 1980 was meant just as much for domestic electoral consumption as it was for that of the Kremlin. The importance of declassified material emerges here, for it was never meant to be public. Declassified material in Foreign Relations of the United States and Vietnam documents housed at the Lyndon B. Johnson Presidential Library are two examples of this, leading the scholar behind the scenes to the minds and conference rooms of the White House and Pentagon.

While primary sources give a picture of how it was --or at least how it was meant to be--presented, the scholar, prior to embarking into the labyrinth of national security primary documentation, must know how to look, where and why. Ironically, to do this, it is necessary to revert temporarily to secondary sources, for these provide earlier distillations and analyses of important events and political actors. Prior to commencing extensive national security/foreign policy research utilizing government documents, it is best to peruse two or three general foreign policy texts. Or, if a specific set of events is being studied, such as the Vietnam conflict, one may rely on volumes devoted to it. This is dependent upon the scope of the research being undertaken. Because the postwar era has witnessed the melding of both national security and foreign policy issues, due to global American commitments, there is no need to consult, at least initially, volumes dealing with military matters per se. Indeed, to do so may cause one to miss the forest for the trees, whereas a good foreign policy text will clue the researcher into major events in both spheres. This initial dependence upon secondary sources is quite helpful, for even the most experienced scholar needs assistance in culling forty years of events and policy development.

Following a compilation of events/documents to be searched, one may, depending upon the nature of the research and the familiarity of the scholar to the field, either consult indices or proceed directly to the sources themselves. If the researcher is not in possession of specifics, such as dates and places, then an index may be appropriate. Two such indices are the Codification of Presidential Proclamations and Executive Orders and the indices for Foreign Relations of the United States, published for the years 1939-1945 by Kraus. Two especially useful indices are The Cumulated Indexes to the Public Papers of the Presidents of the United States, published for Truman through Nixon by Oceana, and the indices to United States Treaties and Other International Agreements, published for the years 1776-1975, and also numerically, chronologically, by country and subject, by Heinz.

In the postwar era, no president has ignored his important role as commander-in-chief and leader of the free world with global responsibilities. While talk of isolation recurs, there is certainly little possiblity of it now. There has been a substantial increase in presidential dealings with national security affairs. Indeed, the term national security is a postwar phenomenon, indicating that it is an amalgam of political, economic, and social factors requiring presidential attention, not merely purely military planning. The key to presidential activity in this and other spheres of policy is Public Papers of the Presidents of the United States, issued one to three times per annum. The volumes contain speeches, reports to Congress, news releases, and other presidential documentation. Each volume possesses an index, but, with the advent of the Carter administration, it must be noted that the indices switched from citing document numbers to citing pages. In addition, they are poorer in quality and, in fact, an error was detected in the first volume published for 1979.

More recent presidential documents may be found in Weekly Compilation of Presidential Documents. As of the Carter administration, Public Papers is merely a compendium of the Weekly Compilations. Earlier versions of Public Papers contained indices only for proclamations and executive orders. The actual documents for these years may be found in the Code of Federal Regulations, Title 3, The President, which is issued every several years. More recent such matters may be found in the Federal Register. The U.S. Office of the Federal Register can provide information regarding these publications.

One can also attempt direct contact with the White House. Usually the point of contact is the White House Office of Public Affairs. However, for purposes of national security research, it may be more appropriate to

consult with the National Security Council. There is a
standing backlog in requests for information received by
the NSC, but it is not unusual to receive a response in a
matter of several weeks. All requests are screened by a
Freedom of Information Mandatory Review Officer in the
NSC's Office of Information Policy and Security Review.
If the information sought is over twenty-five years old,
it has probably been declassified and is in the custody
of the National Archives and Records Administration. If
the material is not as dated, then, depending upon its
sensitivity, it may be releasable or not.

The U.S. State Department publishes the monthly
Department of State Bulletin, containing statements by
the secretary and other officials, analyses, and texts of
foreign agreements. The index became poorer in the late
1970s. Some presidential statements are reprinted here.
Recent foreign agreements are more easily found here, for
United States Treaties and Other International
Agreements, also published by the State Department,
often possesses a long lead time due to ratification and
adherence delays, which can be several years. Several
volumes of _United States Treaties_ are published annually,
each with an easily used table of contents. The volumes
certainly give one an appreciation for the complexity of
international negotiation and transaction.

Foreign Relations of the United States is the most
extensive reference tool produced by the State
Department. It contains internal government memoranda,
which often take the scholar away from public rationales
given for certain actions. For example, discussions
leading up to the adoption of NSC 68, the containment
policy inaugurated by President Truman, as well as the
text itself, may be found here. Each year can have
several volumes, and there are some special series, such
as those dealing with the Geneva Conferences and Vietnam.
However, the confidentiality and classification of many
of its documents require a long lead time, approximately
thirty years. Once again, this tool gives one an
appreciation for the complexity of the issues involved.
It also shows conscientious public servants grappling
with, and debating over, them. Information regarding
these publications may be obtained from the State
Department's Bureau of Public Affairs, Washington, D.C.
20520.

Of course, the U.S. Department of Defense possesses
a wealth of information on national security affairs. The
researcher's initial contact here is the Office of the
Assistant Secretary of Defense for Public Affairs,

located at the Pentagon in Washington, D.C. 20301. This office handles the massive flow of news releases, standard and recurring publications, and referrals. For the scholar wishing to find his way around the Pentagon, a useful publication is the DOD Organization and Functions Guidebook, prepared periodically by the Directorate for Organizational and Management Planning for the Office of the Secretary of Defense, Defense Agencies, and DOD Field Activities. For historical listings of a wide range of Defense officials and general statistics, the DOD Fact Book is issued periodically by the Directorate for Defense Information.

The Organization of the Joint Chiefs of Staff has issued several publications of interest to national security historians. The arm for this activity is the Historical Division of the JCS Joint Secretariat. The Select Bibliography on the JCS contains published and unpublished works, as well as articles, from scholarly and journalistic publications, and memoirs. Short historical treatments may be found in the series entitled "JCS Special Historical Studies." Two shorter works are A Concise History of the Organization of the Joint Chiefs of Staff and The Evolving Role of the Joint Chiefs of Staff in the National Security Structure. A major, detailed work is Chronology, Functions and Composition of the Joint Chiefs of Staff. This is updated when necessary. The latest edition is that following the passage on October 1, 1986 of Public Law 99-433, the Goldwater-Nichols Department of Defense Reorganization Act of 1986.

For annual policy, the Secretary of Defense publishes his Annual Report to the Congress for each fiscal year. This contains broad political-military discussions, as well as the budgetary needs and implications of defense programs. The JCS issues its United States Military Posture every fiscal year. This is a shorter publication dealing with more purely military innovations, highlights, and priorities. Both of these volumes are available to the public, whereas the Secretary's annual Defense Guidance is classified. (It was called Consolidated Guidance under President Carter.) These annual publications reflect the varied character of military policy among the services, dispelling the popular myth of the monolithic Pentagon.

There are other recurring publications. Defense is a bi-monthly magazine distributed to official personnel, but available to the public. Developments over time can be chronicled in Defense's annual Almanac issue. The

U.S. Air Force is the executive agency for DOD in the
production and distribution of Current News, containing
national-security-related news and editorials from
scholarly and journalistic periodicals around the
country. There are also special theme issues.
Unfortunately, Current News is unavailable outside
official channels or special organizational exchange
programs. Finally, Soviet Military Power was inaugurated
by Secretary Caspar Weinberger and has gone through
several editions.

As far as recurring publications and news releases
are concerned, DOD frequently receives requests for names
to be included on mailing lists, or for listings of
publications. Due to budgetary and staff constraints,
DOD is unable to maintain mailing lists or updated lists
of publications. However, a wide variety of material is
made available to the public on an individual request
basis. Requests should be addressed to the Staff
Assistant for Public Correspondence, Office of the
Assistant Secretary of Defense (Public Affairs),
Washington, D.C. 20301, telephone (202) 697-5737. If the
requested material is available for public distribution,
an attempt will be made to provide it or a source will be
named where the information can be obtained.

Although the Joint Chiefs of Staff has issued its
own historical studies, these have been specially
written. Defense historical documents, such as
directives or statements from the secretary, are
generally unavailable from DOD. This includes material
pertaining to the Civil War through the Vietnam conflict.
For example, Secretary Melvin Laird's statement of
January 27, 1973 announcing the end of conscription would
be unavailable from DOD. Historical files of DOD and the
military departments are under the jurisdiction of the
National Archives and Records Administration(NARA), 8th
Street and Pennsylvania Avenue, N.W., Washington, D.C.
20408. Information from records maintained by NARA is
available to the public and documents will be reproduced
for a nominal fee. Ultimately, all records will fall
under NARA's jurisdiction. However, it may in practice
be difficult to obtain them, for DOD unofficially admits
that there is some measure of conflict between it and
NARA over which agency should control access to them, as
well as over procedural questions.

Each military department possesses its own public
affairs office, which handles matters unique to that
particular service. These offices are accessible through
the Pentagon. If the office cannot expedite a particular

request, it will direct the scholar to the relevant service's historical records and information center. Indeed, one may also be directed to the public affairs or history office of a specific component, such as the U.S. Military Airlift Command's Military History Office at Scott Air Force Base, Illinois, to cite one example.

For limited information on retired and separated military personnel, one can contact the National Personnel Records Center, General Services Administration, 9700 Page Boulevard, St. Louis, Missouri 63132. Privacy Act provisions, though, will restrict the information available on specific individuals. In addition, DOD photographs may be purchased from the Defense Audiovisual Agency, Building 168, Naval District of Washington, Washington, D.C. 20374. Finally, no legislation is available from DOD, but this is the subject of the following section.

Congressional Quarterly Weekly Report and Congressional Digest, while not government publications, can clue the researcher into when and how issues were, or are being, resolved. They can also guide one to public laws, that is, the legislation which is the foundation for almost all official national security activity. Legislation may be found in United States Statutes at Large. It is a better reference tool than the United States Code, for United States Statutes gives the legislation as actually passed, for example, the National Security Act of 1947, whereas the United States Code, updated every several years, is a compilation of legislation still in force dissected into the various federal legislative titles and regrouped into the relevant legal order. Thus United States Statutes is geared toward the scholar, while the United States Code is published for the convenience of the practicing attorney. More recent legislation may be found in the Congressional Record, along with debates, reports, and related material. The Congressional Record Index appears many times annually and is a guide to the often complex issues and debates. The U.S. Office of the Congressional Record located at the Capitol can offer specific information regarding these latter publications.

It may occasionally be more convenient to approach legislative business through another channel. Members of the general public may obtain one free copy of congressional publications from the Senate Document Room. The House Document Room no longer distributes documents to the public. Up to six free items may be obtained per contact. Additional material is subject to a nominal fee.

All House and Senate publications, except committee
prints and hearings, are available here thanks to a
cooperative effort of the Secretary of the Senate and the
Superintendent of Documents. Committee prints and
hearings are often available directly from the relevant
legislators and committees. This special Senate Document
Room sales outlet is located in the Hart Senate Office
Building, Room B-04, Washington, D.C. 20510, telephone
(202) 224-7860. It is helpful to provide the publication
type, such as Public Law (PL) or House Resolution (HR),
and the publication number, such as HR 3838. If these are
not known, an abbreviated title is desirable. If over six
publications are ordered at once, the standard
remittance and credit options are available. If one will
be a frequent user of such services, it may be convenient
to establish a Superintendent of Documents Prepaid
Deposit Account, against which orders can be charged as
long as sufficient funds remain on account. To establish
such an account, fifty dollars must be dispatched to the
Special Accounts Branch, Stop: SAOS, U.S. Government
Printing Office, Washington, D.C. 20402, telephone (202)
275-2481. Finally, if committee prints and hearings are
unavailable from committees or legislators, they may be
purchased from the Superintendent of Documents,
Congressional Sales Office--Main GPO, Washington, D.C.
20402-9315, telephone (202) 275-3030. The remittance
policy is the same as for the Senate Document Room.
Recorded information regarding the latest committee
prints and hearings available for sale is reached by
calling (202) 275-5250.

        In all cases, it is best to possess specific
information prior to wading into reference works or
establishing contact with governmental sources. Because
of the many different publications, statements, officials
involved, and document types, it is not difficult to
quickly become lost in an intellectual quagmire. Eight
hours in a federal depository library working with
government documents can be a mind-boggling experience.
Once one becomes familiar with the various reference
works, though, including their formats, strengths, and
weaknesses, they become easy to use, and it becomes
easier to relate one to another. Some documents cite
others, or specific legislation, for example, which
reduces the amount of searching required.

        Federal depository libraries are located in every
congressional district and should contain much of the
material cited in this chapter. If the desired
information is unavailable, the addresses and phone

numbers of sources, such as presidential libraries, can be received from the nearest Federal Information Center. Also, the U.S. Government Printing Office stocks and sells over twenty-four thousand different publications, periodicals and subscription services. A list of periodicals and subscription services is available free of charge. It must be noted, however, that the Government Printing Office and federal bookstores are more difficult to deal with, because they process the entire range of information issued by the government. Their requirements for specific titles, for example, can hamper research efforts.

It is easiest to deal with the component that issued a document, or was related to a particular event, such as a congressional committee, executive department, or military component. The researcher should attempt to pinpoint the optimal level and agency for locating a particular document/event. Also, public affairs offices must be given as much specific information as possible, for they, too, are deluged with paperwork and a backlog of requests. Once dealing with military and civilian public affairs officers, though, the researcher will most often find them to be courteous, competent, and efficient.

This concluding chapter has attempted to steer the national security scholar toward relevant sources, the foundation and, hopefully, strength of the present volume. Primary sources in this specialty will assist one in viewing public displays--and material never intended for public display. They show what political-military actors said and what they meant, for the two do not always correspond. The utilization of such sources can provide the scholar with new insights and a fresh perspective, perhaps discovering what was unknown at the time of a particular event or, thanks to the passage of time, discerning ironies of policy and history. Ultimately, the perspicacity provided by primary national security sources can help the scholar discover the truth, which, after all, is the raison d'etre of scholarship.

References

The following is a listing of the major sources used in this volume. However, this does not repeat all of the citations listed in the volume, since many are based on identical source material. An example of each major source is listed with specific dates and other identifying data as a means of showing the proper listing, and is not intended to show it is the only citation in the volume.

National Security Council, Office of Special Projects, "A Report to the National Security Council," NSC 10/2, June 18, 1948 (mimeographed).

Public Law 85-599, "Department of Defense Reorganization Act," 1958.

The Senator Gravel Edition, The Pentagon Papers, vol. IV, Boston: Beacon Press, 1971.

U.S. Congress, House Armed Services Committee. Statement by Richard L. Armitage, Assistant Secretary of Defense, on Special Operations Forces Reorganization, July 16, 1986 (mimeographed).

U.S. Congress, House, Congressman Boland speaking for the Amendment to the Department of Defense Appropriation Bill, 1983, H.R. 7355, December 8, 1982. Congressional Record, vol. 128, no. 143.

U.S. Congress, Senate, Committee on Foreign Relations, <u>Vietnam Commitments, 1961</u>. Committee Print. Staff Study. Washington, D.C.: U.S.Government Printing Office, 1972.

U.S. Department of Defense, Caspar W. Weinberger, Secretary of Defense, <u>Annual Report to the Congress, Fiscal Year 1985.</u>

U.S. Department of Defense, Caspar W. Weinberger, Secretary of Defense, <u>Executive Summary, Annual Report to Congress, Fiscal Year 1988.</u>

U.S. Department of Defense, National Military Command Center, Message Center, "Deployment of MEB to Danang," February 24, 1965 (mimeographed).

U.S. Department of State, <u>Afghanistan, 18 Months Later</u>, Special Report No. 86, August 1981.

U.S. Department of State, <u>Department of State Bulletin</u>, January 25, 1954, pp. 107-110.

U.S. Department of State, <u>Foreign Relations of the United States, 1950</u>, vol. 1, 1976, pp. 237-265.

U.S. <u>Statutes at Large</u>, vol. 61, pt. 1 (1948), "National Security Act," 1947.

U.S. Department of State, <u>United States Treaties and Other International Agreements</u>, vol. 6, pt. 1, "The Pacific Charter," September 8, 1954.

U.S. General Accounting Office, Comptroller General, <u>Report to the Congress of the United States</u>, "The Defense Budget: A Look at Budgetary Resources, Accomplishments, and Problems," GAO/PLRD-83-62, April 27, 1983.

U.S. President, Executive Order 12333, "United States Intelligence Activities," December 4, 1981. <u>Federal Register</u>, No. 2235, December 8, 1981, 59941-59954.

U.S. President, <u>Public Papers of the Presidents of the United States</u>, Washington, D.C.: Office of the Federal Register, National Archives and Records Service Administration, 1953. Harry S. Truman, 1950, pp. 150-151. This is also the source for citations for

Weekly Compilation of Presidential Documents, Ronald Reagan, 1985, pp. 972-973.

U.S. President, Report of the President's Special Review Board, February 26, 1987.

The White House, Office of the Press Secretary, Text of an Address by the President on Central America, May 9, 1984 (mimeographed).

Select Bibliography

The purpose of this bibliography is to identify the major sources used as background for the framework of this volume. These sources are identified by an asterisk. This also serves as a reading list, identifying some of the most useful works on U.S. national security.

Art, Robert, Vincent Davis, and Samuel P. Huntington. Reorganizing America's Defense. Washington, D.C.: Pergamon-Brassey's, 1985.

Barnett, Frank R., B. Hugh Tovar, and Richard H. Shultz, eds. Special Operations in US Strategy. Washington, D.C.: National Defense University Press, 1984.

Blechman, Barry M., ed. Rethinking The U.S. Strategic Posture: A Report from the Aspen Consortium on Arms Control and Security Issues. Cambridge, Mass.: Ballinger Publishing, 1982.

Bock, Joseph G. The White House Staff and the National Security Assistant: Friendship and Friction at the Water's Edge. Westport, Conn: Greenwood Press, 1987.

Brown, Harold. Thinking About National Security. Boulder, Colo.: Westview Press, 1983.

Coates, James and Michael Kilian. Heavy Losses: The Dangerous Decline of American Defense. New York: Viking, 1985.

Congressional Quarterly, Inc. <u>U.S. Defense Policy</u>, third
edition. Washington, D.C.: The CQ Press, 1983.

Dougherty, James E. and Robert L. Pfaltzgraff, Jr.
<u>American Foreign Policy: FDR to Reagan</u>. New York: Harper
and Row, 1986.

Fallows, James. <u>National Defense</u>. New York: Random
House, 1981.

Halloran, Richard. <u>To Arm a Nation: Rebuilding America's
Endangered Defenses</u>. New York: MacMillan, 1986.

Hartmann, Frederick H. and Robert L. Wendzel. <u>To
Preserve the Republic: United States Foreign Policy</u>.
New York: MacMillan, 1985.

Heyns, Terry., ed. <u>Understanding U.S. Strategy: A Reader</u>.
Fort McNair, Washington, D.C.: National Defense
University Press, 1983.

*Hilsman, Roger. <u>The Politics of Policymaking in Defense
and Foreign Affairs: Conceptual Models and Bureaucratic
Politics</u>. Englewood Cliffs, N.J.: Prentice-Hall, 1987.

International Institute of Strategic Studies. <u>The
Military Balance, 1987-1988</u>. London: ISSS, 1987.

*Jordan, Amos A. and William J. Taylor. <u>American National
Security: Policy and Process</u>, revised edition.
Baltimore: The Johns Hopkins University Press, 1984.

*Kaufman, Daniel J., Jeffrey S. McKitrick, and Thomas J.
Leney, eds. <u>U.S. National Security: A Framework for
Analysis</u>. Lexington, Mass.: Lexington Books, 1985.

Kegley, Charles E., Jr., and Eugene R. Wittkopf, eds. <u>The
Nuclear Reader: Strategy, Weapons, War</u>. New York: St.
Martin's Press, 1985.

Koenig, Louis W. <u>The Chief Executive</u>, fifth edition. New
York: Harcourt Brace Jovanovich, 1986.

Korb, Lawrence J. and Keith D. Hahn. <u>National Security
Policy Organization in Perspective</u>. Washington, D.C.:
American Enterprise Institute for Public Policy
Research, 1981.

Kruzel, Joseph, ed. American Defense Annual, 1987-1988. Lexington, Mass.: Lexington Books, 1987.

*Nash, Harry T. American Foreign Policy: A Search for Security, third edition. Homewood, Ill.: The Dorsey Press, 1985.

*Nathan, James A. and James K. Oliver. United States Foreign Policy and World Order, third edition. Boston: Little, Brown and Co., 1985.

Nelson, Michael, ed. The Presidency and the Political System, Second edition. Washington, D.C.: The CQ Press, 1988.

Oleszek, Walter J. Congressional Procedures and the Policy Process, second edition. Washington, D.C. The CQ Press, 1984.

Palmer, Bruce, ed. Grand Strategy for the 1980s. Washington, D.C.: American Enterprise Institute for Public Policy Research, 1981.

Pfaltzgraff, Robert L., ed. National Security Policy for the 1980s. Beverly Hills, Cal.: Sage Publishing, 1981.

Pfaltzgraff, Robert L. National Security: Ethics, Strategy, and Politics. Washington, D.C.: Pergamon-Brassey, 1986.

Pfiffner, James P. The Strategic Presidency: Hitting the Ground Running. Homewood, Ill: The Dorsey Press, 1988.

Reichart, John F. and Steven R. Sturm, eds. American Defense Policy, fifth edition. Baltimore: The Johns Hopkins University Press, 1982.

*Sarkesian, Sam C., ed. Presidential Leadership and National Security: Style, Institutions, and Politics. Boulder, Colo.: Westview Press, 1984.

Smoke, Richard. National Security and the Nuclear Dilemma, second edition. New York: Random House, 1987.

*Snow, Donald M. National Security: Enduring Problems of U.S. Defense Policy. New York: St. Martin's Press, 1987.

*Spanier, John. <u>American Foreign Policy Since World War II</u>, eleventh edition. Washington, D.C.: The CQ Press, 1988.

Spanier, John and Eric M. Uslaner. <u>American Foreign Policy Making and the Democratic Dilemmas</u>, fourth edition. New York: Holt, Rinehart and Winston, 1985.

Thompson, Scott, ed. <u>National Security in the Nineteen Eighties: From Weakness to Strength</u>. San Francisco: Institute for Contemporary Studies, 1981.

Trager, Frank N. and Philip S. Kronenberg, eds. <u>National Security and American Society; Theory, Process, and Policy</u>. Lawrence: The University Press of Kansas, 1973.

*Watson, Richard A. and Norman C. Thomas. <u>The Politics of the Presidency</u>, second edition. Washington, D.C.: The CQ Press, 1988.

Index

About the Editors

SAM C. SARKESIAN is a Professor of Political Science at Loyola University of Chicago. He also serves as Vice-Chairman of the Research Committee on Armed Forces and Society of the International Political Science Association and he chairs the Research Committee of the National Strategy Forum. He is a member of the International Institute of Strategic Studies. He served as Chairman of the Inter-University Seminar on Armed Forces and Society from 1980-1987. Dr. Sarkesian is author or editor of a number of articles and books on national security, military professionalism, and unconventional conflicts. His most recent publications by Greenwood Press include *America's Forgotten Wars: The Counterrevolutionary Past and Lessons for the Future* and *The New Battlefield: The United States and Unconventional Conflicts*. He served for over twenty years in the U.S. Army with service in Germany, Korea, and Vietnam.

ROBERT A. VITAS is a Fellow of the Inter-University Seminar on Armed Forces and Society and serves as assistant to the Executive Director of that organization. He has published articles on Lithuanian politics and nationalism. His book review essays have appeared in the *Air University Review* and *Presidential Studies Quarterly*. Dr. Vitas serves as Vice-President and Executive Director of the Lithuanian Research and Studies Center. He is a member of the American Political Science Center, the Study of the Presidency, and the Association for Advancement of Baltic Studies. He will receive his Ph.D. in 1989 from Loyola University of Chicago.